# RETHINKING EARLY MEDIEVAL INDIA

# RETHINKING EARLY MEDIEVAL INDIA

## A Reader

*edited by*

UPINDER SINGH

OXFORD
UNIVERSITY PRESS

**OXFORD**
UNIVERSITY PRESS

Oxford University Press is a department of the University of Oxford. It furthers the University's objective of excellence in research, scholarship, and education by publishing worldwide. Oxford is a registered trademark of Oxford University Press in the UK and in certain other countries

Published in India by
Oxford University Press
22 Workspace, 2nd Floor, 1/22 Asaf Ali Road, New Delhi 110002, India



First published 2011
Oxford India Paperbacks 2012
19th impression 2021



ISBN-13: 978-0-19-808606-2
ISBN-10: 0-19-808606-7

Typeset in Adobe Garamond Pro 10.5/12.6
by BeSpoke Integrated Solutions, Puducherry, India 605008
Printed in India by Manipal Technologies Limited, Manipal

# Contents

# Illustrations

## FIGURES



## MAPS

# Preface

This book emerged out of my long engagement with early medieval India, both as a historian and as a teacher. I began my innings in historical research with an epigraphic study of the rural economy of early medieval Bengal and Bihar for my MPhil, went on to study the inscriptions of Orissa for my PhD, and continued to engage with this exciting period in the course of my subsequent research and teaching at the undergraduate and postgraduate level.

And yet, many years ago, when I was first approached by the Oxford University Press (OUP) to produce an edited volume on early medieval India, I confess that my initial reaction was not one of great enthusiasm. The reason was that in the course of my teaching, I had found that the history of early medieval India had in effect become a history of the historiography of the period. I did not want to produce yet another work which focused on the debate over whether early medieval India was feudal or not. In retrospect, I think that this is the reason why I delayed working on the book for many years. At some point, I realized that a volume on early medieval India could actually be a challenging venture if it sought to critically discuss the debate as well as the many important issues that lie beyond it. Once this was clear to me, selecting the essays and excerpts and writing the Introduction proved to be enjoyable tasks.

During the course of working on this book, I benefitted greatly from discussions with many of my colleagues in the History Department of the University of Delhi—Seema Alavi, Sunil Kumar, Farhat Hasan, Raziuddin Aquil, Kesavan Veluthat, Bhairabi P. Sahu, and Parul Pandya Dhar. I am especially grateful to Parul for helping out with glosses on technical terms related to art and dance. My friend Rukun Advani stepped in with very helpful advice at a critical juncture. K.P. Shankaran of the Philosophy Department of St Stephen's College, was, as always, a source of thought-provoking ideas. My husband Vijay Tankha, as usual, pitched in with advice on many points, especially on stylistic issues. I would like to thank them all.

I would especially like to thank the editorial team of the academic division, OUP, for their suggestions, support, trademark efficiency, and strict adherence to schedules, qualities I truly admire and appreciate. I am also grateful to the anonymous readers of the proposal at OUP for their useful comments and suggestions.

A few words on the cover image: Parul Pandya Dhar introduced me to Chedha Tingsanchali's photograph of this sculpture of Rāvaṇa lifting mount Kailāśa in the *maṇḍapa* of the Virupākṣa temple at Pattadakal, Karnataka. I owe thanks to Dr Gautam Sengupta, Director General of the Archaeological Survey of India; Mr Halakatti, Superintending Archaeologist, Archaeological Survey of India, Dharwad Circle; and to the photographer Somu for making available a beautiful photograph of this sculpture. Aditya Arya, friend and photographic adviser, played an important role in ensuring the high quality of the photograph that was finally used. For me, the sculpture in question is much more than something that provides a striking visual for the cover of this book. Conceptualized and executed centuries ago by a brilliant anonymous sculptor, it is a symbol of the cultural creativity and vitality of the early medieval period.

Upinder Singh

# Acknowledgements

The author and the publisher gratefully acknowledge the following for granting permission to reproduce the following articles and excerpts:

Indian Council of Historical Research for

Noboru Karashima, Y. Subbarayalu, and P. Shanmugam, 'Nagaram: Commerce and Towns AD 850–1350', *Indian Historical Review*, vol. 35, no. 1, 2008, pp. 1–33.

Oxford University Press, New York for

Cynthia Talbot, *Precolonial India in Practice: Society, Region, and Identity in Medieval Andhra*. New York: Oxford University Press, 2001, pp. 48–61 and 84–6.
Leslie C. Orr, 'Domesticity and Difference/Women and Men: Religious Life in Medieval Tamilnadu', in Tracy Pintchman (ed.) *Women's Lives, Women's Rituals in the Hindu Tradition*, New York: Oxford University Press, 2007, pp. 109–29.

Jawaharlal Nehru University and Sage Publications India Pvt. Ltd for

Kunal Chakrabarti, 'Cult Region: The *Purāṇas* and the Making of the Cultural Territory of Bengal', *Studies in History*, vol. 16, no. 1, ns, 2000, pp. 1–16.

Indian Economic and Social History Association and Sage Publications India Pvt. Ltd for

Upinder Singh, 'Politics, Violence, and War in Kāmandaka's *Nītisāra*', *Indian Economic and Social History Review*, vol. 47, no. 1, 2010, pp. 29–62.

India International Centre for

Kapila Vatsyayan, 'The Flying Messenger', in H.P. Ray (ed.), *Sacred Landscapes in Asia: Shared Traditions, Multiple Histories*, New Delhi: India International Centre and Manohar, 2007, pp. 225–38.

University of California Press for

Sheldon Pollock, *The Language of the Gods in the World of Men: Sanskrit, Culture, and Power in Premodern India*. Berkeley: University of California Press, 2006, pp. 10–30.

# Abbreviations

| | |
|---|---|
| *EI* | *Epigraphia Indica* |
| *JBRS* | *Journal of the Bihar Research Society* |
| *JESHO* | *Journal of the Economic and Social History of the Orient* |
| *JASB* | *Journal of the Asiatic Society of Bombay* |
| *JAS* | *Journal of Asian Studies* |
| *SII* | *South Indian Inscriptions* |
| *ARE* | *Annual Report on [South Indian] Epigraphy* |
| *TASSI* | *Transactions of the Archaeological Society of South India*, Madras, 1955 |
| *AMCAIO* | *Ancient and Medieval Commercial Activities in the Indian Ocean: Testimony of Inscriptions and Ceramic-sherds*, Tokyo, 2002 |
| *HAS* | *Hyderabad Archaeological Series* |
| *CPIHM* | *Copper Plate Inscriptions in the Hyderabad Museum* |
| *IAP* | *Inscriptions of Andhra Pradesh* |
| *NDI* | *Nellore District Inscriptions (A Collection of the Inscriptions on Copper Plates and Stones in the Nellore District)* |
| *EA* | *Epigraphia Andhrica* |
| *APAS* | *Andhra Pradesh Archaeological Series* |
| | *No. 3: Kannada Inscriptions of Andhra Pradesh* |
| | *No. 9: Select Stone Inscriptions from the AP Government Museum* |
| | *No. 31: Select Epigraphs of Andhra Pradesh* |
| | *No. 38: Perur Inscriptions* |

| | |
|---|---|
| *TAS* | *Travancore Archaeological Series*, Trivandrum, 1910-38 |
| *CN* | *Cenkam Natukarkal* |
| *IPS* | *Inscriptions (Texts) of the Pudukkottai State Arranged According to Dynasties*, Pudukkottai, 1929 |
| *NK* | *Nannilam Kalvettukal*, Madras, 1979-80 |

# Introduction

## Upinder Singh

A striking aspect of the history of the Indian subcontinent between *c.* 600 CE and 1300 CE, often referred to as the early medieval period, is that regardless of the theoretical framework invoked, regional and pan-Indian historical processes emerge with greater vividness and detail than in earlier centuries. Perspectives on this period are linked to larger issues such as the periodization of India's past and the nature of Indian culture and civilization. They are also connected with how historians view the two major political events within which the early medieval is framed—the decline of the Gupta empire at one end and the consolidation of the Delhi Sultanate at the other. Periods between empires tend to be especially prone to neglect and portrayal as periods of decline.[1] The early medieval period was rescued from neglect many decades ago and became the subject of intense debate among historians, managing to shake off some of its image as a dark age along the way. And yet, it presents a classic case of historiography overwhelming history. At the end of a half century of debate, it is time to rethink the way we think about early medieval India.

The tripartite division of India's past into the Hindu, Muslim (or Mahomedan/Mohammedan) and British periods is often seen as the invention and legacy of James Mill's *History of British India* (1817), but it was part of a much more pervasive perception among nineteenth century European scholars about India's past and present, one in which religion merged with other categories such as ethnicity, race, community and culture. The significant shift in the basis of the labels—from 'Hindu' and 'Muslim' to 'British'—reflected an evolutionary perspective in which British rule marked a break that was qualitatively different from earlier ones, when centuries of backwardness and despotic rule, inextricably intertwined with religion, made way for enlightened governance. In this scheme of things, *c.* 600–1300, sliced through by the Ghaznavid invasions, included the later part of the Hindu and the early part of the Muslim period. There were some more calibrated variations on the theme. For instance, writing in the early twentieth century, Vincent Smith divided India's past into five phases—the ancient period, Hindu period, the period of the medieval Hindu kingdoms, the Muslim period, and the British period, confidently asserting that these were self-evident divisions, not susceptible to any questioning.[2]

While many Indian historians accepted the idea of a Hindu period and considered the Turkish invasions a watershed in Indian history, they did not necessarily accept the 'Muslim' period label. This is reflected in *The History and Culture of the Indian People*, an important and influential eleven-volume series containing the writings of the some of the most eminent historians of its time. R.C. Majumdar, the general editor of the series, described the Hindu, Muslim and British period labels as inconsistent and absurd, and suggested their replacement by the terms ancient, medieval and modern. But the main objection seems to have been to the term 'Muslim period', on the grounds that the rule of Muslim elites did not extend over the entire subcontinent. Along with many of his contemporaries, Majumdar associated the history of India with a history of Hindu civilization and considered the advent of Islam as a calamity.[3] The centuries preceding and following the Turkish invasions were viewed through the lens of invasion and resistance, as a bleak period marked by political decline, in which the only positive developments were in the spheres of art and architecture. The volumes of *The History and Culture of the Indian People* were titled on the basis of themes that were seen as central to the periods concerned: *c.* 700–1000 CE was the age of imperial Kanauj and *c.* 1000–1300 CE was marked by a struggle for empire.[4] The view from South India tended to be much less gloomy, largely because of the political and cultural achievements of the Cōḻas.[5]

Starting from the 1950's, Marxist historians inaugurated a major change in the historiography of ancient India, making a strong case for a shift in focus from dynastic history towards economic and social processes.[6] The writings of D.D. Kosambi were especially influential in changing the agenda. This historiographical shift had profound implications for the understanding of *c.* 600–1300. The Hindu/Muslim periodization was firmly rejected as communal, inconsistent, and as giving unnecessary importance to superficial dynastic change. Political history became passé and dynastic labels for the Indian past were questioned. The historian's gaze moved impatiently away from the minutiae of detail towards the big picture of modes of production and changes in economic and social structures.

Kosambi put forward a two-stage theory of Indian feudalism,[7] but it was really R.S. Sharma's writings that sparked off the major debate. Sharma suggested that *c.* 400–1200 CE was characterized by significant structural changes in economy, society and polity, especially connected with the phenomenon of royal land grants. He discussed these changes within the framework of the emergence, maturity and decline of a feudal order. The feudalism model reigned supreme for about three decades, especially within Indian academia. This was in spite of critiques which challenged its presuppositions and empirical basis, and the eventual appearance of alternative frameworks, chief among which were the segmentary state model and the integrative or processual model.[8]

In the course of this debate, most scholars swiftly became habituated to thinking and talking about *c.* 600—1200/1300 CE as a unit and referring to it as the early medieval period, although the precise beginning and end of this period remained fluid. The assumption was that medievalism was associated with major changes in the social, economic, political, and cultural fabric of India and preceded the establishment of the Delhi Sultanate by several centuries.[9] It should be noted, however, that not everyone accepted the designation of *c.* 600–1300 as 'early medieval'. For instance, in the context of South Indian history, Burton Stein and others referred to this period as full-fledgedly 'medieval'.[10] A clear definition of the early medieval was given by B.D. Chattopadhyaya in his introduction to *The Making of Early Medieval India*, where he suggested that historians tended to understand and present this period as the polar opposite of the early historic.[11] This book is important not only for its content, but also for reinforcing a certain use of the term 'early medieval'.[12] It should be noted that this term was and is still used by many of the adherents of various historical models for the period *c.* 600–1300. In the course of the debate, it was not the idea of the early medieval as a distinct stage in Indian history that was questioned, but the *nature* of the changes that this period witnessed.

The beginning and end of this early medieval always remained hazy.[13] If it was seen as extending up to *c.* 1300, it should have included the early part of the history of the Delhi Sultanate, but right from the outset, the early medieval had a split personality—there was not one, but two early medieval Indias, each with its own, largely separate, historiography, both functioning in isolation from each other, scarcely aware of the other's existence.[14] One consisted of pre-Sultanate and non-Sultanate history; the other focused on the history of the Delhi Sultanate, using the term 'early medieval' for the Sultanate period and distinguishing it from the 'later medieval' which was identified with the Mughal empire.[15] A major reason for this divide was the fact that Sanskrit inscriptions were a major source for the former and Persian chronicles for the latter, and few historians had expertise in both languages. Historians involved in the debate on early medieval India largely on the basis of an analysis of Sanskrit land grant inscriptions argued that crucial economic and social changes preceded the Turkish conquest by several centuries, but those working on the Sultanate and Mughal periods took little cognizance of such assertions. In fact, many historians working on the history of the Sultanate, while rejecting the labels of the 'Hindu' and 'Muslim' periods, argued that that the establishment of the Delhi Sultanate did in fact mark a historical watershed, not because of the religious affiliations of the new elites, but because it led to profound economic changes.[16] As a result of these factors, although the old labels (Hindu, Muslim) made way for the new (ancient, medieval), the historiography of the Delhi Sultanate retained a distinct identity, and this tended to perpetuate the very ways of thinking it sought to critique. Although at one time, the term 'early medieval' was often used for the Sultanate period, these days, historians of medieval India are by no means committed to this usage. All this should make it apparent that terminology is a slippery terrain and that an integrated history of *c.* 600–1300 simply does not exist. This book is forced to function within this limitation. It is essentially about pre-Sultanate and non-Sultanate history, although the last essay draws attention to the ways in which the two early medieval Indias can, and indeed must, be brought together, if the idea of the early medieval is to survive in a meaningful way.

Considering that the early medieval period has been the subject of constant reinterpretation over many decades, can a case be made for yet another round of rethinking? For several reasons, the answer is yes. It is necessary to take stock and see whether we are closer to any consensus, or even near consensus, after a half-century of debate. Further, although the debate undoubtedly opened the political, social, and economic aspects of the early medieval period to fresh, intense scrutiny, it also created a curious impasse. For far too long, the history of *c.* 600–1300 has been considered synonymous with the debate on whether or not feudalism existed in India. Researchers have generally marshalled empirical evidence selectively in order to support one or other hypothesis, displaying a disinclination to move beyond existing frameworks, and several significant aspects of the period that are peripheral to the concerns of the debate have not received the attention they deserve. The debate is important and cannot be by-passed; that is why this book begins with it.[17] At the same time, it also directs attention towards the many important issues that lie beyond the pale of this debate. The aim is to raise as many questions as possible, including about the very idea of the early medieval, which can form the basis of new approaches towards understanding this important phase in Indian history.

## I

Part I of this book offers an overview of the three major theoretical models for early medieval India, with special emphasis on their perspective on political processes. These are part of a protracted academic conversation involving many participants, in which ideas were expressed, critiqued, and remoulded over many decades.[18] Here, the most recent and mature formulations of the hypotheses have been included, ones in which the scholars concerned have responded to what they consider the most serious critiques, and in which they have fine-tuned their ideas on the basis of considered reflection. Apart from critically evaluating the strengths and weaknesses of the arguments, questions to ponder over while reading the essays include: how do these recent formulations compare with the initial versions and with each other? Are there new insights and are there issues that remain problematic or unresolved?

Although not the first to write about Indian feudalism, and certainly not the only one to do so, R.S. Sharma has single-handedly done more than any other scholar to develop this hypothesis and establish it within mainstream historiography.[19] His *Indian Feudalism* (1965) was a radical intervention, a bold venture that synthesized an enormous range of epigraphic data and offered a hypothesis that was subcontinental in scope,[20] tracking key processes in Indian history over almost a millennium. At one sweep, the older histories of early medieval India with their dynastic frameworks and mournful view of the advent of Muslim rule appeared superficial. The focus was firmly shifted away from political narrative to political processes and agrarian change. The historiography of early medieval India would never be the same again.

Sharma is an exceptionally prolific scholar, and his writings on Indian feudalism range over about half a century, from a 1958 article to his most recent book, published in 2009.[21] The essay included here represents his most recent, detailed thoughts on the subject.[22] Sharma reiterates some of his earlier ideas, introduces a few new nuances and emphases, and responds to some of his critics. The definition of feudalism that he offers is more succinct than the one in *Indian Feudalism*—he describes it as a mechanism for the distribution of the means of production and the appropriation of surplus in a predominantly agrarian society. He asserts a basic similarity between Indian and Western European feudalism (something that has, throughout, laid the hypothesis open to the charge of Eurocentricism), but also concedes that there were differences. These differences, as well as variations within the Indian feudal order, are more sharply underlined than before. Referring to the need to re-examine the concept of class in pre-capitalist societies, Sharma highlights the differentiation within the peasantry in early medieval times. The emphasis is squarely on agrarian relations, and there is only fleeting reference to the hypothesis of a decline of urban centres, coinage and trade, issues which he had dealt with in greater detail in *Indian Feudalism* and even more so in *Urban Decay in India*—ideas which have been contested.[23] Compared to *Indian Feudalism*, there is a stronger focus on caste, which Sharma understands as a means of sanctioning new social hierarchies. Tension and conflict between donees and peasants were part of the original formulation, but here he also talks of religious movements, ideas and practices that helped deal with this conflict. Further, unlike in *Indian Feudalism*, where he placed the climax and the beginning of the disintegration of the feudal order during *c.* 1000–1200, here he seems to suggest that the essentials of feudal agrarian relations continued to exist till the sixteenth century, when the central authority became stronger with the establishment of Mughal rule.

Reacting to critiques of the feudalism model, Sharma chooses Harbans Mukhia's essay for the most detailed response.[24] He refutes Mukhia's assertion that the peasant in early medieval India had basic control over the means and process of production, and demonstrates that the land grant inscriptions clearly indicate that the donees controlled the entire production process and had political and juridical rights backed by the threat of force. Serfdom remains central to the hypothesis. In *Indian Feudalism*, Sharma identified two kinds of serfs: those whose home and land lay in the donees' estates and who provided them with labour services; and semi-serfs who gave them rent. Here, he asserts that the essence of serfdom was the existence of small satellite farms attached to big ones, the latter being managed by 'manorial magnates' but cultivated by small farm owners. He states that the peasant was deprived of both surplus labour and surplus produce, although he considers the former more important. As earlier, he talks of peasants being attached to the soil and being compelled to work on the estates of their lords, but here he also talks of serf labour being one of *various* kinds of available labour, along with tenants, share-croppers and forced labour. He asserts that feudalism flourished in paddy-producing areas because the requirements of labour were higher there; this counters Mukhia's assertion that the fertility of the soil in India precluded the emergence of serfdom.

In spite of Sharma's spirited rejoinder to Mukhia, the latter's question about whether the subjection of the peasantry is equivalent to serfdom remains valid. The subjection of the peasantry took various forms in different parts of the world, and all these forms cannot be subsumed under a single category. Sharma counters Mukhia's argument that no new mode of production can appear due to measures from the top, and asserts that the Kali crisis was a crisis in the mode of production which led to a critical situation where kings had to resort to making land grants because they were unable to collect taxes and pay priests, administrative officials, and soldiers. But the source of this crisis remains as puzzling as in the initial formulation of the feudalism hypothesis.

Sharma's essay also contains a brief but more hard-hitting critique of Burton Stein's ideas. He questions Stein's association of the Indian feudalism model with Marxist/left historians, and asserts that the criticism of the model emanates from some Western historians who cannot extricate themselves from colonial constructs of Indian history.[25] He suggests that the application of the segmentary state hypothesis to early medieval South India amounts to the resurrection of the theories of the Asiatic mode of production and oriental despotism in new garb. Sharma relegates comments on other critiques of the feudalism hypothesis and alternative theoretical frameworks to footnotes, and there is little serious engagement with them.

Several aspects of the feudalism hypothesis remain problematic. These include the frequent conflation, for instance between the Indian and European historical experience; between hierarchies in politics and rural society; between subordinated peasants and serfs; and between the situation prevailing in the *brahmadeya* and the average village. Early medieval society cannot be meaningfully understood by using the Dharmaśāstric *varṇa* framework, and the spread of the institution of caste requires much more attention. A close reading of inscriptions from different parts of the subcontinent reveals that the nature and degree of social and economic stratification that resulted from land grants depended on several factors that varied across regions. A subcontinental hypothesis has to take this into account. The manner in which Sharma directly links land grants with religion, philosophy, and popular ideas is representative of the reductionist way in which proponents of Indian feudalism have tended to treat the religious and cultural domains.

At the heart of the matter (and this applies to the other models as well) are certain fundamental methodological issues concerning the relationship between the historian and the sources, and between theoretical models and empirical evidence. A nuanced reading of the sources in their entirety, one which is attentive to their idiom and ambiguities, becomes difficult if the main aim is to prove the veracity of a historical model. There is also the question of whether the comparative method is best used in historical analysis to identify similarities and extend the purview of historical models, or to highlight specificities and differences. Sharma's hypothesis may in fact have worked better minus the references to medieval Europe, serfs, seigneurial rights, manorial magnates, and subinfeudation. After all, it does offer important insights into long-term subcontinental patterns of political hierarchies and agrarian relations, even if various aspects of its vision of the early medieval can be questioned.

In the context of South India, it was not Sharma but Burton Stein who shook things up. Stein's *Peasant State and Society in Medieval South India* was published in 1980 (a good fifteen years after *Indian Feudalism*), but Stein had put forward a searing critique of the traditional historiography of South India well before that. It was a hard-hitting but convincing critique, designed to pave the way for a definitive shift in the way in which the South Indian state and society had been theorized. Stein suggested that the segmentary state model, designed by anthropologist Aidan Southall in the context of his work on the African Alur tribe,[26] could fruitfully be applied to South India. The essay included in this book represents Stein's most recent (actually his last) reflections on the segmentary state hypothesis, especially in view of Southall's reformulations. It is noteworthy that he describes this as an 'interim report', indicating that he was open to further thinking on the issue. Stein's hypothesis was largely confined to South India, although he does hint at the possibility of applying it to other areas. Like the feudalism hypothesis, it too gave a long-term view, focusing on the Pallava and Cōḻa periods and extending the discussion to the Vijayanagara empire.

In his earlier writings, Stein had basically engaged with the older, traditional historiography of South India. In this essay, he broadens the engagement, defining the segmentary state in contradistinction to the unitary and feudal state. The distinguishing features of the segmentary state are essentially similar to those outlined in *Peasant State and Society*—the existence of several centres or political domains; a differentiation between political power and sovereignty; the autonomous administrative and coercive capacities of all the domains; and a single ritual centre, an anointed king, being recognized by lesser political centres. Referring once again to Y. Subbarayalu's work on the *nāḍus*,[27] Stein reiterates that these localities were the basic building blocks of the pyramidally segmented society of South India. He sees the chiefdoms and monarchies of the time as layered in a hierarchical ranking within a political sphere characterized by shared sovereignty.

Stein divides his critics into the categories of strong and weak, intellectual and ideological, asserting that some of their criticisms are based on an erroneous reading of his work. For example, he cites B.D. Chattopadhyaya's assertion that he had denied elements of centralization as an instance of a weak intellectual criticism. It is, however, difficult to accept Stein's claim that *Peasant State and Society* draws attention to the highly centralized resource command of the Cōḻa state. Stein rather unfairly alleges a racist bias in some of the critiques, claiming that while Indian scholars delight in comparing their history with Europe, they find comparisons with Africa offensive. He dismisses criticisms from the right and the left (no names are given), apparently correlating the centralized view of the state with right-wing communal ideologies and connecting left-oriented historiography with an obsession with class, class conflict, and the state. Of course, all these points can be contested, but they are for the most part polemical rather than academic.

Stein does not really offer an effective response to the many cogent critiques of his hypothesis. These include its disregard for the differentiation within agrarian society, the role of urban groups including merchants, and the abundant evidence of an administrative and revenue infrastructure in the Cōḻa kingdom. There is also the question of the usefulness of a model that includes within its purview states which seem to have little in common (for example, the Alur tribal polity and the feudal kingdoms of medieval Europe). Stein's critique of the older historiography is much more pertinent than his cavalier treatment of more recent perspectives. While he makes the perplexing statement that the feudalism model has not been elaborated, and that the state is absent in its formulation, he adds the more acceptable point that it overlooks evidence regarding urbanization, trade, and banking. Stein identifies Kulke's integrative model as one of the strong critiques of his segmentary state model, but describes it as 'vague', especially with regard to its explanation of the process of cult appropriation. Nevertheless, he concedes the possibility of a reconciliation of his views with those of Chattopadhyaya and Kulke.

In this essay, Stein focuses squarely on the segmentary state and does not elaborate on the other ideas that were central to *Peasant State and Society*—those of a peasant society, peasant state and the Brāhmaṇa–peasant alliance.[28] He also responds to Southall's recent reworking of the segmentary state hypothesis; he clearly prefers the original formulation and suggests ways in which it can be recast. This includes jettisoning the problematic dichotomy between ritual sovereignty and political sovereignty; elaborating the relationship between segmentary polity and social segmentation; and explaining the element of pyramidality with greater clarity. He acknowledges the existence of different types of segmentary states and gives a longer lease of life to the segmentary polity of South India, asserting that it extended from the sixth to the nineteenth century. Further, he suggests that a comparative analysis must proceed along analogical rather than homological lines.

In spite of his reiteration of faith in the segmentary state model, some new emphases can be discerned in this essay. These include a description of the *nāḍus* as political and social *communities*—'communities' being understood as 'part societies', including people and the place they inhabit, along with shared sentiments, values, and entitlements over human and material resources. Stein argues that the relationship between these communities and the state is a crucial element in understanding Indian societies. Also significant is his emphasis on the importance of the spheres of culture and ideology, and of the moral and political dimensions of the state as expressed in normative texts. These are ideas worthy of careful consideration.

B.D. Chattopadhyaya and Hermann Kulke deserve equal credit for thoughtful critiques of the feudalism model and for proposing an alternative theoretical framework for early medieval India.[29] In the 1980's, their writings presented a major breakthrough in a historiography that had got into the habit of thinking of Indian feudalism as an established fact to which no alternatives were possible.[30] For a long time, their framework was somewhat apologetically referred to as the 'alternative model' in distinction to the 'dominant', that is, the feudalism model. Today, such phraseology may seem unnecessarily hesitant and self-effacing, but it has to be understood against the background of the overwhelming support enjoyed by the feudalism hypothesis among Indian historians at that point of time.

Chattopadhyaya and Kulke convincingly argued that from the political and cultural points of view, the early medieval period was marked by integration, most visible in the process of intensive state formation in areas that were peripheral to the heartlands of the earlier large kingdoms and empires. Chattopadhyaya identified certain important processes that were at work in all phases of Indian history, including the early medieval: the expansion of state society through local state formation; the transformation of tribes into peasants and the expansion of caste; and cult appropriation and integration.[31] In the essay included in this volume, Kulke offers a further refinement and elaboration of the integrative model, which he describes as a processual model of integrative state formation.[32] The diachronic element is present in the feudalism and segmentary state models, but is especially prominent in Kulke's recent formulation. He describes integrative state formation in various geo-political zones as a process of continuous and interactive political development comprising chiefdom, early kingdom, and imperial kingdom, pointing out that integration worked simultaneously at multiple levels—political, administrative, agrarian, ritual, and cultural—with legitimation constituting an important link.

Of the three theoretical frameworks for early medieval India, Kulke and Chattopadhaya's model brings out the relationship between the socio-political, religious, and cultural domains most successfully. In the essay included in this volume, Kulke talks of changes in the ideology of kingship, the influence of the *bhakti* cult on politics, the importance of the king–Brāhmaṇa relationship, and the integrative role of royal patronage of temples and *tīrthas*. Tribes—often mentioned fleetingly in other discussions of the state—have an important place here. They interface with kingdoms, which were dependent on forest resources and recruited forest people into armies. Kulke highlights the transformation of tribal chieftains into Hindu *rājās* and the interactions between states and tribal communities, which were reflected in the patronage of autochthonous cults by upwardly mobile rulers.

What is perhaps most important in his elaboration of the processual integrative state is the fact that he acknowledges that integration also involved war, conquest, and violence, and that, in spite of the systematic expansion and centralizing tendencies of certain states, the writ of the emperor did not run unimpeded. Autonomous localities, defiant tribal chieftains, allies, and independent kingdoms were important parts of the story of imperial expansion and perennial sources of political instability. Kulke also refers in passing to a host of other issues such as the development of regional kinship systems, the codification of regional norms, Sanskritization, Kṣatriyization, Hinduization, the spread of caste, the shift from Sanskrit to the regional languages, and the emergence of new regional identities.

Kulke is the most accommodating of the various participants in the debate when it comes to recognizing the congruence of his model with others. His description of the impact of land grants on tribal areas is essentially similar to Sharma's. In his description of the second stage of early medieval state formation, he acknowledges the validity of Stein's observation that the power of the king diminished with the distance from the capital city. He goes as far as to state that the 'samantaization' of the early kingdoms can be described as an Indian variant of feudalism. At the same time, he emphasizes that this phenomenon did not by any means originate from a decline of an earlier empire. Further, his (and Chattopadhyaya's) interpretation of the rationale and impact of royal land grants remains diametrically different from that offered by the proponents of Indian feudalism.

The integrative/processual model has been found useful in many studies that have focused on specific regions.[33] However, several issues can be raised in connection with the hypothesis. One has to do with the emphasis on legitimation.[34] The focus on legitimation should not allow us forget that land grants effected transfers of land rights and that it is therefore necessary to examine their impact on agrarian relations in detail. There is also the question of instrumentality. Did Brāhmaṇas consciously legitimize the power of local chiefs by crafting genealogies and providing advice and guidance on rule, or did they rather unconsciously and inchoately participate along with chiefs, kings and others in the emergence of a new politico-cultural world? Further, Kulke's discussion of religion tends to be state-centric and his use of homogeneous politico-religious categories such as 'Hindu states' and 'Islamic states' is problematic. The strong emphasis on integrative processes in early medieval India may have been necessary in view of the feudalism school's emphasis on disintegration, but it should be noted that state formation in all periods is necessarily integrative to some degree, the differences lying in the scale and mechanisms of integration. And in the emphasis on integration, the centripetal forces and the elements of resistance, conflict, and violence should not be underestimated.

Continuity and change are the essence of history, but early medieval India has usually been viewed through the lens of change rather than continuity. If we are to open the period, especially its political aspects, to fresh scrutiny, the levels of continuity and disjuncture between the early historic, early medieval, and the centuries in between need to be looked at afresh. Several processes that are often treated as characteristic of the early medieval period, in fact, have older antecedents. These include the connection between kings and Brāhmaṇas, Brāhmaṇas and land, and the phenomenon of Brāhmaṇa migrations.[35] A fresh investigation of earlier states, including the Maurya, post-Maurya, Gupta and Vākāṭaka polities, is long overdue. In fact, the study of the state in ancient India has for far too long been mired in debates about whether states and empires were centralized or decentralized, homogenous or heterogeneous entities, as if the answers to these questions were not fairly obvious. It is also necessary to move beyond treating the existence or absence of a bureaucratized land taxation system and a monopoly over force as the only diagnostic features of the state.[36] Another way of broadening the horizons of the discussion is to bring in fresh sources through a thorough archaeological investigation of early medieval sites and by harnessing the evidence emerging from such investigation to the reconstruction of political processes. Currently, the only Indian state for which there has been an in-depth study of the archaeological data is the Vijayanagara empire.[37]

A re-examination of earlier states would have important implications for how the political processes of the early medieval period are visualized. But it is also necessary to confront the reality that although kingdoms and empires interest historians greatly, there were always vast expanses of forest where the state was absent, where plough-based agriculture was not practised, and where caste society did not penetrate easily or at all. And while acknowledging the importance of the political domain, we also need to look beyond it.

## II

The rural and urban aspects of the early medieval economy and society have both received considerable scholarly attention.[38] However, the importance of the forest and forest people, so vividly visible in ancient Indian texts of all kinds, has been seriously underestimated by most historians. It should be noted that in spite of the land clearance that accompanied the expansion of agriculture, large tracts of land in the subcontinent continued to be under forests which were home to communities of hunters-gatherers. Massive deforestation was actually a feature of the colonial period, when the extension of the railways, population increase, and the commercialization of agriculture led to an unprecedented and dramatic reduction of forest cover.[39] An appreciation of this fact is important for our understanding of Indian history.

The first two essays in the second section of this book focus on agrarian structure, urban patterns, and trade. They exemplify the careful analysis of the epigraphic vocabulary that marks the scholarship on early medieval South India. The state is not absent in Kesavan Veluthat's essay on land rights and social stratification. In fact, he begins (in a similar vein as Stein) with a critique of the idealized picture of the South Indian state in early writings, pointing to internal contradictions in their arguments and their overlooking of the abundant evidence of social distinctions. But this is followed by an even stronger critique of Stein's work on similar grounds, in particular, especially his ignoring of data that contradicts the portrayal of a relatively undifferentiated peasant society and the hypothesis of a Brāhmaṇa–peasant alliance. Although Veluthat ultimately asserts that the picture of agrarian society in early medieval South India fits well with Sharma's feudalism model and with the basic structure of feudal society in Western Europe, he generously welcomes all theoretical perspectives that are thoroughly grounded in the primary sources. The fact that he describes Stein as a representative of 'recent American scholarship' and contrasts his writings with those of 'Asian scholars' indicates a perception of a divide based on continental lines, an idea that is also present in Stein's essay.

Synthesizing the results of his own research with that of other scholars in the field,[40] Veluthat traces changes in land rights from the Pallava inscriptions through the greater complexity reflected in the later Pāṇḍya and Cēra epigraphs, on to the emergence of a new agrarian order in the Cōḻa period. While the existence of the idea of private property can be identified from early historic times, ancient notions of ownership differed from modern ones. Therefore, the search has to be for hierarchies of graded land rights rather than absolute ownership rights. Further, the detailed work of Karashima and Subbarayalu has shown that there were variations and changes in the incidence of private property within the early medieval period.[41] Based on a careful analysis of technical terms in the inscriptions, Veluthat identifies the different kinds of hierarchies that existed in different types of villages (*ur*, *brahmadeya*, *devadāna*, etc.), extending from the king to the agricultural labourer. This is important, as many scholars tend to conflate these hierarchies or take the *brahmadeya* as representing the norm rather than the exception. While there were broad similarities between the agrarian order of north and south, the strong corporate traditions represented in the village assemblies of South India were a distinctive element. Also evident are the differences *within* regions of the south, for example in Kerala, non-Brāhmaṇa peasant proprietors were not as strong, and the level of stratification seems to have been greater than elsewhere.

The importance of caste as a subject of academic inquiry is no doubt due to its contemporary social and political significance. The study of this institution been dominated by sociologists and historical anthropologists, who have primarily focused on its profile in colonial and post-colonial times. But the roots of caste lie in ancient India. Discussions of the early history of this institution have generally focused on two phases: its emergence in the early historic period, and its intensification and spread in the early medieval period. However, this discussion has not been accompanied by the posing of fundamental questions, the most important of which is: what exactly are we looking for?[42] As is well known, the word 'caste' is of relatively recent, sixteenth century Portuguese origin. *Varṇa* is much older and is found in ancient Indian texts, but cannot be translated as caste. *Jāti* can be translated as caste or sub-caste, but the ancient texts often use this word in other senses as well (including birth, type and rank). To make the confusion worse, ancient texts often use *varṇa* and *jāti* interchangeably. In our search for the early history of caste, we need to work with broad definitions and to look for evidence of elements of endogamy, hereditary professions and commensality in social functioning. But we should also be aware of the problems of defining caste and of the difficulties involved tracing its early history through the available sources. The configurations and nature of caste changed over time, the institution had regional variations, it spread to areas and communities with very different types of kinship and family structures, and it intersected in different ways with economic and political factors. At the same time, there were many areas where its impact was minimal or non-existent.

*Varṇa* and caste in early medieval India have to be understood against this background. Veluthat's point about the irrelevance of the *varṇa* hierarchy (apart from the Brāhmaṇas) in South India is well taken, but the questions that require more detailed investigation are: why did some *varṇa* categories travel and others not, and why were some of them turned on their head, as reflected in the category of *satśūdra*, which came to be associated with land-owning *veḷḷāḷas*? Veluthat refers to the transformation of artisans and tribes into *jātis* and argues that many of the occupational terms in the inscriptions can be understood as caste categories. The fact that the *veḷḷāḷas* were almost equivalent in status to Brāhmaṇas directs our attention to the fact that caste has always intersected with other bases of social identity, especially economic power. It is evident that the history of this institution requires much more careful scholarly attention. We cannot simply assume a steady or uniform proliferation and intensification of caste organization in early medieval India.[43]

From the village, we move to the town. The essay by Noboru Karashima, Y. Subbarayalu, and P. Shanmugam focuses on *nagarams* (market/commercial centres) during the Cōḻa period. For the purpose of analysis, the authors divide the Cōḻa period into three sub-phases, within which they discuss several issues such as the relationship between the *nagarams*, *nagarattār* (the members of the *nagaram*'s corporate body), merchant guilds, villages and the state. Their analysis makes it clear that the number of *nagarams* in a *nāḍu* could vary and that there were some *nāḍus* without any *nagaram*. A *nagaram* could, therefore, serve as a marketing or commercial centre for several *nāḍus*.

The statistical data assembled by Karashima, Subbarayalu and Shanmugam enables a diachronic view of the activities of the *nagarams*. In the first phase (850–1000 CE), they were under the firm control and scrutiny of the Cōḻa state, and merchants of most *nagarams* do not seem to have been involved in vigorous commercial activities. The *nagarattār* appear frequently in inscriptions as recipients and custodians of money gifted to temples and participated in temple management along with royal and temple officials and corporate bodies such as the *sabhā* and *ur*. As land-owners, they were involved in various land transactions. The middle phase (1001–1200 CE) saw a significant expansion of the Cōḻa state, the naval expeditions to Southeast Asia, and the building of the Bṛhadīśvara temple at Thanjavur, one of the grandest royal temples of early medieval India, where the *nagarattār* feature as recipients and custodians of monetary endowments. During this phase, they were still involved in land management, and are seen negotiating with revenue officers over tax rates.

The configurations of the political situation changed in the third phase (1201–1350 CE), when Cōḻa power declined and other kings and local chiefs came to the fore. Inscriptions testify to the increasing strength and influence of merchant guilds, especially the Aiñūṟṟuvar. Karashima, Subbarayalu, and Shanmugam demonstrate how local merchants, peasants, and powerful merchant guilds interfaced during this period of expanding trade. Apart from the relationship between *nagarams* and guilds, what are equally striking are the connections between merchants and soldiers, and between guilds and farmers' corporate organizations. The third phase also saw the transformation of certain occupational groups into *jātis*. Tribals from the hills who had joined the Cōḷa army emerged as landowners and local chiefs and were absorbed into the caste fold.

One of the significant features of this detailed account of the *nagarams* of South India is the overlap and interaction between village and city and between people involved in agriculture, artisanal production and trade. The authors point to varying patterns across areas and periods in the relations between merchants, artisans, and rulers. As for caste, we would need to know more about the extent to which social organization and interaction was governed by the principles of hereditary occupation, endogamy and commensality. The increasing importance of India–Southeast Asia trade is more than apparent from this essay; the cultural dimensions of these trade interactions need to be explored in greater detail. [44] At the level of method (as will become increasingly apparent from the discussion that follows), it must be noted that the full potential of a statistical analysis of epigraphic data can only be realized if it is accompanied by a careful interrogation of the perspectives that the inscriptions represent.

In contrast to much of the writing on South India, which tends to focus on Cōḷamaṇḍala, Cynthia Talbot's *Precolonial India in Practice*, from which an extract has been included in this book, deals with Andhra. Talbot in fact criticizes the tendency of historians to generalize about South India on the basis of what was happening in the heartland of the Cōḷa empire. Although her book discusses many aspects of society, religion and identity, including gender and the warrior ethic, the excerpt chosen here deals mainly with *varṇa* and *jāti*.

Talbot highlights the importance of inscriptions as a source for the social history of pre-colonial India and examines the ways in which individuals and groups of people are described in some 1000 donative inscriptions belonging to the Kakatiya kingdom (1175–1324 CE). What is especially refreshing about her approach is the fact that her careful analysis of the empirical data is accompanied by a discussion of the potential as well as the limitations and silences of the epigraphic record. Talbot points out that the inscriptions cannot be read as a straightforward reflection of the society in which they were produced: they essentially indicate how the relatively affluent people on whose behalf they were composed wanted themselves represented. She emphasizes that the social identities mentioned in the epigraphs need not correspond to all the social identities that were current at the time, nor to concrete entities that were central in other contexts. The inscriptions tell us what their commissioners and composers wanted conveyed at that particular place for the purpose of the donative record. This realization should be central to any historical analysis of epigraphic sources.

As significant as the bases of social identity that are emphasized in the inscriptions are those that are not. It has been noted by many scholars that apart from Brāhmaḍas (and the *varṇa* status claimed by some kings), the *varṇa* classification is largely absent in early medieval inscriptions. Andhra further presents us with the interesting phenomenon of leading warrior families, including the Kakatiyas, proudly proclaiming that they were Śūdras. As far as caste is concerned, there are few references in the inscriptions to the term *jāti* or to social categories that can be identified as *jātis*.[45] Of course, there is the problem of identifying what exactly we are looking for in view of the elasticity of meaning associated with the word *jāti* and the problem of the terseness of the epigraphic references, which all too often leave the nature of social identities and interactions ambiguous. In spite of these problems, the few clearly identifiable references to caste in the Andhra inscriptions is intriguing, especially considering the fact that the early medieval period is generally viewed as having witnessed a major expansion and intensification of caste organization. Talbot's analysis of names and titles suggests that in early medieval Andhra, status titles referred broadly to occupational groups rather than to localized communities. Clan and lineage (terms for which often overlap) were central to social identity and there was an emphasis on achieved, rather than ascribed, status. The society of early medieval Andhra appears to have been much more fluid than we would have imagined.

Going by Talbot's own cautionary note that the social categories mentioned in inscriptions were not a mirror image of the society of their time, it could be argued that caste identities did exist, but that their specification was not considered necessary for the purpose of the donative record. However, if caste was central to society, a silence of this kind would be surprising, to say the least. Studies such as Talbot's indicate that we need to carefully examine our assumptions about social processes in early medieval India and that there were significant variations in the trajectories of the institution of caste, not only over time, but also across and within regions. It is apparent that the history of caste in pre-colonial India requires much more extensive and careful investigation.

Devika Rangachari's essay 'Women and Power in Early Medieval Kashmir' is part of this book for two important reasons. First, it deals with a part of the subcontinent that is often bypassed by historians. And second, it talks of the participation of women in the political sphere, an issue that has been marginal to the debate on early medieval India.[46] Modern historians have presented Kashmir politics as an exclusively male domain, so much so, that Aurel Stein's genealogies ignore the Kashmir queens completely.[47] In contrast, early medieval texts contain abundant evidence of women's participation in the political sphere. Rangachari substantiates this through an analysis of three textual sources belonging to very different genres—Kalhaṇa's *Rājataraṅgiṇī*, Kṣemendra's *Samayamātṛkā* and the *Nīlamatapurāṇa*. She points out that Kalhaṇa does not present the queens Sugandhā or Diddā as passive puppets but as ambitious rulers whose actions led to decisive shifts in the line of succession. But apart from queens who ruled the land, built temples and cities, and extended financial support to religious establishments, non-royal women, including courtesans and prostitutes, also played politically significant roles.

Rangachari distinguishes between the texts' narrative and authorial gloss. For instance, although Kalhaṇa's poetic narrative indicates that he considered women significant political actors, his attitude towards this phenomenon was clearly marked by a certain ambivalence. Kṣemendra's *Samayamātṛkā* too can be read against the grain. Ostensibly written in order to instruct prostitutes in their art (and to warn men of their wiles) and to teach the king how to use women as a weapon against his foes, its exaggerated portrayal of prostitutes in fact suggests their importance in the political and social worlds. The *Nīlamatapurāṇa* corroborates the conclusions arising from the analysis of the other two sources, but adds an important dimension in its description of women's participation in festivals and religious ceremonies. Lest we reach extreme or hasty conclusions, Rangachari points out that the description of the *īramañjarī* festival in the *Nīlamatapurāṇa* reflects prevailing prejudices towards widows and unmarried women.

A question posed by Rangachari is: how did certain women of Kashmir bypass the ideological barriers of their time and emerge as politically powerful figures? She argues that the crucial issue was not whether the polity was centralized or decentralized; the answers lie in the gap between theory and practice, the isolation of Kashmir from other kingdoms, and the strong tribal roots of the region. All these factors coalesced to create a social and political fabric marked by 'relatively unstructured gender roles'. However, it must be emphasized that theory and practice are not separate dichotomous domains and that we may be looking at gendered roles that were marked by considerable complexity rather than a lack of structure. The assertion of the 'cultural acceptance' of women rulers needs to be nuanced keeping this in mind. The evidence from other parts of the subcontinent (for example, the Bhauma-Kara queens of Orissa, the Vākāṭaka queen Prabhāvatīgupta, and the Kakatiya queens of Andhra) in fact suggests that the situation in Kashmir was not unique.

The larger point that needs to be emphasized is that early medieval politics cannot be understood, as has been the general trend, with an exclusive focus on kings, chieftains and their officials, allies and retainers. There has been insufficient recognition of the intersection of the private and political spheres, the political impact of kinship and family structures, and the importance of the royal household in ancient and medieval kingdoms.[48] This is in contrast to ancient political treatises such as the *Arthaśāstra* and *Nītisāra* which are quite explicit about the importance of the household, especially queens and princes, in their discussion of statecraft. What is required is a careful study of a wide range of textual and epigraphic sources, one that situates them in their historical contexts and the conventions of their genre, and which highlights their similarities as well as differences in perspective.

It is also time for studies of gender to break out of their cocooned worlds. Between the two extremes of constantly invoking patriarchy to emphasize women's subordination and oppression on the one hand and an exaggerated idealization of their social and political place in ancient societies on the other, there is plenty of room for a nuanced investigation of the complex interplay of the roles and relationships of women and men in predominantly patriarchal and patrilineal societies (which were by no means homogeneous in nature), and for an approach which integrates gender with other bases of identity and with larger political and social histories.

## III

The early medieval period was marked by major developments in religious ideas, practices and institutions as well as exceptional vitality in the spheres of art and architecture.[49] The third section of this book highlights the importance of these issues. During the post-1960s shift in historical agenda towards economic and social history, the old definition of culture came to be considered elitist and hackneyed, and a broader notion of culture, which included all socially patterned aspects of human life and behavior, was invoked. But through a sleight of hand, the aspects that fell within the older, traditional understanding of culture (including literature, art, and religion) were ignored, handed over to other specialists (Sanskritists, literary scholars, and historians of art and religion), or interpreted in a simplistic and reductionist manner. It is not that no one wrote about culture; it was rather a question of a larger, unspoken consensus among historians about what constituted the subjects most worthy of historical inquiry. This coalesced with a much more explicitly expressed idea that 'secular' history was history sans religion.

Currently, there are two broad kinds of scholarship on the history of religion and art in ancient and early medieval India. One emerges from the disciplines of religious history and art history and often lacks a strong historical grounding. The other is primarily devoted to connecting religion and art with changes in the socio-political fabric, and is especially interested in patronage and legitimation, in function rather than content. But religion cannot be understood if treated purely as ideology, disregarding its philosophical and doctrinal underpinnings and the details of religious belief and practice. Similarly, a study of ancient sculpture, architecture or literature, which is insensitive to the language and grammar of aesthetics can only yield superficial results. The time is ripe for a much more direct, analytical and yet nuanced historical engagement with what may be broadly termed the cultural domain,[50] one which is not restricted to elite groups, even if the sources tend to predispose us to such a focus. To start off with, historians would do well to take note of approaches within the disciplines of the history of art and religion. The merging of concerns across disciplines can lead to mutual enrichment and the emergence of new insights and methodologies. Apart from their intrinsic merits, the inclusion of the essays by Leslie C. Orr (a scholar of religion) and Kapila Vatsyayan (a scholar of art and culture) in this book aims at making precisely this point.

Leslie Orr uses thousands of inscriptions to analyse piety and patronage in Tamil Nadu between the ninth and thirteenth centuries, within a gendered framework. It should be noted that Orr's is an inquiry into the religious aspirations and actions of women *and* men, especially the extent to which these reflect a domestic sphere of religiosity. Central to her analysis is anthropologist Susan Starr Sered's concept of the 'domestic' which is not defined by the locale of actions, but by the intent of the performers.[51] The domestic is a personalized sphere of religion in which the concerns of life, suffering and death of specific people, usually loved ones, are at the fore. The focus on aspirations, emotions and sentiments should be noted by historians, who are wont to ignore such things or to reduce them to expressions of class or self interest.

Like the extract from Talbot's book, this essay too is marked by a careful reflection on its sources. Further, unlike most works on religious history which tend to focus on a single religious tradition, Orr's database comprises Hindu as well as Jaina inscriptions and also brings out the cultural variations within South India. Orr combines quantitative analysis with a careful examination of the epigraphic vocabulary, frequently looking towards texts to unravel problematic terms, never reading newer meanings into older words. The many contexts of religious austerities, renunciation and sacrifice are examined in detail, including the phenomenon of extreme self-sacrifice in the form of suicide for the sake of a divine lord.

The temple was an important institution in early medieval India, and much has been written about the connections between the patronage of religious establishments and social and political legitimation. But as mentioned earlier, there is more to religious activity than legitimation, and donative records cannot be understood properly without attentiveness towards the idiom in which piety was expressed and how religious activity was interpreted by those who were engaged in it. Women do not appear as temple priests or managers in the inscriptions, but they do figure prominently as patrons and donors. Orr points to differences between the nature of the pious gifts made by men and women, including women's marked tendency to extend patronage towards goddesses. She also draws attention to the frequent mention of the transfer of merit, an important religious idea which cut across religious and chronological boundaries, reflecting the strength of familial, social and political bonds.

There is the more difficult question of how the religious domain is to be defined or at least broadly understood, and the very fluid and permeable boundaries between this and other domains, issues with which Orr's essay ends. There are problems with the use of the term 'religion' with its moorings in the monotheistic Judaeo-Christian tradition, especially when it comes to Hinduism. Central to the terminological difficulty is the presence, absence, or relative importance of canonically defined belief, doctrine, practice, and priesthood. In the context of early Indian history, which was marked by considerable plurality even within particular religious traditions, we need to recognize the existence of at least two levels of the religious domain—one corresponding to distinctive sectarian belief and practice; the other a larger space arising out of a shared cultural matrix where there was a significant degree of overlap. It is also necessary to move away from the assumption of fully formed mutually exclusive religious identities, understanding them as evolving and interacting parts of larger religious landscapes and historical processes. The nature of this interaction cannot be adequately understood, as has long been the fashion, by invoking religious 'tolerance', 'conversion', or legitimation;[52] nor can it proceed by assuming either complete concord or conflict.

For the purpose of conceptual and analytical clarity, it would also be useful to distinguish between *darśana,* ethics, and cultic practice. This would help us make sense of cults that may have had different foci and forms of worship while sharing certain philosophical and moral orientations. A focus on philosophical traditions is also necessary in order to reverse the utter neglect of philosophical thought in histories of ancient and early medieval India. But if we are dissatisfied with the word 'religion', with what can we replace it? Perhaps we should use it as a short-hand, aware of its limitations, using the terms tradition, cult and sect wherever possible. Or perhaps it is time to take recourse to an indigenous vocabulary which is closer to what we are describing, including words such as *dharma* and *paramparā* for the broader categories and more specific terms such as *sampradāya* for schools, sects and cults.[53]

The settling of politics, religion, language and literature into identifiable regional moulds is usually seen as one of the significant features of *c.* 600–1300 CE. However, these configurations were the outcome of complex processes of interaction between subcontinental, trans-regional, regional and local levels. In his essay, 'Cult Region: The *Purāṇas* and the Making of the Cultural Territory of Bengal', Kunal Chakrabarti uses the *Upapurāṇas* to trace how Brahmanical initiative led to the emergence of a goddess cult, which became (and still is) the hallmark of Bengal's cultural tradition. Although emphasizing the importance of Brāhmaṇa initiative, he underlines the reciprocal nature of the dialogue between Brahmanism and local traditions, reflected, for instance, in the increasing importance accorded by Brahmanical texts to local custom.

The specific case Chakrabarti analyses is the transformation of the popular local goddess Maṅgalā into the Paurāṇic Maṅgalacaṇḍī through a mythological makeover and an identification with the primordial Great Goddess. The polytheistic or monolatrous nature of Hinduism offered great potential for such transformations, and the case of Maṅgalacaṇḍī was by no means unique. Analogous developments can be seen within Bengal as well as in other regions, but there were also significant differences. Chakrabarti draws attention to the fact that although the kings of Bengal built and patronized temples, this region did not witness a royally sponsored regional cult centre similar to that of Jagannātha in Orissa (which, as copious research has shown, was the result of a complex interplay of tribal and Brahmanical traditions) nor the emergence of any major pilgrimage site with a regionally-defined catchment area. Nevertheless, he argues that Bengal did emerge as a cult region centering around the worship of the goddess, and that this process was culturally and socially integrative and transformative.

Although the broad outlines of the processes delineated by Chakrabarti are acceptable, he sometimes sounds as though he is talking about conscious Brāhmaṇa strategizing, which may have been far from the case. The Brāhmaṇa is often understood in historical writings as a homogeneous category or is reduced to a priest, recipient of royal land grants, or a vague and wily agent of legitimation. All these are simplistic characterizations and there is much about the Brāhmaṇa and Brahmanization that remains enigmatic. Chakrabarti acknowledges the limits of the accommodation and integration that were effected by Brahmanization and admits imperfect integration and dissent as well. While the religious processes of the kind he describes are widely acknowledged by historians, his essay explicitly raises several important questions concerning the definition and the emergence of the region, and the relationship between region, religion, community, symbols, culture, and identity. Of special interest is his emphasis on community, which he understands as referring to an internal perception of cultural identity, marked by cultural commonality but not necessarily uniformity, in which shared symbols have an important place. An issue worthy of further investigation is the extent of and the manner in which the sense of community was created within the context of existing social divisions and political hierarchies. Further, it is necessary to move beyond a purely text-based understanding of religion, and a study of material remains, especially sculpture, can contribute in a major way towards reconstructing the religious history of early medieval India.[54]

If the inclusion of the essay by Kapila Vatsyayan ('The Flying Messenger') in a volume on history comes as a surprise, it is because a neglect of India's aesthetic traditions characterizes much of our history-writing. Art is something that is usually left to art historians and is very sketchily taught to students of history. As a result, the enormous historical potential offered by a sensitive and nuanced study of Indian art has scarcely been explored. As mentioned earlier, the historian's focus has generally been on the *function* of art, especially on art as an expression of political and social power relations, without trying to understand its language or idiom. But even the function of art cannot be understood if its aesthetic language is disregarded. Further, it is important to take note of the fact that in pre-modern times, although different art forms were distinguished from each another, art, craft, literature, and the performative traditions were also understood as closely linked and as part of a larger aesthetic and cultural domain. All these issues are crucial for understanding a period of Indian history which was marked by unprecedented maturity and sophistication in canon and expression in the aesthetic-cultural sphere.

The intense, vibrant dialogue between the artistic and performative traditions of South and Southeast Asia is a subject about which we still know far too little. The abandoning of the problematic 'Greater India' framework of the historians of the early twentieth century was succeeded by a long phase of extremely insular India-centric history. Historians concerned with trade (always considered a subject worthy of serious historical inquiry) naturally worked with a larger geographical canvas and often explained cultural interaction solely in terms of trade.[55] But there has been a general indifference towards an in-depth examination of the multi-faceted cultural interactions among various parts of Asia. Vatsyayan's essay should be read against this background.

Vatsyayan's is a very specific inquiry—it concerns a *karaṇa* (a combination of gesture, posture and movement) known as the *vṛścika*, varieties of which were extremely popular in South and Southeast Asian dance, sculpture, and mural painting for over ten centuries. In this short essay, Vatsyayan makes several general statements that are worthy of careful reflection. She begins with an assertion of the close connection in spirit, content and form between dance and sculpture in the Asian cultural traditions. She points out that the *vṛścika karaṇa* is found in many varieties of Indian dance and that examples are abundant in the sculptural and dance traditions of Cambodia, Thailand, Myanmar and Sri Lanka. While recognizing that the codification of artistic style and form may have followed rather than preceded the actual execution, she asserts that all these are variations on the basic principle enunciated in the *Nāṭyaśāstra*.

The transmission of the *Rāmāyaṇa* and *Mahābhārata* to Southeast Asia, displayed in dramatic visual form, for instance, on the walls of Angkor Vat and Angkor Thom in Cambodia, is among the better known aspects of the cultural relations between India and Southeast Asia. Vatsyayan's essay brings out the fact that the interactions among among all these lands extended to literary themes, philosophical and aesthetic ideas, and artistic form and technique. She does not elaborate on the details or avenues of these interactions, but surely this is a subject that historians should be interested in exploring further. Such an investigation of the centuries-old conversations between Asian cultures would require moving beyond trade and beyond simplistic assertions of cultural influence, because themes, motifs, styles and content changed as they travelled and nestled into different milieux.[56]

## IV

The period *c.* 600–1300 was extremely rich in literary production, both in Sanskrit and the regional languages, a fact missed in the larger debate on early medieval India. This lacuna is the combined result of the viewing of this period by some scholars through the lens of decline, and the average historian's lack of interest in literature except to the extent that it provides empirical data to substantiate larger hypotheses. The institutional reasons for the appalling neglect (especially in India) of the histories and journeys of languages, ideas and attitudes are also not difficult to locate. Languages and literature are the focus of study in departments of languages and literature, and are rarely studied as carefully as they should be in the history departments of our universities. The lack of communication among these departments, the deep divide between historians and Sanskritists, and between traditional scholars and those trained in analytical research in the universities, perpetuates this neglect. As a result, the study of ancient and medieval languages and literature, which should be an important bed-rock of historical research, is languishing.

The excerpt from Sheldon Pollock's monumental work, *The Language of the Gods in the World of Men* assumes special importance against this background. Here, Pollock focuses on two important processes which intersected during the early medieval period—the creation of the Sanskrit cosmopolis and the turn towards vernacularization. In doing so, he urges us to think deeply about pre-modern processes of globalization and the relationship between language, literature, power, and culture.

Pollock argues that the beginning of the incredible journey of Sanskrit across South and Southeast Asia can be traced to a momentous development which took place at the beginning of the first millennium—the movement of this language from the sphere of ritualistic/religious texts (the world of the gods) to the secular domain (the world of men). He talks of the relationship between writing and literature, literization (the development of a written form of a language) and literarization (the development of 'imaginative, workly discourse');[57] *kāvya* (literature) and *praśasti* (inscriptional panegyric); and *kāvya and rājya* (the monarchical state). He emphasizes the complex relationship between the cultural and political domains and puts forward a strong critique of interpretations that focus overwhelmingly on legitimation. Highlighting the importance of investigating the 'political imagination', he points out that this does not mean an indifference to core issues related to the exercize of power. Actually, what Pollock is advocating is nothing less than a fundamental change in the historian's attitude towards the sources and processes of history.

While aware of the negative associations of the term 'vernacularization', Pollock thinks it is useful as a contrastive category to the cosmopolitan. In his analysis, it denotes the sense of the local, more specifically to the choice of writing literature in a local language, a process which became marked in the Indian subcontinent from the beginning of the second millennium. While some vernacular languages travelled across regions, none could match the dizzy success story of Sanskrit in the previous millennium.[58] Vernacularization was connected with the emergence of regionalized polities and cultural traits and new kinds of community. Pollock is quite emphatic that the stimulus to the Sanskrit cosmopolis and vernacularization was not provided by religion or the temple, but the royal court.[59] He attaches great importance to the *choices* made by the agents of these processes in the creation of new kinds of 'sociotextual communities'.

An important aspect of Pollock's work is his use of the comparative method. For him, the purpose of cultural comparison is not to suggest equivalence but analogy, in order to help understand historical and cultural specificities. That is why his account of the creation of the Sanskrit cosmopolis and vernacularization is accompanied by a discussion of the similarities and differences with analogous processes in Europe.

Many of the questions raised by this extract are elaborated on in the rest of *The Language of the Gods in the World of Men*, and for the most part relate to degrees of emphasis or points that require additional investigation. We need to know much more about the producers, transmitters, and consumers of literary cultures. While the political domain was no doubt important, perhaps Pollock over-emphasizes it. The audience of *kāvya* and the epics shows the spilling out of Sanskrit beyond the court into a larger, even if restricted, social sphere. Pollock acknowledges the important role of the 'peripatetic literati'; we need to know much more about this literati, especially about Brāhmaṇa institutions and movements, both within and outside India. While he certainly recognizes the importance of orality in the Indian tradition, an overwhelming emphasis on writing and literature should not lead to underestimating the power of the oral, artistic and performative traditions that were important parts of the cultural domain. This also has implications for understanding the downward percolation of ideas produced in the court circle. Further, are ideology and legitimation completely irrelevant categories for understanding pre-modern societies, or are they inadequate?[60] Pollock directs our attention to the emergence of the Sanskrit cosmopolis; much more investigation is required into precisely how this 'transregional consensus' over vast spaces happened without military conquest or an organized ecclesiastical institution.

Such questions aside, the essentials of Pollock's arguments are persuasive. Even more persuasive are the new and creative ways he urges us to look at literature and inscriptions. Scholars would do well to heed his advice to examine the profundity and power of texts such as the epics that swept majestically in many different forms across centuries and regions. Historians of early medieval India have tended to privilege the regional; Pollock shows how the local intersected with the translocal. The end product of his story too is the creation of new regional worlds, but his way of investigating and describing the emergence of these worlds brims with thought-provoking ideas.

My own paper, 'Politics, Violence, and War in Kāmandaka's *Nītisāra*', suggests that it is necessary to move beyond the larger debate regarding early medieval India to examine new questions and issues, especially those related to the exceptionally rich intellectual history of the period.[61] This essay is partly a reaction against the sidelining of the history of ideas in Indian history, and also a critique of the unnuanced way in which historians have often treated texts. It urges a careful reading of texts in their entirety and questions the frequently-posited divide between normative and descriptive sources. Drawing on the insights of Pollock and others, I emphasize the need to incorporate political ideas into the historical constructs of ancient and early medieval India and underline the power of these ideas to mould political practice. At the same time, where my approach differs is the emphasis on identifying not only the commonalities within the larger universe of intellectual and creative production, but also the differences in perspective arising from differences in genre, historical context and the authors' point of view.

The specific focus is on the *Nītisāra* of Kāmandaka, a text that can be placed at the beginning of the early medieval period. Kauṭilya's *Arthaśāstra* forms a counterpoint against which Kāmandaka's ideas are discussed. The *Arthaśāstra*'s vision of the potential state appears much more grandiose than that of the *Nītisāra*, whose tone is more cautious and restrained. Like the *Arthaśāstra*, the *Nītisāra* offers an organic account of the body politic, in this respect showing a keener grasp of political realities than visible in the writings of most modern historians, whose accounts of ancient and medieval Indian polities tend to be king-centred. The text graphically illustrates the political importance of the royal household, especially the harem, the king's kin, courtiers, neighbouring rulers, and forest people. This is a perspective that accords great importance to emotions and sentiments such as love, attachment, loyalty, friendship, anger, jealousy and hate in its explication of the political world.[62] Kāmandaka's description of court protocol illustrates the intersection between the personal and political and reveals a keen awareness of the extreme vulnerability and fragility of the king's power. I argue that the valorization of the ideal of the *rājarṣi* and the emphasis on training and self-control (which feature in many a text) were strongly rooted in a philosophical matrix as well as in a political theorist's concern with how monarchical power could be contained and controlled.

The essay also expands the scope of inquiry into political issues by urging the need to explore how early Indian societies dealt with political violence, especially war. It can be argued that non-violence became an important part of a certain construct of ancient India due to the conjunction of the prominence of *ahiṁsā* in some strands of ancient philosophical and religious thought and practice, and the important place of non-violence in India's nationalist movement. Due to the power of this construct, the element of violence in ancient Indian history has not been adequately recognized or investigated. This is in spite of the fact that considerable violence is implied in the political narrative, in the process of state formation and expansion, as well as in processes considered culturally assimilative and integrative. War was a central feature of the history of the early medieval (in fact it has been central to all human history) and the interplay between violence and non-violence in early Indian thought and history thus forms an important subject for historical investigation. Like other ancient thinkers, Kāmandaka considered a certain amount of violence necessary for the exercise of power. Like them, he was acutely aware of the limits and dangers of the use of excessive force and of the politico-ethical problems inherent in warfare. A careful reading of the text, however, reveals significant differences between him and Kauṭilya on issues related to political violence, specifically in his positions on war, capital punishment and the royal hunt.

Ideas and emotions in ancient and early medieval India offer a wide open and challenging field for historical inquiry. While my essay suggests a certain methodology and raises new questions, its goals can ultimately only be achieved by a close study of a greater number and range of texts and other types of sources. A major problem that besets such a project is the uncertainty of the dates of many texts and the lack of specific information about their authors, but these are problems that we have to live with. Ultimately, it is only when a wide selection of texts and inscriptions of different genres and periods are carefully historicized that the full array of ancient and early medieval Indian political ideas can be understood, and their common ground as well as differences in perspective be identified and appreciated.

B.D. Chattopadhyaya's prolific and thought-provoking writings could easily have found their way into any or all of the sections of this book. However, the essay included here ('Images of Raiders and Rulers') has been chosen because it draws attention to a very specific problem mentioned at the beginning of this Introduction, namely the chasm between histories of the Delhi Sultanate and pre-Sultanate/non-Sultanate histories. As mentioned earlier, the difference in the language of the principal sources is a major reason for the existence of two streams of historiography that rarely meet. But an integrated understanding of the early medieval period requires that they *do* meet. Chattopadhyaya's essay provides an important entry point, one which focuses on the question of attitudes, which considers religion as a relevant category, but demonstrates how it was represented in different ways depending on the political situation.

Although familiar with Islam, Indian sources dating between the eighth and thirteenth centuries do not generally use generic terms for Muslims. On the basis of inscriptions (and a few texts), Chattopadhyaya identifies various terms that *are* used, including Pārasīka, Tājika, Turuṣka, Śaka, *yavana* and *mleccha*. The fact that the Dharmaśāstra texts group the Pārasīkas and *mlecchas* with the Caṇḍālas, Bhillas and others indicates how the categories of outer and inner 'outsiders' blended with each other. The choice of terminology and the attributes, metaphors and imagery used to describe various 'others' tells us something significant about prevailing attitudes. The historian's task is to try to understand why some attitudes changed and why different attitudes sometimes coexisted.

This was a political culture in which boasts of victory over many enemies were considered an essential ingredient of political paramountcy, and it is noteworthy that the Turuṣkas (a term which originally denoted the Turks) feature in the inscriptions of their adversaries as one among many in lists of defeated enemies. But context was crucial – for instance, the bloody, adversarial description of the armies of the Tājikas (an indigenized term of West Asian origin) in the Navasari inscription stands in stark contrast to the eulogies of the virtues of Tājika political subordinates and provincial governors in other epigraphs.

Another significant issue is how the establishment of the Delhi Sultanate was represented in non-royal Sanskrit inscriptions. Thirteenth century inscriptions from the Delhi area employ the same epithets, metaphors and imagery for kings of Śaka, Turuṣka and *mleccha* descent as used in *praśastis* of non-Muslim rulers. The great flexibility of political idiom is evident from newly- coined titles such as *hammīra* and *suratrāṇa*. It is also evident in references to Turuṣkas/Śakas/*mlecchas* constituting the burden of the earth as well as to their relieving Viṣṇu by shouldering this burden. At the same time, in their recurrent allusions to the calamitous nature of *mleccha* rule and the frequent litany of the idea of the earth being submerged by the Turuṣkas or *mlecchas*, inscriptions and texts do reflect a perception of a changed order.

The mingling and interaction of people did not only take place in the royal court or on the battlefield, and political rhetoric or policy cannot be equated with the sum total of religious interactions.[63] Chattopadhyaya successfully shows that there was a wide variety of representations of Muslims in Sanskrit sources, the crucial difference being whether the Muslims in question were political adversaries or established rulers, but he is aware that this explanation is insufficient.[64] Further, he concedes that sectarian and theological tensions and conflicts did in fact exist, but argues that these were accompanied by many complex negotiations. The inquiry clearly has to be pushed beyond these tentative conclusions, in spite of the sensitiveness of the issues it deals with. Apart from the political context of the Sanskrit textual and epigraphic sources, it is necessary to juxtapose their discourse with that of the Persian chronicles, a point made many years ago by Aziz Ahmad in his essay on epics and counter-epics in medieval India.[65] It is also necessary to look more carefully at the creators and audiences of these epics and counterepics, and to unravel the complexities of their context and discourse in greater detail, as has been done, for instance, by Richard H. Davis in his analysis of the creation of the legend of Maḥmūd of Ghazna's iconoclasm at Somanātha.[66] Such an analysis would also have to be stretched forward chronologically and would need to respond to David N. Lorenzen's hypothesis that a self-conscious Hindu identity emerged during *c.* 1200–1500 through the rivalry between Hindus and Muslims.[67]

Decades of imagining Indian history in terms of an inherent conflict between a homogenized Hinduism and Islam on the one hand and ignoring issues related to religious identities (even denying their existence) in the name of secular history on the other, have to rapidly make way for a more serious engagement with religious identities and processes, especially the interface between Hinduism and Islam.[68] The problem is that our's is an age in which the historian is haunted by the ghosts of the past and concerns for the future, and in which the political implications of historical arguments often supercede the dictates of objective historical inquiry. An analysis of the complexities of inter-community interactions in early medieval and medieval India should not be premised on the assumption of an antagonistic interface between two homogenized communities; nor should it lead to an idealization of the early medieval period as an age of communal harmony, a model for our own intolerant times.

## IV

This book presents a very small selection from the vast and diverse scholarly writing dealing with various aspects of the history of the subcontinent between *c.* 600 and 1300. It is partly representative of some of the important work that has contributed to an understanding of this period, but it is even more an expression of possibilities for the future. That is why the aim has been to try to raise as many issues and questions as possible.

Strangely enough, after several decades of debate, the three theoretical models—feudal, segmentary state and integrative/processual—look less different than they did initially. Certainly, there are major differences in perspective, but today there is a likelihood of agreement on some points, for instance, with regard to the existence of political hierarchies and graded land rights. Have we reached a stage where it is possible to combine elements of the various apparently contradictory theories and create a composite model that incorporates some of the insights of all three? Or is it possible to bypass the whole debate and ignore the theoretical models altogether? Is a 'non-aligned' position possible?[69] It is actually difficult to ignore or bypass the debate and choices have to be made. And there is always the possibility of the emergence of a new theoretical framework, especially as historians seem to be more amenable than before to flexible approaches.

The major achievements of the past half-century of historical investigation of early medieval India include a rigorous analysis of political processes, agrarian relations, social stratification and the formation of regional cultures. There is now a need to broaden the canvas. At the level of method, this would require a more equal partnership between theory-building and the analysis of empirical evidence. Instead of treating empirical evidence as its handmaiden, theory has to show a greater commitment to a more careful and nuanced analysis of the whole range of empirical evidence and a greater interest in the specific, the different, the unique. As regards sources, it should be emphasized that early medieval archaeology is a very under-developed field. A thorough archaeological investigation of sites which have evidence of early medieval occupation is essential for a better understanding of the history of this period. What is also required is the abandoning of assertions about the inherent superiority or inferiority of a particular kind of source, reflected for instance in the unnecessary attitude of one-upmanship often displayed by supporters of texts, inscriptions and archaeology. The strategy of using one kind of primary source and looking to others only for corroboration has to be replaced by a much more self-conscious and sophisticated methodology of inter-textuality. This would require greater attentiveness towards the perspectives and voices of texts, inscriptions, artifacts and images, listening to what they are saying as well as noticing what they are concealing or disguising, and asking why they are doing so.

Broadening the canvas should also include thinking more deeply about the relationship between humans and their physical environment; recognizing the importance of the forest; filling the gaps in regional histories; abandoning the presuppositions of urban decline and reconstructing the profiles of urban societies; including women and gender relations into integrated social histories, along with other subordinated and marginalized groups; engaging more meaningfully with the complexities and pluralities of the religious domain; adopting a nuanced approach towards literature, art and other elements of the aesthetic sphere; recognizing and exploring the rich philosophical and intellectual production of this period; and looking historically and analytically at ideas, attitudes and emotions. All this *without* (and this point cannot be emphasized enough) abandoning or minimizing the importance of the range of historical questions that have already been posed and the answers that have already emerged. It is not a patchwork, superficially eclectic history that is visualized, but a more human history, a reversal of the long tradition of the parcelling of the past into small fragments, of emphasizing the importance of some of these fragments and relegating others to the margins. There is also an urgent need to break out of insular habits and to look at the history of the subcontinent within the larger perspective of Asian, even global interactions and histories. The use of the comparative method is likely to play an important part in such investigations, but not, as was the earlier fashion, to provide models to be imposed onto different cultural contexts, but rather to suggest analogies and to delineate cultural specificities, diversities, and contrasts.

Finally, we come back to the question of periodization and labels, to reflect on the very idea of the early medieval. It can be argued that the issue of what we should call *c.* 600–1300 is, at one level, not all that crucial. But we do need to be sure about the basis and logic of the terminology we use, and we should also be aware of its impact.[70] The early medieval was designed as a bridge term, as a response to an older, flawed division of India's past into the Hindu, Muslim and British periods. However, it is time to think about whether it has not given rise to other sorts of complications. In patching together the seven centuries between 600 and 1300 under one label, we may in fact be ignoring important continuities with what came before and after, or papering over major changes that took place during this period. Further, what do we understand by medievalism,[71] and what is so medieval about the early medieval? Why should we privilege the land grant phenomenon while identifying historical disjunctures and transitions? What is the point of an 'early medieval' which is not followed by a 'later medieval', and which most medievalists do not have much use for?[72]

For a long time, the early medieval has, in effect, been synonymous with the post-land grant phase of the old 'ancient' period.[73] But there is no consensus on even this issue. Many historians working on non-Sultanate history, including those whose writings are included in this book, prefer the term 'medieval' to 'early medieval' for these centuries; and as if this were not enough, there is considerable variation in their assessments of when the medieval period began. For instance, Stein's medieval South India extends from the sixth to the late thirteenth century. On the other hand, Karashima suggests that the medieval state and society emerged in this region during the fifteenth century, and describes the thirteenth to fifteenth centuries as the period of the ancient-medieval transition.[74] As mentioned earlier, there has been a long-standing view among a section of scholars writing on Sultanate history that the establishment of the Delhi Sultanate *does* constitute a historical land-mark, not because of the fact that the Sultans were Muslims but because their rule ushered in major changes in the urban sphere and in military technology.[75] Further, the use of the term 'early medieval' for the Sultanate period has made way for a great deal of experimenting with nomenclature, including different uses of the terms early and late medieval, the Middle Ages, the pre-colonial, and early modernity, and an awareness that all these are very fluid categories. As the labeling of periods cannot operate in a vacuum and has to exist within a continuum of at least something that came before and after, all this has implications for the use of the term 'early medieval'. Of course, such issues would have less relevance for long-term histories which do not work within conventional chronological frameworks.

It is easy to reject terminology and much more difficult to coin a new, better one, especially when every word carries many shades of meaning and much conceptual baggage. What are the alternatives to the 'early medieval?' One option is to continue to use it for the sake of convenience, but to be flexible about its chronological limits at both ends, not insisting that these centuries possessed a unity in terms of historical or cultural processes, and allowing for disjunctures and regional variations. Or we could use labels that are connected with what is perceived as a central feature of the period—referring, for example, to the integration, regionalization, feudal, or segmentary state periods, depending on which framework we think most convincing. Perhaps it is time to abandon the search for the perfect labels and simply use chronological markers to indicate which period we are talking about. Alternatively, it is possible to think in terms of different kinds of periodization for different issues and regions. The last two options have certain advantages, because in trying to fit history in its entirety into an overarching unilinear evolutionary scheme, we privilege what we consider the dominant processes and miss out on the complex multilinear character of 'Indian history', which is, after all, a shorthand for a very complex and ever-changing mosaic of historical processes extending over a vast subcontinent. In fact, the analogy of a kaleidoscope, with its mesmerizing, constantly changing patterns of many-coloured jagged-edged glass pieces offers a better image than a mosaic.

To a great extent, the divisions of the past and history itself depend on the direction and nature of the historian's gaze—whether it is looking towards kingdom or forest, village or town, land or sea; whether it is observing political events, social processes, or creative ideas; whether its view spans a small region, a continent, or the whole world. Old habits die hard. But while there is a need for many more histories of early medieval India, it may also be time to let go of the term 'early medieval'. At the very least, we should not take the label too seriously, nor hesitate to transgress its boundaries.

## NOTES

1 This is also the case, for instance, with the period c. 200 BCE–300 CE, which, in terms of political history, corresponds to the post-Maurya, pre-Gupta period. For a discussion of the historical importance and cultural vitality of this period, see Upinder Singh, *A History of Ancient and Early Medieval India: From the Stone Age to the 12th Century*, New Delhi, chap. 8. The eighteenth century, wedged between the decline of the Mughal empire and the establishment of British rule, is another instance. See Seema Alavi (ed.), *The Eighteenth Century in India*, New Delhi, 2007 [2002].

2 Smith's ancient period extended from pre-historic times up to the Maurya dynasty, the Hindu period from the Mauryas till the death of Harṣa, the period of the medieval Hindu kingdoms from the death of Harṣa upto the Ghurid conquests, the Muslim period from the Ghurid conquest till the decline of the Mughal empire, and the British period from the growth of the East India Company's power in the mid-eighteenth century (Vincent A. Smith, *The Oxford History of India*, Oxford, 1919, p. 10). The terms 'imperialist' and 'nationalist' historians have been deliberately avoided in the discussion here. This is because although the political context definitely impinges on historical writing, such labels often result in an unnuanced over-simplification of much more complex and varied perspectives and scholarly contributions.

3 On the inappropriateness of the 'Muslim period' label, see the Preface to R.C. Majumdar (ed.) *The History and Culture of the Indian People:* Volume 1: *The Vedic Age*, Bombay, 1951, pp. 23–4. Elaborating on his vision of Indian history, Majumdar wrote (p. 29): 'This volume attempts a picture of what may be regarded as the dawn of Hindu civilization. To continue this metaphor, we may say that the next two volumes reflect its full morning glory and noonday splendor. In the fourth volume we come across the shadows of the declining day, whilst dusk sets in with the

fifth. Then follows the darkness of the long night, so far as Hindu civilization is concerned, a darkness that envelops it even now.'

4 R. C. Majumdar (ed.), *The History and Culture of the Indian People*, Volume 4: *The Age of Imperial Kanauj*, Bombay, 1955, and Volume 5: *The Struggle for Empire*, Bombay, 1957.

5 According to K.A.N. Sastri, *The Cōḷas*, Madras 1975 [1937], p. 2: '...in its administrative system and in its literary and artistic achievement, Tamil civilisation may be said to have attained its high watermark under the Cōḷa empire...'

6 It should be noted that like the terms 'imperialist' and 'nationalist', the 'Marxist' label also includes a great variety of perspectives.

7 See, for instance, Kosambi, *An Introduction to the Study of Indian History*, Bombay, 1998, pp. 295–6. It should be noted that although for Kosambi, true history was 'the presentation, in chronological order, of successive developments in the means and relations of production' (p. 2), and although in his opinion, feudalism extended from the early centuries CE well into the Sultanate period, he frequently used the epithets 'Moslem' or 'Mohammedan' while describing various aspects of the Sultanate period; this suggests that he considered the religion of the Muslim elites as a historically significant fact.

8 The early critiques included those of D. C. Sircar (see his *Landlordism and Tenancy in Ancient and Medieval India as Revealed by Epigraphic Records*, Lucknow, 1969). Burton Stein was the chief proponent of the segmentary state model, while Hermann Kulke and B. D. Chattopadhyaya are the major proponents of the integrative/processual model. The writings of the latter three scholars are included in this book and are discussed further on in this Introduction.

9 According to Niharranjan Ray, the medieval period in Indian history extended from the seventh to eighteenth centuries. His culturally comprehensive list of medieval features included, among other things, the regional dimensions of polity, language, literature, and art; a feudal agrarian system; a decline in trade and the use of money; a proliferation of religious sects and sub-sects; a disregard for science and technology; a fatalistic and fearful attitude towards life; and a predisposition towards belief in the supernatural (General President's Address, *Proceedings of the Indian History Congress*, 29th session, Patiala, 1967). Some years later, R.S. Sharma ('Problem of Transition from Ancient to Medieval in Indian History', *The Indian Historical Review*, vol. 1, no. 1, March 1974, p. 9) wrote: 'Undoubtedly the establishment of the Muslim Turkish rule introduced certain significant changes in the social, economic and political organization of the country. But most features such as feudal state organization, reversion to closed economy, proliferation of castes, regional identities in art, script and language, *pūjā*, *bhakti* and tantra, which develop in medieval times and continue later, can be traced back to the sixth and seventh centuries. It would then appear that in these two centuries ancient India was coming to an end and medieval India was taking shape.'

10 Note the title of Stein's book, *Peasant State and Society in Medieval South India*, Delhi, 1980.

11 Literacy, cities, and the existence of monarchical states and chiefdoms are central to the idea of the early historic. While the early historic phase in north India can be said to have begun in the sixth century BCE, there are different ideas about its

terminal date. Chattopadhyaya seems to stretch it to the third/fourth century CE (*The Making of Early Medieval India*, New Delhi, 1997, p. 7), but there are good reasons to extend it till the first/second century CE at the most. The early historic phase in South India can be placed between c. 300 BCE –300 CE.

12 Chattopadhyaya's basic argument was that the early medieval period was marked by integrative processes that especially manifested themselves in sustained local and regional state formation and the emergence of regional cultures.

13 For Chattopadhyaya, the early medieval begins in the sixth century; he wavers between extending it up till the twelfth/thirteenth or the thirteenth century. Sharma's *Indian Feudalism* uses the term early medieval for *c.* 500—1200.

14 There are some exceptions which bridge the divide. For instance, André Wink's *Al Hind: The Making of the Indo-Islamic World*, Volume 1: *Early Medieval India and the Expansion of Islam 7th–11th Centuries* and Volume 2: *The Slave Kings and the Islamic Conquest 11th–13th Centuries*, New Delhi, 1999, charts the changes that accompanied the Islamicization of the subcontinent. Cynthia Talbot (*Pre-colonial India in Practice: Society, Religion and Identity in Medieval Andhra*, New Delhi, 2001) looks at the Kakatiya polity in relation to the Delhi Sultanate. John Deyell (*Living Without Silver: The Monetary History of Early Medieval North India*, New Delhi, 1990) examines the monetary systems of various kingdoms that existed in north India from *c.* 750 CE to 1250 CE. Richard H. Davis' fascinating *Lives of Indian Images*, Delhi, 1997, examines the complex worlds of belief and identity associated with religious images from ancient to very recent times.

15 For instance, A.B. Pandey defines the medieval period as the period of 'Muslim domination'. His *Early Medieval India*, Allahabad, 1960, extends from the advent of Islam in India and the Arab invasion of Sind up to the battle of Panipat in 1526. His *Later Medieval India: A History of the Mughals*, Allahabad, 1963, focuses on the Mughal empire and its contemporaries.

16 See, for instance, Mohammad Habib, 'Introduction to Elliot and Dowson's History of India, vol. II', in K.A. Nizami (ed.), *Politics and Society in Early Medieval India: Collected Works of Professor Mohammad Habib* (New Delhi, 1974 [1952], vol. 1, pp. 33–110; Tapan Raychaudhuri and Irfan Habib (eds), *The Cambridge Economic History of India* Volume 1: *c. 1200—c. 1750*, Cambridge, 1982, p. xiii; and Irfan Habib, 'An Economic History of the Delhi Sultanate—An Essay in Interpretation', *Indian Historical Review*, vol. 4, no. 2, 1978, pp. 287–303. For a useful critical overview of the historiography of the Delhi Sultanate, see Sunil Kumar, *The Emergence of the Delhi Sultanate*, Delhi, 2007, chap. 1.

17 In all cases, in this Introduction, 'the debate' refers to the debate on the theoretical framework for *c.* 600—1300.

18 Books containing useful collections of some of the most important contributions to the debate include Hermann Kulke ed., *The State in India: 1000—1700* (Delhi, 1997); Harbans Mukhia (ed.), *The Feudalism Debate*, New Delhi, 1999; D.N. Jha (ed.), *The Feudal Order: State, Society and Ideology in Early Medieval India*, New Delhi, 2000.

19 D.N. Jha (*The Feudal Order*, p. 3) points out that the first Indian historian who wrote about the growth of feudalism in ancient India was B.N. Datta in his books

*Studies in Indian Social Polity*, Calcutta, 1944, and *Dialectics of Land Economics in India*, Calcutta, 1952.

20 It did not actually directly discuss developments in the far south.

21 R.S. Sharma, 'The Origin of Feudalism in India', *Journal of the Economic and Social History of the Orient*, vol. 1, part 1, 1958, pp. 297-328; *Rethinking India's Past*, New Delhi, 2009.

22 This is a re-worked version of an essay published in *The Journal of Peasant Studies* in 1985, and is essentially similar to the contents of chap. 3 of Sharma's *Early Medieval Indian Society: A Study in Feudalisation*, Kolkata, 2001.

23 R.S. Sharma, *Urban Decay in India c. 300–c. 1000*, New Delhi, 1987. For a completely different understanding of trade and urban centres in early medieval India and the hypothesis that this period witnessed a third phase of urbanization, see Chattopadhyaya, *The Making of Early Medieval India*, pp. 130–82. For evidence that counters the hypothesis of urban decay from c. 300 onwards, see Singh, *A History of Ancient and Early Medieval India*, pp. 497–504, 584–7. For a convincing refutation of the idea of a decline in coinage in early medieval times, see Deyell, *Living Without Silver*.

24 See Harbans Mukhia, 'Was there Feudalism in Indian History?' in Mukhia (ed.) *The Feudalism Debate*, pp. 34–80.

25 Any presentation of the debate as one in which Indian and Western historians are ranged against each other is inaccurate. While it is true that the segmentary state hypothesis has not found much favour with Indian historians, the critique of the feudalism hypothesis has come from Indian historians, apart from American and European scholars.

26 Aidan W. Southall, *Alur Society: A Study in Processes and Types of Domination*, Cambridge, 1953.

27 Y. Subbarayalu, *Political Geography of the Chola Country*, Madras, 1973.

28 Peasant society and the Brāhmaṇa–peasant alliance are dealt with in detail in *Peasant State and Society*, but the book has surprisingly little to say about the peasant state, which has a prominent place in its title.

29 See especially B.D. Chattopadhyaya's 'Political Processes and Structure of Polity in Early Medieval India', Presidential Address, Ancient India Section, Indian History Congress, 44th session, Burdwan, 1983; reprinted in Chattopadhyaya's *The Making of Early Medieval India*, pp. 183–63; and Hermann Kulke, 'Fragmentation and Segmentation Versus Integration? Reflections on the Concepts of Indian Feudalism and the Segmentary State in Indian history', *Studies in History*, vol. 4, no. 2, 1982, pp. 237–63.

30 Stein's segmentary state hypothesis did not find much support among Indian historians.

31 Chattopadhyaya, *The Making of Early Medieval India*, p. 16.

32 He uses the word 'processural', which I have, with his consent, changed to 'processual'.

33 See for instance, Upinder Singh, *Kings, Brāhmaṇas and Temples in Orissa: an Epigraphic Study, AD 300–1147*, New Delhi, 1994; Kunal Chakrabarti, *Religious Process: The Purāṇas and the Making of a Regional Tradition*, New Delhi, 2001;

Talbot, *Precolonial India in Practice*; Nandini Sinha Kapoor, *State Formation in Rajasthan: Mewar during the Seventh–Fifteenth Centuries*, New Delhi, 2002.

34 For Kulke's understanding of legitimation, which relies heavily on Max Weber's insights, see the essays in Hermann Kulke, *Kings and Cults: State Formation and Legitimation in India and Southeast Asia*, New Delhi, Manohar, 2001 [1993]. For a comprehensive, detailed discussion of how legitimation operated within an integrative framework at different points of time, see Bhairabi Prasad Sahu, 'Legitimation, Ideology and State in Early India', *Proceedings of the Indian History Congress*, 64th Session, Mysore, 2003, Presidential Address, Ancient India Section.

35 See Upinder Singh, 'Brāhmaṇa settlements in ancient and early medieval India', in B.D. Chattopadhyaya (ed.), *A Social History of Early India* in D.P. Chattopadhyaya [gen. ed.], History of Science, Philosophy and Culture in Indian Civilization series, vol. II, Part 5, New Delhi, 2009, pp. 157–75.

36 That this problem is not confined to the period we are examining here is indicated by the observations made by Farhat Hasan on the historiography of the Mughal state. Hasan points out (*State and Locality in Mughal India: Power Relations in Western India, c. 1572—1830*, Cambridge, 2004, p. 2) that much of the debate on the nature of the Mughal state has focused on its coercive and extractive capacities. In contrast, his own study examines the Mughal state in its local context. For a broad overview of changing perspectives on the Mughal state, also see Muzaffar Alam and Sanjay Subramanyam (eds) *The Mughal State 1526—1750*, New Delhi, 1998, Introduction. Alam and Subramanyam point out (p. 57) that the Mughal state has to be understood as a political process and that it eventually came to resemble a patchwork quilt rather than a wall-to-wall carpet.

37 See, for instance, Carla M. Sinopoli, *Pots and Palaces: The Earthenware Ceramics of the Noblemen's Quarter of Vijayanagara* (New Delhi, 1993). A recent significant contribution to the study of empires is Susan E. Alcock, Terence N. D'Altroy, Kathleen D. Morrison and Carla M. Sinopoli eds. *Empires: Perspectives from Archaeology and History* (Cambridge, 2001). See especially Kathleen Morrison's essay, 'Coercion, Resistance and Hierarchy: Local Processes and Imperial Strategies in the Vijayanagara Empire', pp. 252–78.

38 For an overview, see Singh, *A History of Ancient and Early Medieval India*, pp. 573–603.

39 See Michael Williams, *Deforesting the Earth: From Prehistory to Global Crisis*, Chicago and London, 2003, pp. 346-69.

40 These include Noboru Karashima, M.G.S. Narayanan, Y. Subbarayalu, D.N. Jha, R. Champakalakshmi, and Rajan Gurukkal.

41 See, for instance, Noboru Karashima, *South Indian History and Society: Studies from Inscriptions AD 859-1800* (Delhi, 1984) and Y. Subbarayalu, 'Quantification of Inscriptional Data with Special Reference to the Study of Property Rights in Medieval Tamilnadu', paper presented at the symposium on 'Quantitative Methods in Indian Historiography' organized by the Indian History Congress (Dharwad, 1988), unpublished.

42 For an elaboration of the problems in writing the early history of caste, See Upinder Singh, 'Interrogating *varṇa* and *jāti* in ancient and early medieval India',

Presidential Address, Ancient India section, in *Punjab History Conference Proceedings Volume (40th session), March 14-16, 2008*, Punjabi University, Patiala, 2009. Historians of ancient and early medieval India need to reflect on the implications of the arguments made by Nicholas B. Dirks, *Castes of Mind: Colonialism and the Making of Modern India*, Princeton, 2001; and Susan Bayly, *Caste, Society and Politics in India: from the Eighteenth Century to the Modern Age*, The New Cambridge History of India, IV.3, Cambridge, 1999. Dirks argues that caste as we know it today was the product of the encounter between India and Western colonial rule. According to Bayly, caste was by no means 'a self-serving orientalist fiction', but until the colonial period, much of the subcontinent was inhabited by people for whom caste was relatively unimportant; the crucial changes started taking place in the eighteenth century and were accentuated thereafter. A long-term history of caste has not yet been written.

43 David Ludden's assertion (*An Agrarian History of South Asia*, The New Cambridge History of India, IV.4, Cambridge, 1999, pp. 100-01) that in early medieval times, groups outside caste society comprised the bulk of the population, merits careful consideration and a response.

44 For a useful discussion of some of the political and cultural ramifications of the Cōḷa naval expeditions and India–Southeast Asia–China interactions, see Hermann Kulke, K. Kesavapany and Vijay Sakhuja eds. *Nagapattinam to Suvarnadwipa: Reflections on the Chola Expeditions to Southeast Asia*, Singapore, 2009.

45 Talbot translates *jāti* as subcaste, but recognizes that it can refer to a host of other descent-based units.

46 For important contributions towards engendering the history of ancient and early medieval India, see Kumkum Roy (ed.), *Women in Early Indian Societies*, New Delhi, 1999; Kumkum Roy, *The Power of Gender and the Gender of Power: Explorations in Early Indian History*, New Delhi, 2010; Uma Chakravarti, *Everyday Lives, Everyday Histories: Beyond the Kings and Brahmanas of 'Ancient' India*, New Delhi, 2006.

47 M.A. Stein ed. *Kalhaṇa's Rājataraṅgiṇī*, vol. 1, Bombay, 1988 rpt, Introduction and Appendix, pp. 139-44. II

48 For an analysis of the representation of the king's household in texts such as the *Arthaśāstra* and *Kāmasūtra*, see Kumkum Roy, 'The King's Household: Structure and Space in the Śāstric Tradition', in Kumkum Sangari and Uma Chakravarti eds. *From Myths to Markets: Essays on Gender*, Simla and N. Delhi, 1999, pp. 18-38. The importance of the royal household in the *Nītisāra* is discussed in my essay, 'Politics, Violence and War in Kāmandaka's *Nītisāra*', in this volume. The political importance and authority of women of the royal household is also abundantly clear from epigraphic evidence from many sites and periods of their role as patrons of religious establishments.

49 For a broad overview of religious and cultural developments, see Singh, *A History of Ancient and Early Medieval India*, 603–43. For an excellent, detailed discussion of the art and architecture of this period, see Susan Huntington, *The Art of Ancient India: Buddhist, Hindu, Jain*, New York and Tokyo, 1985, chaps 10–22.

50 This has already started happening. An important recent work which examines court culture between c. 400-1200 is Daud Ali's *Courtly Culture and Political Life in Early Medieval India* (Cambridge, 2006). The larger, more powerful argument about the relationship between culture and power in the first and second millennia has been made by Sheldon Pollock and is discussed later in this Introduction. But apart from the relationship between culture and politics, vast areas within cultural history remain to be explored.

51 Susan Starr Sered, *Women as Ritual Experts: The Religious Lives of Elderly Jewish Women in Jerusalem*, New York, 1992.

52 Terms such as 'tolerance' and 'conversion', which are rooted in monotheistic contexts, are frequently used in a problematic way in writings on ancient and early medieval India. As has been repeatedly emphasized here, legitimation of social and political status is an important process, but all religious activity and interactions are not subsumed within it.

53 Even if we do not use the indigenous vocabulary, it is necessary to at least discover and acknowledge its existence.

54 For a discussion of the archaeological perspectives on religion, see Timothy Insoll (ed.) *Archaeology and world Religion*, London and New York, 2001; and Elisabeth A. Bacus and Nayanjot Lahiri (eds) *The Archaeology of Hinduism*, World Archaeology 36.3, 2004. An example of an excavated site which has yielded very exciting structural and sculptural remains with rich potential for the reconstruction of religious (and political) history from the early historic through to the early medieval period is Mansar in Nagpur district. For details, see Hans Bakker's article on the site in Bakker ed. *The Vākāṭaka Heritage: Indian Culture at the Crossroads*, Groningen, 2004; and http://mansar.eldoc.ub.nl.

55 See, for instance, H.P. Ray, *The Winds of Change*, New Delhi, 1994. Apart from giving a useful overview of trade between India and Southeast Asia, Ray argues (p. 10) for a 'Buddhist trading network' being taken over by the Pāśupata Śaivas from the third-fourth centuries onwards. Such a direct congruence between trade and religious networks can be questioned.

56 That some scholars have finally re-engaged with the cultural interaction between India and Southeast Asia is evident from Parul Pandya Dhar's *The Toraṇa in Indian and Southeast Asian Architecture*, New Delhi, 2009, a detailed comparative study of the form and style of the *toraṇa* in India and Southeast Asia.

57 Pollock (*The Language of the Gods in the World of Men: Sanskrit, Culture, and Power in Premodern India*, California, 2006, N. Delhi, 2007, p. 283), distinguishes between two kinds of language use—'workly discourse', which includes that which is 'imaginative, performative, expressive'; and 'documentary', which is 'informational, constative, contentual'.

58 Pollock also introduces the idea of the 'cosmopolitan vernacular', the stage when a vernacular language started aiming towards localizing the full range of the literary qualities of the superimposed cosmopolitan language (which he demonstrates through a discussion of Kannada) and a second, later 'vernacular revolution' that challenged the cosmopolitan vernacular, and in certain instances, replaced it by a more localized regional vernacular.

59 He assigns a more prominent role to religion in the second vernacular revolution.
60 Pollock suggests that they are irrelevant (see *The Language of the Gods*, pp. 516–24).
61 Elsewhere, I have suggested a connection between the great intellectual output of these centuries and the patronage of Brāhmaṇas by kings through land grants ('Brāhmaṇa Settlements in Ancient and Early Medieval India', p. 163).
62 Scholars are engaging more than before with the cultural configurations of love and sexuality in ancient and early medieval India. See, for instance, Daud Ali, 'Courtly love and the aristocratic household in early medieval India', in Fransesca Orsini (ed.), *Love in South Asia: A Cultural History*, New Delhi, 2007, pp. 43–60; Shalini Shah, *Love, Eroticism and Female Sexuality in Classical Sanskrit Literature: Seventh–Thirteenth Centuries*, New Delhi, Manohar, 2009; Shonaleeka Kaul, *Imagining the Urban: Sanskrit and the City in Early India*, New Delhi, Permanent Black, 2010).
63 Chattopadhyaya looks at the larger range of interactions in his essay, 'Meritorious Deeds, Sacred Sites and the Image of God as the Lord of the Universe', in his *Representing the Other*, pp. 61–78.
64 In another essay, he suggests that the 'curiously contradictory images' can be explained by Brahmanical ambivalence, or by concerns of legitimation and distancing ('Meritorious Deeds, Sacred Sites and the Image of God', p. 84).
65 Aziz Ahmad, 'Epic and Counter-epic in Medieval India', *Journal of the American Oriental Society* vol. 83, no. 4, Sept.–Dec. 1963, pp. 470–6. Ahmad emphasized that the epics and counter-epics did not emerge or operate in *direct* dialogue with each other.
66 Davis, *Lives of Indian Images*, pp. 88–112.
67 David N. Lorenzen, 'Who Invented Hinduism?' in David N. Lorenzen, *Who Invented Hinduism? Essays on Religion in History*, New Delhi, 2006, pp. 2–3. Lorenzen substantiates this hypothesis through an analysis of the works of Kabir, Ekanāth and Vidyāpati.
68 Some scholars have already entered this field. These include David N. Lorenzen, 'Who Invented Hinduism?'; Muzaffar Alam, 'Competition and Co-existence: Indo-Islamic Interactions in Medieval North India', *Itinerario*, vol. 13, no. 1, 1989, pp. 37-59; Richard M. Eaton, *Sufis of Bijapur: Social Roles of Sufis in Medieval India* (Princeton, 1978) and *The Rise of Islam and the Bengal Frontier, 1204—1760*, Berkeley, 1993; and. For a useful collection of essays that brings out the complex nature of religious identities and interactions in pre-colonial India, see David Gilmartin and Bruce B. Lawrence eds. *Beyond Turk and Hindu: Rethinking Religious Identities in Islamicate South Asia*, New Delhi, 2002. The broader terms 'Indic' and 'Islamicate' are useful in helping break out of thinking in terms of the narrower Hindu/Muslim categories.
69 Historians such as R. Champakalakshmi, Noboru Karashima and James Heitzman have not embraced any of the existing models whole-heartedly. It is interesting to note that all these scholars have worked on South India. Further, Kulke has suggested ('Fragmentation and Segmentation Versus Integration?') that different models could perhaps be applied to different areas.

70 In Indian universities, historians still tend to be classified as ancient, medieval or modern historians; post-graduate students are required to choose one of these specializations; advertisements for teaching jobs often indicate which specialization employers are looking for. An unfortunate result is that historians whose expertise lies in transitional phases tend to be looked at askance and may end up falling between two stools in the job market.

71 For a useful discussion of this issue in different cultural contexts, see *The Medieval History Journal*, special issue on 'Contextualising the "Medieval"', Vol. 1, No. 1, Jan.–June 1998.

72 This is like that other term 'early historic', which is not followed by a 'later historic', and perplexingly, in the writings of some historians immediately flows into the 'early medieval'.

73 The term 'ancient' with its rich resonances, has already been replaced in many writings with the more neutral but colourless word 'early'.

74 Noboru Karashima, *South Indian Society in Transition: Ancient to Medieval*, New Delhi, 2009), pp. 1, 23.

75 For instance, in his *Essays in Indian History: Towards a Marxist Perception*, New Delhi, 1997, p.80, Irfan Habib states that "The Ghorian conquests of northern India, leading to the establishment of the Delhi Sultanate (1206–1526), may be said to mark the true beginning of the medieval period in India." He makes the same point and questions various aspects of the Indian feudalism hypothesis in his essay 'Classifying Pre-colonial India', in Harbans Mukhia (ed.) *The Feudalism Debate*, pp. 186–97. On the other hand, in his more recent *Medieval India: The Study of a Civilization*, New Delhi, 2008, Habib accepts the idea of Indian feudalism and demarcates the early medieval period (which he places between *c.* 600 and 1200 CE) from the Sultanate period.

# Part I

## Theoretical Models and Political Processes

# 1

# How Feudal was Indian Feudalism?*

R. S. Sharma

Several scholars have questioned the use of the term feudalism to characterize the early medieval socio-economic formation in India.[1] But the points raised by Harbans Mukhia[2] deserve serious attention. He rightly suggests that unlike capitalism feudalism is not a universal phenomenon. But in my view, tribalism, the stone age, the metal age, and the advent of the food producing economy are universal phenomena. They do indicate some laws conditioning the process and pattern of change. [...]

Tribalism is universal and continues to be followed by different forms of state and class society. [...]

[...]

But there could be enormous variations in tribal society, as also in the nature of feudal societies. It is rightly stated by Marx that feudalism 'assumes different aspects, and runs through its various phases in different orders of succession'.[3] But certain universals remain the same. This is admitted even by critics of Indian feudalism who think of the variants of feudalism.[4] Feudalism has to be seen as a mechanism for the distribution of the means of production and for the appropriation of the surplus. It may have certain broad, universal features, and it may have certain traits typical of a territory. Obviously land and agricultural products play a decisive role in pre-capitalist class societies, but the specificities

*Previously published in Hermann Kulke (ed.), *The State in India 1000–1700*, New Delhi, Oxford University Press, 1997, pp. 48–85. This is an extract from the chapter. In the present version, some portions of the text and notes have been removed. For the complete text see the original version.

of land distribution and the appropriation of agricultural products differ from region to region. It cannot be argued that what developed in pre-capitalist Western Europe was the same as in India and elsewhere. Historical laws, as far as they are known, do not work in this manner nor could one say that feudalism was the monopoly of Western Europe. It is not possible to have a clear-cut formula about feudalism. The most that one could say about the universal aspect of feudalism would be largely on the lines of Marc Bloch and E.A. Kosminsky.[5] Feudalism appears in a predominantly agrarian economy which is marked by a class of landlords and a class of servile peasantry. In this system, the landlords extract surplus produce by social, religious, or political means, which are called extra-economic methods. This seems to be more or less the current Marxist view of feudalism, which considers serfdom, 'scalar property' and 'parcellized sovereignty' as features of the West European version of the feudal system. The lord-peasant relationship is at the heart of the matter, and the exploitation of the estate by its owner, controller, enjoyer, or beneficiary is its essential ingredient. Apart from these basic universal aspects feudalism may have several variations. The particularities of the system in some West European countries do not apply to the various types of feudalism found in other areas. For example, evidence of peasant struggles against landlords in other countries has not been produced in sufficient degree. Similarly, artisanal and capitalist growth within the womb of feudalism seems to be typical of the West European situation where agricultural growth and substantial commodity production created major structural contradictions. The nature of religious beneficiaries, who appropriated a major portion of land, also differs from country to country. Thus the Church owned a substantial amount of land in Portugal. Buddhist and Confucian establishments controlled land in Korea. Buddhist monasteries were also important in eastern India. Temples emerged as estate-owners in south India, and many brāhmaṇas enjoyed a similar position in the upper and middle Gangetic basin, central India, the Deccan, and Assam. In north India religious grantees did not have to pay taxes to the state although they fulfilled other obligations. But in south India in many cases they had to pay taxes. Non-religious landed intermediaries also appear in different forms in various parts of India and outside the country. In certain parts of the country, for example, in Orissa, we find tribal chiefs being elevated to the position of landlords. In other parts many administrative officials enjoyed land taxes from the peasants. But in spite of these variations the basic factor, namely the presence of a controlling class of landlords and a subject peasantry, remained the same in early medieval times and did not 'change until the sixteenth century when the central authority became stronger.

[...]

It is argued that the peasant in medieval India enjoyed autonomy of production because he had 'complete' control over the means of production.[6] [...]

[...]

[...] Peasants may have possessed land, labour, oxen, other animals and agricultural implements. But we have to ascertain how effective was his 'control' over the means of production. Did other conditions such as taxes, forced labour, and constant interference by beneficiaries who were ever present, make the peasant's control really operational? [...]

In fact, land grants leave no doubt that the landlord enjoyed a good measure of general control in the means of production. Why did the landlords claim various types of rents from the peasants and how could they collect the rents? Clearly, they did so on the strength of royal charters which conferred on them either the villages or pieces of land or by imposing various types of taxes. [...]

Generally, the early charters gave the beneficiary usufructuary rights. But the later charters granted such concessions as rendered the beneficiary the de facto owner of the village land. The donated village/villages constituted his estate. For example, the beneficiary was entitled to collect taxes, all kinds of income, all kinds of occasional taxes, and this 'all' (*sarva*)[7] was never specified. Similarly, he was entitled to collect proper and improper taxes,[8] fixed and not fixed taxes,[9] and at the end of the list of taxes the term 'et cetera' *(ādi, ādikam)*[10] was used. All this added enormously to the power of the beneficiary. These extraordinary provisions could serve as a self-regulating mechanism as and when production increased,[11] but they could also interfere with the expansion of production. Some provisions clearly give superior rights to the beneficiary in the land of the peasants. For instance, the land charters of Madhya Pradesh, northern Maharashtra, Konkan, and Gujarat in Gupta and post-Gupta times empowered the beneficiary to evict the old peasants and introduce new ones; he could assign lands to others. A similar provision occurs in Coḷa charters. But it is taken to mean that the beneficiary had the right to vary the rates of taxation and impose additional dues and services in later Coḷa times.[12] In any case all such concessions leave no doubt that the beneficiary was armed with superior rights in land, which was actually occupied by the cultivator. Most grants after the seventh century AD gave away the village along with the lowland, fertile land, water reservoirs, all kinds of trees and bushes, pathways, and pasture grounds. In charters from eastern India the village was granted along with mango trees, *mahuā* (*Bassia latifolia*) and jack-fruit trees, and various other agrarian resources. Cotton, hemp, coconut, and areca-nut trees are also given away in grants, but this happened mostly after the tenth century when cash crops assumed importance. Such provisions connected the agrarian production directly with the beneficiary and, more importantly, transferred almost all communal agrarian resources to him. Since the peasant did not have free access to various agrarian resources, his autonomy in production was substantially crippled.

[...]

Most charters asked the peasants to carry out the orders of the beneficiaries.[13] These orders would relate not only to the payment of taxes which were concerned with the fruits of production but would also relate to the means and processes of production. In a way the blanket authority to extract obedience from the peasant placed him at the mercy of the beneficiary. It implied general control over his labour power which undoubtedly is an essential ingredient of the means of production. This labour could be used either in the fields cultivated by the peasant or in those directly managed by the beneficiary. The beneficiaries could insist on having certain types of produce for their ostentatious and unproductive consumption, and with all the seignorial rights that they possessed they could compel the peasants to produce those cereals or cash crops which they needed.

The law books of Yājñavalkya, Bṛhaspati, and Vyāsa specify four graded stages of land rights in the same piece of land. [...] Multiple, hierarchical rights and interests in land, which was the chief means of production, can be inferred even from Gupta land sale transactions. These transactions mention the interest of not only the king but also that of the local administrative body (*adhikaraṇa*) dominated by powerful men; beneficiaries and the rights of the occupier of the plots are also mentioned.[14] [...] But in the grant system which became widespread in post-Gupta times the local adhikaraṇa disappeared, and was generally not consulted in matters of land grants.

Hierarchical control over land was created by large-scale subinfeudation, especially from the eighth century onwards.[15] This appears in both north and south India. At one stage under the Coḷas, there were as many as five grades in its landed hierarchy. It consisted of the king on top followed by the assignee and then the occupant who leased land to the sub-occupant who finally got it tilled by the cultivating tenant.[16] Subinfeudation gave rise to a hierarchy of landlords, different from the actual tillers of the soil. Such a process seems to be in line with a significant generalization made by Marx about feudalism. According to him, 'feudal production is characterized by division of soil amongst the greatest possible number of subfeudatories.'[17]

The peasantry was divested more and more of its homogeneous and egalitarian character. Many indications of unequal distribution of land in the village are available. We hear not only of brāhmaṇas but also of the chief brāhmaṇa, *mahattama, uttama, kṛṣivala, karṣaka, kṣetrakara, kuṭumbin,* and *kāruka*, land-endowed brāhmaṇas and *agrahāras*. We also hear of *kṣudra prakṛti* or petty peasants, and of Meda, Andhra, and Caṇḍāla. It is obvious that certain people in the villages had a greater share in the sources of production and apparently possessed more than they could manage directly. Such people got their lands cultivated by petty peasants either through lease holding, sharecropping, or the system of serfdom. We have therefore no means of establishing that most of the peasants living in villages were in 'complete' control of the means of production.

[...]

The terms for the peasant used in medieval texts, and particularly in inscriptions, signify the change in the nature of the peasant's relation to the land he cultivated. From the age of the Buddha to the advent of the Gupta period, tax-paying vaiśyas continued as an omnibus order, comprising mostly peasants. However, by early medieval times they were reduced to the position of the śūdras, who in spite of having acquired peasanthood, continued to bear the hallmark of servitude.[18]

[...]

A review of the terms used for the peasant in medieval inscriptions and literature fails to present the peasant's image as a controller of land. On the other hand we have such technical terms as *bhoktā, bhogī, bhogika, bhogijana, bhogapati, bhogapatika, bhogikapālaka, bhogirūpa, mahābhogī, bṛhadbhogi, bṛhadbhogika,* and so on, used generally for those who enjoyed landed property.[19] Here I have not taken into account many other terms connected with *rājā, rāṇaka, sāmanta, maṇḍaleśvara,* and so on, who were powerful landed intermediaries. The contrast between the two types of terms is obvious. Some people were meant for cultivating land and some for enjoying the fruits of production although in this category people did not share the surplus equally. There is nothing to show that the peasants who produced were in firm and independent control of their holdings. And finally there was the state symbolized by the king, whose general authority over land was recognized by numerous epithets used for him in early medieval records.[20]

[...]

An important factor which gave the beneficiaries general control over the means of production was the conferment of seigniorial rights on them. The charters authorized the beneficiaries to punish people guilty of ten offences,[21] including those against the family, property, individual persons, etc., and to try civil cases.[22] Further, royal officers were not allowed to enter their territory[23] and cause any kind of obstruction in their functioning.[24] All these were as good as manorial rights, and could even enable the beneficiaries to force the peasants to work in their fields. It would appear that the right to try cases on the spot involving the imposition of fines could seriously interfere with the process of production. It is therefore obvious that the political and judicial rights, which were non-economic rights, helped the beneficiaries to effectively exploit estate peasants economically. This may have been a successful way of governing the vast population because the perpetrators of crime could be dealt with immediately. At the same time these non-economic rights served to enforce the general economic authority of the beneficiaries over both the means and the processes of production. It may further be noted that in many cases the beneficiaries were empowered to adopt any means of enjoying the benefits accruing from the villages, and the term used for this was *sarvopāya-saṃyuktam*.[25] They were also authorized to enjoy the fruits of production at their own free will. If we carefully examine the phrase *saṃbhogyā yāvadichchā kriyāphalam*[26] it would mean that the donee could even intervene in the process of production. If a person is entitled to enjoy the fruits of production at his discretion, he may develop a natural tendency to control the process (*kriyā*) itself on which the nature and the amount of yield depend. Sometimes whatever belonged to the village (*svasaṃbhoga sametaḥ*) was to be enjoyed by the beneficiary.[27] He was also granted the village along with all its products (*sarvotpattisahitaḥ*).[28] [...]

It is not clear how the peasants were provided with agricultural implements. The charters authorized the beneficiaries to enjoy all that was hidden under the earth. This would amount to giving mining rights to the beneficiaries. It is well known that the mining rights belonged exclusively to the king. The king may have acquired this monopoly at the initial stage as the head of the tribe or the community, but once this exclusive control over iron and other minerals passed into the hands of the beneficiaries, they would be in a position to control the supply of agricultural implements to the peasants. But in pre-feudal times the big landowners did not have such rights. Mining rights belonged to the king who symbolized the community, and the peasants probably did not experience difficulties in procuring agricultural implements.

Not only were the successors of the king and the people in power asked to observe the terms of the grants[29] but also all those who would upset the grants were threatened with the use of force.[30] In some warnings corporal punishment (*śarīradaṇḍam*) is clearly mentioned.[31] The threat to use force is contained mostly in grants from Madhya Pradesh, Maharashtra, Andhra, and Karnataka, and the earliest example is found in a Pallava grant of the fourth century from Guntur district. In addition, the opponents of land grants were threatened with all kinds of curses. The idea that a peasant was the complete master of the means of production is also belied by the philosophical teachings found at the end of most grants. The grants underline the instability of life with regard to not only death but also to the fickleness of fortune. The concept of the fickleness of fortune (or mobility of Lakṣmī) is mainly derived from the frequent transfer of control over the means of production from one person to another. [...]

[...]

[...] I have shown earlier that in the donated villages the beneficiaries enjoyed superior authority over the means of production. Donated fields, many of them very large in area, were without doubt directly and completely controlled by the beneficiaries, who manipulated the production resources and processes. How this influenced the course of production in 'free' villages has to be investigated.

[...]

On the basis of the land charters we can say that in the donated areas, the landed beneficiaries enjoyed general control over production resources. [...] This raises the problem of serfdom. It is thought that feudalism was identical with serfdom, and there seems to be an assumption that serfdom was the only potent method of exploiting the peasants. It may be very effective, but other forms of servitude imposed on the peasantry were equally effective. After all what is the essence of serfdom? In this system small farm units are attached to big farm units, and the two are interdependent for purposes of production. Big farms are directly managed by manorial magnates but are cultivated by those who possess small plots. Therefore, serfdom means giving more surplus labour for less surplus produce. But in the Indian context, surplus produce is extracted more through the general control exercised by landed intermediaries than by the employment of serfs. A serf also occupies some land and provides his family with subsistence. But he not only pays rent in cash or kind for exploiting his unit of production but also spends extra hours labouring on the field of his lord. The extra yield which accrues from these extra hours of labour does not necessarily stay with the cultivator. On the other hand it enables him to pay more rent in cash or kind to his lord.

It has been argued that serfdom is an incidental feature in the case of India.[32] But the evidence cited so far would show that it is more than incidental.[33] In any case if the landlord gets his share without reducing too many people to serfdom, what basic difference does it make to him or to the social pattern. In both systems the landlord is concerned with extracting his share; in both the cultivator is a dependent peasant, exploited by his landlord; and in both the social structure is beset with the contradiction between the landlord and the actual tiller. A beneficiary may not have possessed big plots of land, but he may have possessed too many plots which made management difficult. In fact laws regarding the partition of land became effective in Gupta and post-Gupta times[34] and they may have contributed to the fragmentation of land. The fragmentation of land is also indicated by epigraphic sale transactions found in Bangladesh.[35] Therefore, if a landlord possessed too many plots, tenanting and sharecropping would be more convenient than getting the land cultivated by serfs.

It is held that because soil in India was very fertile there was no scope for the rise of serfdom or forced labour.[36] But we have indications of forced labour in the middle Gangetic basin where the soil is most fertile. Till recent times poor tenants, belonging to the lower castes, were forced by upper caste landlords to work in the fields at meagre wages.[37] Peasants were compelled to plough the land of the landlords and do various kinds of odd jobs for them in other fertile areas. This is known as *harī* and *begārī* in the whole of the Gangetic basin area. The medieval term harī is *halikākara*,[38] and for *begārī is viṣṭi* from which *beṭh-begārī* is derived. The Pāla charters found in Monghyr, Bhagalpur, Saharsa, and Nalanda districts, all part of the middle Gangetic plain, mention the term *sarvapīḍāparihṛta.* This means that the peasants were subjected to forced labour and oppression, and when a village was transferred to a beneficiary he became entitled to these advantages without the interference of the state. Forced labour may have originated in less populated areas but not necessarily in less fertile parts. In any case once its usefulness was recognized it spread to more populated parts.

Feudalism flourished in paddy producing areas. Paddy production requires 50 per cent more man hours than does wheat production. According to a popular saying in Patna and Gaya districts in Bihar, wheat cultivation can be undertaken even by a widow, who represents an image of helplessness in the countryside. Evidently wheat cultivation requires less labour and barley cultivation even less. Therefore, at the time of paddy transplantation there would be scarcity of labour; and it would be necessary to take on forced labour. The term *sotpadyamānaviṣṭi* is used frequently[39] and has been translated to mean the use of forced labour as the occasion demands. But since the term qualifies donated land or a donated village, it might mean the labour generated or produced by the village in future.[40] [...] That there were various types of forced labour is clear from the use of the term *sarvaviṣṭi*[41] in many land grants, particularly in Vākāṭaka grants. These many types may have included the use of labour in the fields in central and western India. However in northern India *viṣṭi* meant the right to compel the rural population to construct forts, roads, etc., and to help the authorities in transport, *veṭṭi* is frequently mentioned in south Indian charters.[...] The evidence from the *Skanda Purāṇa* produced by B.N.S. Yadava leaves little doubt that hundreds of people were compelled into forced labour which was evidently meant for production in medieval times.[42] Hence, serfdom cannot be dismissed as an incidental feature.

If serfdom is understood to mean the compulsive attachment of the peasants to the soil, it prevailed in good part in Madhya Pradesh, eastern India, Chamba, and Rajasthan. In many cases the charters clearly transfer the peasants, artisans, and even traders to the beneficiaries.[43] In most charters the villagers and peasants are asked to stay in their villages and carry out the orders of the beneficiaries. This fact of the immobility of peasants and artisans has not been contested by anybody so far. However, it is argued that even if these people had been allowed to move, what purpose would it have served? If such a view is take then what is the point of underlining the absence of serfdom in the Indian context?

[...]

It is repeatedly stated that no new mode of socio-economic formation can emerge as a result of political, administrative, and judicial measures;[44] this does not take into account the fact that the colonial system in India owed its origin largely to such measures. The king in ancient India symbolized state authority, and the state was backed by priests and warriors who lived on the surplus produced by the peasants and augmented by the artisans. This kind of state and society appeared in the age of the Buddha. It continued to function more or less smoothly till the third century AD. But many passages in the epics and the Purāṇas speak of a kind of social crisis heralded by the advent of the Kali age. These passages are ascribed to the second half of the third century AD and the beginning of the fourth century AD. They depict a state of affairs in which rural people were oppressed with taxes and forced labour.[45] The oppressions of the state coupled with the havoc caused by natural calamities created a state of chaos, and the lower orders, particularly the vaiśyas and the śūdras, refused to perform the functions assigned to them. The peasants also refused to pay taxes.[46] The *Manu Smṛiti*, the *Śānti Parva* and other texts suggested two measures to overcome this social crisis. One was the use of force or *daṇḍa*, which is glorified in these texts. The other was the restoration of the *varṇāśrama-dharma* which was considered to be the bedrock of the class-divided and state-based society.

[...]

[...] The fact cannot be discounted that trade[47] and urbarnism[48] suffered a distinct decline, and the absence of gold coins for three centuries between the seventh and the tenth centuries and the paucity of other types of coins[49] are well known. There is practically no indication of the use of slaves in production. All these are presages of change in the methods and relations of production. Hence the production system as a whole was afflicted with certain maladies, which compelled the state to convert land/land revenues into a general mode of payment for religious and administrative services. The grant system relieved the state of the heavy responsibility of getting taxes collected from all over the countryside by its agents and then of disbursing them in cash or kind. On the other hand, priests, warriors, and administrators were asked to fend for themselves in the villages that were assigned to them for their enjoyment. The system also relieved the state of the responsibility of maintaining law and order in the donated villages which now became almost the sole concern of the beneficiaries. Therefore it would be wrong to assume that political, administrative, and judicial measures, which created new property relations in land, were undertaken by the state entirely on its own.

The social crisis apparently led to the withdrawal of slaves from production, and the provision of land for them as tenants and sharecroppers. This explains to a good extent the elevation of śūdras to peasanthood and their participation in rituals. It seems that landowners converted

Śūdra labourers into peasants and themselves became landlords living on rents. The substantial *gahapatis* of the age of the Buddha probably turned landlords. That the village headman tended to become a landlord has already been indicated,[50] although the causes of this transformation need investigation.

The new socio-economic formation that emerged as a result of the appearance of a class of landlords and of a subject peasantry had its own limitations. [...] But the beneficiary would impose proper and improper taxes as well as fixed and unfixed taxes, would collect 'all kinds' of taxes, and, what is worse, would make additional impositions which were covered by the term *ādi* which meant etc. In certain areas they could also introduce new forms of forced labour. Besides, all communal and agrarian resources hitherto enjoyed by the peasants were transferred to the landed beneficiaries who were always present on the spot. This situation caused constant conflict between those who claimed rent on the strength of their royal charters and the others who claimed immunity on the basis of customary and immemorial rights which would certainly be known to the local people but because of their illiteracy would not be shown in black and white. Hence there was bound to be constant friction, tensions, and struggles between the landed beneficiaries and the servile peasantry. This could lead to litigations between the beneficiaries, and also between the beneficiaries and the peasants.[51] Due to the common practice of land grants and the enormous advantages derived from them the brāhmaṇas forged many charters (*kūṭaśāsana*) and claimed villages as their own on that basis. But there were so many valid charters that conflicts between the landlord and the peasant were always a possibility. In order to settle this conflict Nārada, Bṛhaspati, the *Agni Purāṇa* and other authorities give the final authority to the royal charter in the case of a dispute. They lay down that if there is a conflict between the religious right *(dharma)*, contract right *(vyavahāra)*, customary right *(carita)*, and the right derived from the royal charter *(rājaśāsana)* the royal charter will override all the other sources of the law or authority.[52]

But it seems that the overriding power of the royal charter did not work in all cases. We have the case of the Kaivartas, a fishing and cultivating community in Bangladesh, who rose against Rāmapāla in the eleventh century AD. They fought with bamboo sticks riding on buffaloes. So powerful was their revolt that two dozen vessels had to be mobilized by Rāmapāla in order to put down this rebellion. This is an important example of a peasant revolt.[53] The possibility of a clash is also indicated in some Bengal grants which mention the term *karṣaṇavirodhi sthāna*.[54] At least two grants take pains to show that they do not clash with the existing cultivating rights of the peasants. Therefore, the possibility of a clash between the peasants and the incoming beneficiaries is clearly visualized. Similarly in many grants from Madhya Pradesh and Maharashtra, the people are warned that if they try to upset the grant in any manner they will be punished with force.[55] This point is stated repeatedly[56] in many inscriptions. In some cases this threat is directed towards royal officials, but mostly it is a general threat meant for everybody. Again, in the texts of this period, *brahmahatyā*, that is the killing of brāhmaṇas, is considered to be a great sin and it occurs in many Purāṇas. Why did the murder of a brāhmaṇa become so important in early medieval times? Apparently it was because of his becoming a landed beneficiary and therefore an oppressor. [...]

[...]

[...] the caste system with its features of hierarchy and superiority, not to speak of untouchability, provided ritualistic and ideological sanction for the production and distribution system. The śūdra peasant castes proliferated in medieval times. Although the peasants were exploited in a more or less similar manner, endless caste divisions undermined their solidarity. Ritualistic distinctions distorted the reality of exploitation.

It appears that the *jajmānī* system developed in the early medieval period, and was part of a more or less self-sufficient economy. At the end of harvesting, on the threshing floor, portions of paddy were given to the gods, brāhmaṇas, rulers, and various kinds of labourers, indicated by the term *bhṛtyavarga-poṣaṇam*.[57] The brāhmaṇas, who controlled many 'estates', played a crucial ideological role in penetrating the consciousness of the peasantry and making them behave as they wanted them to. Some medieval religious reform movements apparently sought to improve the status of those who really produced and suffered, but these movements were manipulated to contain the conflicts and ease the tensions; they could not rouse the peasantry to retaliate. In certain parts of the country the survival of bonds of kinship also helped to keep people together. This may be particularly true of Rajasthan and the Himalayan areas. Classes with conflicting interests were kept together through the performance of *pūjā, japa, vrata, tīrthayatrā, saṃskāra,* and *prāyaścitta* as well as through prospects of heaven and hell. The all-pervasive influence of astrology (*jyotiṣa*) and of the doctrine of Vedānta reconciled the people to their lot. These types of factors brought people of opposite interests together.

It is held that lack of 'concentrated social effort' blocked changes in the means, methods, and relations of production.[58] We may not have much idea about the social effort, but we can certainly identify significant changes in the mode of production in early medieval times. This period was undoubtedly an age of larger yields and agrarian expansion.[59] It is possible to count hundreds of states, particularly in those areas which had never witnessed the rise of full-fledged states. A state presupposes an assured source of income which would enable it to maintain a good number of managerial staff. This would not be possible unless the agrarian base was strong enough to pay for the priests, officers, soldiers, and so on.

Urban contraction was an important cause of the dissemination of technology in rural areas. Western India provides many examples of the migration of town-dwelling brāhmaṇas to the countryside where they were donated land by the ruling class.[60] Backward regions would benefit from the better knowledge of agriculture of the beneficiaries. Agriculture would also benefit from the ready availability of artisans who migrated from decaying towns.

Several texts on agriculture such as the *Kṛṣiparāśara* in the north and Kamban's book in the south were composed in early medieval times. Kāśyapa's *Kṛṣisūkti*, though found in the south,[61] could be set in a paddy-producing area either in the north or the south. [...] In addition, detailed instructions regarding agriculture appear in the *Bṛhat Saṃhitā* of Varāhamihira, the *Agni Purāṇa,* and the *Viṣṇudharmottara Purāṇa.*[62] Three crops, first mentioned by Pāṇini, were known widely[63] and better seeds were produced.[64] Meteorological knowledge, based on observation, was of an advanced nature in the *Kṛṣiparāśara.* The knowledge of fertilizers improved immensely, and the use of compost was known.[65] Some other innovations in agricultural techniques are worth noting. The *bṛhadhala* or big plough mentioned in a tenth century inscription from the Ajmer[66] area may have been an important instrument in breaking difficult soil in certain parts of the country. Equally advantageous to agricultural processes may have been the use of the pounder, which was in use in Pāla times.[67]

More importantly, irrigation facilities were expanded. The law books lay down severe punishments for those who cause damage to tanks, wells, ponds, embankments, and so on.[68] The construction of a *vāpī* (step-well) became very popular in Rajasthan and Gujarat. Its importance is also underlined in the work of Kāśyapa.[69] V.K. Jain has prepared a map in which he has shown the distribution of vāpīs in western India in the eleventh–thirteenth centuries.[70] Vāpīs of the tenth and eleventh centuries are also found in good numbers in the Mehrauli area of Delhi. It is interesting to note that the term vāpī is derived from the Sanskrit root *vap* which means 'to sow'. Clearly step-wells were meant for irrigating the fields, but they would be equally useful for supplying drinking water and also for irrigating gardens. Further, the use of the *araghaṭṭa* or the Persian wheel had become widespread in the ninth–tenth centuries, particularly in Rajasthan. The *Kṛṣisūkti* of Kāśyapa prescribes that the machine for lifting water (*ghaṭī yantra*) is to be operated by men, oxen, or elephants.[71] The use of the term *arahaṭṭiyanara* in a lexicon of the twelfth century shows that certain persons were employed to work the water wheel.[72]

Of course the use of iron implements attained a new peak in this period. The *Paryāyamuktāvālī,* a medieval lexicon whose manuscripts have been found in West Bengal and Orissa, mentions as many as half a dozen types or grades of iron.[73] Above all, iron artefacts were manufactured in plenty. They were used as beams for holding the roof and also as memorial pillars which evidently was a non-utilitarian purpose. Several pillars, including the Mehrauli pillar in Delhi, were erected to mark the conquest of victorious princes.

The increase in the number of varieties of cereals including rice, wheat, and lentils as well as in fruits, legumes, vegetables, and so on, is striking. These can be inferred not only from the Amarakośa but more so from the *Paryāyamuktāvalī.*[74] According to the *Śūnya Purāṇa* more than fifty kinds of paddy were cultivated in Bengal.[75] It would thus appear that the introduction of new crops, expansion of irrigation facilities, and innovation in agricultural techniques contributed to the growth of agriculture.

It appears that agriculture and agrarian settlements in the Middle Ages received special attention from the rulers, landed beneficiaries and immigrant artisans. [...] However, a mere increase in production may lead neither to stability nor to structural changes. For this, certain other conditions, including the rousing of consciousness, may be needed.

## FEUDAL VERSUS SEGMENTARY

Burton Stein's latest views have some bearing on the current debate. He states that 'notwithstanding its distinguished paternity by D.D. Kosambi in the middle 1950s and R.S. Sharma a decade later, the feudal concept has never been seriously tested against the claims inherent in it, nor has it been elaborated in any significant way'.[76] Here something is wrong with the chronology. I sent my *Origins of Feudalism in India* (*circa* AD *400–650*) for publication in early 1957, and it appeared in 1958[77] and not 'a decade' after Kosambi's work 'in the middle 1950s'. Incidentally, after 1956, when his *An Introduction to the Study of Indian History* was published, Kosambi wrote two valuable papers on feudalism in 1959.[78] That 'the claims inherent' in the feudal concept have been both 'tested' and significantly 'elaborated' will be amply borne out by the papers, including mine, found in D.N. Jha (ed.), *Feudal Social Formation in Early India,* Delhi, 1987. Since then, several other publications have discussed new dimensions of the subject. The feudal model is being fruitfully applied to the study of art, religion, caste system, language, and literature of medieval times. Yet the concept of Indian feudalism is called a 'convenient residual position'. If it means an unaccountable position, it will continue to be so as long as the coiner of the phrase refuses to take into account the work done on the subject. How I wish a serious scholar would not shut his eyes to relevant publications of not only the last three decades but even earlier.

Feudalism is denounced as an 'article of left historiographical faith'. But the present paper is in response to the criticisms of Mukhia, who is considered a leftist. I also know of a few other similar critics. To attribute feudalism to leftism betrays an appalling ignorance of the work of reputed researchers such as Devangana Desai, Lallanji Gopal, N. Karashima, T.V. Mahalingam, Dasharatha Sharma, and B.N.S. Yadava,[79] who by no means can be labelled as 'leftists'. They have applied the feudal analogy fully or partly to the Indian state and society of different regions and periods. The declamation of the feudal concept in the Indian context has become an obsession with some western historians who cannot extricate themselves from the colonial constructs on Indian history presented in a new garb. The importance of kin, caste, religion, symbolism, segmentation, and so on, is overemphasized and any comparison with the west European experience to bring out historical specificities and universalities is frowned upon. Some western historians and Indologists underline the role of decentralization in early Indian history and assert that Indian rulers were merely the masters of roads, towns, and capitals and not of the hinterland. They do not consider the feudal framework for analysis although it could explain the mechanism through which rent was collected from the rural population and remitted as revenue by the feudal lords to the central treasury in medieval times.

Stein imagines that Indian feudalism is seen by its exponents only in the context of feudatories found everywhere in pre-modern India.[80] If he cares to go through relevant writings he will discover that those who emerged as landlords either on their own or through assignments made by the central authority constituted the crucial component in the feudal structure. The payment of tribute by the feudatories to the central power depended on its strength, which consequently determined the extent of the local exploitation of the peasants. If the tribute was regular the peasant would be taxed more; if it was occasional he would be taxed less. But the landlords superimposed upon the peasants became regular exploiters, whose presence was indispensable for controlling the land as well as the peasants who cultivated it. The feudal infrastructure explains the nature of the state and all the other, superstructural elements such as art, religion, and culture. Feudatories played a supplementary role in the whole system.

Following Southall, Stein adds that 'comparisons with, and even borrowing from Europe had been acceptable, even eagerly sought whereas merely structural comparison of Indian and African forms gives offence to many Indians'.[81] Here he not only ignores the importance of comparative study in history but also the fact that European history has been taught in India for nearly two hundred years; the colonial masters never introduced any African history except that of ancient Egypt or Africa's partition in the 1880s. Indian historians have been influenced by western writings on European history but they are not attracted by such constructs as the one on the segmentary state. The use of anthropology including the African anthropology for explaining historical processes is a comparatively recent phenomenon, and yet it is used by Indian historians in the study of ancient India.[82] Therefore to say that many Indians feel offended by such an exercise is wilful distortion. I very much hope that such allegations are not intended to prejudice the Africanists and educated Africans against Indian scholars, though such an effect, is perhaps unavoidable.

In his enthusiasm for building a model, Stein propounded the distinction between ritual sovereignty and actual political control in the context of the Coḷa 'segmentary' state. But the myth of the ritual sovereignty of the Coḷas as distinct from actual political authority exercised by its different local centres (segments) of power was exploded by several scholars, and now it has been wisely abandoned by its expounder. He is 'now (1989) convinced' that 'the distinction is incorrect' and that political authority forces a lord 'to foster ... ritual actions and services'.[83] Since I happen to be older I reached this conclusion in 1954.[84]

The 'segmentary' supporters may feel happy in their make-believe world. The test of a theory or its refutation lies in the nature of the supporting evidence. The attempt to project the 'segmentary' as a model for the early Indian state and society has proved to be abortive. Almost every segment of the segmentary concept has been examined and dismissed.[85] In the process the study of Indian feudalism has been enriched empirically and conceptually. In exposing the hollowness of the segmentary and similar untenable formulations on Indian history, Indian as well as other historians have done valuable work to rebut the colonialist historiographical dogmas that the Indians were always ruled by despots, that they were always absorbed in the problems of their spiritual lives, that they were not concerned with material life, and so on.

## CONCLUDING OBSERVATIONS

Feudalism in India was characterized by a class of landlords and by a class of subject peasantry, both living in a predominantly agrarian economy marked by a decline in trade and urbanism and by a drastic reduction in metal currency. The superior state got its taxes collected and authority recognized by creating a number of inferior power blocs or even states (that is, landed priests, *maṭhas, vihāras, basadis,* temples, *agrahāras, brahmadeyas,* and so on) who generated the necessary social and ideological climate for this purpose. Unlike the European system most of the power structures within the state did not have to pay taxes. West European feudal lords granted land to their serfs in order to get their own occupied land cultivated. But Indian kings made land grants to get the taxes (surplus) collected. In their turn the grantees collected rents from their tenant peasants who could be evicted and even subjected to forced labour.

The critics of Indian feudalism posit the presence of either a peasant society or peasant control over production resources in medieval times. Both cases could suggest a kind of egalitarian, classless society with prominent tribal traits. There is a tendency, open or concealed, to resurrect the Asiatic mode and even oriental despotism in a new incarnation. Fortunately, on the basis of sound logic and solid empirical evidence the latest full-length study on the subject by Brendan O'Leary convincingly shows that the Asiatic mode cannot be applied to the Indian experience.[86] In my view, during medieval times, the major part of the Indian subcontinent was marked by the strong presence of a surplus-consuming class which lived off the labour of a subject peasantry on the strength of its superior agrarian authority buttressed by ritualistic and ideological mechanisms. In this context the concept of class may be reconsidered. The position of class may be located in the overall system of production. If a class means a category composed of those who either exclusively control the means of production or those who are completely deprived of such control, such a thing can happen only in a full-fledged capitalist system. The application of such a concept to pre-capitalist societies is riddled with difficulties, for even in the feudal society of western Europe the serf enjoyed day-to-day control over his share of the means of production.[87] In such a society, class is best seen in the context of the unequal distribution of the surplus, which was eventually given a lasting basis by the unequal distribution of the means of production and strengthened by ideological, ritualistic, and juridical factors. [...]

## NOTES

1 D.C. Sircar, *Landlordism and Tenancy in Ancient and Medieval India as Revealed by Epigraphical Records*, Lucknow, 1969. Also see *Journal of Indian History*, vol. 44, 1966, pp. 351–7; vol. 51, 1973, pp. 56–9; *Journal of Ancient Indian History*, vol. 6, 1972–73; pp. 337–9; D.C. Sircar (ed.), *Land System and Feudalism in Ancient India*, Calcutta, 1966, pp. 11–23. Irfan Habib discusses 'Indian Feudalism' in *The Peasant in Indian History*, Presidential Address, Indian History Congress, 43rd Session, Kurukshetra, 1982.

2 Harbans Mukhia, 'Was There Feudalism in Indian History?', *The Journal of Peasant Studies*, vol. 8, no. 3, April 1981, pp. 273–310. In this paper the whole medieval period is discussed: but I will confine myself primarily to early medieval times (fifth to twelfth century), about which I have some idea. My task has been made easy because Dr Mukhia's criticisms have been effectively met by B.N.S. Yadava in *The Problem of the Emergence of Feudal Relations in Early India*, Presidential Address for Ancient India Section of the Indian History Congress, 41st Session, Bombay, 1980. In a similar address delivered at the 40th Session of the Indian History Congress held at Waltair in 1979, D.N. Jha anticipated and answered many of these objections in *Early Indian Feudalism: A Historiographical Critique*. Also see Suvira Jaiswal, 'Studies in Early Indian Social History', *Indian Historical Review*, vol. 6, 1979–80, pp. 18–21.

3 Marx–Engels, *Pre-Capitalist Socio-Economic Formations*, Moscow, 1979, p. 23.

4 Mukhia, 'Was There Feudalism?', p. 310, fn. 225. In the discussion on variants Indian feudalism is seen as a distinct possibility.

5 Kosminsky's views based on Marx and expressed in his *Studies in the Agrarian History of England in the Thirteenth Century*, Oxford, 1956, are summarized and discussed in Barry Hindess and Paul Q. Hirst, *Pre-Capitalist Modes of Production*, London, 1975, pp. 222–3, cf. pp. 234–5.

6 Mukhia, 'Was There Feudalism?', pp. 275, 290–1, 293.

7 The terms used are *sarvoparikarakaradānasametaḥ, sarvakarasametaḥ, sarvakaravisarjitaḥ*. See Balchandra Jain, *Utkīrṇa-Lekha*, Raipur, 1961, pp. 56–7. The terms *samastapratyāya* and *sarvāyasameta* also occur (R.S. Sharma, *Indian Feudalism*, 2nd edn, Delhi, 1980, p. 100). Also see *sarvādānasamagrāhya, Epigraphia Indica (EI* hereafter), vol. V, no. 5, line 14.

8 Sharma, *Indian Feudalism*, pp. 98–100.

9 The phrase used is *niyatāniyatasamastādāya*, all specified and unspecified dues. *Epigraphia Indica*, vol. XII, no. 36, line 12.

10 *EI*, vol. XXIX, no. 7, line 42; Jain, p. 52.
11 Mukhia rightly postulates that the village potentates would be the first to notice the rise in productivity and the first to demand a greater share in the peasant's produce, 'Was There Feudalism?' p. 309, fn. 214.
12 R. Tirumalai, *Land Grants and Agrarian Reactions in Cola and Pandya Times*, Madras, 1987, p. 31.
13 The phrase *ājñāśravaṇavidheyībhūya* is common in north Indian grants.
14 *Sel Inscr.*, bk III, nos 16, 18, 19,41, 42, 43, etc.
15 Sharma, *Indian Feudalism*, pp. 73–5, 185–7.
16 R. Tirumalai, *Land Grants and Agrarian Reactions in Coḷa and Pāṇḍya Times*, p. 60.
17 Marx-Engels, *Pre-Capitalist Socio-Economic Formations*, p. 22.
18 R.S. Sharma, *Śūdras in Ancient India*, 2nd edn, Delhi, 1980, ch. vii.
19 Sharma, *Indian Feudalism*, pp. 12–13, 216.
20 These terms are *avanīśa, avanīndra, kṣitipati, kṣitendra, kṣitīśa, kṣiteradhipa, pārthiva, pṛthivīpati, pārthivendra, pṛthivīnātha, bhūpa, bhūpati, bhūbhuj, bhūmipa, bhumīśvara, mahīpa, mahīpati, mahīpāla, mahīndra, mahāmahendra, urvīpati, vasudhādhipa, vasudheśvara, sāmanta-bhumīśvara*, etc. R.S. Sharma, 'From Gopati to Bhupati: A Review of the Changing Position of the King', *Studies in History*, vol. 2, no. 2, 1980, p. 8 with fns. 81–2.
21 Sharma, *Indian Feudalism*, p. 3; the common term used is *sadaṇḍadaśāparādhaḥ*.
22 Ibid., the term *abhyantarasiddhi* is used.
23 Ibid., p. 2.
24 *Sel. Inscr.*, bk III, no. 62, lines 21–2.
25 Mukherji and Maity, *Corpus of Bengal Inscriptions*, no. 47, line 62.
26 Ibid., line 63.
27 Ibid., no. 46, line 22.
28 *EI*, vol. V, no. 20, line 54. The village, situated near Nagpur, was granted by Kṛṣṇa III in AD 940–41.
29 D.C. Sircar (ed.), *Select Inscriptions Bearing on Indian History and Civilization*, vol. I, Calcutta, 1965, (abbrev. as *Sel. Inscr.*), bk III, no. 49, lines 18–28; no. 50, lines 15–23.
30 ... *sadaṇḍanigrahaṃ kariṣyāmah*. This phrase is found with slight variations in many charters. Ibid., no. 61, II. 22–4; no. 62, II. 32–4; no. 64, II. 21–4; no. 65, II. 39–41; no. 67, II. 24–5.
31 Ibid., no. 67, II. 24–5.
32 Mukhia, 'Was There Feudalism?' p. 286.
33 Sharma, *Indian Feudalism*, pp. 19, 31, 40–3, 56, 60, 67–8, 99–101, 109, 195–8; B.N.S. Yadava, *Society and Culture in Northern India in the Twelfth Century*, Allahabad, 1973, pp. 164–9; 'Immobility and Subjection of Indian Peasantry in Early Medieval Complex', *Indian Historical Review*, I, 1974, pp. 18–27. A good deal of evidence can be obtained from G.K Rai, *Involuntary Labour in Ancient India*, Allahabad, 1981, but the passage from Vātsyayāna's *Kāmasūtra* (V.5.5) is inaccurately construed and translated.
34 Sharma, *Indian Feudalism*, pp. 118–19.
35 Ibid., p. 49.

36 Mukhia, 'Was There Feudalism', pp. 286, 289, 303, fn. 124.
37 This was the case in north Bihar until the abolition of the Permanent Settlement.
38 Y.B. Singh, 'Halikākara: Crystallization of a Practice into a Tax', Paper presented to the 43rd Session of the Indian History Congress, Kurukshetra, 1982.
39 Sharma, *Indian Feudalism,* pp. 99–100.
40 The term *upatsyamāna* would suit this interpretation better, although even *utpadyamāna* means the same thing. I owe this suggestion to R.C. Pandeya. Palaeographically there is very little difference between the two terms.
41 *Sel. Inscr.,* bk III, no. 61, line 19; no. 62, line 28.
42 Yadava, *Society and Culture in Northern India,* pp. 164–6.
43 Sharma, *Indian Feudalism,* p. 188 with fn. 6.
44 Mukhia, 'Was There Feudalism', pp. 274, 286.
45 The Kali passage in the Cr. edn of the *Mahābhārata* (III. 188.71) amended by me on the basis of the Gita Press edn reads: *nirviśeṣā janapadā karaviṣṭibhirarditāḥ.* Apparently taxes *(kara)* affected the vaiśyas and forced labour (*viṣṭi*) the śūdras.
46 R.S. Sharma, 'The Kali Age: A Period of Social Crisis', S.N. Mukherjee (ed.) *India, History and Thought: Essays in Honour of A.L. Basham,* Calcutta, 1982, pp. 186–203. Also see *Śūdras in Ancient India,* 2nd edn, Delhi, 1980, pp. 233–9.
47 In addition to the material presented regarding the decline of trade in my *Indian Feudalism,* 2nd edn, chs. I and III, further evidence appears in B.N.S. Yadava, *Society and Culture in Northern India in the Twelfth Century,* pp. 270–5. Speaking of early medieval Bengal, M.R. Tarafdar says: 'The period between the eleventh and thirteenth centuries shows distinct signs of the decay of trade and urban centres, a process which must have started earlier' ('Trade and Society in Early Medieval Bengal', *Indian Historical Review,* vol. 3, January 1978, p. 282). However, in western India trade shows revival in this period (V.K. Jain, 'Trade and Traders in Western India', PhD thesis, Delhi University, 1983); this seems to be the case with south India also (Kenneth R. Hall, *Trade and Statecraft in the Age of the Coḷas.* I postulate decline of trade mainly in the seventh–tenth centuries.
48 B.D. Chattopadhyaya in 'Trade and Urban Centres in Early Medieval North India', *Indian Historical Review,* vol. 1, 1974, pp. 203–19 doubted the decline of urbanism, but in 'Urban Centres in Early Medieval India', Sabyasachi Bhattacharya and Romlia Thapar (eds), *Situating Indian History: For Sarvapalli Gopal,* Delhi, 1986, pp: 8–33, he postulated a 'third urbanization' which presupposes de-urbanization in Gupta and post-Gupta times. Almost all Sātavāhana towns decay and disappear after the third century AD. A.H. Dani informs me of a similar fate of the Kuśāṇa towns in Pakistan, and the Soviet archaeologist V. Masson tells me that five central Asian urban centres of around the first to the fourth centuries AD become either villages or castles afterwards. Some recent books such as those of O.P. Prasad, *Decay and Revival of Urban Centres in Medieval South India,* New Delhi, 1986, and B.P.N. Pathak, *Society and Culture in Early Bihar,* New Delhi, 1988, discuss de-urbanization in different parts of the country. R.N. Nandi convincingly shows that many of the decaying towns were convened into *tīrthas* or places of pilgrimage in early medieval times. 'Client, Ritual and Conflict in Early Brahmanical Order', *Indian Historical Review,* vol. 6, 1979–80, pp. 100, 103–9. For a detailed review

of the archaeological and other types of evidence see R.S. Sharma, *Urban Decay in India (c. 330–c. 1000)*, New Delhi, 1987.

49 R.S. Sharma, 'Indian Feudalism Retouched' (review paper), *Indian Historical Review*, vol. 1, 1974, 320–30. For additional evidence regarding the paucity of coinage, see M.R. Tarafdar. This point has been elaborated further in my two lectures on 'Paucity of Metal Money in India' (c. 500–c. 1000) delivered in the Indian Museum, Calcutta, in 1989 (unpublished).

50 Sharma, *Indian Feudalism*, pp. 41–2.

51 In 1214, a temple in Karnataka claimed the land of its neighbours, but the local authorities decided against the temple. S. Sethar and G.D. Sontheimer (eds) *Memorial Stones*, Dharwad, 1982, p. 303.

52 R.S. Sharma '*Rājaśāsana:* Meaning, Scope and Application', *Proceedings of the Indian History Congress*, 37th Session, Calicut, 1976, pp. 76–87.

53 Sharma, *Indian Feudalism*, p. 220.

54 Mukherji and Maity, *Corpus of Bengal Inscriptions*, no. 6, line 18; no. 7, line 19.

55 *Sel. Inscr.*, bk III, no. 61, lines 22–4.

56 Ibid., no. 62, lines 32–4; no. 63A, lines 21–4; no. 67, lines 24–5.

57 Gy. Wojtilla (ed.), *Kāśyapīyakṛṣisūkti*, verses 491–2.

58 Mukhia, 'Was There Feudalism', p. 292. However this statement is qualified by the phrase 'change completely' (ibid.).

59 R.S. Sharma, *Urban Decay in India (c. 300–c. 1000)*, ch. x.

60 Ibid., Appendix I.

61 Gy. Wojtilla (ed.), *Kāśyapiyākṛṣisūkti, Acta Orientalia Academiae Scientiarum Hung*, vol. 33, no. 2, 1979, pp. 209–52. The usual term for cultivator in this text is *kṛṣīvala*, which occurs in early medieval texts and inscriptions. Most of the material in this work probably belongs to medieval times, and its core is placed in the eighth–ninth centuries, Wojtilla, tr., ibid, vol. 39, no.1, 1985, p. 85, fn. 1.

62 Ibid., pp. 358, 361, 363. The *Agni Purāṇa* belongs to the ninth–tenth centuries. The *Viṣṇudharmottara Purāṇa* is attributed to the eighth century.

63 D.M. Bose et al. (ed.), *A Concise History of Science*, pp. 356–61.

64 Ibid., pp. 358–9.

65 Ibid., pp. 358–60.

66 B.P. Mazumdar, 'Industries and Internal Trade in Early Medieval North India', *Journal of the Bihar Research Society* (*JBRS*, hereafter), vol. XLV–XLVI, 1979–80, p. 231.

67 Discovered in the Pāla stratum of Taradih and reported orally to me by A.K. Prasad.

68 These texts belong to the early centuries of the Christian era. See R.S. Sharma, *Perspectives in Social and Economic History of Early India*, New Delhi, 1983, pp. 158–9.

69 Wojtilla (ed.), *Kāsyapiyākṛṣisūkti*, pp. 219–20.

70 'Trade and Traders in Western India' (unpublished PhD thesis), University of Delhi, 1983.

71 Wojtilla (ed.) *Kāsyapiyākṛṣisūkti*, verses 167–8. The *ghaṭī-yantra* operated by oxen is considered to be the best, that by men to be the worst, and that by elephants to be of middling quality.

72 B.N.S. Yadava, *Society and Culture in Northern India in the Twelfth Century*, p. 259.
73 The text was edited by T. Chowdhury in *JBRS*, vol. 31, 1945 and vol. 32, 1946. The earliest ms. used by him belongs to 1851–62. Composed by Haricaranasena, the text is based on the *Paryāyaratnamāla* of Mādhavakara (*JBRS*, vol. 31. 1945, Introduction, p. i). Since it is strikingly indebted to Amara in chs. 22, 23 (ibid.) and since potato and tobacco are not mentioned in it, it seems to be pre-Mughal. The synonyms for iron and other metals are found in ch. (*Varga*) 6 (*JBRS*, 1945).
74 T. Chowdhury, ch. 18 (*JBRS*, 31. 1945, pp. 31–3) speaks of twenty-four types of *śtmbīsukadhānyagaṇa* (p. 33), but the varieties, when counted, come to nearly 110 types of cereals including wheat, barley, lentils and so on. Ch. 19 (ibid., pp. 33–4) speaks of ten types of *śālidhānya* (transplanted paddy) and nineteen types of *tṛṇaśālidhānya* (untransplanted paddy), but on counting, the various types of paddy and allied cereals come to nearly sixty-four.
75 T.C. Dasgupta, *Aspect of Bengali Society*, pp. 249–50 quoted in B.N.S. Yadava, *Society and Culture*, pp. 258–305 fn. Yadava has cited several other pieces of evidence (pp, 258–9).
76 Burton Stein, 'The Segmentary State: Interim Reflections', Seminar on State Formation in the Pre-Colonial South India, Jawaharlal Nehru University, New Delhi. 1989.
77 *Journal of the Economic and Social History of the Orient* (*JESHO* hereafter), vol. 1, 1958. pp. 297–328.
78 'Indian Feudal Trade Charters', *JESHO*. vol. 2, 1959, pp. 281–93; 'Origins of Feudalism in Kashmir', *The Sardhasatabdi Commemoration Volume*, Asiatic Society of Bombay, Journal of the Asiatic Society of Bombay (*JASB* hereafter) n.s., vols 31–2,1959, pp. 108–20.
79 Devangana Desai, *Social Dimensions of Art in Early India*, Presidential Address. Section I, Indian History Congress, 50th Session, Gorakhpur University, 1989; Lallanji Gopal, *Economic Life of Northern India (c.* AD *700–1200)*, Banaras, 1965; N. Karashima, 'Nayakas as Lease-holders of Temple Lands, *JESHO*, vol. 19, 1976, pp. 227–32; *South Indian History and Society*, Delhi, 1984, Introduction; 'Nayaka Rule in the Tamil Country During the Vijayanagara Period', Seminar on State Formation in Pre-Colonial South India, Jawaharlal Nehru University, New Delhi, 1989 (unpublished), T.V. Mahalingam, *South Indian Polity*, revised edn, Madras; Dasharatha Sharma, *Early Chauhan Dynasties*, second edn, Delhi, 1975; B.N.S; Yadava, *Society and Culture in Northern India in the Twelfth* Century, Allahabad. 1973.
80 Stein, 'The Segmentary State'.
81 Ibid.
82 Romila Thapar, *From Lineage to State*, Delhi, 1984; Suvira Jaiswal, 'A Survey of Research in Social History of Ancient India', in R.S. Sharma (ed.), *A Survey of Research in Social and Economic History of India*, Delhi, 1986; K.M. Shrimali, *Religion, Ideology and Society*, Presidential Address, Ancient India Section, Indian History Congress, 49th Session Dharwad, 1988; R.S. Sharma, *Origin of the State in India*, Department of History, Bombay, 1989.
83 Stein, 'The Segmentary State'.

84 'Superstition and Politics in the *Arthaśāstra* of Kautilya', *JBRS*, vol. XL, 1954, pp. 223–31. In his work on medieval Orissa Hermann Kulke rejects religion as a substitute for political authority; on the contrary he sees it as a promoter of political power ('Fragmentation and Segmentation versus Integration: Reflections on the Concepts of Indian Feudalism and the Segmentary State in Indian History', *Studies in History*, vol. IV, no. 2, 1982, p. 254).

85 R Champakalakshmi, *Indian Economic and Social History Review*, vol. XVII, nos 3 and 4,1983, pp. 411–26; D.N. Jha, 'Validity of brāhmaṇa-Peasant Alliance and the Segmentary State in Early Medieval South India', *Social Science Probings*, vol. 4, no, 2, June 1984, pp. 270–95; R.N. Nandi, M.G.S. Narayanan, 'Review Article: South Indian History and Society', *Tamil Civilization*, vol. 3, no. 1, 1985, pp. 57–91; Vijaya Ramaswami, *Studies in History*, vol. 4, no. 2, 1982, pp. 307–19; Kesavan Veluthat, 'Power Structure of Monarchy in South India (*c.* AD 600–1300)', PhD thesis, University of Calicut, 1989.

86 *The Asiatic Mode of Production*, London, 1989. See particularly chs VII and VIII.

87 Yadava, *The Problem of the Emergence of Feudal Relations in Early India*, p. 46, fn. 1, draws attention to the position of the serf as stated by E.J. Hobsbawm on the basis of Karl Marx: 'The serf, though under the control of the lord, is in fact an economically independent producer', *Karl Marx: Pre-capitalist Economic Formations*, London, 1964, p. 42.

# 2

# The Segmentary State

## *Interim Reflections**

Burton Stein

Aidan Southall formulated the segmentary state model for his study of the Alur in highland East Africa in 1956[1] for the same reason that I adapted his formulation for the Cholas of south India almost two decades later: in order to provide a conception of 'state' that satisfied empirical conditions in our respective researches as well as the desire to theorize political relationships in our different fields in new ways. Thirty years after his Alur formulation, when Southall addressed the matter once again, he confessed to being surprised, then astonished, that his African solution was taken up by Richard Fox to discuss Rajput polities in northern India and later by me. The reformulation that Southall produced in 1988[2] was, he says, partly to 'repay' my refinements of his earlier conception: similarly, this essay is in part my reply in the reciprocal exchange with Southall, but it is also something else.

First of all this discussion seeks to answer some of the accumulated criticisms of nearly a decade about my use of the segmentary state concept in several papers and in my books, *Peasant State and Society in Medieval South India* and *Vijayanagara*.[3] Secondly, the purpose is to clarify my present position on segmentary political relations in pre-modern India while remaining open about its final definition, and hence it is an interim report.

* Previously published in Hermann Kulke (ed.), *The State in India 1000–1700*, New Delhi, Oxford University Press, 1997, pp. 134–61.

Easily the most difficult question confronting the historians of India has been how to characterize the state in pre-modern times, and the difficulty persists because it is only very recently that the question has been perceived as being problematic. Thirty years ago when I began my research on medieval south India, it became obvious to me that research on the Chola, Vijayanagara and other medieval kingdoms was flawed conceptually and empirically with respect to the treatment of the state. This was not a widely held conviction when I began my work, but I think it is fair to say that it is now widely accepted, though my proposed characterization of political relations in that earlier south Indian society as 'segmentary' is not. Older historical views insisted on seeing polities of the time as centralized and to a degree bureaucratized; lurking behind much of the writing of that time was a very modern, unitary state form. Indeed, this was the explicit formulation of the best of modern historians, K.A. Nilakantha Sastri,[4] and it was and remains an implicit understanding among many other historians still.

Given my discontent with that received wisdom, it became necessary to delineate another sort of state form, one that met the constraints of extant evidence on these early kingdoms and the underlying structure of material relations in the societies of each, and also one that could be theorized—provided with structure and content—in a way that made it a candidate form for other Indian societies and perhaps societies other than Indian as well.

At the time that I adopted the segmentary formulation I was insufficiently alert to a major discordant theoretical element which still remains a part of Southall's formulation. This is the relationship between what I was calling political segmentation or a 'segmentary state' and something called 'segmentary society'. For Richard Fox, a fellow debtor at Southall's African bank, this was less a problem because his ruling Rajputs were organized politically as segmentary lineages, but even for Fox there was a similar problem since these Rajput lineages did not extend from the bottom to the top of the political order, as the African Alur lineages do; moreover, the state regimes of Rajput houses have historically nested within larger political orders in which lineage principles were weak, or almost wholly absent—that of the Mughal state and its successors, the Marathas and the British.[5]

But mine was a more serious sort of difference at the level of theory, for I predicated segmentation of an altogether different sort from the segmentary lineages of Southall's Alur or Fox's Rajputs. Still, I did this within Southall's general formulation where he introduced the notion of pyramidal segmentation:

Several levels of subordinate foci may be distinguishable, organized pyramidally in relation to the central authority. The central and peripheral authorities reflect the same model, the latter being reduced images of the former. Similar powers are repeated at each level with decreasing range.[6]

In *Peasant State and Society*, I took the hundreds of local societies—called *nāḍu* in the inscriptions and literature of Chola times as the fundamental components, or pyramidally organized segments, of the society; I saw these nadus as social and political communities and I also saw, and continue to see, the relationship between these hundreds of communities and the state, as crucial for an understanding of this Indian Society, or, perhaps of other pre-industrial societies.

It is essential, however, to accept that *community* is understood according to the usual English signification of being simultaneously a people and a place, rather than in its limited and debased usage as sub-caste or religious group. Hence, community is to be understood as *janapada*, not *jāti*, and pertains to shared sentiments and values; however, community is also about shared rights or entitlements over human and material resources, and thus, in its particularities, pertains to smaller, local spatial entitles under conditions of pre-modern technology. It is because very localized affinities, sentiments and, especially, entitlements—*and the cultural, social, and political means for defending them*—continued to persist in India until well into contemporary times, that I have been encouraged to see segmentary political forms as extending well into the last century, thus giving the concept considerable historiographical reach.

At the level of theory, the relationship between segmentation in the political order and a segmentary social base is as ambiguous in my previous formulations as it was in Southall's. Segmentary lineages do not figure in his first definition of the 'segmentary state'; it was only later that he examined this issue and concluded that political segmentation need not be based on segmentary lineage systems.[7] This view is reconfirmed in Southall's most recent formulation where he notes the contrastive treatments of Indian political segmentation by Fox and me, and appears to be untroubled by the differences. Nevertheless, the theoretical question remains. Its shadow is cast over some of what follows, and it must be readdressed below.

## THE SOUTH INDIAN SEGMENTARY STATE AND ITS CRITICS

The concept I have used can be outlined in the following terms, though detailed understanding must depend on a reading of my *Peasant State and Society in Medieval South India*, 1980 and my volume on the Vijayanagara kingdom.[8]

The segmentary state refers to a political order which is distinguished from others. It is distinguished from the usual model of polities that lurks anachronistically in all of our heads—the unitary state with its fixed territory, its centralized administration and coercive power; it is also distinguished from the favoured alternative genus of the polity of historians, 'feudal', by which is meant a variety of political relationships, but most usually—as the Anglo-French species—a form of prebendalism based upon a high degree of political centredness. In positive terms, the segmentary state is a political order in which:

1. There are numerous centres or political domains;
2. Political power (in Indian classical reference, *kṣatra*) and sovereignty (or *rājadharma*) are differentiated in such a way as to permit appropriate power to be wielded by many, but full, royal sovereignty, only by an anointed king;
3. All of the numerous centres, or domains, have autonomous administrative capabilities and coercive means;
4. There is *a* state in the recognition, by lesser political centres, often through ritual forms, of a single ritual centre, an anointed king.

An additional defining statement is required to complete the outline of the system which I have postulated. The political order of medieval South India to which I applied the concept of the 'segmentary state' is based upon a segmentary social order, which I called 'pyramidal', following Southall.[9] In the medieval south Indian segmentary state, the numerous political centres of the polity appeared to be based upon internally differentiated localized social structures, usually designated as nadu during the Chola period (ninth to thirteenth century). These were stratified and ranked, occupationally diverse, and culturally varied territories which displayed what I took to be complementary oppositions. Hence, based upon the admittedly fragmentary evidence of that time, it could be argued that lineage and other kinship affinities were internally opposed and also balanced by occupational and sectarian principles of affiliation; the interests of peasant groups were opposed and, again, balanced, by the interests of herdsmen or artisanal producers; and among the latter, between those producing for markets and those whose products or services were locally consumed and mediated by the clientage relations usually designated by the terms, *jajmānī*. Moreover, I argued that the enstructuration of localized, pyramidally-organized segments was obedient to and fundamentally shaped by varied social, political and cultural developments as well as by ecological or ecotypic conditions. This resulted in three different types of localities which I designated as 'central', 'intermediate', and 'peripheral' zones of the segmentary political system of Chola times.

Criticisms of this formulation have taken several different forms, and at times, what may have been intended as appreciation seems, paradoxically, to be the opposite. Take, for example, the banal appreciation of the segmentary state concept as valuable in bringing to our notice the tendency in all political systems for central authority to weaken at their peripheries. Why this should be considered valuable, or even interesting, escapes me. A segmentary state, or political order, is *not* a centralized political or administrative order, hence to find the segmentary political concept valuable merely for noting the peripheral attenuation of central rule is to reduce a segmentary political system to an imperfect manifestation of centralized authority under paleotechnical conditions of transportation and communication.

More explicit critics of the segmentary state argument that I have made can be divided into the categories, strong and weak and intellectual and ideological.

Some of the weak, intellectual criticisms that have been lodged are the following. That in my formulation, I have denied any central features or forces at work in the kingdoms of the Cholas and Vijayanagara; that I am actually speaking, as B.D. Chattopadhyaya puts it, of a 'State *sans* politics'.[10] This, I submit, is a flawed reading of *Peasant State and Society*, where I drew attention to the highly centralized resource command of the Chola kings in the heartland of their kingdom, the wealthy Kaveri valley, and illustrated the point by reference to the massive mobilizations of Rajaraja I and Rajendra I for building their great royal shrines in Tanjavur and Gangaikondacholapuram. In *Peasant State and Society* I also spoke of the significant political sovereignty enjoyed by the numerous chiefs (*uḍaiyar*) of the Chola age as evidenced by their pooling and redistribution of resources, and I referred to the increased appropriative capacity and authority of post-Chola chiefs culminating in the Vijayanagara-age chiefs who, along with kings of the age, enjoyed a very high degree of coercive command over the varied institutions and ranked social groups within their domains.

The capacity of chiefs, *as well as kings*, to centralize resources is an important historical fact that is easily overlooked or trivialized because the simultaneity of enhanced power and authority by lesser and greater lords does indeed appear like a denial of centralization, as some critics charge. But that seems to me to essentialize central authority, forcing all historical kingdoms into the mould of the absolutist states that historians see in sixteenth to eighteenth century Europe, as well as in parts of southern and western Asia, where increased central authority always appeared to come at the expense of lesser lordships.[11]

Another criticism is cultural as well as essentializing and racist: it is that no theoretical formulation that arises from sub-Saharan Africa can be given serious consideration in and for India, with its ancient reflective as well as normative texts and with its distinctive institution and ideology of caste and *varnāshramadharma*. Notice that this is not a xenophobic caveat when it comes from Indian critics, because most, like K.A. Nilakantha Sastri, have been quite pleased to find Fustel de Coulanges' city-state structures and even Byzantine bureaucracies in medieval South India, much as D.D. Kosambi, R.S. Sharma and others were pleased to find European feudal institutions and ideology. Comparisons with, and even borrowings from Europe have been acceptable, even eagerly sought, whereas merely a structural comparison of Indian and African forms gives offense to many Indians.[12]

Moreover, I have sought to demonstrate the ways in which a segmentary formulation of the sort that I have proposed is not only consistent with the medieval *dharma* and *niti* texts of India, but, arguably, may be the only political formulation that adequately captures the textual understandings of Indian kingship and the primary lines along which political affiliations can occur, according to these texts.[13]

Then there are criticisms from scholars with what I take to be programmatic objections to the segmentary state proposal. From the ideological right have come objections to this as to any proposal that even questions, much less repudiates, the substantialized conception of Indian society hyperthrophized as caste and varnāshramadharma. I am referring here to scholars in India whose communalist views are known and whose historical understandings reflect these views. A similar programmatic bias comes from the left, from some Marxist scholars who ask of work on the cholas what they ask of any other historical society: an analysis of classes, class conflict and relations between classes and the state and who also ask how the segmentary state formulation advances our understanding of the transition to capitalism at some very later time.

Such critics offer no research hypotheses, no historiographical formulations to be examined seriously and confronted with evidence; their views preserve certain formulations for their contemporary ideological utility only. To be sure, all of our histories are and must be framed by the interests and purposes of our time, but these must be expected to yield to the corrective of disciplined historical scholarship. In fact, however, almost no work has been done nor is being done on the state in pre-modern India by most ideologically committed scholars, and as a consequence, there is little scope for such formulations of ideological convenience to the right or the left to be challenged.

Of course, there is an obvious difference between naive Marxist pronouncements, such as those of Kathleen Gough's proposals about a Chola 'slave economy',[14] and the sort of nuanced criticism I have been pleased to have from others, Marxists and non-Marxists, the cogency of whose comments on my segmentary state is related to their active studies of historical state systems.

I shall mention first among these strong criticisms of the segmentary state formulation those from S.J. Tambiah and Hermann Kulke with both of whom I have had rewarding and challenging discussions over the years. The former's 'galactic' state model, worked out for pre-modern Thailand, is, in its theoretical and descriptive specification, kinship generated—its sole filiational principle is blood.[15] That suggests an affinity with Southall's formulation, as the latter has recognized.[16] Whether or not Tambiah's formulation is satisfactory for Thai kingship and state I cannot say, but kinship—usually lineage affiliation—is only one of several principles that are seen to operate in the polities of early South India. I shall return to this question shortly, but for now it is also necessary to consider Kulke's criticisms of the segmentary state model. Like Tambiah who gives major importance to forms of ritual incorporation, Kulke has considered my formulation, but in the end rejected it for its lack of fit with the specific polity he was examining, that of medieval Orissa. There, he finds no intermediate forms resembling the nadu of Tamil country in Chola times that formed the basis, in my view, of the peripheral 'centres' of the segmentary polity. Kulke proposes something he calls an 'integrative polity' where the sole specified means of royal incorporation seems to be the symbolic capture of local, 'tribal' godlings by the royal cult of Vishnu as Jagannatha of whom the first worshipper was the Ganga or Gajapati ruler. How this incorporation was achieved and whether it was or can have been the sole political process at work is left unclear.[17]

In contrast to Tambiah and Kulke there are a set of critics of the segmentary state formulation whose reservations stem from their commitments to a modified, or 'Indian' feudalism. Adherents of the feudal formulation include not only many Indian scholars of medieval states, but also scholars of modern India who find in an 'Indian feudalism' a convenient foundation for their twin concerns with the rise of nationalism and the development of capitalism in modern India. Yet, notwithstanding its distinguished double paternity by D.D. Kosambi in the middle 1950s[18] and R.S. Sharma a decade later,[19] the feudal concept has never been seriously tested against the claims inherent in it nor has it been elaborated in any significant way.[20] Hence, the feudal conception remains either an article of left historiographical faith or a convenient residual position for those scholars who cannot accept that early Indian states were embryonic modern, unitary states. In either case, an Indian feudalism is flawed by the absence in any of the applications of the concept to what might have been the 'feudal state' which presumably expressed and preserved the interests of the host of what are called 'feudatories' allegedly found everywhere in pre-modern India. In other words, to alter a criticism of the segmentary state as 'a state without polities', in 'Indian feudalism' there is a highly variegated set of political forms, but no feudal state. Nor have any advocates of an Indian feudal polity given serious attention to the theoretical implications of the considerable evidence which exists on the processes of urbanization, trade and banking during the early and later medieval age in India.

The most incisive criticisms of the feudal conception of pre-modern Indian politics have been elucidated by Harbans Mukhia, who has attacked the feudal formulation from the point of view of its economic as well as political claims[21] and by B.D. Chattopadhyaya, who proposed an alternative model which he calls 'the samanta-feudatory system',[22] at least for the early medieval period of Indian history. From both of these scholars, too, have come the most probing queries about the segmentary state proposition: Mukhia asking for an analysis of the interests—class or other—represented in and protected by the segmentary states I posit; and Chattopadhyaya asking where lineage-based political entitles, the ancient and ubiquitous *sāmanta* of India—including the south—are to be found in my theory.

If the segmentary theory is to stand against the diffusely conceived feudal theory of political organization in pre-modern India, then these and other criticisms must be met. To Mukhia's question about the class character of the state, my response is that I see the medieval south, and perhaps other parts of the subcontinent, as a generalized polity of chiefdoms, that is as a system of enduring (but not necessarily permanent) political structures, based on strong hereditary regimes with extensive authority over wide areas and over varied and internally ranked local social segments; chieftains occupied the apex of pyramidal segments and derived their authority from local landholding groups or from conquest over such localities. However, chieftainship in medieval India cannot be taken as either a complete system of authority nor as adequately theorized; for that the principle of monarchy is crucial. But, monarchy in its turn must be properly understood in its medieval Indian sense. For, ranked and ruling hereditary chiefs claimed to be kings (rājā or swāmī) and while they differentiated themselves from other, greater kings who held an exalted status through vedic anointment, these lesser or 'little' kings were deemed to share sovereignty with the greater ones.[23] The latter, far fewer in number, are *the* kings of those Indian polities which we designate as historical kingdoms, and a condition of being for these anointed kings was the preservation of the sub-stratum of chiefdoms, or 'little kingdoms', of which the great historic kingdoms consisted.

But, in answering Mukhia's question and objection about the interests protected and advanced in the segmentary state of my imagining, have I not conceded Chattopadhyaya's? For what is a *sāmanta* polity if not a polity of chiefdoms? Answering this hypothetical objection would be easier if we had a clearer idea of what the 'samanta-feudatory system' was and according to what principles it worked. Unfortunately we have had no greater specification of its workings than that afforded by Kulke, and Chattopadhyaya, in the end, falls back on Kulke's vague 'integrative polity', even though he deplores Kulke's failure to specify a 'political mechanism of integration'.[24]

That there have been historical political orders based on segmentary lineages in which the term 'sāmanta' and 'ruling lineages' figured importantly is not disputed. Among these are those whom Fox wrote about in the Gangetic plain and those of Rajasthan on which Chattopadhyaya, among many others, have worked and therefore about which a great deal has come to be known from James Tod's time, a century and a half ago. But even here, extensive regimes, 'kingdoms', have rarely emerged from the expansion of single lineages and in places other than Rajasthan, where there is the appearance of something like this occurring, it turns out to be something different, as Chattopadhyaya admits.[25]

Still, even where the sāmanta term is rarely encountered, as in south India, lineage political formations were important. From late Chola times in south India, lineages of powerful chiefs became so decisive as to bring the Chola regime to an end; and they continued to be important through the entire Vijayanagara period. Timing is important here, for such lineage-based regimes never displaced the control of high caste, corporate assemblies in the riverine valley cores of the Chola kingdom, but only in the dry, upland parts of the southern peninsula that were gradually opened then and later. Lineage polities arose from and were the political authority in societies of the moving agrarian frontier of the peninsula, those mixed pastoral and agricultural communities that converted jungle bush and pastures into arable land with the aid of tank irrigation and that retained martial characteristics which were available to greater lords, such as the Vijayanagara kings.[26]

Chattopadhyaya's concerns about the idea of 'feudal polity' and some of his criticisms of the feudal model reflect his laudable intention to launch upon or to participate in the construction of a generalized model of polity during India's medieval era. This intention is reflected in the seriousness of his judgements about specific elements of both the feudal and the segmentary state formulations. Notwithstanding his reservations however, he feels the major task for historians is to chart the evolution of state formations during the medieval era, and to 'plug the gap between polity and society' then.[27]

Before turning to an examination of changes in what I am calling a segmentary political order that must be made to meet the more serious criticisms against the formulation, I should say that I believe that a reconciliation of the views of Kulke and Chattopadhyaya with my own are possible as well as promising, and I do not mean by the usual compromise method of observing that we three are studying different places at somewhat different times, hence variations are to be expected. Of course, they are, but it is at the level of theory that I believe a convergence of views is both promising and likely, since I believe that each of us is actually dealing with evolving structures within a single broad form and in our own ways we are privileging certain elements and neglecting others.[28]

It may be useful therefore to briefly review how such a political evolution can be viewed in south India within a segmentary frame by considering the Chola and Vijayanagara kingdoms upon which I have worked.

The major core of Chola political authority from the late tenth to the thirteenth centuries was in the Kaveri basin, with secondary 'central zones' of the Chola segmentary state in other river valleys of the southern peninsula: the Ponnaiyar and Cheyyar in the northern Tamil plain, and the Vaigai and Tambraparni valleys in the south. The major core of the Vijayanagara kingdom, contrarily, was in the dry upland and watershed region of the peninsula, opened over several centuries by a process of agrarian expansion along a moving frontier. The corresponding state resource catchments thus varied in significant ways: in the Chola kingdom principal reliance was upon a share of the rich irrigated agriculture under corporate control in the collegial assemblies of Brahmanas and Vellalas; in the Vijayanagara kingdom, principal reliance of all lordships was increasingly upon the wealth of trade within that broad region between and connecting the two trade coasts and less upon agrarian production from the largely dry cultivation of frontier zones under the control of the tough warrior chiefs of the upland. During the Vijayanagara period, also, the former riverine zones of Chola dominance were reduced to subjugation to upland state regimes, a condition that was begun in the time of the Hoysala kingdom of Karnataka and brought to fulfillment by the Vijayanagara successors to the Hoysalas. Social organization and ideology of the riverine cores of the Chola kingdom nevertheless remained largely hierarchical in post-Chola times, while in intermediate zones of the kingdom (including parts of the Tamil plain and its upland extensions) society and ideology tended to be pluralistic and less hieratic; it was here that the dual division of lower castes in those of the right and left (*valañgai* and *iḍangai*) were entrenched.

By Vijayanagara times, fundamental changes in society and economy, dating from the thirteenth century, had altered a great deal; forces of urbanization and commercialization generated by political and religious changes created opportunities for new groups to advance their standing against older elite groups, and widespread social conflict as a result of this and other factors can be documented. For example, more ambitiously centralizing chiefs of the lower Kaveri incited widespread local uprisings in 1429–30 as reported by N. Karashima and Y. Subbarayalu.[29]

There were also important changes in military organization. In Chola times there were local militias maintained by entrenched communally organized local societies with only a small standing force under royal control (*velaikkārar*) drawn from the heartland segments (*valanāḍu*) of the Kaveri basin. Vijayanagara military formations, under pressure to imitate the highly successful fourteenth century Muslim invaders into the southern peninsula, had adopted firearms and imported war-horses and came to maintain larger standing forces than ever before. Commanders of these enlarged and standing forces assumed increasing political roles, and a powerful generalissimo like Saluva Narasimha was able to seize royal authority in the late fifteenth century, founding a new

Vijayanagara dynasty. Later, two of his commanders were to do the same during the sixteenth century.

To support such enhanced military capabilities required a greatly enlarged money revenue, and this was found in the expanding commerce of the age. Trade in the peninsula was stimulated by the dominating consumption centre of the Vijayanagara capital and by new chiefly and temple centres that proliferated as the royal style of Vijayanagara spread; another source of commercial stimulation was the expanding international trade around the coasts of the peninsula and the increasing number of commercial centres founded during the age. Commerce and temple developments went together to add to the forces of urbanization and monetization, and temples, which had a more modest political role during the Chola period (in contrast to the large Brahmana settlement or brahmadēya), now became centres of political, administrative, and commercial activities and were among the most important civil institutions of that later society.

This brief outline has the obvious purpose of showing that major structural changes in the southern peninsula between the Chola and Vijayanagara ages were accommodated within the framework of the segmentary state in south India. To be sure, the Vijayanagara state was a different kind of segmentary state from that of the Cholas, but it was segmentary nevertheless in the critical sense that its royal power never attained that degree of centralized control over the constituent chiefdoms of the kingdom as to enable the kingdom to transform itself into something other than a segmentary state.

There is considerable evidence of efforts made to achieve substantially greater centralization of royal authority in Vijayanagara times. The kings Devaraya I and II in the first half of the fifteenth century strove for this transformation by creating a more centralized military force based on mercenaries, including Muslim horsemen and gunners, under royal commanders and by seeking to mobilize part of the international trade wealth to provide the fiscal means of supporting these technological innovations. Military modernization along lines first presented by Muslims and later by Europeans is easily dismissed as having failed to attain the efficiency and impact of foreign armies and that handguns and cannons were more decorative than destructive of the foes of Vijayanagara. A close study of the reports that exist on the campaigns of Krishnadevaraya suggests otherwise, but even if this denigration is accepted, the measures taken to modernize their armies committed the Vijayanagara kings of the fifteenth and sixteenth centuries to new resource mobilizing strategies.

Paradoxically, however, a major effect of these measures was to simultaneously strengthen the chiefdoms of the realm. These became more centralized within their domains, and military chiefs regularly transformed prebendal service entitlements into hereditary entitlements. Military commanders of royal armies pursued separate, often anti-royal ends and local rulers along both coasts garnered the greatest part of the wealth from international trade. The most vigorous effort to centralize royal authority came under Krishnadevaraya who employed Brāhmaṇa administrators and fortress commanders against the territorial chiefs of his realm. His efforts foundered soon after his death as a result of the dynastic machinations of his son-in-law, Aliya Rama Raja; the latter restored and strengthened the independent authority of chiefs in the Andhra tracts of Rayalseema and Telengana as a means of gaining their support for his own campaign for the Vijayanagara throne. Military commanders usually affecting the title of *nāyaka* have been converted by historians into royal servants in the so-called *nāyaṇkara* system. Actually, these commanders remained their own men, seeking advantage for themselves and their families in the tracts where they were appointed to serve royal interests. In these places they either pursued their own advantage by establishing independent lordships loosely linked to Vijayanagara kings, or these chiefs formed lethal coalitions against royal authority. Nor, apparently, was such independence from royal authority taken as illicit by the later rulers of Vijayanagara, for during the highly successful southern campaign during the 1550s of Vithala, the nephew of Rama Raja, no effort was made to limit the expansion of the emerging Madurai kingdom, or *samasthānam,* of Visvanatha Nayaka. The Madurai nāyakaship became a realm as large and as wealthy as the homeland of the Vijayanagara kings of the Aravidu dynasty of the late sixteenth century, and Madurai was only one of several such so-called 'nāyaka kingdoms' that began its coalescence in the late days of the great Krishnadevaraya.

The failure to achieve that royal centralization sought by some rulers in imitation of the more centralized regimes of their Muslim enemies of the Deccani sultanates is one reason for adhering continuity in the segmentary state formed during the Chola era. Another reason for holding to a segmentary political conception was the vigour with which communal entitlements everywhere continued to be protected by all sorts of local groups in south Indian society. Not only were many ancient entitlements preserved, but new communal rights were granted by the more powerful, military rulers of local societies in the south, partly to fortify their local rule and partly, too, in order to attract migrant soldiers and artisans to their mini-realms to enhance their autarchic wealth. These extensive communal awards survived into the nineteenth century as *in' am* and were a legacy which such ambitious and powerful centralizers as Haidar Ali Khan, Tipu Sultan, and finally the East India Company sought unsucessfully but with great determination to abrogate.

This structure and ideology of communal or community entitlements together with the force to protect them grew during the eighteenth century and were largely intact during the early nineteenth century. They are the social, economic, and moral side of the political question about the nature of the state in early and late medieval south India. And this structure of entitlements remains another reason for holding on to the conception of the segmentary state.

## A RETURN TO THEORY AND REVISION OF THE CONCEPTION

As this is partly a colloquy with Aidan Southall, several points raised by his recent reformulation of the segmentary state concept require comment. One has to do with his invocation of a mode of production argument in order to close the conceptual gap opened by differences in the levels of economy of such diverse candidate 'segmentary states' as the Alur and Indian ones, and even Tambiah's Thailand and Geertz's Bali. His proposed solution is to postulate something called 'a kinship mode of production' and even a 'foraging mode of production'[30] for the Alur and possibly for other African societies, and, not surprisingly, an Asiatic mode for the others. But mode of production solutions merely confound political and economic processes, and there is the suspicion created that the former can be reduced to the latter. Given that Southall provides the barest outline of what he means by the 'Asiatic mode' and even less about what the 'kinship' or 'foraging' modes are, uncertainty is bound to exist, and this uncertainty is deepened by his suggestion that the kinship mode of production is an 'embryonic version' of the Asiatic mode.[31] Finally, he poses an empirical difficulty for me as well as I am sure for Noboru Karashima who has worked on the cholas by adopting Kathleen Gough's characterization of the latter kingdom as an example of Asian despotism under the Asiatic mode of production.[32]

This leads to a second comment on Southall's reformulation. As I understand it, his position confuses conceptual levels. I cannot now understand whether he is saying that the 'segmentary state' concept is a formal system of political structure or whether it is a type of political organization entailed by particular modes of productive relations (say, 'kinship', 'foraging', 'Asiatic'), but not others. As my definition at the beginning of this paper confirms, I consider Southall's original proposal to have been formal in character, one that is free of any *necessary* relationship or conditionality arising from any particular social or economic configurations, except, as I have already said, a segmentary political structure has seemed to me to presume related forms of social segmentation. Nor am I certain about how important it is at the conceptual level that I, or another scholar, agree with Southall about what Marx might have meant by the Asiatic mode or whether Gough's application of the notion to the imperial Cholas is valid.

Some confusion is additionally engendered in Southall's reformulation with respect to which two somewhat different notions of social morpology guide his theoretical statements. Southall appears now to be more concerned about the origins and development of structures than their typological characteristics. Approving as I do of Southall's desire to bring into a single comparative frame the 'idiosyncratic interpretations' of Tambiah and Geertz, I do not see how this objective can be advanced by his evolutionary apperception that the 'kinship mode of production' of the Alur was an 'embryonic version' of the 'Asiatic mode of production' even as Alur shrines were 'embryonic versions' of temples in south India.[33] Morphological questions are certainly important, especially in our age when the zealots for a cultural-based social science hold such influence as they distressingly do in the US and increasingly in the UK. Only a serious comparative social science can check the drift into a nihilism of culturally hegemonic explanations. But a comparative analysis must be generated more along analogical lines than the homological lines that Southall seems to be advocating now.

Stemming from Southall, but also apart from his recent reformulation, are questions about segmentation and the very appropriateness of deploying segmentary terminology at all. This is not an obvious problem for Fox, nor for that matter would it be for Chattopadhyaya, because Rajput ruling lineages and the ideal typical sāmanta are based upon segmentary lineages for them, much as they are for Henri Stern in his analyses of what he purports is the 'traditional' Indian polity of Rajasthan.[34] However, the segmentary conception based exclusively on patrilineage politics cannot be taken as a generalized political form in pre-modern India without first resolving certain questions. Southall drew attention to two of these questions by observing that Fox's Rajput lineages do not extend from the base to the summit of Rajput principalities, but pertain to ruling lineages alone and that these Rajput polities always exist within (and are probably not conceivable outside of) larger political formations—Mughal or British—where segmentary lineages were not important features.

These caveats to Fox's application of the segmentary state concept are not reasons for Southall's rejection of that application, nor should they be, though we may regret that Fox did not clarify the relationship between Rajput lineages and the societies that they ruled and did not consider the implications of Rajput politics being embedded in larger political formations. On these and other questions it is doubtful that Fox or anyone else who had not studied the histories of these particular Rajput-ruled societies could tell us how ruling patrilineages were related to the sub-structure of their political societies. This must depend on memories beyond the recall of the anthropological present of Fox and other anthropologists. Norman Ziegler has offered valuable understanding of the consequence for Rajput houses involved in the Mughal system, and this was important in shaping Rajput understanding of themselves as later discovered by Fox and Stern.[35] The other relationship—from the Rajput chief or king downward—is only now being uncovered in the work on the rich historical documentation of archives such as that of Jaipur. If, as a result of this research, the dominant political alignments of groups within these lineage polities are discovered not to have been segmentary, and these were not segmentary societies, then we must ask: what was the social sub-structure, how were Rajputs beneath ruling lineages and non-Rajputs in these places linked to the ruling lineages there, and how, finally, was the pan-Indian ideology of hierarchy accommodated?

I am taking ideology to pertain to the reasoning of historical subjects about what values they considered of first importance and how such values were attained. In a long section of *Peasant State and Society*, I undertook to relate the theory of the segmentary state to moral as well as political conceptions that were current in normative texts of the age. On the strength of that examination in relationship to pre-modern, south Indian polity, I reassert my conviction that the segmentary state form was the only one that fits the evidence that we have of the broad pattern of political relations and of the ideology in pre-modern peninsular India.

I also realize that this stress upon ideology puts me at odds with Southall, who has revised the theoretical grounding of his segmentary state concept in accordance with material relations—modes of production. This opening to material factors may be dictated by, or at least responsive to, questions arising from African ethnology. However, this is not a movement forward in the Indian context for two reasons. The first is the confused status of the 'Asiatic mode' concept and its unacceptability to almost all scholars in India, including Marxists; Gough's application of the concept has, if anything, confirmed the irrelevance of that mode of production argument. Moreover, an extended debate a few years ago on modes of production in India concluded in such disarray that an opening in that direction, at least for the present, holds little promise.[36]

The opening from the present conception of the segmentary state and of state formations more generally in pre-modern India must be of another sort; it must be in the direction of culture and ideology. As never before, the scholarly resources for this line of inquiry into pre-modern states arc adequate to the task. All bear critically upon the segmentary state concept and all, being the work of anthropologists, are centrally concerned with culture.[...]

[...]

I wish to conclude by briefly suggesting some of the ways I think my formulation on the segmentary state should be recast in light of all that I have said above.

First is the idea that a segmentary polity must depend upon a significant degree of social segmentation, though social segmentation is never a condition unmediated by ideas about authority and politics.[37] The particular sort of segmentation (that is, whether it is the sort of pyramidal segmentation based on local, territorial assemblies of the Chola kingdom or segmentary lineages found everywhere in the dry upland of the peninsula after the Cholas) is not important, but the segmentation must be related to formal political processes as the nādu in Chola times was and as the systems of chieftainships in later times were, and there must be an ideological interface between dominant forms of segmentation and formal political processes and institutions.

Secondly, and accordingly, it is necessary to reject Southall's proposition that the 'spheres of ritual suzerainty and political sovereignty do not coincide'.[38] I am now convinced that in India the proposition is incorrect, that lordship for Hindus always and necessarily combined ritual and political authority. That is, the practice of political authority, or appropriate power, made it incumbent upon any lord to foster and to be involved with ritual actions and services, whether this was in relation to gods or to their subjects.[39] And this is true irrespective of whether we are speaking about great kings or minor chiefs, or whether we are speaking of the ritual of the *abhiṣekha* or that of receiving the first honours of a tutelary goddess. Insisting on the coincidental relationship of ritual and political authority has the additional clarifying advantage of reinforcing Southall's pyramidal principle. As restated at the beginning, this had to do with the authority of greater and lesser lords, it being posited that the nature of the authority of both was the same—that of the lesser being but a reduced version of the greater lord; hence it was the scope of authority, rather than its quality that was different.

Thirdly, there is need to be more clear about what is meant by 'pyramidality'. This remains an essential element in my thinking about the segmentary state. Indeed, the notion of pyramidality has taken on an enhanced import as a result of reviewing the work on south India by Beck, Dirks, Appadurai, and Reiniche, and by considering the work and the criticisms of Chattopadhyaya and Kulke. Community in the sense outlined at the beginning inhabits the core of the notion of pyramidal segmentation, both socio-economic and political. Entitlements derived from as well as based in community structures do not merely reflect the nature of varied community structures in pre-modern south India but can be deemed constitutive of these structures. Shared social group rights were established by the political enactments of *mānya* and later of *in'am* grants from kings and chiefs, and these rights were confirmed, as well as contested, in temples. In *Peasant State and Society* as well as in my recent study of the Vijayanagara kingdom, I have sought to show how community-defining entitlements varied according to ecologically prefiguring contexts in medieval south India. In being the socio-economic foundation of that medieval metasociety, these locality societies should not be thought of as isolated or complete in themselves; all were part-societies, linked to more extensive formations in ways dictated by historical contingencies in relation to their own attributes. Communities or localities were thus linked by political and cultic affiliations to the protection of great or small kings and gods and, increasingly, in later times, by commercial ties to even quite distant places in India and beyond. Still, as part-societies these communities of pre-modern south India retained historic identities and the capability to act with considerable independence regarding their internal constitutions and their external linkages.

This territorial imperative is admittedly a new and not easily assimilated emphasis for scholars of India as may be seen in Dirks' insistence, when reviewing and criticizing Dumont on the Kallars, that territoriality encompassed kinship and political allegiances inflected all relationships.[40] Pyramidality is a concept that permits us to engage the saliency of territory and community as the archetypal foundation (*urbild*) of pre-modern south Indian society and thereby confirms the validity of something like the segmentary state I continue to see there.

## NOTES

1 Aidan Southall, *Alur Society: A Study in Processes and Types of Domination*, Cambridge, 1956.

2 Aidan Southall, 'The Segmentary State in Africa and Asia', *Comparative Studies in Society and History*, vol. 30, January 1988, pp. 52–82.

3 Published, respectively, by Oxford University Press, New Delhi, in 1980 and by Cambridge University Press as vol. 1.2 of The New Cambridge History of India, in 1989.

4 K.A. Nilakantha Sastri in *The Cōḷas*, Madras, 1935–37, and in *A History of South India*, Madras, 1935.

5 R.G. Fox, *Kin, Clan, Raja and Rule*, Berkeley, 1971, pp. 56–7. Southall draws attention to these aspects of Fox's analysis in 'The Segmentary State in Africa and Asia', pp. 69 and 71.

6 Southall's definition is found in *Alur Society*, pp. 248–9; in Fox, *Kin, Clan, Raja and Rule*, p. 56; and in my *Peasant State and Society*, p. 265 and elaborated from pp. 265 to 285.

7 Aidan Southall, 'A Critique of the Typology of States and Political Systems', in Michael Banton, *Political Systems and the Distribution of Power*, New York, 1965, p. 126.

8 Entitled *Vijayanagara*, published in, The New Cambridge History of India.

9 Being insufficiently aware that Southall did not question whether a segmentary political order can exist without segmentary social forms, I simply proceeded on the basis that there must be a congruent relationship between political and social segmentation, and I saw no difficulty in attempting to specify this congruence, but in an Indian, rather than African idiom. Others have attempted to define similar differences in other ways, for example Sahlin's distinction between tribal orders and chiefdoms, in his 'The Segmentary Lineage and Predatory Expansion', *American Anthropologist*, vol. 63, no. 2, 1963, pp. 32–45.

10 'Political Processes and the Structure of Polity in Early Medieval India', Presidential Address, Ancient India Section, Indian History Congress, 44th Session, Burdwan, December, 1983.

11 Even here of course there is not perfect unanimity; Perry Anderson sees these 'absolutist sates' as the highest stage of feudalism, the very antithesis of centralism! *Lineages of the Absolute State*, London, 1974.

12 Some western scholars, with their own hegemonic notions about the concept of culture, have also criticized this African model on the basis of the literacy of India. This essentialization of cultural differences is then made to stand for a qualitatively different (that is, lower) level of African culture, hence comparisons involving non-literate Africa and literate India are not like with like. That there are genuine differences between the historical societies of South Asia and those of sub-Saharan Africa is not denied, but that these differences are reducible to literacy and literate

traditions can scarcely be credited when one considers the reach of Islam into Africa from the seventh century.

13 *Peasant State and Society*, pp. 275–85.

14 Kathleen Gough in 'Modes of Production in Southern India', *Economic and Political Weekly*, vol. XV, nos 5–7 (Annual Number), February 1980, pp. 337–64; and her *Rural Society in Southeast India*(Cambridge: Cambridge University Press, 1981).

15 S.J. Tambiah, *World Conqueror and World Renouncer*, Cambridge, 1976.

16 Southall, 'The Segmentary State in Africa and Asia', p. 53, where he also mentions Geertz's 'theatre state' as another 'idiosyncratic' ethnographical interpretation.

17 Kulke's paper entitled 'Fragmentation and Segmentation versus Integration? Reflections on the Concepts of Indian Feudalism and the Segmentary State in Indian History', a manuscript version of which the author sent me some years ago and since published in *Studies in History*, vol. IV, no. 2, 1982, pp. 237–64.

18 D.D. Kosambi, 'The Basis of Ancient Indian History', *Journal of the American Oriental Society*, vol. LXXV, no. 1, 1955.

19 R.S. Sharma, *Indian Feudalism: c. 300–1200*, Calcutta, 1965.

20 Despite the recently edited work of D.N. Jha, *Feudal Social Formation in Early India*, Delhi 1987, containing essays by Sharma and Kosambi as well as several writers on South India: N. Karashima, Y. Subbarayalu, M.G.S. Narayanan and Kesavan Veluthat.

21 Harbans Mukhia, 'Was There Feudalism in Indian History?' and 'Peasant Production and Medieval Indian Society', in T.J. Byers and Harbans Mukhia (eds), *Feudalism and Non-European Societies*, London, 1985.

22 Chattopadhyaya, 'Political Processes and the Structure of Polity'.

23 The term *dayada* is important here and is explored by Andre Wink in his *Land and Sovereignty in India: Agrarian Society and Politics under the Eighteenth-century Maratha Svarajya*, Cambridge, 1986; a translation of an important source dealing with the concept is found in V.D. Rao, 'Ajnyaparra Re-examined', *Journal of Indian History*, vol. 29, 1951, pp. 63–89.

24 Chattopadhyaya, 'Political Processes and the Structure of Polity', p. 19 and note 116.

25 Chattopadhyaya discusses this in an interesting if somewhat cryptic manner in 'Political Processes and the Structure of Polity', pp. 11–14.

26 Several recent works elucidate this history: David Ludden's *Peasant History in South India*, Princeton, 1985, especially ch. 2; Pamela Price's '*Rajadharma* in 19th Century South India: Land, Litigation and Largess in Ramnad Zamindari', *Contributions to Indian Sociology*, vol. 13, 1979, pp. 204–39; Nicholas Dirks' study of the Pudukkottai kings of south India, *The Hollow Crown: Ethnohistory of an Indian Kingdom*, Cambridge, 1987, who achieved their differentiated status as 'king' in the late seventeenth century from the legitimate superior royal authority, the last ruler of the Vijayanagara kingdom.

27 'Political Processes and the Structure of Polity', p. 4. Among his criticisms the latter pertains to the claim that sāmantas and other candidate 'feudatories' received 'feudal' assignments of land from greater lords. He doubts the existence of a contingently 'contractual' basis usually implied in feudal assignments, and he also denies that contract was an important element of political affiliation in early medieval

India, though service assignments became important in later medieval times. This conforms with my own judgements in the analysis of the Chola kingdom and in marking the difference between the Chola and, as I continue to call it, the Vijayanagara segmentary state.

28 For instance, Chattopadhyaya is more attentive to urbanization in the evolution of early medieval polities than either I or Kulke are, and therefore provides a more balanced appreciation of the material basis of early polities than we do with our emphasis upon ritual forms of integration and incorporation in the evolving political structures of medieval Orissa and the far south. B.D. Chattopadhyaya, 'Urban Centres in Early Medieval India: An Overview', in S. Bhattacharya and R. Thapar (eds), *Situating Indian History,* Delhi, 1986.

29 'Valangai Idangai, Kaniyalar and Irajagarattar: Social Conflict in Tamil Nadu in the 15th Century'. Originally published in N. Karashima (ed.), *Socio-Cultural Change in Villages in Tiruchirapalli District, Tamilnadu, India,* Tokyo, 1983; reprinted in Jha, *Feudal Social Formation,* pp. 284–307.

30 Southall, 'The Segmentary State in Africa and Asia', pp. 53–4.

31 Ibid., p. 66.

32 Karashima, *South Indian History and Society,* p. xxix.

33 Southall, 'The Segmentary State in Africa and Asia', pp. 64–6.

34 'Power in Traditional India: Territory, Caste and Kinship in Rajasthan', in R.G. Fox, *Realm and Region in Traditional India',* Durham, North Carolina, Duke University, Monograph and Occasional Papers Series, No. 14, 1977.

35 Norman P. Ziegler, 'Some Notes on Rajput Loyalties During the Mughal Period', in J.P. Richards, *Kingship and Authority in South Asia,* Madison, 1978.

36 See the percipient and succinct summary of that debate by John Hariss in his *Capitalism and Peasant Farming; Agrarian Structure and Ideology in Northern Tamil Nadu,* Bombay, 1982, pp. 10–16.

37 I am unable, however, to go as far as Raymond Jamous in stating that the segmentary order of the Moroccan Iqar'iyen is based upon the concept of honour, its representations and values, for this seems to me to privilege ideology and culture over structure and, morphology unacceptably and to diminish the prospect of comparative analysis: *Honneur, et Baraka: Les structures sociales traditionelles dans le Rif,* Paris, editions de la Maison des Sciences de I'Homme, 1981, p. 184.

38 Southall, 'The Segmentary State in Africa and Asia', p. 52.

39 The conceptions of A.M. Hocart on caste and kingship remain as persuasive and influential for me as for others like Dirks, *The Hollow Crown,* pp. 284 and 426 and Jamous, *Honneur et Baraka,* p. 10. A.M. Hocart, *Caste: A Comparative Study,* London, 1950 and *Kings and Councillors,* Chicago, 1970.

40 Dirks, *The Hollow Crown,* pp. 258–61.

# 3

# The Early and the Imperial Kingdom

## *A Processual Model of Integrative State Formation in Early Medieval India**

Hermann Kulke**

### I

After the decline of the Gupta empire and of the 'transient' successor state under King Harṣa in the early seventh century, the overwhelming majority of the early medieval states of India emerged from a process of continuous agrarian expansion and political integration. Since the middle of the first millennium AD this development took place mainly in those areas of the South Asian subcontinent which had lain at the periphery or even outside the core areas of ancient state formation. This process started from local nuclei of early socio-economic and political development and increasingly came to include their hinterlands.

Generally speaking this process of integrative state formation in early medieval India pertained to three concentrically connected geographical areas and accordingly went through three chronologically distinct stages of state development. These geographical zones were (i) the local nuclear area from which the political development issued, (ii) its surrounding

*Previously published in Hermann Kulke (ed.), *The State in India 1000–1700*, New Delhi, Oxford University Press, 1997, pp. 233–62.

**I am indebted to Pamela Price for her considerable help to improve the English translation of my paper originally written in German. I am particularly grateful for her valuable comments and for suggesting 'processural model' as a subtitle of this paper. The original German version began with a lengthy introduction into existing theories of state formation in early medieval India.

peripheral zones, and (iii) beyond these peripheral zones the nuclear areas of (originally) independent 'neighbours' (*sāmanta*). These three spatial zones found their chronological dimension in three successive stages of state formation, which may be termed as chiefdom, early kingdom, and imperial kingdom.[1] In Sanskrit terminology this process would somewhat correspond with the evolution from 'king' (*rājā*) to 'great king' (*mahārāja*) and 'supreme king of great kings' (*mahārāja-adhirāja*). Four factors will receive special attention: (i) the foundation and extension of chiefly power within a nuclear area, (ii) the emergence of the early kingdom through a stepwise penetration into, and integration of, the peripheral zones and, to a lesser extent, of the neighbouring nuclear areas respectively, (iii) the emergence of the imperial kingdom with a considerably enlarged core region, consisting of the original dynastic nuclear area and its conquered and integrated hinterland, and (iv) processes of integration during these three stages of state formation with particular references to aspects of 'ritual policy'.

The following delineations emphasize aspects of a continuous and multifarious process of state formation rather than static structural features of the state and its society. The conceptual model of integrative state formation which emerges from an analysis of the dynamics of these interdependent socio-economic, political, and cultural processes is a model which may be called processual. It stresses diachronic development and change rather than synchronic structures and their static nature. For analytical purposes, however, it operates with the heuristical tool of three successive stages of *state formation*. This combined method of historical and structural analysis may give a wrong impression of the existence of three successive stages of distinct *states* or even social formations. This however, apparently, was not the case although distinct traits of structural changes *within* the early medieval state are clearly discernible.

## II

For centuries, the local nuclear areas of future early medieval kingdoms had been under Hindu and, at least right into the Gupta period, at times also under Buddhist influence, or had indirect contact (for example, through trade) with remote centres of higher state and cultural development. In the first centuries of the first millennium AD, the Sātavāhana kingdom played for central India as significant a role as the tribal principalities and early kingdoms of the Sangam period in South India during periods of marked Hinduization. For the further development of the whole of India, then, the Gupta empire was of immense significance:

although its political influence extended only temporarily beyond the Vindhya mountains, its culture radiated perceptibly into the distant South India as well as into South-east Asia. But it was characteristic of the further early medieval development of the post-Gupta period that the vast majority of the early medieval kingdoms did not arise from the centres of the Gupta empire or from its provincial capitals. They arose rather in their autonomous peripheral hinterland and in intermediate regions which had not yet been conquered, but which had already come under a wide range of influences of the Gupta empire. These were therefore regions in which local princes had the chance to establish their local rule under the influence (or better, on the model) of more advanced forms of economic and political development and to consolidate it undisturbed over many generations. Initially, wandering Brāhmaṇas might have offered their 'higher' knowledge to the chiefs of these local nuclear areas in the hinterland of the earlier kingdoms. However, it may have been the local chiefs themselves who far more frequently invited the Brāhmaṇas 'deliberately' as the most highly qualified 'development specialists' at that time.

It is of the greatest importance for the process of early medieval state formation that these developments usually originated from inside local nuclear areas and evolved further from here in concentric radiation. This development was only seldom thrust forcibly from outside, as for example through conquest by neighbouring kingdoms. However, even in the few cases in which an emigration or conquest is assumed (for example, Pallavas), usually several generations elapsed before these new dynasties had consolidated their rule within a conquered nuclear area to such an extent that they could make their influence prevail beyond their peripheral regions or into external regions.

Let us have a look at the local nuclear regions which form the nuclei of incipient state formation. So far, scarcely any systematic investigation of the origin and early history of these nuclear areas exists.[2] Their topography and their early history, however, make it clear that they lay mostly in the ecologically favourable riverine landscapes, for example, those of the entire east coast with its numerous rivers, which enabled agrarian extension through paddy cultivation and, thereby, led to an increase in population.[3] Another factor of their early development was the occasional participation in early inter-regional trade. This appears to apply in particular to the early local nuclear areas in the western highland of the Deccan, of which some lay strung like pearls in a chain on the 'southern path' (*dakṣiṇāpatha*) which formed a north-south axis since Mauryan times. The upsurge of nuclear areas lying near the eastern coast of the lower courses of the rivers of South India, too, seems to have been influenced by international sea trade.[4] All these variables indicate that the economic factor played a considerable if not a decisive role in the early development of the local nuclear areas. This development may have led to a professional differentiation and—strengthened by Hindu influence—to a nascent social stratification. However, this process of social differentiation might have been considerably slower than is often presumed. Even when in inscriptions of this period the adherence to the *varṇa* system is mentioned, there is no justification in most of the cases for inferring the existence of all four varṇa castes. The terms Śūdras and Vaiśyas and names of the real *jāti* castes appeared in epigraphical documents only centuries later.

For early medieval India it is not yet possible to answer the question, heatedly discussed by sociologists and anthropologists, as to whether these economic and social factors led to new political formations in order to protect class privileges,[5] or whether classes represent only sequels of preceding political developments.[6] So far scarcely any separate investigation in these matters exists. But what matters more is that the first inscriptions from these nuclear areas originate in a period in which these developments had already progressed considerably and therefore permit only very limited *a posteriori* conclusions for earlier periods. In spite of this uncertainty, many things point to the fact that the founding of local rule was far more frequently the result of a physical coercion, for example, of the eldest tribal prince of a clan or—in exceptional cases—of a conqueror, rather than the result of a voluntary agreement of the people (or more likely, the elite) as is traditionally maintained by Hindu *śāstra* texts and the Buddhist theory of the origin of the state.[7] Furthermore it can be inferred from the epigraphical evidence that in most cases this decisive political change in the early history of the local nuclear areas coincided with the migration of the Brāhmaṇas settled in the immediate neighbourhood of the new seat of power who were invited to do so. They were not only highly qualified ritual specialists, but also, by virtue of their monopolistic access to the *śāstra* texts, had a command of a considerable body of knowledge on state administration and political economy.

Most important appears to have been the legitimizing function of the Brāhmaṇas during this early phase of local political development. For, the material reproduction of this new form of political authority demanded—as is widely agreed—a continuously increased appropriation of socially produced surplus which required new forms of religio-political legitimation. Creating such legitimation was pre-eminently the task incumbent on an invited Brāhmaṇa.[8] Raising the status of the new rulers was a most urgent necessity in order to legitimize the claim to a regular system of imposts and, later, revenues. This happened in different ways. One way was for the Brāhmaṇas to create genealogies which traced the origin of the new local ruling 'dynasty' (*vaṃśa*) back to a mythical progenitor of remote epic antiquity or even directly, to a god.[9] Further, Brāhmaṇas vested the new rulers with the paraphernalia of Hindu royalty. To these belonged, for example, the obligatory royal umbrella (*chattra*) and the construction of the first Hindu temples. Even if these temples or shrines were initially insignificant edifices, inside of them the Brāhmaṇas held sway over a cult which differed impressively from local village and tribal cults.[10] This new Hindu cult comprised, on the one hand, a *regular* sequence of daily rites and was directed, on the other hand, to a permanently 'present' god who was worshipped either in the form of an *anthropomorphic* divine idol or as a Śaivite liṅgam.[11] This god, who was always present and visible, required also regular offerings. In contrast, the local tribal deities manifested themselves just now and then in their non-iconic symbols or in a priestly medium and received offerings only on these definite occasions. This comparison between the Hindu temple cults and the cults of the autochthonous local deities of the nuclear areas might have induced the people of the early nuclear areas to also draw comparisons between the status of their earlier tribal chiefs and that of a new Hindu rājā. In the basically egalitarian tribal societies the chiefs could assume a more elevated position only temporarily and in certain functions (as, for example, while waging war). Only in this functional position could they expect some regular presentations and services from people outside their own clan (villages?). The Hindu rājā claimed an altogether different position. In the Brahmanical theory of society he occupied an elevated rank which towered above that of his former tribal brethren. In this new 'representation' he demanded regular tributes—as the ever present 'new' Hindu god in the temple nearby demanded worship continuously. This kind of legitimation was successful not only in India for transforming voluntary offerings into the demand for regular levies!

However, with all these new forms of legitimization of Hindu royalty, in no way was only the status of the rājā and his 'dynasty' elevated. An exclusive elevation of the ruling family might have led to the reverse of the stabilization of rule and could have instigated rebellions leading to the fall of the 'newly rich' parvenu. Therefore the inhabitants of the nuclear area or at least the privileged groups participated in the 'elevation' of their new ruler. Thus the origin of a clan as a whole was directly associated with the mythical 'history' of a rājā, by, for example, claiming that the entire clan was one of the 'lost tribes' of the epic times of the Mahābhārata. Still more important and effective in the long run was the 'royal' promotion of autochthonous local and tribal cults, since such a promotion involved concrete social advantages for those concerned. Of particular importance in this connection was the Great Goddess who was equally feared and venerated for her power (*śakti*) by the local population. Usually no temples were set up to these tribal gods in the early phase of the local evolution of power. But their tribal priests were invited on certain occasions to the court where their deity then manifested itself through the medium of one of its priests. Or the deity would be carried along to the royal court by the tribal priests in a holy object into which the deity had already 'entered' at its place of origin, as for example in Orissa in a long bamboo stick (*khila muṇḍa*)[12] During their presence at court, the tribal priests and their deity were hosted by the king and rewarded with gifts. The king and his *rājaguru* also made a visit to the deity in its place of origin on the occasion of religious festivals. An important characteristic of the courtly cults of these early local nuclear areas was thus the incorporation of mighty local cults and the (temporary) integration of their non-Brāhmaṇa priests into the courtly circle.

The major aim of this integration of local cults into the courtly cult was to create a 'vertical legitimization' in order to legitimize the new rule within the nuclear area and its people. The Hindu temple at the court, the creation of Kṣatriya genealogy, and other symbols of Hindu kingship also served, on the other hand, the purpose of 'horizontal legitimization'. It aimed at equating the status of the 'new' rājā and his dynasty (*rājāvaṃśa,* which originally implied 'lineage of the rājā') with that of the neighbouring princes and Hindu rājās. The task of the court Brāhmaṇas consisted mainly in uniting these different areas and functions of the courtly cult into a system which would be comprehensible even to the non-Brāhmaṇa inhabitants of the nuclear area. This task brought about integration in two respects: on the one hand, the integration of local cults, in the manner described, into the courtly cult and on the other hand the integration of this courtly cult into the sacral Hindu topography of the near and far precincts of the nuclear area.[13]

As mentioned above, we have little evidence about socio-economic causes and the impact of this early political development on the local population. It appears to be doubtful that the Brāhmaṇas and their privileged position as landowners and court officials had already at this early stage a significant influence on the social structure of the local population, as postulated by the concept of Indian feudalism. However, it is very likely that their settlement had a direct impact on the agrarian extension. As these Brāhmaṇas depended solely on the agrarian surplus produced by their 'villages', at least some of them would have tried to increase this surplus through an improvement in agricultural methods, particularly through irrigation and rice production. But the rulers of these chiefdoms and early kingdoms, too, are known to have improved the irrigation system of their nuclear areas. The Cōḷa ruler, Karikala of the Śaṅgam age, was praised for his irrigation work in the Kaveri valley and the inscriptions of the early eastern Gaṅgas of Kalinga provide ample evidence of 'royal' initiative in local irrigation works.[14] Another important consequence of the increasing number of settled Brāhmaṇas in the newly developing nuclear areas must have been the opening up of new channels of translocal communication and trade. All these factors may have had a stronger influence on the social differentiation and incipient social stratification of the rural population than the mere settlement of Brāhmaṇas.

The most important characteristic of the early development of the state was thus the founding as well as the consolidation and legitimization of political authority *within* the local nuclear area. In contrast to this, the relations with the peripheral zones and the still remoter neighbouring areas played only a subordinate role. What was certainly of importance in this respect was the increase in the barter and trade relations with the peripheral zone of the nuclear area. This barter trade may have taken place in those times in the same way in which it can still be observed in the weekly markets, for example, in Orissa at the outskirts of tribal areas. Further, it is also probable that even in this early period, tribal warriors were occasionally recruited in the peripheral zones for the troops of the local nuclear area. In those cases in which the local rājā himself came from one of the tribes of the area, his rule was based to a large extent on institutionalized relations with this tribe.[15] Common campaigns and division of the booty may then likewise have been normal, as the already mentioned integration of the tribal cults in the courtly cult of the nuclear area. Of particular relevance in these cases were the ritual privileges of these tribes during the coronation of the rājās and during the annual festivities as, for instance, in later centuries during Durgāpūjā. But everything points to the fact that even if a tribal chief rose to the status of a Hindu rājā of a local nuclear area, the tribes of the peripheral zones endeavoured to preserve their independence.

The relations with the nuclear areas of neighbouring princes, often separated by extensive forests, created no problems in this early phase. They were mainly limited to marriage relations and sporadic campaigns, which, however, remained in this early period without any significant long-term consequences. Permanent subjugation and annexation after a military victory were still scarcely conceivable. Considering the power potential at the disposal of the early local principalities, the neighbouring seats of the rulers were still far beyond their sphere of permanent political control.

III

This situation was to change appreciably only in the second phase of state formation in early medieval India—with the emergence of the early kingdoms. The important characteristics of this second phase of the development of the state are: (i) intensification of political control through hierarchization in the nuclear area, (ii) its (at least partial) extension to peripheral zones, and (iii) the attempted enforcement of conditions of tributary dependence on the neighbouring chiefs and rājās.

With the emergence of the early kingdoms there began the fight—proverbial in India—following the 'law of the fishes' (*matsya-nyāya*): the big fish swallows the small one. The question of which local nuclear area would attain success in this fight, when the risky 'war of elimination' for 'trans-local' hegemony began, depended in this incipient phase of development certainly to a large extent on the charisma of the rājā and the abilities of his advisers. However, sustaining for several generations a hegemony—and thereby the founding of a dynasty—came to be based then entirely on the powers and economic resources of the original nuclear area. The latter continued to remain the major, if not the sole, basis for the new regional power.

Since in the preceding period of local rule the entire nuclear area had in no way been under direct control in its full geographical extent, it must have been the urgent concern of the ruler who had been able to upgrade his position to that of a 'great king' (*mahārāja*) to subjugate his original nuclear area as far as possible to his central and direct rule. Here, at least, the claim of the monopoly of legitimate and uncontested physical power and more or less direct revenue collection had to be established and—even though mostly in a protracted process—successfully implemented. The inscriptions of this period show that the 'great kings' of these early kingdoms were obviously zealously engaged in creating hierarchically graded administrative levels from a 'provincial' administration of districts down to the village and in associating these levels with a hierarchy of administrative powers and officials. Even if the ideal prescribed in the *śāstra* texts and repeated in the inscriptions was only rarely realized even within the nuclear area, there can be no doubt that the efforts to translate this ideal into reality contributed considerably to the extension of royal authority within the extended nuclear areas.

The astonishingly large number of land gifts to Brāhmaṇas was another striking characteristic of these early kingdoms. While in the early phase of the development of the nuclear area mostly individual Brāhmaṇas were settled in the immediate neighbourhood of the seat of the ruler, mahārājas now bequeathed entire villages (*agrahāra* or *brahmadēya*) in the whole nuclear area to increasingly larger groups of Brāhmaṇas.[16] However, the lavish conferment of immunities and privileges did not necessarily lead to a loss of these privileges by the king, as presumed by the adherents of the 'school of Indian feudalism'. Rather the exact opposite may have happened—at least at the period of the endowment. The copper-plate inscriptions mention in great detail and in a standardized manner the future rights of the Brāhmaṇas. What is perhaps most important in this context: the levies devolving on them were, probably for the first time, by means of these gift deeds unified norms of royal dominion proclaimed for the whole nuclear area. In fact the king may have transferred privileges which he himself was not yet in a position to enjoy fully in the areas where the endowments were made. Most significant in this connection is that every donation of land to Brāhmaṇas and the public proclamation of its legal conditions and implications for the villagers can be equated with the setting up of legal norms for the whole environs of the Brāhmaṇa villages. By enmeshing the entire nuclear area in a net of such privileged Brāhmaṇa settlements with standardized rights with regard to the taxes and services on the part of the local inhabitants, obligatory standards were—most likely for the first time—created also for those 'royal' areas which were not under the levying power and administration of the Brāhmaṇas. Moreover, the kings unequivocally handed over the power to implement these 'manorial' claims in these Brāhmaṇa villages to the Brāhmaṇa donees, for in all endowment inscriptions entry into the donated land was forbidden for royal administrative officials. Thus, it devolved upon the Brāhmaṇas the difficult task not only to create validity for the 'royal' rights transferred to them, but also to develop a village-level administration necessary for the implementation of these demands. Further, the judicial power to punish dilatoriness on the part of the village population was conferred upon the Brāhmaṇas. In a pre-modern state, police or even military means could have been scarcely more effective than this form of intensification of royal authority by means of a group of loyal Brāhmaṇas whose existence depended on their implementation of the *rājadharma*. In the long run of course, these Brāhmaṇa villages deprived (in the sense of 'Indian feudalism') the state of the administrative hold on the land and people and certainly became (in the sense of the 'segmentary state') part of the constellation of local power. However, persistence in exercising their own 'royal' privileges, existentially necessary for the Brāhmaṇas, continued to strengthen those of the king, too. Brāhmaṇa settlements were and remained, therefore, in this sense foremost pillars of the normative order of Hindu kingdoms and, one should add, inexpensive and efficient ones.[17]

The extension of royal authority in the extended nuclear area was accompanied by an intensification of the royal presence within the nuclear area itself, so that one can speak for the first time of the capitals of these kingdoms. This development was promoted as much by the extension of the residential area of the expanding court as by the intensification of craft and trade within the nuclear area. As a basically new element of town-planning, there appears in this period the building of new, bigger temples which were erected throughout Central and South India, for the first time built of stone. In certain cases—as for example, with the Pallavas of Kanchipuram, the Cāḷukyas of Aihole/Badami and in Orissa—a definite synchronism can be ascertained between the emergence of the early kingdoms in the late sixth century AD and the first appearance of freestanding sacral Hindu stone architecture. Quite a number of early capitals may have increasingly become sacral centres too with the settlement of new groups of temple priests and the celebration of temple festivals. The latter were 'public' in contrast to the early royal Vedic sacrifices and their influence on the hinterland also increased correspondingly. This over-all temple development was further strengthened by the fact that, with the central power's penetration of the nuclear area and its peripheral zones, autochthonous cults met with growing royal patronage. Some of these cults of mighty local gods were elevated in the course of the development to the status of dynastic family divinities (*kuladevatā*). Thus, in the phase of the early medieval kingdoms too the integration of local autochthonous cults formed an important characteristic of the courtly cults. This trend received a strong impetus from the bhakti cults which were spreading from South India in these centuries and by means of which the local gods acquired the dignity of being manifestations of the great Hindu divinities. This process was repeated in various respects by the rise of local princes as manifestations of great Hindu rājās.

## IV

In addition to the systematic extension of royal power within the entire nuclear area, there emerged in the second phase closer relations between the 'centre' and the peripheral zones and neighbouring areas. The relations of the central nuclear area with its peripheral zones were determined by their geographical conditions and their inhabitants. These regions were often covered by the thick jungles and chains of hills which surrounded the riverine landscape of the nuclear area. These were usually occupied by tribes who were frequently feared for militancy.[18] Thus, these areas, which often barrier-like encircled the early local nuclear areas, remained 'excluded' for centuries from the development of the nuclear areas in the river valleys. In the thirteenth rock edict, Aśoka referred to the 'forest dwellers' (*āṭavi*) who allegedly lived within his empire, and Samudragupta too in his famous Allahabad inscription proudly claimed that he 'had made all kings of the forest kingdoms [his] vassals' (*paricārakīkṛta-sarva-āṭavika-rājasya*).[19] However, both inscriptions indicate that the 'forest dwellers' of these two mighty empires of Indian antiquity had preserved their nearly unlimited autonomy. In the sixth century AD several kings in Central India and Orissa also identified 'forest kingdoms' (*āṭavi-rājya*) as a part of their kingdoms[20] which lay obviously in the peripheral zones of their nuclear areas. Even in these cases, however, we may legitimately doubt whether these 'forest kingdoms' were subjected to the actual control of the respective early kingdoms. But it is significant that the references to tribal principalities emerged around AD 600 just in that period when the evolution of states in these areas entered the second phase and the expanding royal power of the nuclear areas advanced for the first time to the peripheral zones.

There may have been mainly two causes for expansion into the peripheral zones. Firstly, these zones formed the hinterland for the expanding population of the nuclear area which required arable land for the increase of area under cultivation. Secondly, it was through these peripheral zones that the lines of communication with the outside world passed, particularly with the *sāmantas*, the 'neighbours' and future tributary princes. Gaining new areas for agrarian extension and securing lines of communication[21] might therefore have been important objectives for the population and the rājās of the nuclear areas. However, the penetration of the peripheral zones was quite a laborious process. At first it took place mainly in the immediate neighbouring regions of the nuclear areas and in 'outposts' which lay inside the peripheral zones in the valleys of tributary rivers and on transit roads. The extension of cultivable area was certainly not always peaceful and was carried out mainly by the peasants of the adjacent neighbourhood who were concerned with the extension of their economic basis. This effort was promoted by means of *temporary* tax concessions which, as we know from many *śāstra* texts, new settlers obtained. The settlers were followed by Brāhmaṇas. The privileges granted to them on a *long-term* basis played a similar role in the establishing of administrative institutions as has been described above for the nuclear areas.

While an expansion of the nuclear area took place by stages in the regions which lay in the immediate neighbourhood of the riverine landscapes, development in the 'outposts' may have proceeded differently. Here, winning new land for cultivation through settlers from the nuclear area was not as important as gaining settlements of traders in the area around already existing seats of power of the tribal leaders. Sooner or later Brāhmaṇas certainly followed them, too. But at least in the early period of this development they may have been invited by these tribal chiefs themselves, rather than having been sent out by the kings of the nuclear area. Even when the king of the nuclear area was mentioned in the documents of land grants, they may have represented in this case the subsequent sanctioning of local *fait accompli* rather than an act of direct royal control.[22] However, it would be wrong even in these cases to belittle the long-term results of such land grants to Brāhmaṇas. In the tribal area as well they led to the formation of administrative institutions previously unknown to the tribes. The spreading of these administrative forms was of use to the tribal chief in equal measure as it was to the king of the nuclear area. It may have been the gradual development of these seats of local tribal chiefs, under the influence of the nuclear areas, which was entered as *āṭavika-rājya* in the inscriptions around AD 600. Some of these tribal princes found themselves similarly involved in the process of Hinduization and rose to become tributary princes (*sāmanta*) in the course of further development, while others in their turn could preserve their autonomy for centuries right up to the threshold of the third, the imperial phase.

## V

Beyond the peripheral zones the 'neighbours' (*sāmanta*) ruled over their own nuclear areas. The expression *sāmanta* (from *sāmanta* 'all around', 'adjacent') referred at first to the *independent* neighbours, as for example in Aśoka's second rock edict to the Cōḷas, Pāṇḍyas, Satiyaputras, and Keralaputras in the distant, unconquered south. However, a significant change of meaning took place in the course of the following centuries, when, in the seventh century at the latest, the expression *sāmanta* had become generally prevalent as the title for 'neighbouring tributary princes'.[23] The institution of tributary princes were certainly as old in India as the known history of the subcontinent. But it was new that *neighbours* were simply identified with *tributary princes* in the period of the early medieval kingdoms. This semantic change implied that for the rulers of a nuclear area, at least theoretically, there were no longer independent neighbours—only independent nuclear areas could exist beyond these subjugated neighbours. Thus the rājās of the nuclear areas were confronted with the choice of either conquering their immediate neighbours or themselves becoming a *sāmanta* tributary prince of a mighty neighbour. Exactly this development set in the second phase of early medieval state formation. Such a politico-military struggle of subjugation is certainly nothing unusual. But it is characteristic for India that this development led to a new political institution, the *sāmantacakra.* The 'circle of tributary princes' who surrounded the kingdom became an established part of the early medieval kingdoms and their ideology. No true kingdom could exist without a circle of illustrious tributary princes, for only the brilliant ornaments on their heads let the Mahārāja shine in his entire greatness—a favourite theme in the *praśasti* panegyrics of the inscriptions. The *sāmantas* were once again installed in their allodial rule after their subjugation, but they had to pledge themselves to the payment of a (rather nominal) tribute (*kara-dā*), to a participation in the royal assemblies and to the donation of damsels (*kanyā-dāna*) to the royal harem.[24]

These *sāmantas* were a product of the genesis of the medieval kingdoms of India as their institution influenced permanently the structure of these kingdoms. For, the early kings of the nuclear areas were, in spite of increased revenues from their now extended nuclear areas, seldom capable of controlling directly their militarily overthrown 'neighbours' nor of replacing them by followers of their own court. An important reason for this weakness was the fact already mentioned that the opening up of the peripheral zones proceeded only very hesitantly and therefore a permanent control of all *sāmantas* beyond these peripheral zones often failed as a result of spatial-logistic problems. Thus the *sāmantas* continued to remain at first autonomous rājās in their own nuclear areas, they had their own centre of power and some of them also independently made land donations to Brāhmaṇas. However, they had to mention always in their inscriptions their mahārāja and 'overlord' and as the date of donation mostly his year of reign. If such a reference to the king of the central nuclear area is missing in an inscription and instead the *sāmanta* assumes royal titles (for example, mahārāja), it always points to a weakening of the central power and frequently also to the attempt of the *sāmanta* to attain unrestricted independence or even to wrest for himself the supremacy over the *sāmantacakra*. In this period of early kingdoms Stein's assertion is certainly valid: that with increasing distance from the centre the chances of tributary princes entering into alliances with hostile neighbours also increased.[25]

The period of early kingdoms marked at the same time the peak of the power of the *sāmantas*. Their almost unbroken power in their own principalities was enhanced in this period still further by their increasing influence in the central royal court. Loyal princes of the *sāmantacakra* were appointed *mahāsāmantas* by the kings; they sent daughters to the royal harem and took over high offices at court. This power and high status enjoyed by the *sāmantas* could not remain without affecting the structure of the royal nuclear area. For, in the face of the rise of the *sāmantas* in the royal union, the status of the officials of the central administrative apparatus, as for example that of the provincial governors (*upārika*), declined increasingly. It could therefore be only a question of time till they also strove for the *sāmanta* title and looked upon their provinces more and more as their 'fief'.[26] Thus a 'sāmantaization' of the early kingdoms took place, which could be termed an 'Indian variant' of feudalism so far as the political structure is concerned. The origin of this development, however, is to be sought less in the decline of earlier empires than in a development 'from below' as once pointed out by D.D. Kosambi in a different context.[27]

The 'sāmantaizing' of the early medieval kingdoms certainly also led to a strengthening—and in many cases even to the founding—of new local centres of power. This structural development in the peripheral zones and in the *sāmantacakra* resulted also, in a very few cases, in a fragmentation of the central political power. But this development of new local centres was rather the consequence of a general growth of governmental institutions which was not restricted to the royal nuclear area. And it was this process of extension of the local basis of governmental institutions which created the political and also economic conditions for the rise of future regional empires. These future empires were built on the basis of already existing local centres of power, which—to a certain extent, if not even in their overwhelming majority—originated in the period of local autonomy from the *sāmantacakras* of the various early kingdoms.

It should further be mentioned that in the period of these early kingdoms there began for the first time in large parts of India a process which slowly led to the integration of 'scattered' local centres into considerably enlarged regional core regions, as far as various economic, cultural-religious, social, and political matters were concerned. The centripetal forces which slowly emerged and which became more strongly effective in the future regional kingdom, created the basis for regional developments, the precursor of the present-day regional cultures and regionalism.

## VI

The imperial kingdoms represent the third and final stage in the development of Hindu statehood before the founding of Islamic states in India and the rise of 'patrimonial-bureaucratic' states in late medieval India.[28] Among these imperial kingdoms of early medieval India the kingdoms of the Cōḷas, Rāṣṭrakūṭas, Cāḷukyas of Kalyāṇī and Pālas have to be mentioned, as well as Eastern Gaṅgas and later the Sūryavaṃśa Gajapatis in Orissa. An important characteristic of these states is that the establishment of their regional hegemony was often closely associated with significant ruler personalities. As examples could be mentioned King Dharmapāla of the Pālas, King Rājarāja and Rājendra of the Cōḷas and King Anantavarman Coḍagaṅga of the Gaṅgas of Orissa. All of them expanded, sometimes by several times, their original realms by means of successful campaigns. Nevertheless, even these empires were no new creations of warlords. They too emerged from a continuous process of integrative state formation which had its origin in the development of local centres of power. As earlier in the development from local chieftaincies to early kingdoms, the development to the imperial level was also characterized by a strong continuity of structural traits. Nevertheless, new factors and characteristics made their appearance, a few of which turned into distinct structural features in the course of the development.

Among these structural features, which varied in their appearance in the imperial kingdoms, were:

1. A considerable extension of the directly controlled area by the union of two or several earlier nuclear areas or even early kingdoms and their intervening zones to a new 'core region'.
2. Shifting of the capital to the centre of this core region.
3. Expansion of the central administration within this enlarged core region.
4. Systematic enlargement of an apparatus of legitimation directed towards the imperial centre.
5. Increasing integration of the whole system.

A decisive new characteristic of the imperial kingdom was the considerable extension of the directly controlled area far beyond the 'natural' frontiers of the original nuclear areas of the early kingdoms. Since all the imperial kingdoms emerged from a violent dynastic change, certain similarities can be identified in the course of these imperial state formations.[29] In most of the cases, the dynasty of the old nuclear area (weakened by preceding battles) was overthrown by a powerful tributary prince who had already come to occupy a strong place in the central court. Examples of this are the overthrow of the Pallavas by the Cōḷas or that of the Cāḷukyas of Badami by the Rāṣṭrakūtas and in turn their overthrow by the Cāḷukyas of Kalyāṇī. As opposed to this, the cases in which independent neighbouring princes conquered the weakened kingdoms 'from outside' are rare, occurring, for example, in Orissa in the overthrow of the Bhauma-Karas of central Orissa by the Somavaṃśīs of Dakṣiṇa Kośala and later of the Somavaṃśīs by the Eastern Gaṅgas from southern Kaliṅga. Whether the dynasty was overthrown by a tributary prince or by a neighbouring king, in both cases this conquest associated with dynastic change, usually led to the unification of at least two nuclear areas: one of the conqueror and the other of the conquered. The conqueror thus contributed his own nuclear area towards the founding of the new kingdom. While in the phase of the early kingdom the conquered 'neighbours' were mostly reconfirmed as *sāmanta* tributary princes in their largely autonomous rule, the conquered ruler of a neighbouring nuclear area met with an entirely different fate in the phase of imperial kingdoms.[30] For in order to merge a conquered nuclear area permanently with that of the victor, the removal of the conquered dynasty from power was unavoidable. No doubt the descendants of overthrown dynasties sometimes succeeded after generations in temporarily reviving the ruling power of their ancestors.[31] However, from the fact that in most cases we hear nothing more about the overthrown dynasties, we may draw the conclusion that the loss of power would usually have been radical and complete.

A similar fate overtook most of the little autonomous principalities which had existed between these unified nuclear areas. Confronted now by imperial dynasties that had been considerably strengthened, their autonomy had a chance of survival only if the principalities lay in remote, rather inaccessible areas. But in contrast to the annexation of neighbouring kingdoms, the 'union' of these intermediary zones was not always accompanied by violence. Instead, the earlier peripheral zones and the large areas of the early *sāmantacakra* of the victorious dynasty usually underwent processes of intense integration. Important means of integration were further agrarian extension, inclusion into translocal trade networks and the spread of the 'state society'[32] of the dynastic core region. Tribals from the forests and mountain regions were increasingly recruited as troops of the empires. The means of communication through these former peripheral zones were further improved and sometimes secured by means of fortified garrisons. Beyond these peripheral zones, in the earlier *sāmantacakras*, the process of the increasing erosion of allodial rule continued. It often started with marriage alliances with the central royal family and the rise of *sāmantas* to mahāsāmantas and generals at the court. But in contrast to similar developments in the preceding phase, this time the process often led to the replacement of the allodial rulers by members of the central dynasties or their courts. Thus from earlier tributary principalities of the *sāmantacakra* there gradually evolved provinces or districts of the extended core region of the imperial kingdom. A good example of this 'provincialization' is offered by the semantic change of the term *maṇḍala.* During the period of the early kingdoms in Orissa, maṇḍala was always a term for an autonomous principality or the area of an allodial *sāmanta* prince. But in the period of the imperial kingdom of the Gaṅgas it came to indicate unequivocally a province of the imperial kingdom under a governor appointed by the central power.[33]

## VII

After the setting up of an imperial kingdom by conquest, the annexation of neighbouring kingdoms and the initiation of the process of integration of intermediary zones, the new 'imperial dynasty' was soon confronted with the question of enlarging, shifting, or re-establishing its capital. There were basically three alternatives: maintaining one's own old capital, taking over and expanding the conquered one, or founding a new capital. Examples of all three possibilities are known to us from medieval history. But in this respect too a clear difference is evident between the early kingdoms and their 'imperial' successors. The early kingdoms usually preserved their original capitals around which they then established their *sāmantacakra.* It was different in the case of the imperial kingdoms. With the conquest and annexation of neighbouring kingdoms, the original ancestral land and its capital often lost its central position in the framework of the extended imperial kingdom. It was necessary to overcome this marginality by the founding of a new, more centrally situated capital. The Rāṣṭrakūṭas offer a good example. About a hundred years after their victory over the Cāḷukyas of Badami, in the middle of the eighth century, they founded a new capital in the centre of their new empire in Mānyakheta. It lay almost equidistant from Badami, the capital of the conquered Cāḷukyas in the south, and their own ancestral land in the north. The Eastern Gaṅgas also shifted their capital from Kalinganagara in southern Kalinga to the central deltaic region of Orissa in Cuttack after their victory over the Somavaṃśa dynasty of central Orissa in the early twelfth century. From the beginning of the thirteenth century they proudly called their new capital 'New Benares' (*Abhinava Vārāṇasī*).

The shifting of the capitals aimed, however, not only at the acquisition of a geometrically exact central location. Some cases show that this shifting of the capital was accompanied by the successive development of the state. The capitals of the Cōḷas offer a good example of this. During their early history up to the time of the Pallava hegemony (seventh and eighth centuries), when the Cōḷas were tributary princes, Uraiyur in the upper 'head' of the Kaveri delta was their capital. King Vijayālaya, the founder of the 'Imperial Cōḷas', shifted the capital in the late eighth century to Tanjore (Tanjāvūr) in the centre of the Kaveri delta area. This became the nuclear area of the Cōḷa empire in subsequent centuries. In the beginning of the eleventh century, King Rājendra however went even a step further and founded Gaṅgaikoṇḍacōḷapuram down the river as the new capital, as if, at the height of the policy of overseas expansion by the Cōḷas, he was striving to also bring the coastal area under the direct control of the capital. The shifting of the capital of the Gaṅgas after their conquest of central Orissa appears to have also aimed mainly at exchanging their small ancestral nuclear area at the lower course of the Vamsadhara river with the considerably larger deltaic area of the Mahanadi river, which became the centre of the new core region of the 'Imperial Gaṅgas'. The major intention of shifting the capital of a regional kingdom was the penetration into a larger, potentially richer nuclear area, bringing it under the direct control of the new 'imperial' dynasty, thus gaining a considerably larger hinterland of the new capital. The shifting or founding anew of the capitals of the imperial kingdoms was thus often directly connected with the creation of an extended core region and the attempt to control it directly.

## VIII

These central areas of the imperial kingdoms were not, however, unified state territories, subjected exclusively to a central administration which was equally effective everywhere. Autonomous local administrative areas, which were only loosely connected with the central administration, continued to exist. Allodial principalities and tribal chiefdoms in remote forests and mountainous regions lay 'interspersed' in the extended core regions of the imperial kingdoms. Thus, in the final analysis, the concentric model of the processural state with its political authority decreasing in its outer 'rings' continued to apply also to the core region of the imperial kingdoms.[34] However, there were considerable differences here from the early kingdoms. First, it seems as if the court and its officers in all these states lived mainly on their own landed property and on benefices which might have been limited in time or heredity. This decentralized system of extracting socially-produced surplus had already existed in the nuclear areas of the early kingdoms. But the major difference between the early and the imperial kingdoms in this regard was the fact that the imperial court was able to extend this system into the annexed provinces of the enlarged core area. According to the growth of this core area and the centre's power of disposal, the number of courtiers and officers grew without changing the decentralized system as such. But the mere increase in the number of courtiers who obtained a living from 'their' villages in the countryside increased—directly or indirectly—the impact of the centre on its hinterland. There may indeed have been only little 'resource transfers of a political nature' from the more distant places of the core area to the centre. However, what was new was the dense network of mutual dependency which linked the centre and its enlarged core area to an hitherto unknown degree. Whereas the court of the early kingdom depended mainly on the resources of its direct hinterland, the whole enlarged core area of the imperial kingdom was linked with the centre by a system of decentralized collection of duties and their redistribution. Second, the radius of these 'imperial power rings' had widened considerably, whereby the power potential of the inner circle, particularly at the capital seat of the ruler and its immediate surroundings, also increased correspondingly. Third, the degree of the decrease of central power could be reduced considerably in the outer regions of the central area. Or, in other words and expressed less 'theoretically': At the height of political authority of imperial kingdoms there existed in the rather far-extended core regions, in spite of still existing local autonomy, no potential putsch-leader and also no centrifugal tendencies with the goal of entering into alliances with a neighbouring kingdom. The unity of the imperial kingdom was not challenged any more for long periods.[35] Even a dynastic change (as for example that of the Rāṣṭrakūṭas to the Cāḷukyas of Kalyāṇī in the tenth century) implied only a geographical displacement or just an enlargement of the central core region through the inclusion of the homeland of the new dynasty.

The core regions were often surrounded by a quite amorphous conglomerate of autonomous polities (often 'successors' of the earlier *sāmantas*), allies, and independent kingdoms which lay in the intermediary zone separating the next imperial kingdom. The differences in definition between tributary states and allies, and independent kingdoms fluctuated continuously. The partial instability of the political system of the imperial kingdoms had its origin mainly in these geographical intermediate and peripheral zones. Incursions which could also have an effect on the stability of the central core region took place here through a change in alliances and through the striving for independence of dependent kingdoms. Most of the fights between imperial kingdoms therefore aimed at the control of these 'forefields'.

More extensive and detailed studies would be needed in order to arrive at comparative and sufficiently accurate conclusions about the function and effectiveness of the central administrative apparatus of the regional empires. For we are aware that questions about the structure of the central administration and revenue collection within the core region, or the extent of the subordination of the conquered areas to this administration and questions as to whether and under which circumstances autonomous forces could maintain or even strengthen their autonomy, are some of the most vehemently discussed controversies of the various schools of Indian historians. The concepts of Indian feudalism and of the segmentary state succeeded in effectively destroying the 'conventional' picture of the medieval regional kingdoms as centrally governed unitary states for North as well as South India. Nevertheless, recent investigations show that some rulers of the larger imperial kingdoms were at least temporarily successful in their attempt to overcome the 'structural weaknesses' of the kingdoms by systematically improving the central administrative apparatus and also by appointing more local officers and leaders who could be controlled from the centre. An example for these centralizing measures for Orissa is the introduction of the ministerial *pātra* and *parīkṣā* systems in the twelfth and thirteenth centuries.[36] The success of these endeavours of the centre was repeatedly challenged by local forces or even nullified by them. But this power struggle not only demonstrates the weakness of the central rulers, but quite often also gives evidence of the occasional triumph of their attempts which, however, soon evoked corresponding counter-forces. But the lack of long-term success of these measures of the central dynasties justifies the designation of the imperial kingdoms of medieval India as exclusively segmentary states as little as the occasional success of these measures of the centre does not prove these states to be strong 'unitary states'. We will be doing justice to the structure of these regional kingdoms only if we are willing to analyse them as historical processes of various structural historical developments. Certainly it is as much legitimate to interpret these regional kingdoms 'from below', viewing them from the perspective of the local segments and their continuity, as it is permissible to explain them 'from above', from the point of view of the centre and its successes. Both these 'one-sided' approaches will do only partial justice to the overall structure of these states and their societies. The structural history of the imperial kingdoms—as that of nearly all pre-modern states—was as much the expression of the continuance of local power groupings as of a stage by stage extension of the organs of the central power.

## IX

The elevation of the Hindu 'great kings' (*mahārāja*) to 'imperial lords' *(mahārājādhirāja)* was accompanied also by a change in the ideology of the Hindu kingship. It is true that even the kings of the early kingdoms were praised in the *praśasti* eulogies of their inscriptions for their divine-like qualities. But this was done in an allegorical way for the most part. The kings of the large kingdoms rose, on the other hand, more and more to the status of earthly representatives of the tutelary deity *(rāṣṭradevatā)* of the kingdom who was mostly Śiva, and since the twelfth century, Viṣṇu. Under the influence of the Bhakti cult these deities had also been elevated to the status of great gods *(mahādeva)* in the preceding centuries. In the way that the *Mahārājas* underwent some sort of 'deification' as their earthly representatives, the mahādevas went through a process of 'royalization'. They were increasingly transformed into imperial lords by fitting them out with all the symbols of an earthly *mahārāja* and by assimilating their temple rites increasingly to the palace rites. For, the greater the ostentation of the mahādeva and his divine court, the more legitimate was the splendour and power of his earthly representatives and his royal court. This development contributed decisively to the legitimation of the *mahārāja* who, while not really deified, was brought, nevertheless, nearer to divinity.[37]

This new royal ideology is abundantly evident in the new temple architecture.[38] In the period between c. AD 1000 and 1250 when the large regional kingdoms were at the height of their power, there arose a series of monumental imperial temples ('Reichstempel') which exceeded in their dimensions several times over the temples of the earlier medieval kings of the respective regions. Among them are the Kaṇḍarīya Mahādeva temple of Khajuraho (about 1002), the Rājarājeśvara temple in Tanjore (about 1012), the Udayeśvara temple in Udaipur, and the Liṅgarāja temple in Bhubaneswar (both about 1060/70), the Jagannātha temple in Puri (after 1135) and the Sūrya temple in Konarak (about 1250).

Their cults developed into imposing state cults which were increasingly oriented towards the rulers, as is evident from the central liṅgas in the temples of Tanjore and Udaipur which were named after their respective donors, Rājāraja and Udayāditya. Tanjore is moreover a good example of the extent to which an entire kingdom could be drawn into this cult. Hundreds of priests, temple guards, dancers, musicians, book-keepers, and craftsmen, mentioned in the large inscriptions of Tanjore by name and place of birth were brought to Tanjore from various parts of the kingdom. While most of the craftsmen and temple guards had to be further provided for with food by their native villages, King Rājarāja instituted for the maintenance of the priests and dancing girls tax revenue villages which were distributed over the extended core area of the kingdom. Thus the kingdom was covered by an additional network of relationships directed towards the royal-sacral imperial centre—relationships which were as much economically as politically legitimate. Surplus revenues and profits from the temple were loaned to the surrounding villages and districts, which utilized this finance for agricultural developmental projects as well as for other purposes, leading to a further economic strengthening of the Cōḷas' own hereditary lands.[39] Rājarāja's successors also built further monumental temples in the proper ancestral land of the Cōḷas in the lower course of the Kaveri river: his son Rājendra in Gaṅgaikoṇḍacōḷapuram, Rājarāja II (1146–1173) in Darasuram and Kulottuṅga III (1178–1216) in Tribhuvanam. As a result of the establishment of these large temples in the extended dynastic hereditary land they came to increasingly assume the character of sacral zones of the empire within the larger core region.

Since the late eleventh and the beginning of the twelfth century, however, more important than the building of new monumental temples was the systematic enlargement and embellishment of already existing holy places (*tīrtha*) which had turned into centres of pilgrimage of regional importance under the influence of the Bhakti cult in the preceding centuries. By the continuous extension of the temple lay-out, construction of numerous new subsidiary temples and halls, corridors for promenade and (in South India) tall temple gateways (*gopuram*), these centres grew into substantial temple cities. Cidambaram, the centre of the cult of the dancing Śiva-Naṭarāja, and Puri, the seat of Viṣṇu as 'Lord of the World' (Jagannātha), are particularly good examples of the systematic royal expansion of local cult centres by generous royal patronage since the early twelfth century.[40] Therefore, it need not surprise us that these temple towns became in ever greater measure also centres of royal influence and thus assumed in some respects the function of the imperial palatine of German Middle Ages. This political function of the temple towns became particularly evident at places where huge 'thousand pillar halls' were constructed which occasionally (as for example in Cidambaram) bore the name 'royal hall' (*rājasabhā*). By means of this systematic enlargement and the promotion of numerous temple cities which were distributed over the entire core area of the empire, the kings covered this vast area with an 'additional' network of direct royal, political, and ritual influence.

But the political significance of the temple towns was in no way limited to their being occasionally also 'royal towns'. Far more important was their role as cosmic centres and the source of the highest legitimation of the royal authority.[41] Very soon the founder kings were included in the temple legends in which they were elevated to mythical heroes of the hoary past. In a temple māhātmya of the temple of Puri it is mentioned still more clearly that only by the construction of the (first) Jagannātha temple by the mythical king Indradyumna, famines and mass deaths came to an end in Orissa and therefore mankind had happily submitted itself to his rule. On the other hand, it is expressly stated in the same text about the other kings that they were interested only in the collection of unjust taxes but not in the welfare of the people.[42] Which greater legitimation could the dominion of the kings of the Gaṅga dynasty of Orissa have enjoyed in the period around 1300 when this māhātmya was written down? The priests and pilgrims did look upon the kings of the Gaṅga dynasty as direct successors of the mythical king Indradyumna. And many of them still knew that Anantavarman Cōḍagaṅga, a member of this dynasty, had got constructed 'anew' only a few generations earlier the great temple admired by them. The message of these temple legends, which the priests propagated to the pilgrims during their visits to the temple cities, were carried by them to villages even in the remotest areas of the kingdom.

A further, perhaps even more important aspect of the temples (and also of the kings' 'temple policy') was their integrating function within the regional kingdoms. The great temples were associated 'vertically' in an often closely meshed network of ritual and legendary relations with 'sub-regional' and local cults of their hinterland, as well as 'horizontally' with other temples of the region. Thus, for example, in South India the liṅgas of five great Śaivite temples were assigned to the five elements: Kancipuram to the earth, Jambukesvara to the water, Tiruvannamalai to the fire, Kalahasti to the wind, and Cidambaram to the spirit-ether (*akāśa*). Again in Orissa, the biggest temples of the five important cults were brought together into a system of the 'five gods' (*pañcadevatā*): Viṣṇu/Jagannātha in Puri, Śiva/Liṅgarāja in Bhubaneswar, Durgā/Virajā in Jaipur, Sūrya in Konarak, and Gaṇeśa (here vicarious for the tribal cults) in Mahavinayaka. What is of significance is that all these 'regional' temples lay inside the extended core areas of the respective regional kingdoms. The effect of this 'temple policy' was to link local loyalties of the earlier nuclear areas and their peripheral zones with the cults of the central temples and then, at the level of 'horizontally interlinked systems', to integrate them into a new regional cult as a basis of a new regional loyalty.

This regional integration similarly took place in numerous other spheres, through the development of regional kinship and caste systems ('sanskritization'), by the codification of regional norms (*deśa dharma*),[43] by the social and economic integration of the tribes ('kṣatriyaization') and by the inclusion of tribal deities and rituals ('Hinduization') into Hindu cults. The medium in which the new 'regional loyalty' was propagated was no more the Brahminic-court Sanskrit, but the regional languages. Non-Brahminic itinerant preachers, sectarian leaders, and holy men emerged more and more as the propagators of the new 'mission'. The growth and history of the medieval imperial or regional kingdoms were thus accompanied—and in some cases even accomplished—by the emergence of a new regional identity. It was the forerunner of today's regional cultures of India and thus perhaps the most important heritage of medieval India.

## X

Summarizing these delineations on a processual model of integrative state formation in early medieval India, the three successive stages of spatial and socio-political development may be characterized by three key terms, that is, rājavaṃśa, *sāmantacakra*, and maṇḍala. Rājavaṃśa pertains to the chiefdom and the establishment of local rule under a 'royal' lineage (*vaṃśa*) in a nuclear area. *Sāmantacakra* refers to the early kingdom and the process of extending political authority within the nuclear area and the establishment of tributary relations with the circle (cakra) of formerly independent neighbours (*sāmanta*), without however annexing them. The term maṇḍala stands for the imperial kingdom and the process of annexation of the *sāmantacakra* and its, partly, administrative transformation into maṇḍala provinces. This political development is as well based on, as accompanied by, continuous processes—emanating from the central nuclear area—of agrarian extension, social stratification ('*jātification*'), political hierarchization, and cultural integration.[44] In its final stage of an imperial kingdom the early medieval state in India was therefore based on an impressively enlarged and centrally dominated core region with its own 'state society' and a highly developed integrative cultural identity, a stage, however, which only few historical kingdoms were able to reach.

## NOTES

1 See also Hermann Kulke, 'The Early and the Imperial Kingdom in Southeast Asian History', in Kulke (ed.) *Kings and Cults: State Formation and Legitimation in India and Southeast Asia*, New Delhi, 1993, pp. 262–93.

2 For South India, see C. Maloney, 'Archaeology in South India: Accomplishments and Prospects', in B. Stein (ed.), *Essays on South India*, Honolulu, 1975, pp. 1–40; Nicholas B. Dirks, 'Political Authority and Change in Early South Indian History', *Indian Economic and Social History Review*, vol. XIII, 1976, pp. 125–57; S.D.S. Senaviratne, 'Kalinga and Andhra: The Process of Secondary State Formation in Early India', *Indian Historical Review*, vol. 7, 1980, pp. 54–69; Burton Stein, *Peasant State and Society in Medieval South India* Delhi, 1980, pp. 90*ff*; G. Berkemer, *Little Kingdoms in Kalinga Ideologie Legitimation und Politik regionaler Eliten*, Stuttgart, 1993, pp. 83–152.

3 An almost ideally typical description of the expansion of such a 'nuclear area' is contained, for example, in the Prithu legend in the Viṣṇupurāna: 'Prithu accordingly uprooted the mountains. Before his time there were no defined boundaries of villages or towns, upon the irregular surface of the earth there was no cultivation, no highway for merchants: all these originated in the reign of Prithu. Where the ground was made level, the king induced his subjects to take up their abode. Before his time, also the fruits and roots which constituted the food of the people were procured with great difficulty ... Thence proceeded all kinds of corn and vegetables upon which people subsist now and perpetually.' *The Vishnupurana*, translated by H.H. Wilson London, 1840, pp. 86*ff*. (I, 13, 81*ff*).

4 C. Maloney, 'Archaeology in South India', p. 19.

5 M.H. Fried, *Evolution of Political Society*, New York, 1967.

6 E.R. Service, *Origins of the State and Civilization: The Process of Cultural Evolution*, New York, 1975.

7 On Gopāla, the founder of the Pāla dynasty, it is reported in the Khalimpur inscription of his son Dharmapāla that he had been elected by the 'people' (*prakrti*) in order to put an end to 'the law of the fishes' (*matsya-nyāya*). R.C. Majumdar, *The History of Bengal* 1971, p. 97, presumes quite probably with justification that this election was made by the 'leading chiefs'. However, whether it is possible then to speak of a 'bloodless revolution which both in its spirit and subsequent results reminds us of what happened in Japan about 1870 AD' is questionable.

8 Probably Max Weber was the first to emphasize this important legitimizing role of the Brāhmaṇas: See H. Kulke, 'Max Weber's Contribution to the Study of "Hinduization" in India and "Indianization" in Southeast Asia', in Kulke, *Kings and Cults*, pp. 240–61.

9 See Romila Thapar, 'Origin Myths and the Early Indian Historical Tradition', in Thapar, *Ancient Indian Social History: Some Interpretations*, New Delhi, 1978, pp. 294–325; Nicholas B. Dirks, 'The Past of a Pālaiyakārar: The Ethnohistory of a

South Indian Little King', *Journal of Asian Studies* (*JAS* hereafter), 41, 1982, pp. 655–83; S. Sinha 'State Formation and Rajput Myth in Tribal Central India', in Hermann Kulke (ed.), *The State in India: 1000–1700*, New Delhi, 1995.

10 A. Eschmann, 'Hinduization of Tribal Deities in Orissa', in *The Cult of Jagannath and the Regional Tradition of Orissa*, A. Eschmann, H. Kulke, G.C. Tripathi (eds), Delhi, 1978, pp. 79–97.

11 Often an anthropomorphic image is put in front of the original aniconic idol. For further derails, see Hermann Kulke, 'Tribal Deities at Princely Courts: The Feudatory Rajas of Central Orissa and their Tutelary Deities (iṣṭadevatās)', in Kulke, *Kings and Cults*, pp. 114–36.

12 See Hermann Kulke, 'Legitimation and Town planning in the Feudatory States of Orissa', in Kulke, *Kings and Cults*, pp. 93–113 and B. Schnepel, 'Durga and the King: Ethnohistorical Aspects of the Politico-Ritual Life in a South Orissan Jungle Kingdom', *Journal of the Royal Anthropological Institute* (*Man*), vol. 1, 1995, pp. 145–66.

13 J. Rösel, 'Sakralstädte als Kristallisatoren regionaler Tradition—das Beispiel der indischen Tempel-und Pilgerstadt Puri', in H. Kulke and D. Rothermund (eds), *Regionale Tradition in Südasien*, Wiesbaden, 1985, pp. 149–70.

14 Thus the inscriptions of Indravarman of Kalinganagara of the late sixth century mention a *rājataṭāka* and a *kṣatriyataṭāka* (tank) and interesting details about sluices (*taṭāka-udara-bandha*), water regulations, and so on. (S.N. Rajaguru (ed.) *Inscriptions of Orissa*, vol. II, Bhubaneswar, 1960, pp. 24*ff*). For Rajasthan see B.D. Chattopadhyaya, 'Irrigation in Early Medieval Rajasthan', in B.D. Chattopadhyaya (ed.), *The Making of Early Medieval India*, New Delhi, 1994, pp. 57–88.

15 A good example is provided by Keonjhar in north Orissa and its relations with the tribe of the Hill Bhuiyas; see S.C. Roy, *The Hill Bhuiyas of Orissa*, Ranchi, 1935. For south Orissa, see B. Schnepel, 'The Nandapur Suryavamshis: Origin and Consolidation of a South Orissan Kingdom', *Orissa Historical Research Journal*, 1992, pp. 170–99.

16 It was mainly R.S. Sharma's contribution (*Indian Feudalism*, Calcutta, 1965) which has explained this change in the land policy of Indian kingdoms.

17 For a more detailed study see Hermann Kulke, 'Some Observations on the Political Functions of the Copper-Plate Grants in Early Medieval India', in B. Kolver (ed.), *The State, the Law, and Administration in Classical India*, Munich, 1977, pp. 237–43.

18 For the theory of the five landscapes (*tiṇai*) in early Tamil Literature and their socio-economic and cultural relevance; see G.D. Sontheimer, *Pastoral Deities in Western India*, New York, 1989.

19 Allahabad inscription of Samudragupta, line 21, in D.C. Sircar, *Select Inscriptions*, vol. I, Calcutta, 1965, p. 265.

20 Koh inscription of Samkshobha from the year AD 529, verse 8, in ibid., p. 395 and Kanas inscription of Lokavigraha from the year AD 599, in *Epigraphia India* (*EI* hereafter), vol. 28, p. 329.

21 For example, an inscription of Indravarman of the Gaṅga dynasty of Kaliṅga mentions in the late sixth century a 'royal road' (*rājamārga*), *EI*, vol. XXV, pp. 194–8.

22 This interpretation follows B. Stein's concept of 'ritual sovereignty' of the central king. (Burton Stein, 'The Segmentary State in South Indian History', in R.G. Fox (ed.), *Realm and Region in Traditional India*, Durham, 1977, pp. 3–51.

23 L. Gopal, '*Sāmanta*—Its Varying Significance in Ancient India', *Journal of the Royal Asiatic Society*, vol. 5, 1963, 21–37. For further studies on the role of the *sāmantas* in early medieval India, see the introduction to Kulke (ed.), *The State in India*.
24 These duties of the 'frontier kings' (*pratyantanṛpati*) are best depicted in Samudragupta's Allahabad inscription.
25 Stein, 'The Segmentary State', p. 10.
26 Sharma, *Indian Feudalism*, p. 159.
27 D.D. Kosambi, *An Introduction to the Study of Indian History* Bombay, 1956, pp. 353*ff.*
28 See S.P. Blake, 'The Patrimonial-Bureaucratic Empire of the Mughals', in Kulke (ed.), *The State in India*, and the relevant portions of the introduction to that book.
29 Here also the Pālas appear to be an exception. The long list of the *sāmantas* who are mentioned in the Rāmacaritam and whose support King Rāmapāla could 'buy' in his fight against the Kaivartas only by giving huge presents, shows their unbroken power. The power of the Pālas in Bengal rested obviously not on a strong central area, but on a power balance within or above the allodial local princes, a balance which had to be constituted anew time and again. On the structure of the Pāla empire, see S. Bhattacharya, *Landschenkungen und politische Entwicklungen im früh-mittelalterlichen Bengalen*, Wiesbaden, 1986.
30 Thus the late Cāḷukyas of Kalyāni traced their lineage to the early Cāḷukyas of Badami. In contrast to the Pāṇḍyas who continued to exist in their capital of Madurai even at the height of the Cōḷa power, the Pallavas appeared at first to have been completely destroyed by the Cōḷas and their capital Kanchipuram became the second capital of the Cōḷas. Nevertheless, Kopperuñjiṅga, who claimed to be a descendant of the Pallavas, succeeded temporarily in the early thirteenth century in taking prisoner the Cōḷa king, Rājārāja III, and conquering extensive parts of the Cōḷa empire, K.A.N. Sastri, *The Cōḷas*, 1955, pp. 422*ff.*
31 Relations between the regional kingdoms and the tribes of the mountainous hinterland were not always smooth. There are several examples of the violent insurrections of tribes against Hindu māharājas. It appears, for example, that at the end of the thirteenth century there was a regular invasion of Kaliṅga by the Śabara tribes living in the hills (vide *EI*, vol. VI, p. 260).
32 This important term was introduced by B.D. Chattopadhyaya, 'Political Processes and the Structure of Polity in Early Medieval India', in Kulke (ed.), *The State in India*. Also see the introduction.
33 For Orissa, see S.K. Panda, *Herrschaft und Verwaltung im östlichen Indien unter den späten Gaṅgas (c. 1038–1434)*, Wiesbaden, 1986, pp. 60–86 and more recent, 'From Kingdom to Empire: A Study of the Medieval State of Orissa under the Later Eastern Gangas, AD 1038–1434', *Indian Historical Review*, vol. 17, 1993, pp. 149–60; for the Cōḷas, see Y. Subbarayalu, 'The Cōḷa State', *Studies in History* vol. 4, no. 2, 1982, 269–306 and J. Heitzman, 'State Formation in South India', in Kulke (ed.), *The State in India*, pp. 162–94.
34 For the important issue of spatial differentiation of agrarian and political processes within the core region of South Indian kingdoms which was first raised by Y. Subbarayalu (1973) and B. Stein (1969, 1977), see the introduction to Kulke (ed.), *The State in India*.

35 Cf. on this also what O.W. Wolters says on the founding of the empire of Angkor in the year 802: 'Local independence was no longer the acceptable objection as it had been in the eighth century. The integrity of the Angkorian kingdom was no longer in question', O.W. Wolters, 'Jayavarman II's Military Power: The Territorial Foundation of the Angkorian Empire', *Journal of the Royal Asiatic Society*, 1973, p. 30.
36 S.K. Panda, *Herrschaft and Verwaltung im östlichen Indien unter den spätenGangas (ca. 1038-1434)*, Stuttgart, 1986, p. 175. For similar centralizing tendencies in the Cōḷa state Heitzman's paper in Kulke (ed.), *The State in India*, and Subbarayalu 'The Coḷa State', *Studies in History*, vol. 4, no. 2, 1982, pp. 269–306.
37 In their recent study on the political culture of Nāyaka Tamil Nadu, V.N. Rao, D. Shulman and S. Subrahmanyam agree that in early medieval South India there existed a 'culturally given distinction between the king and the god'. However, this distinction has been transformed since the seventeenth century when the Nāyaka kings 'assumed the identity of the god in his shrine'. (V.N. Rao, D. Shulman, S. Subrahmanyam, *Symbols of Substance. Court and State in Nāyaka Period of Tamil Nadu*, New Delhi, 1992), p. 187.
38 Hermann Kulke, 'Royal Temple Policy and the Structure of Medieval Hindu Kingdoms', in A. Eschman, H. Kulke, and G.C. Tripathi (eds), *The Cult of Jagannath and the Regional Tradition of Orissa*, New Delhi, 1978. pp. 125–38.
39 K.A.N Sastri, 'The Economy of a South Indian Temple in the Cōḷa Period', in *Malaviya Commemoration Volume*, 1932, pp. 305–10; see also G.W. Spencer, 'Temple, Money Lending and Livestock Redistribution in Early Tanjore', *Indian Economic and Social History Review*, vol. V, 1968, pp. 279–93 and Spencer, 'Religious Networks and Royal Influence in Eleventh Century South India', *Journal of the Economic and Social History of the Orient* (*JESHO* hereafter), vol. 12, 1969, pp. 279–93; J. Heitzman, 'Ritual Polity and Economy: The Transactional Network of an Imperial Temple in Medieval South India', *JESHO*, vol. 34, 1991, pp. 23–54.
40 J.C. Harle, *Temple Gateways in South India: Architecture and Iconography of the Chidambaram Gopuras*, Oxford, 1963, pp. 31*ff*.
41 Hermann Kulke, *Cidambaramāhātmya. Eine Untersuchung der religionsgeschichtlichen und historischen Hintergründe für die Entstehung der Tradition einer südindischen Tempelstadt*, Wiesbaden, 1970, pp. 126*ff*; see also D. Shulman, *Tamil Temple Myths: Sacrifice and Divine Marriage in South Indian Śaiva Tradition*, Princeton, 1980, pp. 40–55 and Friedhelm Hardy, 'Ideology and Cultural Contexts of the Śrīvaiṣṇava Temple', in Burton Stein (ed.), *South Indian Temples*, New Delhi, 1978, pp. 119–52.
42 *Puruṣottamamāhātmya of the Skanda Purāṇa*, XI, pp. 125*ff*, Venkatesvar Press, VS, 1966; see also R. Geib, *Indradyumna-Legende: Ein Beitrag zur Geschichte des Jagannātha-Kultes*, Wiesbaden, 1975, pp. 97*ff*.
43 A. Wezler, 'Dharma und Deśadharma', in H. Kulke and D. Rothermund (eds), *Regionale Tradition in Südasien*, Wiesbaden, 1985, pp. 1–22.
44 The most recent and comprehensive evaluation of the whole range of parameters of structural change and continuity in early medieval India is B.D. Chattopadhyaya's introduction, in *The Making of Early Medieval India*, Delhi 1994, pp. 1–37.

# Part II

## Village, Town, and Society

# 4

# Land Rights and Social Stratification*

Kesavan Veluthat

Historians in the past have tended to view society in early medieval south India as generally smooth and free from any contradictions. In fact, K.A. Nilakanta Sastri would go as far as to glorify the 'political spirit of the time … [which] aimed at securing the harmony of classes, rather than their equality'[1], and the 'healthy society … which was free from the glaring economic oppression of one class by another'.[2] He seldom recognized the contradiction between these statements on the one side and the rich empirical data he has marshalled in his own writings about the class distinctions and contradictions on the other. The situation is not any better in the case of later studies by Appadorai, Minakshi, and Mahalingam.[3] In Appadorai's work, which is on the economic conditions of southern India in the first half of the second millennium AD, one would naturally expect a picture of class differentiation and contradiction, but in vain.

Recent American scholarship, which starts with the avowed purpose of offering a corrective to the kind of historiography represented by Nilakanta Sastri, hardly makes the position different. For instance, Burton Stein in his major work on peasant state and society in medieval south India characterizes society in the Pallava and the succeeding Cōḻa ages as organized into a large number of peasant localities and cultures.[4] Naturally, one would look for a picture of the structured relationship within such a highly developed peasant society, especially as this work is

* Previously published in Kesavan Veluthat, *The Early Medieval in South India*, New Delhi, Oxford University Press, 2009, pp. 83–99.

the extension and fulfilment of a scathing attack on the historiography represented by Nilakanta Sastri and his disciples, which appeared as a 'prolegemenon' a few years earlier.[5] But the whole work is professedly about 'peasants without lords'.[6] Perhaps Stein is right in characterizing his own work as 'somewhat perverse in theoretical and historiographical senses!'[7] Actually, Stein is unabashedly indifferent to the rich data on the differentiation within the peasantry in making the assumption of a world of peasants without lords. He seems to push under the carpet the subject nature of a major chunk of peasantry while describing the relationship between the Brāhmaṇas and the peasants as an alliance. True, it was one of co-operation if we take the Gandhian idea that in every situation of oppression there has to be the co-operation of the oppressed! The conception of an undifferentiated monolithic peasantry obviously springs from [a] perverse theoretical position and a total indifference to data. However, there is a happy development in recent years represented by the works of a few Asian scholars, Noboru Karashima, M.G.S. Narayanan, Y. Subbarayalu, D.N. Jha, R. Champakalakshmi, and Rajan Gurukkal among them.[8] This is not to say that every one of them shares the same frame of reference and the same set of assumptions; on the contrary, their theoretical positions and tools of analysis vary considerably. Every one of them is conversant with the primary sources and has also his/her own philosophy of history, which makes it a happy feature for south Indian historiography.

The copper plate records of the Pallavas and the Pāṇḍyas in the seventh and eighth centuries AD provide information on the various shades of rights on land and concomitantly the position of different sections in society depending upon the nature of right that one enjoyed on a particular piece of land. Most of the Pallava copper plates record the grant of land to Brāhmaṇas. Inevitably they are related to the creation and transfer of certain superior rights over land. This is expressed in the case of a few Pallava records by the expression *kuṭi nīkki*,[9] which means, literally, removing the earlier occupants. The same idea is conveyed by another expression *mun-peṟṟārai māṟṟi*[10] found in a couple of other Pallava records. Both these signify that the recipients of the land were at liberty to evict the earlier occupants of the land and settle it with new occupants of their own choice. R. Tirumalai has argued that these expressions need not signify the eviction of the earlier occupants in a physical sense.[11] On the other hand, he suggests that it may indicate the extinction of the existing rights of the occupants over the land which was granted. L.B. Alayev, on the other hand, seeks to explain the expression *kuṭi nīkki* as 'except *kuṭi*', that is, when a piece of land was alienated the *kuṭis* would not form part of it.[12] It is significant that apart from the handful of records speaking of land with earlier occupants—whether they were physically removed or their earlier rights were extinguished or they were not touched at all is another question—the vast majority of Pallava charters do not speak about the fate of the earlier settlers. This would suggest that what was granted to Brāhmaṇas was relatively unsettled land where all the rights were given to the donees.

The land grants of the Pallavas, therefore, indicate the beginnings of a structured relationship in the matter of land rights. In many cases there is no mention at all of the earlier occupants on the land indicating thereby that the donees were granted unsettled land. Here it is clear that what was granted was to be enjoyed by the donees, with the right to get the land cultivated with the help of tenants if they would. In the other records, which do speak of the pre-existing occupants, it is by making it possible for the donees to get it cultivated by the earlier occupants, in whatever way the expression *kuṭi nīkki* is interpreted. Even here the situation is as if there was the state at the top enjoying an overall suzerainty and final right over the land and the occupant-tenant at the bottom who cultivated the land with one stratum of intermediary, that is, the donees of the grant, in between. On them were conferred not only the right to get the land cultivated and its rights enjoyed but also other fiscal and administrative rights such as the collection of numerous imposts and the maintenance of law and order.[13]

As we come to a slightly later situation obtaining in the Pāṇḍyan kingdom, we have a clearer picture of a more evolved system of land rights, thanks to the excellent study of the agrarian system and socio-political organization under the early Pāṇḍyas undertaken by Rajan Gurukkal.[14] Most land grants of the Pāṇḍyas are concerned with the creation or maintenance of *brahmadēya*, *devadāna*, or *paḷḷiccantam*. They speak of the conferment of two kinds of rights: the *mīyāṭci* and the *kārāṇmai*. These two expressions indicate, respectively, the superior possessive right and the right to cultivate. The phrase in the Pāṇḍyan records, *kārāṇmai mīyāṭci uḷḷadaṅga* in the Tamil portions and *kārāṇmai mīyāṭciyutam* in the Sanskrit portions, indicating the right to cultivate the land and/or get it cultivated, is an exact translation of the expression *karṣayataḥ karṣāpayataśca* occurring in the same context in inscriptions from northern India.[15] Below these two shades of rights there appears to have been a third one, namely, that of occupancy (*kuṭimai*). In a stone inscription from Ambasamudram it is clearly stated that the *mīyāṭci* alone was transferred while the *kārāṇmai* was retained by the earlier tenants of the land.[16] It is explicitly stated in the record that the land in question was to be a *mutal kuṭi nīṅṅā dēvadānam*, a *dēvadānam* where the earlier occupants were not be disturbed. This would show that *kuṭimai*, or occupancy right, differed from *kārāṇmai*. There are expressions such as *āḷaḍanga* (literally 'including the men') found in the grants indicating the transfer of agrestic labourers also along with the land. This is a clear evidence of labour tied to soil, in the same way as we have in the Sanskrit charters from northern India expressed by the phrase *dhanajanasahitā*.[17] In the Pāṇḍyan records, therefore, one can see the further evolution of land rights into the next stage. In certain records from the Pāṇḍyan kingdom the expressions *mērpāti* and *kīḻpāti*, literally the 'upper share' and the 'lower share', are used in the place of *mīyāṭci* and *kārāṇmai* respectively.[18] This, incidentally, would dispel the misunderstanding created by Stein with regard to the expressions *mēlavāram* and *kīḻvāram* in the Cōḻa records.[19] This discussion of the land rights in the Pāṇḍyan records helps in the reconstruction of the structured relationship with various shades of tenurial rights. With the help of a diagram, Rajan Gurukkal has demonstrated this hierarchy with the *kuṭis* (occupants) on the bottom of the scale and the king at the top and a graded hierarchy of intermediaries placed between the two. This class of intermediaries consisted of, according to Gurukkal, the chiefs, the *nāḍus*, the *ūrs* and the *dēvadānas* or the *brahmadēyas* as the case may be who had the *mīyāṭci* rights, and the *kārāḷars* (the cultivating tenants) in that descending order.[20]

The situation in the Cēra kingdom was comparable. M.G.S. Narayanan's research into various aspects of the history of Kerala in this period has brought out a detailed picture of the structured relations in land obtaining in the early medieval Cēra kingdom.[21] In a study of the traditional land system in Kerala undertaken by Narayanan and the present writer, the following representation is given with the help of a diagram.[22] The Perumāḷ or the king was at the top. He had his own land known as *cērikkal* (something of a demesne) in which there were the *kārāḷar* or tenants and the *kuṭiyāḷar* or the occupants. Below the *kārāḷar* were the labourers attached to land known as the *aṭiyalār*. A portion of the *cērikkal* land may have been granted as *virutti* or service tenure to religious and secular functionaries but the pattern of *kārāḷar-kuṭiyāḷar-aṭiyalār* hierarchy remained the same in such cases also. In other areas where the local chieftains obtained, even they had the *cērikkal* land and had granted *virutti* tenures carrying with it the same pattern of subject peasantry. In certain cases between the *kārāḻar-kuṭiyāḻar-aṭiyālar* peasantry on the one side and the local chief or the king himself on the other, there was another tier, that is, the significant group of intermediaries in the Brāhmaṇa settlements owing right over land as either *brahmasvam* (Brāhmaṇa's property) and *dēvasvam* (god's property) and marginally the trading groups in the *nagarams*. Thus we get the picture of a stratified peasantry which was itself subjected to several shades of superior rights. Although the number of records available in the case of the Cēra kingdom is too limited to make any precise generalization, the picture of land relations obtaining there presents a slightly more complex and presumably more evolved structure than what we found in the Pallava and Pāṇḍya situations. However, there is a major difference in Kerala as we do not come across the strong non-Brāhmaṇa peasant proprietors who characterize the agrarian structure of the rest of south India.

Coming to the situation in the Cōḻa country, we are in a much better position on account of the vast amount of evidence and the varied literature on the subject. Long before Nilakanta Sastri had published his studies on the Cōḻa history, K.M. Gupta had completed his work on the land system in south India between 800 and 1200 AD.[23] Starting from Gupta till the most recent publication of R. Tirumalai on land grants and agrarian relations/reactions in Cōḻa and Pāṇḍya times, a vast body of literature has grown around this topic. Among them the most significant ones either for the new light they shed or for the refreshing questions they raise are those by D.N. Jha,[24] Y. Subbarayalu,[25] N. Karashima,[26] Dharma Kumar,[27] and R. Tirumalai.[28]

The systematic analysis of epigraphic material undertaken by Noboru Karashima presents a pattern of the evolution of tenurial rights on land. In the studies of earlier historians and those who followed their frame of reference it is the land relations in the *brahmadēya* type of villages that had received greater attention. Karashima takes up the question in relation to the non-*brahmadēya* villages also.[29] This is important in two respects. For one thing, since the non-*brahmadēya* villages were more ancient than the *brahmadēya* villages, they have a greater significance in a study of the historical development of tenurial rights over land. Second, as we have seen, since the non-*brahmadēya* villages far out-numbered the *brahmadēyas*, the basic determinant of the social relations will have to be looked for in the relations of production in such villages. In a comparative study of the nature of landed property in a non-*brahmadēya* village and a *brahmadēya* with the help of nine inscriptions from the former and twenty-one from the latter, Karashima argues that private property was not as well developed as it was in the *brahmadēya* villages.[30] Land was held in common by the community in the non-*brahmadēya* villages. In the case of the *brahmadēya* villages there was individual landholding and the landholders and the cultivators were separate entities there. This would suggest that in the beginning of the Cōḻa rule individual holdings of land by non-Brāhmaṇa peasant proprietors were not fully developed. This is supported by further studies made by Karashima and Subbarayalu.[31] In a quantified analysis of details available in the 260 Cōḻa inscriptions registering the sale of land, Subbarayalu has brought out the increasing proportion [of] non-Brāhmaṇa individuals selling land in the four periods of Cōḻa rule in a 1.5 : 4.2 : 7.7 : 37 ratio in percentage. This would show that, in the earlier periods of Cōḻa rule, individual landholding was not common in the non-Brāhmaṇa villages while it became increasingly prevalent in the later years of Cōḻa rule.

In fact, this strong section of non-Brāhmaṇa landed magnates is represented in the Cōḻa records. With the help of the now classic *Concordance of the Names in Cola Inscriptions*, it has been shown that about 20 per cent of the entire population figuring in Cōḻa records bear a name or title signifying the possession of a village, for example, *uḍaiyān, kiḻān, kiḻavan.* This, obviously, means 'possession' of some land in the village. It has been shown that the frequency of such titles goes on increasing as Cōḻa rule progresses, a pattern which conforms to the findings of Subbarayalu in relation to increase in the private ownership of land. This is true of similar titles such as *vēḷān*, *mūvēnta-veḷān*, *araiyan*, and the like, all sported by landed magnates in the Cōḻa country. It has been shown that these landed magnates were identified by the Cōḻa state and co-opted as its agents.[32]

The fact of individual non-Brāhmaṇa landowners being on an increase in the later periods of the Cōḻa rule is further supported by Karashima's examination of a large number of inscriptions recording the sale or donation of land to the Jambukēśvaram temple in Tiruchirappalli.[33] This has yielded significant information about the growth of huge landed magnates owning in certain cases whole villages. Karashima has brought out, significantly, that patterns of landholding in the same village underwent a transformation of this kind. He seeks to explain this phenomenon in the light of two economic factors:

> First, accumulation of wealth brought by the imperialistic expansion of Cōḻa power during the reigns of Rajaraja I and Rajendra I, which was distributed to the people of the heart of the Cōḻa country, the Lower Kavery Valley. Second, an

increase in agricultural productivity was made possible by the introduction of new agricultural techniques such as the construction of dams, the maintenance of water tanks, and channels, etc.[34]

The grant of land on a large scale to secular functionaries of the state on service tenure may have helped in this process. In a further analysis of more inscriptional details, Karashima has laid bare the pattern of some people accumulating large extents of land and becoming big, locally influential, landlords and others losing possession of their land and slipping into the position of tenants and landless cultivators.[35] He has rightly identified in this pattern 'the emergence of a new agrarian order'. Though he is 'still unable to say whether this means the appearance of a feudal system or not, this new agrarian order seems to have brought changes in the relations of many communities belonging to the locality.'[36]

This discussion would dispel any doubts about whether or not there existed private property in land in this period in south India. The weighty evidence presented by Karashima in relation to non-*brahmadēya* villages and non-Brāhmaṇa peasant proprietors has its counterpart in the information concerning individual Brāhmaṇa landowners as well as their corporate bodies such as the *sabhā*, the *pariṣad*, etc. looking after the *brahmadēya* and the *dēvadāna* properties. It is well known that temples had developed into huge landed magnates in this period.[37] In the circumstances, to still support the notion of the Asiatic Mode of Production based on the idea of the absence of private property in land is to close one's eyes towards reality.[38] At the same time, to say that absolute property existed in land will be tantamount to ignoring the various shades of rights that different sets of people enjoyed on the same piece of land, a situation that social anthropologists characterize as multiplexity of rights.[39] That would entail consideration of the structured relationship based on land rights as gleaned from the Cōḻa records.

As in the case of land rights existing in the Pāṇḍyan kingdom, records granting land to *brahmadēyas* in the Cōḻa country also speak of land being granted with the rights of both *kārāṇmai* and *mīyāṭci*. As we saw above, these were, respectively, the rights to cultivate the land and to get it cultivated. Another distinction that one notices in land rights, mostly in the case of non-*brahmadēya* villages, is the almost opposing bipolarity of *kārāṇmai* and *veḷḷāmai*. From the contexts in which the expression *veḷḷāmai* occurs, it would appear that this was the right which could be more or less compared with peasant proprietorship. *Veḷḷāmai*, literally that state of being a *veḷḷāḷa*, is interesting as it is presented as a binary opposite of *kārāṇmai*, literally the state of being a *kārāḷa*.[40] However, the facts of the existence of peasant proprietors and of the increase in the strength and number of such peasant proprietors are beyond dispute.

Again, *kārāṇmai* is seen to be of two different kinds in the situation in the Cōḻa country as elsewhere in the Tamil-speaking region. These are expressed by the phrases *kuṭi nīkki* and *kuṭi nīṅṅā*. In the latter case, the *kuṭi nīṅṅā*, the previous settlers were not to be disturbed. Burton Stein has strangely translated the expression *kuṭi ningaya* to mean an arrangement where 'the previous cultivators are said to have been removed from the land and village at the time of being granted'.[41] R. Tirumalai has shown that even in the *kuṭi nīkki* tenure there was not necessarily a physical eviction of the earlier occupants involved but only a renewal of the terms of occupancy rights.[42] However, this form of tenure may have meant a greater latitude to the new class of intermediaries placed above them, for it is only natural that demands should be enhanced at the time of the renewal of the terms. The same argument is made by Dharma Kumar in her separate study of Cōḻa property rights.[43] In any case, they represented the primary producer with a right over land.

Another element that we come across in the records relating to agrarian relations is the agrestic labour. Given the nature of our records concerned with the upper classes, details about the agrestic labourers are hard to come by. In a masterly analysis of documents pertaining to the villages granted to the Bṛhadīśvara Temple in Tanjavur by Rājarāja I and those granted to the Gaṅgaikkoṇḍacōḻapuram by Vīrarājēndra, it has been shown that in the former list, where forty villages are involved, nineteen of them had a *paṟaiccēri* (separate residential quarters of the *paṟaiyas* who were the agrestic labourers) each and in the latter list involving seven villages there was one, apart from the residential quarters of other communities and occupational groups.[44] Many records speak of the transfer of land together with the labourers attached to it (*āḷadaṅga*).[45] If one can go by the indications in the records, which are heavily biased in favour of the upper sections in society, it would appear that these labourers who present themselves to have had a bonded nature occupied the lowest rung in the hierarchy of land rights. By all indications it was these sections who were made use of in redeeming the obligation to pay the service rent, namely *veṭṭi*.

The following structural representation of the complex relationship obtaining in the world of agrarian relations may be made by summarizing our discussion of the nature of land rights in the Cōḻa country. The king was at the top of the hierarchy with his right, which was exercised occasionally, to appropriate the title to grant land both settled and unsettled and also to create superior rights over it.[46] There were different kinds of hierarchies below him. On the one side there were the large number of *nāḍu* groups which were themselves congeries of peasant villages known as the *ūrs*. Each of these villages had a number of magnates who had a share in the arable land there. To begin with they shared common property in the village, but as time progressed individual peasant proprietors also emerged. Most of them had their land cultivated by labourers attached to their land but it is probable that, in certain cases between them and the labourers, there was another tier of sub-tenants. In another hierarchy below the king were the local chiefs. Either below every chief or directly under the king were the huge landed magnates who came to sport bombastic titles and functioned as the state's agents in the Cōḻa political structure. Below these magnates were their tenants, below them the occupants, and still below them the agrestic labourers. Again, directly below either the king or one of the chiefs were the different kinds of eleemosynary villages such as the *brahmadēya*, the *dēvadāna*, the *paḷḷiccandam*, the *śālābhōgam*, the *kaṇimuṟṟūṭṭu*, and the *veṭṭāppēṟu*. Even in these the tenurial pattern was the same—the *kārāḷas* (tenants), the *kuṭis* (occupants), and the *paṟaiyas* placed one below the other.

This structured relationship of land rights in early medieval south India, beginning to emerge in a rudimentary form under the Pallavas and getting elaborated by the time we come to the Cōḻa state, is seen extending specially to cover the whole of south India. This compares well with the picture of land rights in early medieval north India as outlined by R.S. Sharma.[47] Again, this strikes a favourable comparison with the situation in medieval Europe:

> The tenant who—from father to son, as a rule—ploughs the land and gathers in the crop; his immediate lord, to whom he pays dues and who, in certain circumstances, can resume possession of the land, the lord of the lord, and so on, right up the feudal scale—how many persons there are who can say, each with as much justification as the other, 'That is my field!'[48]

Though one can no longer cling to the idea of the absence of private property in land as the protagonists of the Asiatic Mode of Production would,[49] one cannot be very assertive about the existence of absolute proprietorship over land as Dharma Kumar has tended to suggest in a recent study.[50]

Burton Stein describes this society as a peasant society. His conception is shown to have been taken from economists, sociologists, and anthropologists of varying ideological positions such as Chayanov, Eric Wolf,

Marshall Sahlins, and Theodore Shanin.[51] He completely misses the subject nature of peasantry. The burden of his theoretical assumptions constrains him to stretch the evidences to such an extent as to force him identify an alliance between the Brāhmaṇas and peasants.[52] In reality, however, the case was far from being such an unchanging monolith. We have seen that varying shades of relationships existed between the Brāhmaṇas (themselves not an undifferentiated lot) on the one hand and the different levels of peasantry on the other, varying at different points of time. But stratification within [the] peasantry is one thing which Stein does not recognize at all. As pointed out by D.N. Jha, to speak of massive peasant support to Brāhmaṇas one will have to ignore the solid evidence that comes out of the entire corpus of published Cōḻa inscriptions, which are largely concerned with arrangements about land; there are only seven identifiable cases of *veḷḷāḷa* peasants granting lands to Brāhmaṇas.[53] The picture that we have seen above is that of a structured relationship where the land-owning class, both Brāhmaṇa and *veḷḷāḷa*, occupied the upper stratum exploiting the surplus in agricultural produce by cultivating tenants and agricultural labourers.

Such a structured society with a graded hierarchy of infinite variations in status based on the extent of control over the means of production found its expression in the *jāti* formula. Based on the near total absence of caste designations for those other than Brāhmaṇas named in the temple records of the Cōḻas, B. Suresh has argued that 'the caste system had not yet set'.[54] This confusion is comparable to a similar one in the case of Cēra records from Kerala where, again based on the absence of caste suffixes, Elamkulam P.N. Kunjan Pillai argued that several temple committee members were non-Brāhmaṇas.[55] In the latter case, the researches of M.G.S. Narayanan and the present writer have shown that this is a clear misunderstanding.[56] Even in the case of the Cōḻa country, Subbarayalu has shown that a large number of occupational groups identified in so many words as belonging to different castes make their appearance in the records.[57]

This *jāti* formula, which articulated social stratification, had the contact of each caste with the Brāhmaṇa as the point of reference in fixing the social and ritual status, the assumption there being that the Brāhmaṇas constituted the highest caste. But in reality we see that the *veḷḷāḷa* caste, which is identified significantly as of the Śūdra *varṇa*, is seen to be enjoying an almost equal status with the Brāhmaṇa caste on account of the control of land they had. For instance, in making important decisions concerning land-revenue and allied matters, these two groups are always mentioned together in a premier position. An inscription from Uttaramērūr, recording a decision of the *sabhā* relating to fines to be collected from different castes, gives the following order: Brāhmaṇa, Śiva-Brāhmaṇa, *kaṇakkar*, *veḷḷāḷa* and others.[58] The equal prominence given to Brāhmaṇa and *veḷḷāḷa* is brought out by a couple of records from Mannārguḍi,[59] one dated AD 1118 and the other AD 1239. However, the fixing of the ritual status was always with reference to the contact with the Brāhmaṇas. An inscription of Rājarāja I, dated AD 1002, orders that the landholdings of the members of all castes below the Brāhmaṇas (*Brāhmaṇarkku kīḻapaṭṭa jātikaḷil*) should be sold away in the particular Brāhmaṇa village.[60] This reference certainly includes the *veḷḷāḷas* also, for they were the most prominent landholders.

There is a major lacuna in our sources that we do not get a true picture of the caste hierarchy because, given their concerns, the inscriptions in the temples do not identify the large number of persons mentioned in them by their castes. This is only natural considering the purpose of those records. Thus while the statistical method may be very systematic, in view of the above difficulty in relation to the sources there is the likelihood that one is misled by the results of such analyses. For instance, Y. Subbarayalu has calculated that in the Cōḻa inscriptions the highest frequency of caste obtains in the case of the cattle-keepers or *manṟāḍis* (228/663) while the Brāhmaṇas (110/663), the *veḷḷāḷas* (76/663), and others occupy a much lower position.[61] If one were to go blindly after such analyses, the conclusion might be that the cattle-keepers were more than twice as important as the Brāhmaṇas and three times as the *veḷḷāḷas*! But when it is realized that a large number of temple inscriptions are concerned with the endowment of livestock for the maintenance of 'perpetual lamps', the role of a large number of individual cattle-keepers entrusted with the upkeep of such animals in the inscriptions can be appreciated. It is not as if pastoralism was thrice as strong as agriculture! However, even this methodology is far superior to the kind of impressionistic, speculative argument of Suresh and Kunjan Pillai mentioned above.

We have seen that the Brāhmaṇas occupied the highest position in the *jāti* hierarchy. This is only natural. For one thing, *jāti* was a Brāhmaṇical paradigm at least in the historical context in south India. Second, they were not only among the most powerful in terms of economic resources but also as the custodians of religious ideas and institutions centring around the temples which were themselves huge landed magnates. Second to the Brāhmaṇas in the ritual status were the *veḷḷāḷas* who, on account of their land control, occupied an equally influential position in society. Irfan Habib has marvelled that the *veḷḷāḷa* peasants were not accorded the Vaiśya status.[62] This is not necessary. By the period of our study, the *varṇa* principle had become at best a mere theoretical construct irrespective of the question whether or not it ever had any real significance as a representation of social stratification even in northern India. Second, the Vaiśyas, like the Kṣatriyas, even as a category, have not migrated in numbers to south India, and hence one cannot expect a network of the group representing the Vaiśya *varṇa* there such as it was in northern India. Thus it is natural that these peasants of all grades were designated to the residual category of the Śūdras. At the same time not all of them were subjected to the kind of disabilities that the Śūdras in northern India had been[63] for the obvious reason that the *veḷḷāḷa* peasantry constituted a major force as the owners of the means of production. In fact, many of them were granted the status of *satśūdras*, a curious category by the standards of the *varṇa*. This is evidence enough to show that although social stratification expressed itself in the *jāti* formula, the determinant factor was not caste nor the various shades of connection with the priestly class. On the contrary, it was the control of the means of production in the case of both agriculture and trade that decided the status. This would call into question Romila Thapar's assertion that 'what was immutable in Indian society was … caste'.[64]

In accommodating the semi-tribal population that was getting transformed into peasants, and other occupational groups into so many *jātis*, the model that was followed was the one prescribed by the *Dharmaśāstras*, that is, that of the *saṅkīrṇajātis*. This allowed for the infinite variations in the graded hierarchy of ritual and social status. Thus we have the different artisan groups being identified as various *saṅkīrṇajātis*. There are also cases of the same artisanal group being given different *jāti* statuses on different occasions, showing thereby that there was nothing rigid about it except the principle. Once this principle was accepted the tribes living in the twilight zones were brought under it and assigned to particular castes. The Paḷḷi, the Curutimān, the Kaḷḷar, the Maṟavar, and so on, from the tenth century AD onwards, start getting known as so many castes.[65]

Irfan Habib has raised an important question, 'given the structure of the caste system, who were its chief beneficiaries?'.[66] The truistic answer, that it was the Brāhmaṇas, has been often given by historians including Kosambi and sociologists like Dumont. However, Habib has tried to look at the economic consequences of caste in a different way,

By its repression of the menial castes, it cheapened labour available for agriculture. At the village level, by providing especially for the services of hereditary village artisans and servants, it reduced the necessary expense on the tools, goods, and services that the peasant needed. By thus reducing the portion of agriculture needed for the peasant's subsistence, it enlarged the surplus product, out of which the revenues of the ruling class came. At the same time through hereditary skill-transmission, caste cheapened artisan-products, and thus reduced wage-costs generally. The primary economic consequence of the caste system was, then, a substantial enlargement of the income of the ruling class from both agriculture and crafts.[67]

Thus, within the existing social formation, the standardization of stratification through the *jāti* formula became very handy for the upper classes in society for whom this social institution had a tremendous significance in terms of their interest of the maximization of revenue. This is, however, not to suggest that a crude application of such a calculated material interest was adopted by the powers that be. On the contrary, the acceptance of this formula of social stratification by all sections of society was achieved by subtler means. This took the form of religious ideology which went a long way in validating the stratified social order.[68]

## NOTES

1 K.A. Nilakanta Sastri, *The Cōḻas*, Madras, 1975, p. 508.

2 Ibid.

3 A. Appadorai, *Economic Conditions in Southern India (1000–1500 AD)*, Madras, 1936; C. Minakshi, *Administration and Social Life under the Pallavas*, Madras, 1938; T.V. Mahalingam, *South Indian Polity*, Madras, 1955.

4 Burton Stein, *Peasant State and Society in Medieval South India*, Delhi, 1980.

5 Burton Stein, 'The State and Agrarian Order in Medieval South India: A Historiographical Critique', in Burton Stein (ed.), *Essays on South India*, Delhi, 1975.

6 Stein, *Peasant State and Society*, Preface.

7 Ibid.

8 See R. Champakalakshmi, 'Peasant State and Society in Medieval South India: A Review Article', *Indian Economic and Social History Review*, vol. XVIII, nos 3–4, 1981, pp. 411–27; Rajan Gurukkal, 'The Agrarian System and Socio-Political Organisation under the Early Pandyas *c.* AD 600–1000', unpublished PhD thesis, Jawaharlal Nehru University, New Delhi, 1984; D.N. Jha, *Studies in Early Indian Economic History*, Delhi, 1980; D.N. Jha, 'Relevance of "Peasant State and Society" to Pallava–Chola Times', *Indian Historical Review*, vol. VIII, nos 1–2, 1981–1982, pp. 74–94; Noboru Karashima, *South Indian History and Society: Studies from Inscriptions AD 859–1800*, Delhi, 1984; M.G.S. Narayanan, *The Perumals of Kerala: Political and Social Conditions of Kerala under the Cera Perumals of Makotai (c. AD*

*800–1124)*, Calicut, 1996; Y. Subbarayalu, 'The State in Medieval South India', unpublished PhD thesis, Madurai Kamaraj University, Madurai, 1976.
9 T.N. Subrahmanyan (ed.), *Thirty Pallava Copper Plates,* Madras, 1966, p. 29, l.53; p. 166, l.107; p. 187, ll.20–1.
10 Ibid., p. 166, l.106; p. 187, l.20.
11 R. Tirumalai, *Land Grants and Agrarian Relations in Cola and Pandya Times,* Madras, 1987, pp. 93–8.
12 L.B. Alayev, 'An Interpretation of Terms Dealing with Land and Revenue (Rent) Rights in South Indian Inscriptions (AD 900–1300)', paper presented at the Workshop on 'Socio-Economic Terms in Ancient and Medieval Indian Inscriptions', organized by Indian Council of Historical Research, Mysore, 1989.
13 Subrahmanyan (ed.), *Thirty Pallava Copper Plates.* See also C. Minakshi, *Administration and Social Life*, but she does not appreciate the significance of such alienation.
14 Gurukkal, 'The Agrarian System', pp. 109–25.
15 Cf. D.D. Kosambi, *An Introduction to the Study of Indian History,* Bombay, 1956, p. 323.
16 *South Indian Inscriptions*, vol. XIV, no. 95.
17 Cf. D.C. Sircar, *Indian Epigraphical Glossary,* Delhi, 1966.
18 Gurukkal, 'The Agrarian System', p. 113 n2.
19 See Stein, *Peasant State and Society*, pp. 167–8.
20 Gurukkal, 'The Agrarian System', p. 135, diagram.
21 Narayanan, *Perumals of Kerala.* See the chapter on 'Economic Conditions' under Land Tenures.
22 M.G.S. Narayanan, 'The Traditional Land System of Kerala: Problems of Change and Perspective', paper presented to the Logan Centenary Seminar on Land Reforms in Kerala, Calicut, 1981.
23 K.M. Gupta, 'The Land System of South India between about 800 and 1200 AD', Lahore, 1933 (completed as a PhD thesis in 1926, London University).
24 Jha, *Studies in Early Indian Economic History.*
25 Subbarayalu, 'The State in Medieval South India'.
26 Karashima, *South Indian History.*
27 Dharma Kumar, 'Private Property in Asia? The Case of Medieval South India', *Comparative Studies in Society and History,* vol. 27, no. 2, 1985, pp. 340–66.
28 Tirumalai, *Land Grants.*
29 Karashima, *South Indian History,* pp. 1–35.
30 Ibid., p. 12.
31 Ibid., pp. 15–35; Y. Subbarayalu, 'Quantification of Inscriptional Data with Special Reference to the Study of Property Rights in Medieval Tamilnadu', paper presented at the Symposium on 'Quantitative Methods in Indian Historiography' organized by the Indian History Congress, Dharwad, 1988.
32 For a fuller discussion on how landed magnates were identified as state agents in the Cōḷa country, see Kesavan Veluthat, *The Political Structure of Early Medieval South India,* New Delhi, 1993, chapter III, 'The King and His Men'; also, Kesavan Veluthat, 'Landed Magnates as State Agents: The Gavudas under the Hoysalas in Karnataka', *Proceedings of the Indian History Congress,* Gorakhpur, 1989, for testing the model in the context of medieval Karnataka.

33 Karashima, *South Indian History*, chapter II.
34 Ibid., p. 20.
35 Ibid., pp. 26–7.
36 Ibid., p. 31.
37 Jha, *Studies in Early Indian Economic History*, pp. 74–89.
38 This is what Kathleen Gough does in 'Modes of Production in Southern India', *Economic and Political Weekly*, vol. XV, nos 5–7 (annual number), February 1980, pp. 337–64.
39 Kumar, 'Private Property'.
40 *Kārāḷa* is generally translated as peasant, tenant, etc.; the etymology being not clear. Is it possible to derive it from Sanskrit *karṣaka*? In that case, he would be a cultivating tenant which indeed he appears to have been. *Kār* in the Dravidian languages signifies black and *veḷ* is white. Could therefore *veḷḷāḷa* be treated as the opposite of *kārāḷa*, that is, a peasant proprietor? In any case, *veḷḷāḷa* was one.
41 Stein, *Peasant State*, p. 168, note 74.
42 Tirumalai, *Land Grants*, pp. 93–8.
43 Kumar, 'Private Property'.
44 Karashima, *South Indian History*, pp. 44–5; Chart 1.
45 This is a common feature in the Pāṇḍya, Cēra, and Cōḷa records.
46 For a fuller discussion, see Veluthat, *The Political Structure of Early Medieval South India*, chapter III.
47 R.S. Sharma, *Indian Feudalism*, Delhi, 1980.
48 Marc Bloch, *Feudal Society* (tr. L.A. Manyon), vol. II, London, 1961, p. 116.
49 Gough, 'Modes of Production'.
50 Kumar, 'Private Property'.
51 Jha, 'Relevance of "Peasant State and Society"', pp. 74–5.
52 Stein, *Peasant State*, chapters II and III.
53 Jha, *Studies in Early Indian Economic History*, pp. 78–9.
54 B. Suresh, 'Historical and Cultural Geography and Ethnology of South India (with special reference to Chola Inscriptions)', unpublished PhD thesis, Deccan College, Poona, 1965.
55 P.N. Kunjan Pillai, *Janmisampradayam Keralattil*, Kottayam, 1959, pp. 18–50.
56 Narayanan, *Perumals of Kerala*, chapters on 'Police and Revenue' and 'Social Systems'; Kesavan Veluthat, 'Aryan Brahman Settlements of Ancient Kerala', unpublished MA dissertation, Calicut University, Calicut, 1974, Appendix II.
57 Subbarayalu, *The State*, p. 86 (Table).
58 *Epigraphia Indica*, vol. XXII, no. 33.
59 *South Indian Inscriptions*, vol. VI, no. 57; nos 48, 50, 58.
60 Ibid., vol. V, no. 1409.
61 Subbarayalu, *The State*, p. 86.
62 Irfan Habib, 'The Peasant in Indian History' (General President's Address), *Proceedings of the Indian History Congress*, Kurukshetra, 1982.
63 For the disabilities which the Śūdras in northern India were subjected to, see R.S. Sharma, *Śūdras in Ancient India*, Delhi, 1980.
64 Romila Thapar, *A History of India*, vol. I, Harmondsworth, 1968, p. 77. Thapar takes a position different from Kosambi, *An Introduction*, pp. 313–14.
65 For a list of the different *jātis*, see Subbarayalu, *The State*, pp. 84–111.

66 Irfan Habib, *Interpreting Indian History*, Shillong (n.d.), p. 19.
67 Ibid., p. 20.
68 M.G.S. Narayanan and Kesavan Veluthat, 'The Bhakti Movement in South India' in S.C. Malik (ed.), *Dissent, Protest, and Reform in Indian Civilization*, Simla, 1978, have argued that the bhakti movement in south India was an attempt to standardize and legitimize this kind of a social stratification, the upper sections providing the necessary ideological bulwark.

# 5

# *Nagaram*

## *Commerce and Towns* AD *850–1350**

Noboru Karashima, Y. Subbarayalu, and P. Shanmugam

Royal orders of the Chola state engraved on copper plates and recording grant of land/village to Brahmanas or temples or some other matters concerning a certain locality are usually addressed to *nāṭṭār* (representatives of the *nāḍu* from *veḷḷān-vagai* villages called *ūr*), *brahmadēya-kiḻavar* (representatives of *brahmadēya*), *ūrār* (representatives of *ūr*) of *dēvadāna, paḷḷichchanda, kaṇimuṟṟūṭṭu* villages, and *nagarattār* (representatives of *nagaram*). *Nāḍu* is a basic topographical and territorial unit in which the agricultural production was organized, and *brahmadēya*, *ūr* and *nagaram* are categories of village and town included in *nāḍu*. *Brahmadēya* is the village granted to Brahmanas, and *ūr* includes both the *veḷḷān-vagai* village controlled by the *Vellala* landholders and the villages granted to Hindu temples (*dēvadāna*), those to Buddhist or Jain temples (*paḷḷichchanda*), and those granted to astrologers (*kaṇimuṟṟūṭṭu*). *Nagaram*, same as the Sanskrit *nagara*, is the town.

In the past socio-economic studies of ancient and medieval south India, historians including K.R. Hall and R. Champakalakshmi have paid due attention to *nagarams* in relation to the development of commerce, trade, and urbanization, since the *nagaram* is the town in which merchants lived and carried out their activities.[1] Notwithstanding their

*Previously published in Noboru Karashima, *South Indian Society in Transition: Ancient to Medieval*, New Delhi, Oxford University Press, 2009, pp. 165–95. Originally published in *The Indian Historical Review*, vol. 35, no. 1, 2008, pp. 1–33.

efforts, however, the full picture of the *nagaram* has not yet been depicted, as the text-publication of most of the relevant Tamil inscriptions remains very unsatisfactory. In this essay, therefore, we have examined many unpublished inscriptions[2] also to gather more information on activities of the *nagarattār*. We have tried to find out the general tendency of activities of the *nagarattār* and merchants by dividing our study period into three sub-periods, that is, the early (850–1000), the middle (1001–1200), and the late (1201–1350) sub-periods. For the topographical distribution of *nagarams* found in inscriptions of the period, see Map 5.1.

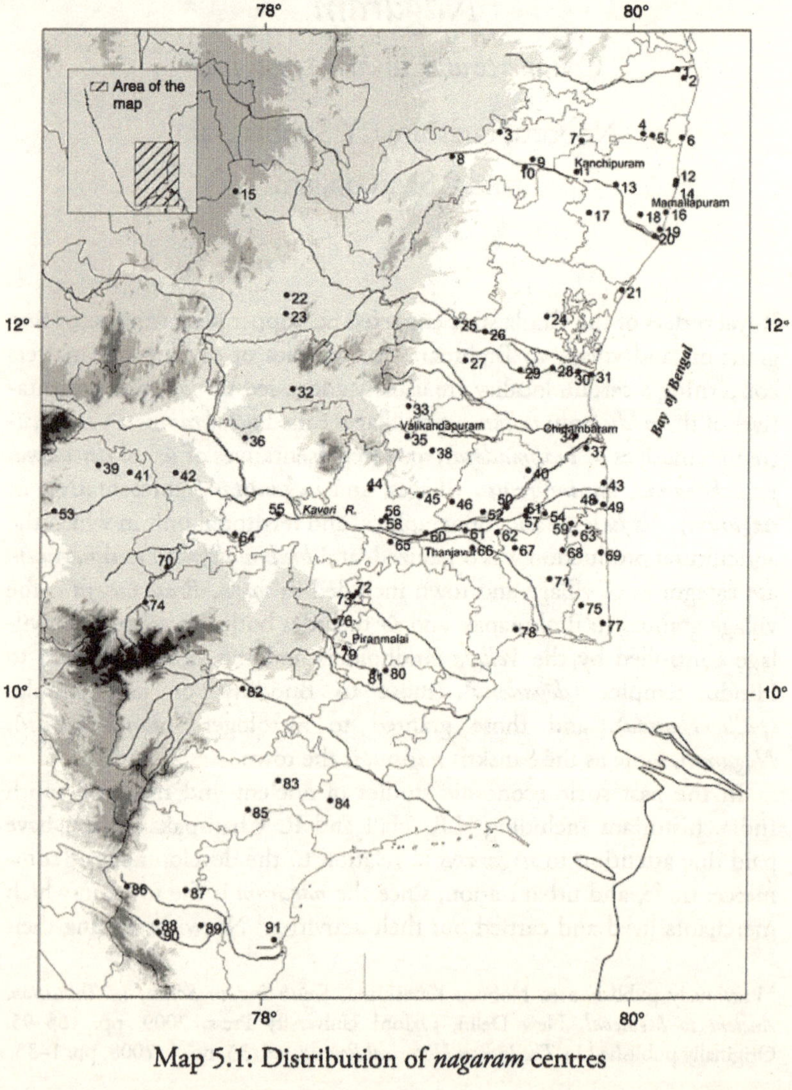


Map 5.1: Distribution of *nagaram* centres

## INDEX TO MAP

| *No.* | *Nagaram* | *No.* | *Nagaram* | *No.* | *Nagaram* |
|---|---|---|---|---|---|
| 1 | Tiruppalaivanam | 32 | Salem | 63 | Tirukkannapuram |
| 2 | Kattur | 33 | Aragalur | 64 | Chinnadharapuram |
| 3 | Melpadi | 34 | Chidambaram | 65 | Tiruchirrappalli |
| 4 | Tirumalisai | 35 | Venganur | 66 | Thanjavur |
| 5 | Puntamalli | 36 | Tiruchengodu | 67 | Kovil Venni |
| 6 | Mayilappur | 37 | Achchapuram | 68 | Tiruvarur |
| 7 | Takkolam | 38 | Valikandapuram | 69 | Nagapattinam |
| 8 | Virinchipuram | 39 | Annur | 70 | Dalavaypattinam |
| 9 | Kaverippakkam | 40 | Gangaikondacholapuram | 71 | Kottur |
| 10 | Sakkaramallur | 41 | Avinasi | 72 | Kodumbalur |
| 11 | Kanchipuram | 42 | Vijayamangalam | 73 | Kovilpatti |
| 12 | Kovalam | 43 | Kavirippumpattinam | 74 | Kotumam |
| 13 | Palur | 44 | Singalantapuram | 75 | Kalyanapurangonda-pattinam |
| 14 | Tiruvidandai | 45 | Uttatur | | |
| 15 | Hosur | 46 | Melappaluvur | 76 | Tuvarankurichi |
| 16 | Mamallapuram | 47 | Paiuvur | 77 | Vedaranyam |
| 17 | Uttaramerur | 48 | Tillaiyadi | 78 | Adirampattinam |
| 18 | Tirukkalukunram | 49 | Tarangampadi | 79 | Piranmalai |
| 19 | Saturangappattinam | 50 | Tiruppurambiyam | 80 | Pillaiyarpatti |
| 20 | Vayalur | 51 | Tribhuvanam | 81 | Tiruppattur |
| 21 | Marakkanam | 52 | Kamarasavalli | 82 | Vikkiramangalam |
| 22 | Kadagattur | 53 | Perur | 83 | Aruppukkottai |
| 23 | Adiyamankottai | 54 | Konerirajapuram | 84 | Kamudi |
| 24 | Vikkiravandi | 55 | Karur | 85 | Sattur |
| 25 | Jambai | 56 | Tiruvellarai | 86 | Kuttalam |
| 26 | Kilur (Tirukkoyilur) | 57 | Tirunagesvaram | 87 | Ukkirankottai |
| 27 | Rishivandhyam | 58 | Tiruppangili | 88 | Mannarkoil |
| 28 | Tiruvadi | 59 | Koyil Tirumalam | 89 | Tirunelveli |
| 29 | Tirunamanallur | 60 | Anbil | 90 | Kallidaikkurichi |
| 30 | Tiruvendiram | 61 | Tiruvaiyaru | 91 | Korkai |
| 31 | Kadalur | 62 | Tirukkarugavur | | |

One of the important points of our study is the relations among the *nagarattār* who were supposed to have been local merchants, the itinerant merchants who were organized in such supra-local merchant guilds as *maṇigirāmam* (*maṇigrāmam*) or *aiñūṟṟuvar*, and the state. In other words, what were the relations between the *nagaram* and the state; the merchant guild and the state; and the *nagaram* and the merchant guild? Though it is rather difficult to answer all of these questions satisfactorily in this study, we have tackled the issue of trade and commercial settlements, holding these questions in mind.

In relation to the above questions, a reference to the recent trends in the studies of urbanization of medieval Europe may be relevant here. Though the focal points in the past studies were the revival of long-distance trade for the true urbanization of the medieval period, and the medieval communes as the product of deliberate strivings towards modern democracy, recent stress is more on natural and multi-linear urbanization discarding the idea to discover anything new in the development of towns. Supporting a feudalistic interpretation of medieval Europe, R.H. Hilton admits the difference between villages and towns, but he regards both as integral parts in the feudalistic structure and does not find the role of the medieval town separate and antagonistic within feudal society.[3] S. Reynolds, who is strongly against the use of the concept of feudalism, does not find much difference between villages and towns, or any revolutionary ideas in the medieval community. She asserts that the basis of urban community, like the basis of community in nucleated agricultural settlements, was geographical propinquity, fortified by the traditional practices of law and local government.[4] In this study also we have kept these points in mind.

## *NAGARAMS* IN THE EARLY PERIOD (850–1000)

### *Nagaram* and *Nāḍu*

The relation of *nagaram* to *nāḍu*, namely, how many *nagarams* existed in one *nāḍu*, has been an issue discussed by previous scholars. According to Hall, there was a maximum of one *nagaram* for each *nāḍu* in Chola times.[5] R. Champakalakshmi accepted this as generally true but at the same time she pointed out that there is also evidence of more than one *nagaram* in some *nāḍus*.[6] Our examination of inscriptions also supports the latter point. Puraiyur-nadu in South Arcot district had two towns, in which the existence of a *nagaram* in an interval of fifty years can be verified from inscriptions. The two towns and inscriptions which refer to a *nagaram* in the town are Paravaipuram *Annual Report on South Indian Epigraphy* [*ARE* hereafter], 1917-319: SA, Panaiyakulam, 1058) and Bhuvanamanikkapuram (*ARE*, 1915-285: SA, Vikkiravandi, 1102).

If we take the period of existence of more than one *nagaram* in one and the same *nāḍu* longer than fifty years but less than 200 years, we find a few more *nāḍus*. Tiraimur-nadu in the Kumbakonam area had two towns, namely Kumaramattandapuram and Tiruvidaimarudur, and inscriptions of Tirunagesvaram (*South Indian Inscriptions* [*SII* hereafter], iii-91: Tj) and Tiruvidaimarudur (*SII*, xxiii-200: Tj) testify to the existence of *nagaram* in these towns in 873 and 1016 respectively. Likewise, Umbala-nadu in the Vedaranyam area had three towns in which *nagaram* existed respectively in *c.* 970 (*TASSI*, 1958/59, pp. 84–110), in 1137 (*SII*, xvii-463), and in 1210 (*SII*, xvii-458), and Oyma-nadu (Tirunallur-nadu) in the Tindivanam area of South Arcot district also had two such towns in 964 (*SII*, xiii-169) and in 1021 (*ARE*, 1913-253 and -254).

As regards the numerical relation of *nagaram* to *nāḍu*, however, the available evidence is not so explicit. An analysis of the large corpus of inscriptions available for Chola-mandalam, the central part of the Chola state, shows that many *nāḍus* do not have *nagaram* settlements.[7] A quick glance at the tables of *nagarams* given by Hall and Champakalakshmi provided in their respective works would themselves suggest that there were several *nāḍus* without any *nagaram*. Champakalakshmi's table (IV), which has been more systematically made, shows that there were only ninety-two *nāḍus* in the entire Tamil Nadu with a *nagaram* during one or more of the five periods from 600 to 1350.[8]

As stated above, *nāḍu* was a basic topographical and territorial unit in which the agricultural production was organized and the number of *nagarams* included in one *nāḍu* is a crucial point for understanding the function of *nagaram* in the state economic policy as well as its local administration. Though there is evidence to reveal that the Chola kings encouraged the establishment of new *nagaram* settlements in certain places from the eleventh century onwards, it seems that there was no deliberate state policy to make one *nagaram* in each and every *nāḍu*. In these circumstances the obvious conclusion would be that a *nagaram* served several *nāḍus*, localities to say, as a marketing or commercial centre. It neither seems to have had much importance in local administration unlike the *brahmadēya* that played an important role in local administration.[9]

The survey of inscriptions referring to the *nagaram*, though tentative, shows the following distribution of *nagarams* in the Tamil country for the three sub-periods of this study (see Table 5.1). The increase in number of the *nagarams* from period I to period II may be explained in two ways. First, it is the effect of the increase in the number of inscriptions themselves, and second, it reflects the active nature of *nagaram* in

Table 5.1 *Nagaram*

| *Period/District* | *I* | *II* | *III* | *Total* |
|---|---|---|---|---|
| Cg | 3 | 13 | 4 | 15 |
| SA | 6 | 10 | 5 | 10 |
| NA | 3 | 6 | 1 | 7 |
| Tj | 7 | 7 | 6 | 18 |
| Tp | 5 | 5 | 11 | 18 |
| Pd | 1 | 5 | 8 | 12 |
| Cb | | | 2 | 2 |
| Rd | 1 | | 4 | 5 |
| Md | | 1 | 2 | 2 |
| Sl | 1 | | 2 | 2 |
| Tn | 1 | 1 | 8 | 9 |
| | 28 | 48 | 53 | 100 |

period II.[10] In the last column is given the district-wise total excluding the period-wise repetition of one and the same *nagaram*.[11]

## Recipient of Money

The first thing we notice while reading inscriptions of the early Chola period concerning *nagarams* is the frequent appearance of *nagarattār* (people of the *nagaram* as a corporate body) as the recipients of money donated to temples. For example, a Tiruvadi inscription (*SII*, viii-308: SA, 885) records that an *arayan* title-holder[12] deposited eighty *kaḷañju* of gold to the *nagarattār* of Adiaraiyamangalam for repairing a temple and for burning a perpetual lamp in the temple. The interest from the money deposited would be used for that purpose. Another Tiruvadi inscription (*SII*, xii-71: SA, 887) records that the same *nagarattār* received 750 *kaḷañju* of gold from Varagunamaharaja, a Pandyan king, to offer four sacred meals daily to the deity of the temple with the interest from that money. A Kilur inscription (*SII*, vii-926: SA, 887) records that the *nagarattār* of Tirukkovalur received thirty-two *kaḷañju* of gold from a donor to feed three persons for the maintenance of a flower-garden in the temple.

While the above three inscriptions all date to the latter half of the ninth century, we have some inscriptions for the tenth century also. Three Tiruvaiyaru inscriptions (*SII*, v-541: Tj, 921; *SII*, v-543: 950 and *SII*, v-542: 955) record that the *nagarattār* of Sivapuri received gold from donors, including a Chola queen, to supply oil for burning a lamp in Tiruvaiyaru temple. A Tiruppalanam inscription (*SII*, xix-105: Tj, 986) records that *nagarattār* of Tiruppalanam received gold from an arayan for burning a lamp, and a Melappaluvur inscription (*SII*, xix-105: Tp, 986) records the promise made by two *nagarattārs* to burn a lamp in the temple with the money they received.

There are many Chola inscriptions recording similar deposit of money with other corporate bodies such as *sabhā* or *ūr* for some charity deeds including temple repairs and conducting a festival, but none of those inscriptions, including the ones relating to *nagaram*, give us any information on how they secured interest from the money deposited. Even though the *nagaram's* way of profit-making was presumably different from those of the *sabhā* and *ūr*, the function of the *nagaram* in supporting charity deeds in the locality by providing interest was not different at all from that of other corporate bodies, which, as bodies of landholders, were mainly concerned with agriculture.

## State Control

The second thing we notice is the control of *nagaram*'s activities by the Chola state. For example, a Tillasthanam inscription (*SII*, v-588: Tj, 932) records that a king's officer investigating temple affairs (*śrīkāriyam ārāykinṟa*) imposed a fine on the people who did not attend the committee (*vāriyam*) meeting of the *nagaram*.[13] Another Tillasthanam inscription (*SII*, v-592: 950) records a similar case in which another officer investigating temple affairs imposed fines on an accountant of the *nagaram*, a shroff, and an oil supplier for some mischief. These inscriptions, particularly the former, clearly indicate that *nagarams* were placed under the strict vigilance of the state.[14]

Though a bit different from direct state control, a Melappaluvur inscription (*SII*, xiii-208: Tp, 966) tells us that a local chief agreed to collect fines in Avanigandharvapuram in the way practised in the old Nandipuram (a town near Palaiyaru, the old Chola royal centre) and that the *nagarattār* of Avanigandharvapuram had this order engraved on stone. A similar case is recorded in another inscription (*SII*, xiii-215: 967) of Melappaluvur. These inscriptions seem to suggest that these *nagarams* were able to get concessions from the local chief in the payment of fine, but they also reveal that *nagarams* were under state control and that they did not enjoy freedom to the extent some medieval towns in Europe and Japan did.

## Temple Management

There are many inscriptions which show us that the *nagarattār* cooperated with state officers, temple authorities, and corporate bodies such as *sabhā* and *ūr*, in the management of temples. A Tiruvidaimarudur inscription (*SII*, v-721: Tj, 934) states that an officer investigating temple affairs, *sabhaiyār* of Tiraimur, *nagarattār* of Tiruvidaimarudil, temple representatives, and temple priests, gathering in a temple hall, decided to assign a plot of land to the drummer who beat drums during the procession of the deity. Another Tiruvidaimarudur inscription (*SII*, iii-124: 950) records that on the occasion of the renovation of a temple, the people of similar composition, including *nagarattār* and a state officer, decided to re-engrave on a new stone the record of lamp-burning engraved on an old discarded stone.

There are two more Tiruvidaimarudur inscriptions which record similar transactions. According to one (*SII*, v-716: 959), Tiraimur *sabhaiyār*, Tiruvidaimarudil *nagarattār*, temple representatives, and an officer investigating temple affairs decided to assign a number of girls to various services in the temple, and the other (*SII*, v-718: 960) tells us that the same five bodies decided to assign a plot of temple land to a dancer for his dancing service in the temple. The officers appearing in these two transactions have the title of *pallavaraiyan* (716) and *mūvēndavēḷān* (718) respectively, indicating their high status. A copper-plate inscription, called Madras Museum Plates (*SII*, iii-128: 986), of Uttamachola records the royal order concerning the management of a Kanchipuram temple. Four groups (*nagarams*) of *sāliyar* who weave royal cloth living in four streets in Kanchipuram were assigned the work of supervising the temple management such as the realization of the interest on the temple money deposited with outsiders.

## *Nagarattār* as Landholders

There are some inscriptions which suggest that *nagarattār* held land in their town. A Tiruvaiyaru inscription (*SII*, v-535: Tj, 892) seems to record, though not clearly owing to damage to the stone, that *nagarattār* transferred the land they had reclaimed in their town for the purpose of burning a lamp. A Tiruvidaimarudur inscription (*SII*, v-713: Tj, 942) records that a pallavaraiyan purchased twenty *vēli* of land from Tiraimur *sabhaiyār* and Tiruvidaimarudil *nagarattār* and donated it to a temple for various services, including feeding Brahmanas in the temple. A Tiruvaiyaru inscription (*SII*, xiii-116: Tj, 950) seems to record, though not clearly owing to damage, that a lady purchased land from Sivapuri-*nagarattār* for twenty-five *kaḷañju* and donated it to the temple, making it free from taxes.

The Madras Museum Plates examined above also reveal that the temple purchased land from the *nagarattār*. From these, therefore, we can presume that *nagarattār* who were primarily merchants were also landholders, which suggests that there was no substantial difference between *nagaram* (town) and ūr (village) in this respect, too. As to the landholdings by *nagarattārs*, though it is not clear whether they held land individually or jointly as a corporate body, we find in the middle-period inscriptions a case of common landholding (Melpadi) and two possible cases of periodical redistribution of land (Mamallapuram and Tirukkonam), as will be seen later.[15]

## Communities, Professions, and Guilds

There are some inscriptions which reveal the professions of *nagarattār* or the communities engaged in commerce. A Tiruvaiyaru inscription (*SII*, v-530: Tj, 911) records the donation of land to a temple by a ruby merchant of a bazaar in Thanjavur. He must have been a member of the *nagarattār*.[16] A Tillasthanam inscription (*SII*, v-583: Tj, 950) records that a big merchant (*mānāyan*) of the *saṅkarapāḍi* community received thirty *kaḷañju* of gold from a Pandyan queen and allotted ten *kaḷañju* each to three *saṅkarapāḍis* of the village for burning lamps in the temple. During the tenth and eleventh centuries *saṅkarapāḍi* seems to have denoted either the individual oil merchant or the guild of oil merchants and not the *jāti*. The Madras Museum Plates give mention to them together with *sāliyar* who were weavers.

An Uttaramallur inscription (*SII*, vi-295: Cg, 922) reveals an interesting thing, namely the local *sabhā*'s decision on the election of shroffs (*pon kāṇpār*) of their village. According to it, *māḍavīdiyār* (merchants living in the street of two-storeyed houses), *sēnai* (betel-leaf merchants?), and *saṅkarapāḍi* (oil merchants) should elect respectively four, two, and three qualified members of their group. The qualifications relate to age and ability to test the gold. Uttaramallur is the famous *brahmadēya* village where there are a good number of inscriptions recording well-organized corporate activities and the strong control of its *sabhā* in local administration, and this inscription also testifies to the *sabhā*'s control of some economic matter, which in other places would have been dealt with by *nagarattār*. No *nagaram* seems to have been formed in Uttaramallur.

A Valikandapuram inscription (*ARE*, 1964/65-308: Tp, 900), which records the killing of a man by a merchant (*vaḷañjiya*), states that fifteen *kaḷañju* of gold paid by the killer for burning a perpetual lamp for expiation was deposited with two merchant guilds called *maṇigirāmam* and *sēnaiyār*. The killer must have been a member of either *maṇigirāmam* or *sēnaiyār*. According to this inscription, these guilds seem to have composed the bigger *aiyavoḷe* organization called *aiñūṟṟuvar* (five hundred) in Vannadu. A Tillasthanam inscription (*SII*, v-590: Tj, 934) also records donation of land to temple by a merchant (*viyāpāri*) of Adittapuram-*maṇigirāmam*. The land was forfeited to him without being redeemed by two Brahmanas who had borrowed money from him submitting their land for surety.

Though some detailed information on the *maṇigirāmam* is obtainable from a few Kerala inscriptions, many references to *maṇigirāmams* are found in the inscriptions of Pudukkottai district and other interior places in this period. *Aiñūṟṟuvar* appears in a Tiruvidaimarudur inscription (*SII*, xix-4: Tj, 972), which records the construction of a part of a temple hall by the regiment called *kaikkōḷa-perumpāḍai*. *Kaikkōḷas*, who became a leading weaving community in the later period, seem to have been soldiers in this period. The windows, door, and the like, constructed by the *kaikkōḷa* regiment were named after *aiñūṟṟuvar*, whom the *kaikkōḷas* refer to as their leaders. Many soldiers were associated with the *aiñūṟṟuvar*, working for them in protection of their trade which involved carrying precious commodities on a long journey.[17]

## Findings

What can we say from the above on the characteristics of the *nagaram* and the nature of merchant activities in the early period? First of all, the actual commercial activities of merchants in *nagarams* do not seem to have been vigorous except in the case of Kanchipuram, former capital of the Pallavas in Tondaimandalam. In most places *nagarattārs* are simply described as having performed the same role as other village assemblies did in local administration. This inactive or negative picture of the *nagaram* is quite contrastive to the picture we get in the inscriptions of the late period.

Another striking fact is that *nagarams* were placed under state control, their transactions being scrutinized by the state officers. In Uttaramallur, merchants' activities were under the control of its *sabhā*, which is known to have had close relations with the state administration.[18] This state control might explain to some extent their inactiveness in their commercial activities in this period, though there are some inscriptions which refer to the activities of merchant guilds. Relations between *nagarams* and merchant guilds such as *maṇigirāmam* or *aiñūṟṟuvar* and those between the state and merchant organizations remain unclear. Anyway, the state control of *nagarams* in this period is also contrastive to the freedom they enjoyed or tried to enjoy in their functioning in the late period.

## THE CHOLA STATE AND MERCHANTS IN THE MIDDLE PERIOD (1001–1200)

### State Expansion Policy

Eulogies of Rajaraja I in his inscriptions tell us that after defeating the allied forces of the Pāṇḍyas, Kerala, and Sri Lanka, he occupied the Pandyan country, the northern part of Sri Lanka, and the southern parts of Karnataka, and sent his army further north to Kalinga. Likewise, we know from the inscriptions of Rajendra I, son and successor of Rajaraja I, that he expanded the Chola territory further and sent his army even to the banks of the Ganga. He also sent a naval expedition, besides, to Sri Lanka and the Maldives, to the Malay Peninsula and Sumatra, conquering Kadaram and other towns in around 1025. His son, Virarajendra is also said to have sent his forces to Kadaram in 1069 to help a Kadaram ruler. These things make it clear that the Chola kings of the middle period followed a policy of expansion to enlarge the jurisdiction of their state.[19]

In China the names of the three envoys sent by Rajaraja I and Rajendra I are recorded in the official annals of the Song dynasty,[20] which enables us to presume that their attack on the Maldive islands, Sri Lanka, and the Malay Peninsula was meant to get hegemony in the East–West maritime trade that rapidly developed from the ninth century when the Abbasids in the West and the Tang dynasty in the East were flourishing.[21] An inscription discovered in Barus in Sumatra dated to 1088 records the activities of Tamil merchants, transacting under the banner of the aiñūṟṟuvar guild in that town famous for camphor trade, though the relation of those merchants to the Chola state is not clear.[22]

### Thanjavur Temple Inscriptions

Rajaraja I built a big Shiva temple in Thanjavur, his capital, by installing a *liṅga* named Rajarajesvara after his own title. This temple can certainly be called a state temple different from the royal *paḷḷipadai* temples built earlier and the purpose of building this temple must have been to proclaim the strength of his state.[23] It is natural, therefore, that there remain on the temple wall and pedestal a large number of inscriptions which record grants of land revenue by the king and that of gold, jewellery, and other precious things by royal ladies and others. Rājāraja's grant included the revenue of forty villages in Chola-mandalam and that of sixteen villages in other *maṇḍalams*, namely Pandi-mandalam, Ganga-mandalam (Karanataka), and Ila-mandalam (Sri Lanka). The tremendous amount of wealth thus donated to this temple was partly distributed by royal order to the local assemblies such as *sabhaiyār* and *ūrār* of several villages in the Chola-mandalam, inducing agrarian productivity. The largesse shown in the donation to this temple is thus well related to the state expansion policy.

Besides members of the royal family, there are many others who donated gold and other objects. Among those donors, other than the royal members, a conspicuous number was made up of high officials and various regiments of soldiers. Out of about twenty-five individual donors, twenty-three were high officials such as *adikāri, sēnāpati, śrīkāriyam, tirumandira-ōlai, naduvirukkai,* or just broad categories of *perundaram* and *paṇimakan*. We find only two *viyāpāris* (merchants) in contrast to this large number of officials. The local assemblies which received money from the temple by royal order include *sabhaiyār* of several Brahmin villages, *ūrār* of a few ordinary villages in Chola-mandalam. Four *nagarattārs* of Thanjavur, the capital city, also received the money, which, however, was meant for supplying plantains to the temple and not for investment in any big enterprise. These Thanjavur temple inscriptions, therefore, seem to suggest that the Chola state of this period was still basically an agrarian state depending mainly on agricultural production.

## Land Control in the *Nagaram*

Of the two Thanjavur temple inscriptions which record the receipt of money by *nagarattār*, one (*SII*, ii-24) states that the *peru-nagarattār* (big *nagarattār*) of Tribhuvanamadevip-perangadi (bazaar) received money from an officer of Rajaraja I and promised him to supply cardamom seeds and *champakā* buds to be put into the water meant for the idol's bathing. The other (*SII*, ii-37) records that *nagarattārs* of four bazaars, that is, Nittavinodap-perunteru, Mummudicholap-perunteru, Virasikamanip-perunteru and Tribuvanamadevip-perunteru, have to supply a large number of plantains to the temple by receiving certain amount of money from the king, Rajaraja I.

The interest accruing from the money deposited with merchants was presumably realized through their commercial activities. A Jambai inscription (*SII*, xxii-82: SA, 1037) gives us somewhat more detailed information on the commercial activities of merchants. According to it, *nagarattār* of Nittavinodapuram decided to meet the cost of burning lamps from the commissions for commodities specified in terms of measure, weight, number, and so on. In the case of areca nuts, ten out of 1,000 should be given by sellers and purchasers. Merchants were thus carrying out their trade in their towns (*nagaram*).

As stated above, however, merchants seem to have concerned themselves equally, if not more, with land control as landholders. There are many inscriptions testifying to it in this period, too. A Mamallapuram inscription (*SII*, i-40: Cg, 1009) is quite informative in this regard. *Nagarattār* of that town together with *pēriḷamaiyār* (cultivators) decided to divide all sorts of taxable land in the town into four divisions (*kūṟu*), each of which was to be held by a group of twenty-five households (*maṉai*).[24] One division was assigned to *saṅkarapāḍiyār* (oil merchants) comprising twenty-five households, the rest was to be enjoyed by the remaining seventy-five households. The people belonging to these 100 households were thus landholders paying taxes on their land, and it is also stipulated that those who did not have any land (some merchants, cultivators, workers, and others) had to pay a certain fixed amount of money on an annual basis.

Two more Mamallapuram inscriptions (*SII*, iv-377: 1061 and *SII*, vii-536: 1147) record the decision made by *nagaram* and *pēriḷamai* together concerning tax remission and land grant respectively. *Pēriḷamai* seems to have been the assembly of *Vellala* agriculturalists who cultivated the land of their own and that of the *nagarattār*. A Tiruvannamalai inscription (*SII*, viii-68: NA, 1039), however, tells explicitly that the *nagarattār*, which was composed of six *viyāpāris*, should cultivate the temple land and pay *kaḍamai* tax to the temple.

As to the land control by *nagarattārs*, there are three Tirukkonam (Tp) inscriptions which give some information. One of them (*Avanam* 1, 10-1: 1049) records that *nagarattār* of Madurantakapuram made rearrangements of their landholding (*kūṟu*) with the help of an influential personage (officer?) who possessed his *jīvitam* (a prebendal tenure) in this town. Among the signatories to this document we find some *cheṭṭiyār* (general merchants), *saṅkarapāḍiyar* (oil merchants), and *sāliyar* (silk weavers). The second one (*Avanam* 1, 10-3a: 1070) records that praying for the victory of the king, *nagarattār* of Madurantakapuram assigned some lands to various temples for services by deciding, for tax purposes, the equivalent standard area of those lands according to their present class (*taram*). The last one (*Avanam* 1, 10-2c: 1127) records that considering difficult conditions that prevailed after a certain calamity, the *nagarattār* changed the tax rate exempting certain unclaimed (?) land from the total taxable land through negotiation with the revenue officer. All these inscriptions of Tirukkonam reveal that *nagarattārs* were eager to control the agricultural production as landholders.

Three inscriptions of Tirumanikuli (SA) record land sale by *nagarattār*. The first (*SII*, vii-776: 1112) states that *nagarattār* of Vanavanmadevipuram sold the land to a temple and made agreement with the temple for tax payment. The second (*SII*, vii-785: 1119) records the sale of land (paddy field and garden land) by *nagarattār* to a *maṭha*. Four *mūvēndavēḷāns* signed the document. The last (*SII*, vii-774: 1121) records that a temple purchased both wet and dry land from six people of Vanavanmadevipuram and the land purchased was converted into a *dēvadāna* after separating it from the town. A Tiruvidaimarudur inscription (*SII*, xxiii-287: Tj, 1122) also records similar sale of land by the *nagaram* of that place for making a *maṭha*. A Tirukkonam inscription (*Avanam* 1, 10-2b: 1055) records that Madurantakapuram-*nagarattār* assigned a land to a Durga temple for three worship services, and a Melpadi inscription (*SII*, iii-16: NA, 1014) records a grant of their common land by *nagarattār*. In these inscriptions too, the *nagarattārs* appear just as landlords.

## Merchant Communities and Guilds

As mentioned above, a Tirukkonam inscription (*Avanam* 1, 10-1) gives the names of *cheṭṭi*, *saṅkarapāḍi* and *sāliya* as signatories to a *nagaram* document. There are some inscriptions which inform us of the individual members who composed the *nagaram* mentioned in the respective document. According to a Kalahasti inscription (*SII*, xvii-313: Ct, 1012) a decision was made on some temple affairs in the town (Mummudicholapuram) by the state officers sent by the king and some local bodies, including the *nagarattār*, which was composed of four *viyāpāris*, of whom two were *cheṭṭis* and one, *kavaṟe-cheṭṭi*, and of one *māyileṭṭi* of *saṅkarapāḍi*. Two more Kalahasti inscriptions (*SII*, xvii-310: 1035, and *SII*, xvii-326: 1035) reveal that the *nagarattār* of the first inscription was composed of more than two *viyāpāris* and one *saṅkarapāḍi* and that of the second by nine *viyāpāris* including five *cheṭṭis* and two *māyileṭṭis*. According to a Tirukkalukunram inscription (*SII*, v-465: Cg, 1044), the *nagarattār* which was composed of two *viyāpāris*, one *sāliyan*, and two *saṅkarapāḍiyān* sold land to a lady who donated it to the hill-top temple of the town.

It may be clear from the examination above that *viyāpāri* (general merchants?), *saṅkarapāḍi* (oil merchants), *sāliya* (weavers) were the important members of a *nagaram* or composed their own special *nagaram* along with or under the more general *nagaram*. Jambai (*SII*, xxii-81: SA, 1050) and Tirukkonam (*Avanam* 1, 10-2a: Tp, 1055) inscriptions record the existence respectively of *saṅkarapāḍi-nagaram* in Valaiyur and Madurantakapuram, and the Madurantakapuram inscription reveals that it existed along with the non-specified *nagaram*, as we have already seen. *Cheṭṭi* and *māyileṭṭi* seem to have been titles given to some important merchants in this period.

The inscription at Barus in Sumatra, already referred to, records the decision made by the merchant guild called *aiñūṟṟuvar* ('500 people') in 1088 in that town. It seems to have stipulated the rate of the contribution of fee to be given to their local agents, denoted by the term 'our son', and the like, of this merchant guild by some members of the guild such as ship owner, ship captain, and boatmen. Inscriptions of this type are found in plenty in Sri Lanka, Tamil Nadu, and Karnataka during the twelfth and thirteenth centuries. We find in them many names of the merchant groups or communities along with the group names of artisans and soldiers.[25]

A Jambai inscription (*SII*, xxii-80: SA, 1055) recording the suicide of a merchant lady harassed by a revenue officer states that the assembly of *nānādēsi* (a merchant guild, same as the *aiñūṟṟuvar*) ordered the revenue officer to burn a lamp for the expiation of his fault. The money for that purpose was deposited with *saṅkarapāḍi* (oil merchants) and *vaṇigirāmam* (same as *maṇigirāmam*), who were to supply oil in lieu of money. This *saṅkarapāḍi* must be the same as the one described as *saṅkarapāḍi-nagaram* in another Jambai inscription above (*SII*, xxii-81). The guild *nānādēsi* must have comprised, besides *vaṇigirāmam* and *saṅkarapāḍi*, many other groups and communities of merchants, though their names are not mentioned in this inscription.

## Call for New *Nagarams*

A Chidambaram inscription (*SII*, iv-223: SA 1036) records that a concubine of Rajendra I purchased a hamlet of the Chidambaram town and made it a new *nagaram* (town) naming it Gunamenagaipuram, to which she invited merchants, cultivators, and other professionals and entrusted to them the responsibility of conducting services (festivals) to the temple of Chidambaram. The invitees included *viyāpāri* (merchants), *veḷḷāḷar*, *saṅkarapāḏiyar* (oil merchants), *sāliyar* (weavers), *paṭṭinavar* (weavers?),[26] who were grouped as *kuḏi*, and *tachchar* (carpenter), *kollar* (ironsmith), *taṭṭār* (goldsmith), and *kōliyar* (weaver), who were grouped as *kīḻ-kalanai* (low-ranking service groups). On the basis of forty-four *vēli* of taxable land and shops in this new town the people were asked to pay 304 *kāsu* for the temple festivals.

The above inscription gives us a picture somewhat different from that obtained from other inscriptions of the early and middle periods, namely that of *nagarattār* being rather a conspicuous body of merchants. This Chidambaram inscription seems to be a precursor of the inscriptions of the later period, which describe vigorous commercial activities of merchants organized as *aiñūṟṟuvar* or appearing as *kāsāya-kuḏi* (*kāsāyavargattār*), that is, those who pay tax in money.

## DOMINANCE OF *AIÑŪṞṞUVAR* IN THE LATE PERIOD (1201–1350)

### Political Situation in the Thirteenth and Fourteenth Centuries

The Pandyan state which was under the Chola rule for nearly two centuries recovered its territory under Maravarman Sundarapandya (1216–44), who invaded the Chola country up to the Thanjavur area. Rajaraja III was captured by his own subordinate chief Kadava Kopperunjinga, a Pandya ally, for some time in his headquarters in South Arcot district. The Cholas were in turn helped by the Hoysalas who advanced to the Tamil country for that purpose under Narasimha II (1220–38) and who established their power base in Kannanur near Srirangam. The allied forces fought also against, besides the Pandyas, the Kakatiyas whose army attacked Kanchipuram during the long reign of Ganapati (1199–1262). Thus the Cholas were invaded both from the south and north and declined rapidly. The last inscription bearing the name of the Chola king dates to 1279 indicating the end of the Chola state.

Afterwards the southern part of the Chola state was ruled by the Pandyan kings and the northern part, by some local chiefs including the Sambuvarayas. The Sevunas, Hoysalas, and Kakatiyas who established their power in the Deccan and the Pandyas, who ruled the southern part of the peninsula, fought each other to get hegemony, but in the beginning of the fourteenth century there occurred invasions of the armies of the two Delhi Sultanates, namely, the Khaljis and Tughluqs. The Sevunas and the Kakatiyas were ruined first and the Pandyas also disappeared following the attack of Madurai by the Tughluq army in 1323. In Madurai a small Sultanate was born after the short rule of the Tughluqs. However, the Vijayanagar state established in 1336 in the Tungabhadra valley in Karnataka sent its army to the Tamil country and after subduing the Sambuvarayas, who were ruling in the Kanchipuram area, took Madurai, ruining the Sultanate around 1370. Afterwards the Tamil country was put under the Vijayanagar rule till the middle of the seventeenth century.

## *Aiñūṟṟuvar* and *Periyanāṭṭār*

Among the late-period inscriptions concerning merchants' activities those of the *aiñūṟṟuvar*, the most important merchant guild, are dominant.[27] We have already examined some of them above, as their activities started from the early tenth century. Though we have seen in the first-period three inscriptions referring to either *aiñūṟṟuvar* (*SII*, xix-4) or *maṇigirāmam* (*SII*, v-590) and both (*ARE*, 1965-308), none of them, however, describes their commercial activities. Among the second-period inscriptions examined above there are two referring to *aiñūṟṟuvar* (Barus) or *aiñūṟṟuvar* and *maṇigirāmam* (*SII*, xxii-80), but only the Barus inscription describes the merchants' sea-borne activity.

There are many more inscriptions which refer to the guilds in the early and middle periods, but most of them in the early period record the donation to a temple by individuals belonging to a guild and do not reveal the commercial activities of the merchants. Though many of the middle-period guild inscriptions describe commercial activities of the guild merchants, we examined only two of them including the Barus inscription. We have many more late-period guild inscriptions, and the period-wise distribution of the inscriptions referring to *aiñūṟṟuvar* and other merchant guilds is given in Table 5.2 below. If we compare this table with that of the *nagaram* shown above (Table 5.1), it is noticeable that activities of these merchant guilds became more vigorous in the third (late) period, while the number of *nagaram* inscriptions increases from the second (middle) period.

Among the *aiñūṟṟuvar* inscriptions we discern a type of inscriptions which record the brave deed of the soldiers (*erivīrar*) who fought for the *aiñūṟṟuvar* merchants and the merit given to them by the merchants in return for such a deed. This type of inscriptions can be called *eṟivīra-paṭṭinam* type inscriptions[28] and there are many of this type in Sri Lanka and Tamil Nadu during the middle period, particularly in the latter half of the eleventh and early half of the twelfth centuries. These inscriptions clearly show that soldiers (also called *vīrar*, *vīrakkoḍiyār*, *nāṭṭu-cheṭṭi*, and so on) were employed by the guild merchants as their guards in their

**Table 5.2** Guild

| *Period/District* | *I* | *II* | *III* | *Total* |
|---|---|---|---|---|
| Cg | | 3 | 2 | 5 |
| SA | 1 | 3 | 4 | 8 |
| NA | 1 | 3 | 2 | 6 |
| Tj | 4 | 4 | 4 | 12 |
| Tp | 8 | 2 | 9 | 19 |
| Pd | 3 | 3 | 3 | 9 |
| Cb | 2 | 2 | 7 | 11 |
| Dp | 1 | | 1 | 2 |
| SL | 1 | 2 | 1 | 4 |
| Rd | 1 | | 5 | 6 |
| Md | | 3 | 4 | 7 |
| Tn | 2 | 3 | 2 | 7 |
| Total | 24 | 28 | 44 | 96 |

long distance travel even across the ocean to various countries carrying precious commodities. The Barus inscription may be counted among *eṟivīra-paṭṭinam* type inscriptions, though any brave deed of soldiers are not described. Rather it is closer to the second type of *aiñūṟṟuvar* inscriptions, definable as the *paṭṭanappakudi* type.

Inscriptions of the second type record that many groups of the guild *aiñūṟṟuvar*, often together with agriculturists organized as *chitramēḻi-periyanāṭṭār*, assembled in the town (*paṭṭinam/paṭṭanam*) and decided to assign a certain share (*pakudi*) of their income from each of the members for the purpose of temple repair or festivals. Contributions are usually fixed in terms of the commodities enumerated in inscriptions, sometimes in great number.

Inscriptions of both types—*eṟivīra-paṭṭinam* type and *paṭṭanappakudi* type—record a good number of groups of merchants, soldiers, and others, assembled in the town for making their decision. An inscription at Viharahinne in Sri Lanka assignable to the first half of the twelfth century and belonging to the *eṟivīra-paṭṭinam* type, enumerates the following groups:

*tāvaḷam-cheṭṭi* (merchants of the locality)
*cheṭṭi-puttiran* (merchants)
*kavarai* (merchants)
*kātrivan* (betel-leaf merchants)

*kāmuṇḍasvāmi* (headmen among landholders)
*ōṭṭan* (messengers)
*pana*... ( ? )
*aṇgakkāran* (soldiers)
*āvaṇakkāran* (shopkeepers)
*pāvāḍai-vīran* (select soldiers)
*āriyattōṭarun tamiḻ valla ca*...(those who are conversant with Sanskrit and Tamil?)
*kaḻutai mēva*... *vanum* (those who ride on an ass?)

If we check other inscriptions also, we can get many more groups assembled in the *aiñūṟṟuvar* meeting, including artisans such as goldsmiths, potters, and the like.[29] As already mentioned, *chitramēḻi-periyanāḍu*, a big peasant organization, also joined the merchant assembly in many cases. This peasant organization was formed initially by Vellalas but later it was joined by old hill tribes that became landholders after they joined the Chola army, and also by artisans such as weavers and smiths who became economically powerful. This indicates that commercial activities developed rapidly in and after the twelfth century in south India influenced by the development of trans-regional maritime trade and that this development made the merchants join with artisans and peasants also. In some inscriptions the joining of *valaṅgai* (right hand) and/or *iḍaṅgai* (left hand) group(s) in their assembly is also mentioned.[30]

Inscriptions of the early and middle periods examined above did not give any information on the relations between the *nagarams* and the merchant guilds such as *maṇigirāmam* and *aiñūṟṟuvar*. A Kovilpatti inscription (*ARE*, 1965-286: Tp, 1305), however, casts some light on this issue. Though it states in the beginning that *aiñūṟṟuvar*, including soldier groups and *chitramēḻi-periyanāṭṭār*, jointly decided to do a charity deed (*paṭṭanappakudi* donation), it tells later that some four *nagarattārs* (all their towns are found in the present-day Pudukkottai district) agreed to do this charity for the deity in a Shiva temple. We are able to know from this inscription, therefore, that each *nagaram* was a component of, or closely associated with, the *aiñūṟṟuvar* organization. In a Piranmalai inscription (*SII*, viii-442: Rd, *c.*1300) also, sixteen *nagarams*, whose names are given and which were in Pudukkottai, Ramanathapuram, Tiruchirappalli, and Coimbatore districts, are said to have joined in the *aiñūṟṟuvar* assembly in order to make a charity deed.

According to some early-period inscriptions, Thanjavur had four *nagarams*, each belonging to a bazaar (street) and Tirukkonam had *saṅkarapāḍi-nagaram* along with the general *nagaram*. These inscriptions suggest that *nagarams* were often formed bazaar-wise or community-wise in the early period. It is noticeable in this relation that a later Mannargudi inscription (*SII*, vi-40: Tj, 1264) records that the *paṭṭanappakudi* donation of the commission of the arecanut trade was decided by the *nagarattār* of Buvanekaviranmadigai (bazaar) along with the *padineṇ-vishayattār* (*aiñūṟṟuvar*). These late-period inscriptions clearly show that *nagarams* were incorporated into the merchant network of *aiñūṟṟuvar* and their activities were carried on as those of commercial towns.

## Commodities of Trade

Many of the *paṭṭanappakudi* type inscriptions enumerate the commodities in relation to the fixing of the cess in terms of commodities.[31] The longest list of the commodities traded is found in the Piranmalai inscription, and a fairly long list in the Kovilpatti inscription, both mentioned above. The list of commodities in the latter is as follows:

*agil* (aloe), *arisi* (rice), *avarai* (beans), *erudu* (bull), *erumai* (buffalo), *kaḍugu* (mustard), *kampi* (iron), *kana mālai* (garlands ?), *kaṟpūram* (camphor), *karu alai mālai* (garlands ?), *kastūri* (musk), *kiḍā* (cattle), *kudirai* (horse), *mayir* (hair), *miḷaku* (pepper), *nel* (paddy), *oṭṭai* (camel), *pasu* (cow), *pākku* (arecanuts), *puḍavai* (saree/long cloth), *pul* (grass), *puḷi* (tamarind), *sāmai* (millet), *sandanam* (sandal), *saṅgu* (conch), *tantam* (ivory), *tuvarai* (dhal), *ulaṇḍu-puḍavai* (woollen cloth), *uppu* (salt), and *varagu* (millet),

Camphor, frankincense, musk, rose-water, and so on, are the important items to be used in various services in temples. The number of temples increased greatly during the Chola period by new constructions, and the services in them were enriched by the elaboration of rituals, which demanded these perfumes and essences. Pepper, arecanuts, rice, and cloth are the important items exported from south India. The reference to the weavers and tax on looms in inscriptions increases remarkably from the eleventh century as we shall see below. Import of horses from Arabia and the Persian Gulf, which started from the ninth century, increased remarkably from the thirteenth century with the establishment of Muslim states in India, whose military power depended largely on cavalry. Another thing we can know from the lists of commodities is that along with the precious commodities traded with overseas countries there were local commodities for daily consumption such as betel-leaf and nuts, rice, grains, pulses, and salt. This indicates the involvement of local merchants and peasants in the Tamil country in this large network of merchants organized as *aiñūṟṟuvar*.

### *Vāṇiyar*

Another conspicuous thing we notice in late-period inscriptions is the rather frequent reference to *vāṇiyar* or *vāṇigar* (oil merchants). A Vembavur inscription (*Avanam* 15, 24-9: Tp, 1198) refers to the street (*teru*) of *vāṇigar* of Vembar in relation to the donation of the commission (*taragu*) on their (?) transactions. Another inscription of the same town (*Avanam* 15, 24-10: 1207) gives the name of *vāṇiga-nagarattār* of some street in relation to the *paṭṭanappakudi* donation. A Tiruppangili inscription (*ARE*, 1939-163: Tp, 1225) records the decision made in a big assembly of *vāṇiya-nagarattār* belonging to several *nāḍus* of the area to bear the *kaḍamai* (tax) on two *sekkus* (oil-press mills) assigned to a temple for burning lamps by distributing among its members the responsibility of paying it to the government. In this record they call themselves as *jāti*, indicating that oil merchants of this area had become a new *jāti* by this time.

An interesting case comes from a Tirukkachchur inscription (*SII*, xxvi-276: Cg, 1171) which records that *vāṇiyar* composing *mānagar* (big *nagaram*) in Tirukkachchur, which was a satellite centre of the *mānagar* of Kanchipuram, decided together with twenty-four *nagarattārs* of this *manḍalam* (big area) to contribute the *kaḍamai* tax on an oil-press mill for lamp-burning and food offering in the temple. They also call themselves *jāti*. The number twenty-four is fictitious indicating 'many', and twenty-four *nagarattārs* must have been just the *nagarattār* of several *vāṇiyar* towns. This inscription, together with the Tiruppangili inscription above, shows that they had established a well-woven network of their organization forming themselves as a *jāti* by this time.

A similar case is recorded in a Tiruppasur inscription (*ARE*, 1930-120, Cg, 1207), according to which *vāṇiya-nagarattārs* of Nellur, Kanchimanagar, Arkkadu, Mayilapur, Tiruvorriyur, Pundamali, Tiruninravur, and others, and *nagarattār* of Narayanapura, Nedumpirai, Tamarcheri, and Perungalur seem to have granted with the permission of Pottappichola, a local chief, a village to Tiruppasur temple for making its compound wall and Pottappichola made the village tax free. Though some of the *nagarams* are specified simply as *nagaram*, they also seem to have been *vāṇiya-nagaram*. Anyway, this inscription also shows a well-woven network of *vāṇiya-nagarattārs*. The said places were distributed over a big area, notably corresponding to the northern part of Tondaimandalam. The designation *darma-tāvaḷavan* given to the compound wall may suggest the relation of *vāṇiya-nagarattar* to *aiñūṟṟuvar* as *tāvaḷam* is the place of periodical fair or market where the *aiñūṟṟuvar* visited for their transactions.

In a Valikandapuram inscription (*ARE*, 1944-276: Tp, 1227), which records the solidarity resolution of the *iḍangai, 98* people, including *vāṇiya-nagarattār* are mentioned as having joined in the resolution with other communities like *nattamakkaḷ*, *malaiyamāngal*, *andaṇar* (Brahmana), *pannāṭṭār* and *kaikkōḷar* (weavers). It is striking in this relation that coinciding with the appearance of this *vāṇiyar-jāti*, the references to *saṅkarapāḍi* who figured rather frequently in the earlier-period inscriptions disappeared in this period. It seems that *saṅkarapāḍi* changed its name to *vāṇiyar* to display its strength like many new groups, each of which asserted itself as a new *jāti*.

## *Kāsāya-kuḍi*

References to *kāsāya-kuḍi* or *kāsāyam* also began to appear in this period. *Kāsāya-kuḍi*, meaning people who pay *āyam* tax in cash (*kāsu*) is juxtaposed with *uḷavu-kuḍi* (cultivators) in a fifteenth-century inscription (*ARE*, 1944-278: Tp, 1416) indicating that they were merchants and artisans distinguished from cultivators. In Tiruvattur inscriptions (*SII*, vii-103: NA, 1211 and *SII*, vii-98: 1234) recording tax remission by Sambuvaraya in favour of a temple, the taxes are categorized into *nel-āyam* (*āyam* to be paid in paddy) and *kāsu-āyam* (*āyam* to be paid in cash). An inscription of Virinchipuram (*SII*, i-64: NA, 1244), recording again the tax remission of a village granted to temple by a Sambuvarayar, categorizes the taxes into *nel-āyam* and *kāsu-kaḍamai*. The latter includes *veṭṭi-pudavai* (tax on cloth), *mudatiramam* (tax on capital?), *vagainda-kāsu* (some cash levy), *paṭṭōlai-kāsu* (fee for document), *mullaḍi-chinnam* (?), *vēlippayaṟu* (tax on pulses), *tāppaḍi-arisi* (tax on rice?), *achcha-taṟi* (tax on *achchu* looms), *sāligai-taṟi* (tax on looms of Saliyas), *tūchaka-taṟi* (tax on looms of the *tūchakas*), *paṟai-taṟi* (tax on looms of Paraiyas), *chekku-kaḍamai* (tax on oil mill), *āśuva-kaḍamai* (tax on soldiers). This clearly shows the development of industries and commerce, especially weaving in villages.

Another inscription of Sambuvaraya coming from Tiruvennainallur (*ARE*, 1921-454: SA, 1350), recording tax remission again, enumerates the merchants and artisans who composed *kāsāya-vargam* (same as *kāsāya-kuḍi*) as follows: *cheṭṭi* (merchants), *kaikkōḷa* (weavers), *vāṇiyar* (oil merchants), *sēnai-aṅgāḍigaḷ* (betel-leaf sellers), *kōyil-angāḍigaḷ* (temple merchants). Yet another inscription of Sambuvaraya in Nerkunam (*ARE*, 1935-218: SA, 1353) records that the taxes to be paid by *kāsāya-kuḍis* settling in a temple street will be granted to a temple. The taxes are specified as *pēr-kaḍamai* (per head), *taṟi-kaḍamai* (on looms), *ālavari* (concession?), *kāṇikkai* (presents), *vāsal-paṇam* (on houses), *taraku* (commission), and *kaḍai-āyam* (on shops).

Apart from the Sambuvaraya inscriptions, there are some more interesting *kāsāya-kuḍi* inscriptions coming from northern districts. A Ponnur inscription in North Arcot district (*ARE*, 1929-391: 1293) records the *nāṭṭavar*'s order of tax (*āyam*) remission in favour of the people of *taṟi* (weavers) and *kāsāya-kuḍi* who came to live in the houses in the three streets of the temple. Another Ponnur inscription (*ARE*, 1929-415: 1293) records that *nāṭṭavar* decided to remit *kaḍamai* and *āyam* of *kuḍi* (cultivators?) and *kāsāya-kuḍi* including *tari* (weavers) who came to live in the precincts of a Jain temple for services and repair of the temple. Merchants and artisans began to be found in more numbers in temple streets from the thirteenth century, and they as well as their workshop areas were called *paṭṭadai*, the references to which we find increasingly in Vijayanagar inscriptions.[32] As in the case of Sambuvaraya inscriptions, there appear no *nagarattār* in these inscriptions, and significance should be given also to the fact that the order was issued by the *nāṭṭavars*.

## Merchants and Political Power

The emergence of new communities such as landholders, artisans, and merchants took place in and after the twelfth century. The new landholding communities were mostly old hill-tribes who joined the Chola army under the expansion policy of the middle-period kings. They are *paḷḷis*, *nattamāns*, *surudimāns*, *malaiyamāns*, *kaḷḷans*, and the like, by *jāti*, and some of them, acquiring a large extent of land, grew to form chiefly families in the thirteenth century such as Kadavarayas in South Arcot district, Banas in Tiruchirappalli district, and Sambuvarayas in North Arcot and Chingleput districts.

These local chiefs seem to have had close relations with merchants and artisans by encouraging their activities. The Sambuvaraya inscriptions examined above clearly show that they were eager to develop industries and commerce in their territory and invited them to temple streets. There is an inscription in Chakramallur (*ARE*, 1941-40: NA, 1207), though damaged, in which Sambuvaraya seems to have converted a village into a *paṭṭinam* (town) probably by accepting the request of merchants and receiving money from them. The town was named *chitramēḻi-padineṉbūmi-paṭṭinam* and designated as *vijaya (vīra)-paṭṭinam*. Sambuvaraya made two *vēlis* of its land tax-free and the people were allowed to sell and mortgage the land as *kāṇiyāḷar*. This inscription is of much importance showing the relation of Sambuvaraya with the *chitramēḻi* organization and the *padineṉbūmi* (*aiñūṟṟuvar*) merchant guild.

Another example comes from Tiruchirappalli district. An Uttattur inscription (*ARE*, 1912-521: Tp, 1199) records that *nāṭṭārs* and *nagarattārs* of the area assembled as *79-nāḍus* (*periyanāḍu*) and decided to change a village into a town giving it a new name, Tayilunallapuram, after the name of a local chief. This local chief is known from a Valikandapuram inscription (*ARE*, 1944-266: Tp, 1220), which records a land grant to a temple for the health of this chief, as Tayilunallaperumal alias Kulottunga Vanakovaraiyan. A Vembavur inscription (*Avanam* 15, 24-8: Tp. 1250) records the protection given to the Tayilunallaperumal temple by a Kerala merchant of *chitramēḻi* organization. This Bana chief, after whom the temple is named, must have greatly encouraged merchants in their activities.

Two Ponnur inscriptions examined above show the strength of *nāṭṭavars* in the control of merchants and artisans grouped as *kāsāya-kuḍi*. Though the *nāṭṭārs* (*nāṭṭavars*) in the early Chola period were basically Vellalas who were landholders as well as cultivators, they changed their composition in the later period and many new *jātis* seem to have joined the *naṭṭavar*.[33] A Madam inscription (*ARE*, 1916-246: NA, 1290) records the remission of *kāsāyavargam* and *nūlāyam* including *kaḍamai* tax on weavers and oil merchants by the *nāṭṭavar*, *pal-nāṭṭavar*, and *paḷ-mudaligaḷ*. We do not know which *jāti* or how many *jātis* composed the *nāṭṭavar*, but *paḷ-nāṭṭavar* (*pannāttavar*) is the *nāṭṭavar* of *paḷḷis* and *paḷ-mudali* is the representative of *paḷḷis*. This inscription, therefore, shows the control of merchants and artisans by the new dominant *jātis*.

Royal control of merchants is also recorded in this period. A Tiruvottur inscription (*ARE*, 1940-97: NA, *c.*1300) states that Vira Pandya ordered that the tax on cultivators as well as merchants and artisans including *cheṭṭi*, *vāṇiya*, *kaikkōḷa*, *sāliya*, *kōliya*, and *sekkukkuḍi* in a temple village should be remitted. Though not a royal order, an Avur inscription (*ARE*, 1919-302: NA, 1288) records the order issued to the *nāṭṭavar* by a Tennavarayan on the mode of *kaḍamai* collection from the people including *cheṭṭi*, *vāṇiyar*, *niyāyattār*, *manṟāḍi*, *kuḍimakkaḷ*, *kuḍumban*, and *āśupodumakkaḷ*. These inscriptions show the state control of merchants and artisans, who were, however, not organized as *nagarattār* in the town, but lived in villages as *kāsāyavargattār*.

All the inscriptions examined above show that merchants and artisans were gaining power owing to the development of trade in the later period, that is, from the middle of the twelfth century to the end of the fourteenth century. A Kakatiya inscription (*EI*, xii-22: thirteenth century) of Motupalli, on the Andhra coast, records the king's assurance of his fair treatment for merchants coming from foreign countries. In Motupalli there is another inscription recording a similar order issued by a Reddi chief in the middle of the fourteenth century (*SII*, xxii-635). Sambuvaraya also established a *paṭṭinam* having a relationship with a merchant guild. Political powers including local chiefs became eager to control activities of merchants in order to share the profit from their trade.

Broadly speaking, however, we may be able to discern two types of relationship having existed between merchants (and artisans) and political powers. In the central and southern districts,[34] where there remain many *aiñūṟṟuvar* inscriptions, merchants and artisans, often associated with peasants organized as *chitramēḻi-periyanāṭṭār*, seem to have tried to keep independence from political powers as shown by their non-referring to the ruling king in many of their inscriptions, though they were never freed from the state control, as inferred from their payment of *kaḍamai* to the state.

In contrast to this, merchants and artisans in the northern districts seem to have been placed under more direct control of the political power as shown by the inscriptions recording the order or permission of the king, chief, and *nāṭṭavar*. We find there many merchants and artisans not organized as *nagarattār* in the town, but living in villages as *kāsāyavargattārs*. This probably derives from the fact that after the decline of the Cholas, the local chiefs established their power more strongly in the northern districts. Otherwise, it may show the difference in the degree or the direction of the socio-economic development between the two regions. However, we shall reserve the clarification of this point to our future studies in relation to the examination of *nagarams* during the Vijayanagar period.[35]

## TRANSFORMATION OF THE *NAGARAM* DURING THE CHOLA AND PANDYAN PERIOD

The first thing we notice from the above examination is that the *nagaram* changed its characteristics with the progress of time, and we find much difference in the *nagaram's* character between the early period (850–1000) and the late period (1201–1350), the middle-period *nagaram* showing a transitional character. In the early period we find its similarity to villages represented by *ūr* and *brahmadēya*. Such activities of *nagarattār* of this period as custodians of money donated to the temple for some charity or participation in temple management were almost the same as carried out by *ūrār* and *sabhaiyār*, that is, mainly as participants in local administration. The holding and control of land by *nagarattār* is also similar to that conducted by *ūrār* and *sabhaiyār*. Another noticeable point for the early period is the state control of the *nagaram*. The *nagaram* was supervised by state officers, the *ūr* and *brahmadēya*. So far as these points are concerned, therefore, we find basically no difference between *nagaram* (town) and *ūr/brahmadēya* (village) in the early period, though the *nagaram* was composed of people who engaged themselves in commerce. Though the existence of merchant guilds such as *maṇigirāmam* or *aiñūṟṟuvar* is known even in the early period, their relation with the *nagaram* was not clear and the two bodies seem to have conducted their activities rather independently.

In contrast to this trend in the early period, we find in the late period more vigorous activities of merchants in relation to the *nagaram* as well as guild in consequence of the development of East–West maritime trade. The *nagaram* seems to have been incorporated into, or at least have cooperated with, the guild of *aiñūṟṟuvar* in and after the twelfth century. In the central area, this is shown by Piranmalai and Kovilpatti inscriptions, in which we find several *nagarams* joined in the assembly of *aiñūṟṟuvar* forming a network. In the northern area we find the Tiruppasur inscription which records the joint activities of *vāṇiya-nagarattār*, and also the latter's relationship with the *aiñūṟṟuvar*. Merchant guilds such as *aiñūṟṟuvar* must have been the most important motive power to let *nagarams* make a network among themselves, but at the same time, *jāti* formation also seems to have been a factor which made possible a linkage among *nagarams* of different localities, as suggested by the Tiruppasur and Tirukkachchur inscriptions above.

*Nagarams* becoming active commercial towns and the emergence of their networks in relation to their association with merchant guilds or to the *jāti* formation of some merchant groups reveal the significant transformation of *nagarams* in the late period. However, we find a subtle difference in the situation of merchants between the central (and southern) and northern regions. *Aiñūṟṟuvar* in the central region showed an inclination to independence from the state by not referring to the ruling king in their inscriptions. In the northern region, however, they seem to have been placed under the control of some political power. Moreover, the inscriptions which refer to *kāsāya-kuḍi* or *kāsāyavargattār*, merchants, and artisans in the village, who were controlled by local chiefs and *nāṭṭavars*, are conspicuous in the northern region. The meaning of this difference is yet to be studied.

According to Hall, the *nagaram* was under the control of the *nāḍu* and served the state as a commercial centre in the locality till the eleventh century, but after the establishment of the *periyanāḍu* that controlled large areas competing with the state, the *nagaram* began to be associated with it. *Periyanāḍu* and *nagaram* jointly contributed to the decline of the Cholas in the thirteenth century. Although our understanding of the *nagaram* may look somewhat similar to this interpretation of Hall's, it is different from his in the following two points. First, we do not admit much importance to the tie between *nāḍu* and *nagaram*, as there were many *nāḍus* without a *nagaram*. Second, though Hall regards *periyanāḍu* as the elite organization of Vellala agriculturists following Stein,[36] we take it basically as the organization of new *jātis* who were originally hill-tribes, and therefore, our assessment of the historical role it played is quite different from that which Hall admits to.[37] Champakalakshmi does not focus her argument on the change in the character of the *nagaram* in different periods, as she discusses the *nagaram* more in general terms in the context of urbanization of ancient and medieval Tamil Nadu.[38]

If we confine the object of our study only to the *nagaram*, we may have to say that the *nagaram* was one of the organizations utilized by the state for its local administration during the early and middle Chola periods, but in and after the twelfth century the *nagaram* transformed its character to the promoter of commerce by associating itself with the itinerant merchant guild *aiñūṟṟuvar*. *Jāti* formation also accelerated the process of their network formation. The two organizations, *nagarams* (towns) and *aiñūṟṟuvar* (merchant guilds), became symbiotic to a certain extent in the wake of the economic growth brought by the new developments in East–West maritime trade as well as the disappearance of the powerful states such as the Cholas. This situation, however, seems to have begun to change again towards the end of the fifteenth century under the Vijayanagar *nāyaka* rule, and that deserves a separate study by itself.

## ABBREVIATIONS FOR DISTRICTS (OLD) IN TAMIL NADU, KARNATAKA, AND ANDHRA PRADESH

Bj = Bijapur
Cb = Coimbatore
Cg = Chingleput
Ct = Chittoor
Kl = Kolar
NA = North Arcot
Nl = Nellore
Pd = Pudukkottai
Rm = Ramanathapuram
SA = South Arcot
Sl = Salem
Tj = Thanjavur
Tn = Tirunelveli
Tp = Tiruchirappali

## NOTES

1 Kenneth R. Hall, *Trade and Statecraft in the Age of the Colas*, New Delhi, 1980; R. Champakalakshmi, *Trade, Ideology and Urbanization: South India 300 BC to AD 1300*, New Delhi, 1996.

2 For this survey, the unpublished inscriptions were first checked for selection by using T.V. Mahalingam (ed.), *A Topographical List of Inscriptions in the Tamil Nadu and Kerala State*, 9 vols, New Delhi, 1985–95, which depends on the brief information given in the *Annual Report on Epigraphy* of the Archaeological Survey of India. The Tables given in Hall and Champakalakshmi were also consulted.

3 R.H. Hilton, *English and French Towns in Feudal Society*, Cambridge, 1992.

4 Susan Reynolds, *Kingdoms and Communities in Western Europe 900–1300*, 2nd edn, Oxford, 1997.

5 Hall, *Trade and Statecraft*, p. 124.

6 Champakalakshmi, *Trade, Ideology and Urbanization*, p. 214.

7 Y. Subbarayalu, *Political Geography of the Chola Country*, Madras, 1973, p. 34.

8 It may be mentioned that there were about 500 *nāḍus* in the whole of Tamil Nadu by the twelfth century and therefore the *nāḍus* with *nagarams* form less than 20 per cent of the total *nāḍus*.

9 As for *brahmadēya*, it seems there was a policy to create at least one *brahmadēya* in one *nāḍu*. Noboru Karashima, *South Indian History and Society: Studies from Inscriptions AD 850–1800*, New Delhi, 1984, pp. 36–40.

10 R. Champakalakshmi attributes the proliferation of *nagarams* to the expansion of the Chola power. Champakalakshmi, *Trade, Ideology and Urbanization*, p. 43.

11 For instance Kanchipuram, a *nagaram* in Cg, appears in all the three periods, but for counting the total, only one occurrence is included.

12 For *arayan* title-holders such as Pallavarayan and Brahmarayan, see Introduction, Noboru Karashima, *South Indian Society in Transition: Ancient to Medieval*, New Delhi, 2009, and *South Indian History and Society*, pp. 55–68.

13 The work of the *vāriyam* is not specified in this inscription, though we find *āttai-vāriyam* (annual committee) of a *nagaram* in a copper-plate inscription (*SII*, iii-128, p. 275) as checking accounts annually. In case of the *sabhā* there were several different *vāriyams*, each dealing with specific affairs like road, water channel, garden, gold, etc.

14 Hall has discussed this point to some extent in his *Trade and Statecraft*, p. 74*ff*.

15 For periodical redistribution, see note 24.

16 According to a Thanjavur inscription (*South Indian Inscriptions* hereafter *SII*, New Delhi, Archaeological Survey of India, 1890, ii-37: 1014), there were four bazaars in Thanjavur, each of which composed an independent *nagaram*.

17 See Karashima, *South Indian Society*, p. 216.

18 K.A. Nilakanta Sastri, *Studies in Cola History and Administration*, Madras, 1932; Karashima, *South Indian History and Society*, pp. 36–40.

19 G.W. Spencer discussed this point in his book, *The Politics of Expansion: The Chola Conquest of Sri Lanka and Sri Vijaya*, Madras, 1983.

20 In the Song annals, a translation of which is given in *South Indian Society*, chapter 13, another envoy from the Chola country is recorded to have arrived in 1077 and though the king who sent this envoy has long been identified with Kulottunga I, this envoy was actually sent by a Kadaram king. See Karashima, *South Indian Society*, p. 276*ff*.

21 Indrapala, who studied the overseas expeditions of Rajaraja I in the light of Sri Lankan evidence, has made a similar observation. Indrapala, 'Overseas Campaign of Rajaraja I', *Tamil Civilization*, vol. 3, nos 2 and 3, 1985, pp. 48–59.
22 Y. Subbarayalu, 'The Merchant-Guild Inscription at Barus, Sumatra, Indonesia: Rediscovery', in Claude Guillot (ed.), *Histoire de Barus: Le Site de Lobu Tua, I, Cahiers d'Archipel*, vol. 30, Paris, 1998, pp. 25–33.
23 Yasushi Ogura, 'The Changing Concept of Kingship in the Cola Period: Royal Temple Constructions, *c.* AD 850–1279', in Noboru Karashima (ed.), *Kingship in Indian History*, New Delhi, 1999. However, G.W. Spencer regards this, on the contrary, as an expression of the weakness of the state. Spencer, *The Politics of Expansion*, p. 42.
24 This Mamallapuram inscription and the Tirukkonam inscription to be examined later suggest the practice of periodical redistribution of land in those towns.
25 See chapter 10, Karashima, *South Indian Society*.
26 *Paṭṭinavar*, otherwise called *āyōgavar*, is stated as engaged in weaving in a Tirubhuvanai inscription (*PI*-159: 1127).
27 See chapter 10, Karashima, *South Indian Society*.
28 Inscriptions of this type record grant of the name, *erivīra-paṭṭinam* (town of brave soldiers), by the guild merchants to the town where merchants and soldiers lived, in appreciation of the brave deed of the soldiers. See Karashima, *South Indian Society*, pp. 204–5.
29 N. Karashima and Y. Subbarayalu, 'Ainurruvar: A Supra-local Organization of South Indian and Sri Lankan Merchants', in Noboru Karashima (ed.), *Ancient and Medieval Commercial Activities in the Indian Ocean: Testimony of Inscriptions and Ceramic-sherds* (*AMCAIO* hereafter), Tokyo, 2002, p. 78.
30 These are the multi-caste organizations composed of the castes classified either right hand or left hand. While *chitramēḷi-periyanāḍu* was an organization basically of agriculturists, these two groups included merchant and artisan groups, and were composed of castes classified lower than Brahmanas and Vellalas. See chapter 6, Karashima, *South Indian Society*.
31 P. Shanmugam, 'Pattanappagudi: A Voluntary Impost of the Trade Guilds', *AMCAIO*, pp. 89–100.
32 P. Shanmugam, 'Pattadai and Industries in the Tamil Country Under the Vijayanagar Rule', *Journal of Asian and African Studies*, vol. 37, 1989, pp. 31–49.
33 Noboru Karashima, 'Nattavars in Tamilnadu during the Pandya and Vijayanagar Period', *Journal of the Epigraphical Society of India*, vol. 22, 1996, pp. 21–7.
34 For southern districts, see also Champakalakshmi, *Trade, Ideology and Urbanization*, pp. 216–17.
35 There is a Vijayanagar inscription (*SII*, xvii-679) dated to 1521 in Nagalapuram (Cg), which records a charity deed conducted by *nagarattārs* of the northern regions including *paṭṭaṇaswāmi* (leading merchants of a port town) of Pulicut.
36 Hall, *Trade and Statecraft*, pp. 203–5.
37 In relation to this, it should be noted here that I notice the change of *nāṭṭār* themselves towards the end of Chola rule as stated above in the discussion on *kāsāya-kuḍi*. See note 33.
38 Her emphasis on the religious factor such as creation of *brahmadēya* and *dēvadāna*, not to speak of the construction and renovation of temples, as the promoter of urbanization is also to be noted. Champakalakshmi, *Trade, Ideology and Urbanization*.

# 6

# The Society of Kakatiya Andhra*

Cynthia Talbot

Stone inscriptions have rarely been utilized in attempts to understand the social structure of pre-colonial India, although they record the names and activities of many thousands of people who made religious endowments. Instead, much of our reconstruction of Indian society before the advent of colonial rule has been based on two types of sources: the brahmanical literature (especially the *dharmaśāstra* [law books]) and modern ethnographic studies. The fact that brahmanical literature presents only the normative views of one segment of society has long been recognized; yet, because of the presumed centrality of the brāhmaṇa in 'traditional' Hindu India, scholars have continued to rely heavily on such works. Similarly, the projection of present-day ethnographic realities back into the precolonial period has been justified on the grounds of the alleged continuity of Indian society. Both types of sources are attractive in the relative richness of their information, since the law books offer a detailed indigenous conceptualization of social organization while ethnography provides insights into actual special interaction not readily available elsewhere. The fragmentary glimpses into the social system obtained via inscriptions are, by contrast, far less immediately rewarding as sources of knowledge.

*Previously published in Cynthia Talbot, *Precolonial India in Practice: Society, Religion and Identity in Medieval Andhra*, New York, Oxford University Press, 2001, pp. 48 and 84–6. By permission of Oxford University Press, New York. This is an extract from the chapter. In the present version, some portions of the text and notes have been removed. For complete text see the original version.

Recent research on the early colonial period has, however, increasingly called into question the accuracy of images of 'traditional' South Asia derived from ethnographies and brahmanical literature. In the revisionist view, brāhmaṇa dominance was greatly heightened by colonial policies of the nineteenth century. The cultural hegemony of the brāhmaṇa was strengthened by the colonial creation of a legal system applied to all Hindu communities which was based on the brahmanical norms expressed in the *dharmaśāstra*. The legal validation of brāhmaṇa authority, accentuated by British employment of large numbers of brāhmaṇas as clerks and assistants in their administration, extended the influence of the caste system into areas where it had not previously intruded. The British suppression of the alternative lifestyles and values of pastoralist and martial communities further contributed to the elevation of the brāhmaṇa during the nineteenth century.[1] If these assertions are correct, it follows that the modern caste-dominated social system does not reflect the precolonial situation but instead is a colonial product. A further implication is that neither brahmanical literature nor modern ethnography can be accepted as reliable guides in reconstructing India's precolonial past.

Inscriptions offer an alternative means for recovering the social world of precolonial India, one that is not distorted by the transformations caused by colonial rule nor restricted to the viewpoint of the elite brāhmaṇa. What little evidence is available on the production of inscriptional texts does suggest that their composers were often brāhmaṇas, although at other times temple scribes may have been responsible for their composition. The strong linkage between brāhmaṇa status and literacy in precolonial India thus accounts for a certain commonality in rhetorical expression throughout the subcontinent, most notably in Sanskrit inscriptions. Yet the fact that medieval inscriptions may have been composed by brāhmaṇas, who therefore framed regional discourse at least partially through the lens of the Sanskrit cosmopolis, does not mean that inscriptions reflected solely, or even primarily, the brāhmaṇa perspective. The desires of the people who commissioned these documents displayed in highly visible public arenas of social interaction had to be accommodated by epigraphic composers, who were after all only hired hands. Whereas the documentary portion of donative inscriptions—specifying the exact nature of the object gifted, as well as its purpose and its recipient—was largely technical and thus not amenable to much variation, the representation of a donor's identity in an inscription was undoubtedly dictated by the donor's wishes.

My reconstruction of medieval Andhra society hence begins with an examination of how individuals and groups commissioning inscriptions chose to have themselves described in these public records. It is largely immaterial for our purposes whether the status claims of inscriptional patrons were widely accepted by other parties, since in either case we learn what social identities were considered pertinent in Kakatiya Andhra. The social typology implicit in the names and titles borne by donors of religious endowments should inform our own models of medieval social organization, rather than preconceptions derived from brahmanical texts or from more recent data. Thus, a second theme of this chapter concerns the way in which the picture of Andhra society derived from inscriptions differs from standard constructions of traditional India in its greater social fluidity and emphasis on earned status instead of ascribed rank. Third, to anticipate my conclusions, I argue that the degree of dynamism in medieval India has been underestimated largely because the actual extent of social and physical mobility has not been sufficiently appreciated.

## *VARṆA, JĀTI,* AND CLAN IN ANDHRA INSCRIPTIONS

Any discussion of the people of precolonial India must address the issue of caste, for caste has been most persistently and consistently presented as the essence of Indian society in the secondary literature. The typical portrayal of Hindu society recognizes two major levels in the caste system: the four *varṇas* and the myriad subcastes, or *jātis.* The *varṇa* system described in classical Sanskrit literature—with its orderly division of society into the four tanks of the brāhmaṇa (priest and scholar), *kṣatriya* (king and warrior), *vaiśya* (herder, trader, or cultivator), and *śūdra* (menial servant)—bears little resemblance to the complex realities of modem society. Whether the theory of the four *varṇas* was ever an accurate description of social divisions is a moot point; at any rate, it is evident that the identification of specific groups as *kṣatriya*, *vaiśya*, or even *śūdra* has been ambiguous for over a millennium.[2] Hence, many modern commentators regard the *varṇa* scheme as an idealized paradigm of societal functions. In contrast, the subcaste (*jāti*) is largely ignored in ancient social theory and appears to be a comparatively late phenomenon.[3] This social grouping—whose boundaries are demarcated on the basis of endogamy, commensality, and hereditary occupation—is seen as the true operative unit of the Hindu social system in more recent times.

If *varṇa* and *jāti* were indeed the two most significant aspects of social organization in traditional India, we would expect to find numerous references to them in medieval Andhra inscriptions. Yet few of the donors of the endowments recorded in these document choose to describe themselves in these terms. Instead, persons figuring in inscriptions commonly only provide their names and those of their parents, and occasionally the names of their overlords and patrons. In the relatively rare instances when *varṇa* status is indicated in inscriptions, the individual involved is usually a brāhmaṇa. Brāhmaṇa *varṇa* claims are often indirectly expressed by phrases such as 'born of the mouth of (the Creator) Brahma' (*South Indian Inscriptions* [*SII* hereafter]10.316) or through reference to membership in a brahmanical *gōtra,* sometimes along with further mention of the Vedic school *(śākhā)* and scripture (*sūtra*) in which the person was trained. Far fewer people made claims in these records to royal *kṣatriya* or mercantile *vaiśya* rank. In only a couple of cases did people say they were *vaiśyas* (*SII* 10.357 and 446). Genealogical links with the ancient lunar and solar dynasties of kings described in the Purāṇas and other Sanskrit literature were the means by which *kṣatriya* rank was most often asserted. The alleged *kṣatriyas* were usually members of minor princely lineages in Andhra, with names derived from the great imperial families of South India such as the Chalukyas, the Pallavas, and the Cholas.[4]

One peculiarity of Andhra society is that many of the leading warrior families made no pretensions to *kṣatriya* status but instead proudly proclaimed their descent from the creator Brahma's feet. This is an allusion to the famous origin myth first found in the *Ṛg Veda* wherein the four *varṇas* are said to have originated from different portions of the body of Purusha, the primordial man (For example, *SII* 6.95, *SII* 10.281). It was from the creator's feet that the fourth, or *śūdra*, class sprang, and another way of expressing *śūdra* status was to say that one belonged to the fourth order of society (For example, Hyderabad Archaelogical Series [*HAS* hereafter] 19 Mn.46, *SII* 4 1053). The pride in *śūdra* origin is especially prominent in two records from the second half of the fourteenth century, in which *śūdras* are said to be the best of the four *varṇas* because they are the bravest (*Copper Plate Inscriptions in the Hyderabad Museum* [*CPIHM* hereafter] 1.17 v.8) or the purest (*Epigraphia India* [*EI* hereafter] 13.24 v.7).[5] Families in what was theoretically the lowest social category, and not the *kṣatriya* lineages of the coastal subregion, possessed the greatest degree of actual political power in medieval Andhra, despite their relatively humble ancestry.

The prevalence of *śūdra* ranking among politically prominent lineages in medieval Andhra is exemplified in the case of the Kakatiya dynasty. The majority of inscriptions in which the Kakatiya genealogy is presented make no specification of their *varṇa* affiliation. But when a *varṇa* ranking is assigned to them, in most cases the Kakatiyas are said to have been born in the fourth class, that which emanated from Brahma's feet. The following excerpt is representative of the general tenor of Kakatiya Sanskrit inscriptions:

> The four-faced Brahma, having sprung from the center of Vishnu's navel-lotus, created the celestial beings. Then from his own mouth, arms, thighs and lotus-feet, he produced the brāhmaṇa, the king, the *vaiśya* and the *śūdra*, respectively. The Kakatiya dynasty, praised by the entire world and belonging to the fourth *varṇa*, then came into existence. In it was born the king named Prola, who was renowned for being exceedingly judicious (*HAS* 13.14).

Only a handful of records, almost all inscribed on copper plates, attempt to provide this ruling family with a more illustrious ancestry.[6] In these inscriptions the Kakatiyas are linked with the solar dynasty of the ancient *kṣatriyas*, stemming from Ikshvaku through Dasharatha and Rama, in what seems to be an imitation of the genealogy of the imperial Chola rulers.[7]

The lack of consistency regarding the *varṇa* rank of the Kakatiya dynasty is noteworthy, as is the fact that their *kṣatriya* claims were put forth primarily in documents associated with gifts to brāhmaṇas. Other records of the thirteenth century produced by families possessing political power similarly reveal little interest in asserting high *varṇa* rank. Had this rank been crucial to social recognition and prestige during that time, we would observe a greater number of royal and chiefly lineages advancing claims to *kṣatriya* status. That they did not indicates the relative insignificance of *varṇa* for non-brāhmaṇas in the thirteenth century. In other words, the classical *varṇa* scheme was meaningful primarily to those who considered themselves brāhmaṇas. Current research suggests that consciousness of *varṇa* became stronger during the colonial period, partially as a result of the listing of castes according to *varṇa* affiliation in the Census of India.[8]

*Jāti* is, if anything, even less visible in thirteenth-century records than *varṇa*. In modern South Asia, the term *jāti* is employed in a wide range of applications. Besides designating an endogamous group, jāti also refers to categories of persons differentiated by language, regional origin, and religion. In effect, *jāti* simply signifies a kind, category, or sort of person. We also find this broad usage of the word in thirteenth-century Andhra. On the rare occasions when the term *jāti* figures in the epigraphic sources, it has a very general meaning. The phrase *padunenmidi jātula praja,* literally meaning 'the people of the eighteen *jātis,*' is equated with the more frequently occurring *aṣṭādaśa praja,* or 'the 18 (kinds of) people' (For example, *HAS* 19 Km.6 and 7).[9] A few lists in contemporary literary sources name the units comprising the collective of eighteen, but the lists do not agree with each other.[10] Thus the number eighteen appears to be formulaic, indicating either a variety of (unspecified) communities or the totality of social groups in a locality or village.[11]

In the general scholarship on South Asia, *jāti* is depicted as a social group with a definite character, clear-cut boundaries, and an immutable quality. However, the accuracy of the common Western perception of *jāti* and the caste system (in the sense of a ranked social order composed of a number of *jātis*) is questioned, even for the modern period, by specialized works on caste. While a closed marriage-circle may indeed exist as the outcome of a succession of discrete marriage choices, the *jāti* as such may have little concrete reality in the eyes of its participants, according to some observers.[12] Other scholars dispute the very notion that an actual marriage-circle can be specified, despite the perception of participants that such groups of people exist.[13] Lower-ranking communities today, particularly those in service occupations, are often said to lack a clear *jāti* organization of their own and have less defined forms of endogamy.[14]

Not only is the word *jāti* rarely found in thirteenth-century inscriptions from Andhra, but there are also no references to specific subcastes by name. Particularly notable is the failure to mention the territorial divisions of the dominant landed castes of modern Andhra, although Burton Stein has alleged that all major landed communities in South India were territorially subdivided into local segments.[15] Given a situation today where the subcaste unit may be amorphous, it is most likely that well-articulated social organization at this level had not yet developed in thirteenth-century Andhra, even among higher-ranking groups. To be sure, the absence of references to specific *jātis* in thirteenth-century inscriptions does not prove that distinct subcaste units were also non-existent in this period but, rather, it shows us that subcaste membership was not an outstanding or memorable feature of an individual's identity in his/her transactions with the larger society. This 'argument from silence' can thus attest to the irrelevance of subcaste affiliation for the purpose of enhancing prestige in publicly displayed records.

There are other social units besides the *varṇa* and the *jāti*—clans and lineages, for example—whose study has languished because of the academic preoccupation with *jāti*. Some of these other social categories may prove to be of greater significance in certain localities than the jāti...

Numerous references to clans occur in Andhra inscriptions of the thirteenth century; *kula* is the term most widely used, with at least seven different *kulas* named in the records.[16] These *kulas* appear to be broad groupings of lineages with alleged kinship ties that stem from a shared eponymous progenitor. Thus, Durjaya is cited as an ancestor by many chiefly lineages from Telangana—including the Kakatiyas (*Inscriptions of Andhra Pradesh* [*IAP* hereafter]-W.29), Malyalas (*HAS* 13.8), Viryalas (*IAP*-W.27)—as well as by lineages from coastal Andhra such as the Konakandravadis (*SII* 4.780), the Ivani Kandravadis (*SII* 10.253), the Kondapadmatis (ARE 346 of 1937–38), the Parichchhedis (*SII* 10.430), and the Chagis (*SII* 4.748). *Kula* may also denote a social unit far larger than a clan, as when it is used in connection with the solar and lunar divisions of the ancient north Indian *kṣatriya varṇa* (*SII* 5.61, *IAP*-C 1.137). So claims to membership in a particular *kula* may simply reflect status aspirations, rather than any actual belief in ancestry.

Some individuals in Kakatiya Andhra cited their *vaṃśa* name, in addition to that of their *kula*, implying that these two words denoted distinct levels of kinship or group affiliation (*SII* 6.588; *SII* 10.265, 278, and 442). *Vaṃśa* is sometimes glossed as 'race' in English and is the word most closely associated with the solar/lunar distinction among *kṣatriyas*. But occasionally *kula* and *vaṃśa* are used interchangeably to refer to the same named group (*SII* 10.398). No systematic differentiation between *kula* and *vaṃśa* can therefore be made since these two terms do not consistently apply to different units of social organization. Some overlap of meaning is also witnessed with a third term for clan, *gōtra* (For example, *SII* 5.55, *SII* 10.197 and 312). On the whole, however, *gōtra* affiliation is more straightforward, with a few princely families of *kṣatriya* rank using the names of brahmanical *gōtras* like Bharadvaja, Kashyapa, and Manavyasa. Non-brahmanical *gōtras* are cited by a number of individuals who were merchants, some with the title Lord of Penugonda.[17] This community of merchants, who resided in the coastal territory, considered themselves *vaiśyas* and are regarded as the precursors of the modern Komati community.[18]

The way people appearing in the epigraphic records identified themselves tells us much about the social categories that were considered important at the time, and in thirteenth-century Andhra the clan and/or lineage was the most frequently mentioned kinship unit. Donors who cited clan names in inscriptions, with the exception of the few merchants noted above, were almost always members of lineages that possessed political and military power. Their political prominence places them in a position homologous to the dominant castes of modern ethnography, among whom strong clan and lineage organization is characteristic.[19] As in more recent times, the people in medieval Andhra who were most likely to possess a strong identity as members of a clan or lineage had the greatest control over land and landed income. This comes as no surprise since, in Laurence W. Preston's words, 'while anyone can construct his biological genealogy (given, of course, adequate historical records or traditions), only with a shared descent of property does this have a social relevance'.[20]

The absence of well-articulated social groups above the lineage or clan level in thirteenth-century Andhra inscriptions may result from the instability of the period. Much of inland Andhra was newly settled, and local societies were still in the process of emerging. The physical movements of people migrating to frontier areas would naturally have led to a great degree of social fluidity in the hinterland. But even the local societies of the delta region were affected by the changing balance of power and the intrusion of warrior lineages from the inland territories. Research on lineages elsewhere in India suggests that kinship networks were more restricted in the earlier phases of their history. So, for instance, kinship ties were less significant among Rajput lineages in the initial stages of power building, for often the founder of a lineage would have migrated to a new territory with a small number of kinsmen. Only in the later stages of the developmental cycle of a Rajput lineage, when it had succeeded in dominating a sizable area of land, did a large body of kinsmen organized into stratified and distinct tiers appear.[21] The same phenomenon was observed in the Pudukkottai region of the Tamil country. Separate kin groups who migrated into Pudukkottai gradually began to form larger affinal networks because of their territorial proximity. Through these marriage ties, originally separate groups of families gradually developed into a subcaste unit.[22] Hence, it is possible that clearly defined subcastes had not yet emerged from among the evolving lineages of Kakatiya Andhra.

On the other hand, doubt has also been expressed about the presence of the caste system in Tamil Nadu during the Chola era, from the ninth through thirteenth centuries.[23] Since the wet zone of the Tamil country was more densely populated and had a longer history of agrarian settlement than did most of Andhra, it should exhibit signs of organized subcaste activity if stable political conditions typically led to the formation of subcastes. In this connection, Ronald Inden's statement that castes 'in something resembling their modem form [do not] appear until the thirteenth or fourteenth century, at the earliest' is worthy of further consideration (1990: 82).[24] Whether or not we believe the caste system, as such, existed in late medieval India, it is obvious that we need to pay greater attention to the lineage level of social grouping.

## A TYPOLOGY OF STATUSES

We have seen that neither *varṇa* nor *jāti* was a prominent element in the public identity of individuals who figured in religious endowments from medieval Andhra. The only markers that are consistently found, the only items that would situate a person in a social context, are sometimes a lineage but most often just the individual's name and those of his/her parents. Hence names are the most direct form of social identification available, as labels or signifiers invariably possessed by every person. Admittedly, though names cannot tell us a great deal, particularly about social relations among groups and individuals, they do constitute a significant method by which people represented themselves to the society at large. Given the emphasis placed on naming in the ancient Indian tradition and the widespread belief in an ontological correspondence between a person's name and the person himself, we must assume that names were considered highly meaningful by medieval Andhra elites.[25] Because men's names generally contained components beyond the merely personal (that is, what we would consider a first name), analysis of them gives us some insight into the social classifications that were prevalent in medieval Andhra.

Names possessed by men varied considerably in length and in structure. The following inscription provides three examples, each somewhat different:

In the 1,218th year of the Shaka era [1296 CE.J, on the 5th (day of the) dark (fortnight of the lunar month) Chaitra, a Sunday, at the time of *uttarāyaṇa saṅkrānti*[26]

Tammili Bhimaya Raddingaru's son Chodaya Raddingaru gave land to the illustrious great lord Kshirarameshvara for a midday service, for his own religious merit. Fields in the lands of the village Pallavadapalli were purchased from Hanungi Kuchenangaru (to wit): a plot of 1 *kha(ṇḍuga)* in the fallow land to the south of the village and 2 *kha(ṇḍugas)* to the east of Udukula canal. Another *kha(ṇḍuga)* in the lands of Peddavipara near the village Modalikudulu was purchased from Hanungi Kuchenangaru. Out of this total of 4 *kha(ṇḍugas)* of land, I (Chodaya Raddingaru) will supply 1 *tūmu* of paddy grain for the food offering and 3 *gūnas*[?] 1 *sōla* of butter daily to the temple of the lord, for as long as the moon and sun endure.

Also given by Chodaya Raddingaru for this midday service: a metal plate (weighing) 3 *visya* 14 *pa*(*lamu*), a large censer weighing 2 *visya* 2 *pa*(*lamu*), a plate for burning camphor (weighing) 10 *pa*(*lamu*), a bell (weighing) 1 *visya* 4 *pa*(*lamu*), and a conch shell (weighing) 1 *visya* 10 *pa*(*lamu*). (*SII* 5.131)

According to this inscription, a man called Chodaya Raddi (*gāru* is a Telugu honorific) purchased land from Hanungi Kuchena, ostensibly to give to the Kshirarameshvara temple at Palakol in West Godavari district. In reality, however, the terms of the endowment reveal that Chodaya Raddi would retain the land and instead supply a stipulated amount of foodstuffs to the temple. He also gave a number of ritual implements for use in the worship of the deity. Chodaya Raddi's father is said to be Tammili Bhimaya Raddi.

The father and son pair, Tammili Bhimaya Raddi and Chodaya Raddi, share a common last component to their names—Raddi, a variant of the better-known Reddi. This component is known as the *gaurava-vācakamu* (literally, 'honorific word') in modern Andhra, a term I translate as 'status title'.[27] Immediately preceding the status title are the men's personal names, Bhimaya and Chodaya. In the case of the father Bhimaya we also find an extra prefix, Tammili. This was an *inṭi-pēru,* 'house-name', derived from the place-name of the family's ancestral village or from an illustrious predecessor.[28] The third man also had an *inṭi-pēru* (Hanungi) and a personal name (Kuchena) but possessed no status title as a suffix. The individuals figuring in this record thus had up to three components to their names: *inṭi-pēru,* personal name, and status title.[29]

Eminent persons often had an administrative title that preceded all other parts of the name. The administrative title indicated possession of an 'official' position such as that of general or minister, as we see in the case of Mahapradhani Mallala Vemadri Raddi (*SII* 4.1333). This man had the official or administrative title *mahāpradhāni,* which showed that he was a minister; the *inṭi-pēru,* or house-name, Mallala; and the personal name Vemadri followed by the status title Raddi. It was not uncommon for men to bear administrative titles in lieu of *inṭi-pēru* (for example, Mahapradhani Muppadi Nayaka, Nellore District Inscriptions (*A Collection of the Inscriptions on Copper Plates and Stones in the Nellore District*) hereafter NDI Kandukur 25), as well as in addition to them. The length of the name was not always a marker of prominence, for some important subordinate chiefs under the Kakatiya rulers of Telangana lacked administrative titles.[30] Some men also placed their father's name prior to their own personal name, so that we find instances like Marayasahini Rudradevaningaru—the man Rudradeva who was the son of Maraya Sahini (*ARE* 307 of 1934–5).

Of the various components of masculine names in medieval Andhra, the last element, the status title, is the most useful in establishing a social typology. Personal names are numerous and, with a few exceptions, seem to bear no status connotations.[31] The house-name may have been used to regulate marriages, for nowadays lower-ranking Andhra subcastes (who lack clan organization) prohibit marriage between families with the same *inṭi-pēru*.[32] Except in the case of a few powerful lineages, however, for whom it functioned as a dynastic label, the house-name was of limited significance in medieval Andhra. Administrative titles are fairly rare in Kakatiya Andhra inscriptions and their exact meanings are unclear. Status titles, on the other hand, are both widespread and limited in number, which makes it possible to conduct statistical analyses and attempt categorization of them. Of the 723 individual male donors represented in the body of data from the Kakatiya period, 514 men (71 per cent) have this component in their names. (Status titles are very rarely possessed by women.) Table 6.1 provides information on the variety and distribution of status titles found among men who made religious endowments, as well as on male donors without titles and on female donors.[33]

Particular sets of status titles were adopted by men in roughly the same type of occupation. This becomes especially evident when we examine the titles used by medieval Andhra brāhmaṇas, who differentiated themselves according to the means of their livelihood. One set of titles, the Sanskrit terms *bhaṭṭa* and *paṇḍita,* were reserved for individuals knowledgeable in religious matters. Charakurikardi Narayana Bhatta is one of these brāhmaṇa religious specialists who is said to have performed the Vajapeya sacrifice (*SII* 6.205). Another example is Mahadeva Bhattopadhyalu, whose brāhmaṇa rank is alluded to by his claim as belonging to the Bharadvaja *gōtra* (*SII* 10.452). A second set of status titles seems to have been used for brāhmaṇas of a more secular bent. *Pregaḍa*, *amātya*, and *mantri* all had administrative or clerical connotations and thus imply literary skills. Considerable indirect evidence indicates that these three titles were restricted in their social range, since men with these title often claim brāhmaṇa *varṇa* rank or cite their membership in brāhmaṇa *gōtras*.[34] It seems likely for this reason that the status titles *amātya*, *mantri*, and *pregaḍa* could only be borne by brāhmaṇas with non-religious means of livelihood.

**Table 6.1.** Classification of Individual Donors

| *Title* | *Donors* | | *Endowments* | |
|---|---|---|---|---|
| | *No.* | *%* | *No.* | *%* |
| Nāyaka | 114 | 14 | 129 | 13 |
| Rāju | 86 | 11 | 131 | 13 |
| Reḍḍi | 77 | 10 | 92 | 9 |
| Mahārāja | 53 | 7 | 95 | 9 |
| Seṭṭi | 50 | 6 | 56 | 5 |
| Bōya | 46 | 6 | 51 | 5 |
| Pregaḍa | 20 | 2 | 23 | 2 |
| Śivācārya[a] | 14 | 2 | 26 | 3 |
| Leṅka | 10 | 1 | 12 | 1 |
| Cakravarti | 8 | <1 | 16 | 2 |
| Bhaṭṭa | 5 | <1 | 5 | 1 |
| Misc. titled men[b] | 31 | 4 | 45 | 4 |
| Untitled men | 209 | 26 | 229 | 22 |
| Women | 87 | 11 | 109 | 11 |
| Total | 810 | | 1,019 | |

a. Includes Shaiva sectarian leaders with other titles such as rāśi, śambhu, and the like.

b. Includes the title *amātya, bhakta, camūpati, dāsa, dēsaṭi, mantri, ōju, paṇḍita, rautu, sāhiṇi, sēnāpati,* and *vaidya.*

We also find a number of individuals claiming to be brāhmaṇas who bear the status title *rāju,*[35] the Telugu equivalent of the Sanskrit *rājā* and most often used by princely lineages. *Rāju* could also designate an individual prince, however. Of the eighty-six men called *rāju* in the body of data, fifty can be identified as having royal or noble descent (whom I label royal *rājus*), while the remaining thirty-six are ministerial or clerical (and almost certainly brāhmaṇa) *rājus*. The distinction made in modem Andhra between brāhmaṇas engaged in secular occupations, known as *niyōgi,* and those who are religious specialists, called *vaidiki* (Vedic brāhmaṇas), is reflected in the two sets of status titles possessed by medieval Andhra brāhmaṇas. The religious specialists were known as *bhaṭṭa* or *paṇḍita,* while secular brāhmaṇas were variously called *amātya, mantri, pregaḍa,* or *rāju*. The interchangeable character of titles within a given set is shown in the case of the man Induluri Annaya, who bears the status title *pregaḍa* in one inscription (*SII* 5.110) and *mantri* in another (*Epigraphia Andhrica*, hereafter 4.12).

Similarly, there are a number of titles associated with royalty. The most well-known, *mahārāja*, was used by the Kakatiya dynasty and by several other noble lineages located south of the Krishna river or in the interior portion of Andhra.[36] The Telugu variant *rāju* was the preferred appellation among royal families of the northern coastal territory.[37] The more elegant Sanskrit word *cakravarti* (universal emperor) was adopted by minor lineages descended from the imperial Eastern Chalukya kings who still flourished in East Godavari and West Godavari districts during the twelfth and thirteenth centuries.[38]

A last set of titles has military connotations. *Camūpati, sāhiṇi, sēnāpati*, and *rautu* all point to command of armed forces of some type. *Leṅka* also refers to a warrior, although it seems to mean a member of a lord's own private troops rather than a commander. The *leṅka* lived, fought, and died with the lord to whom he had sworn his services.[39] The most prevalent status title of all—*nāyaka*, literally meaning 'leader'—is part of this military set. One individual in our sample was known both as Jaya Senapati (*SII* 6.214) and as Jaya Nayaka (EI 5.17). *Nāyaka* is an ambiguous term, however, that also encompassed local notables, as well as military leaders.[40] The majority of the *nāyaka* men in the corpus of inscriptions mentioned the name of their royal overlords, and roughly one-third of them possessed administrative titles such as *mahāpradhāni* (minister), *sāmanta* (allied subordinate or feudatory), and *sēnāpati* (general). *Nāyakas* hence ranked below kings and princes, to whom they generally owed allegiance. Because the title *nāyaka* was adopted by a wide range of important persons, variant versions of it—*nāyaka, nāiḍu, nāik*—are employed today in the names of diverse castes in South India and Orissa.[41]

Up to this point I have been describing sets of status titles that circulated within certain specific social classes—Vedic brāhmaṇas, secular brāhmaṇas, royalty, and the military elite. The status titles themselves are obviously not the names of distinct castes since they have overlapping referents. For instance, the titles *pregaḍa* and *mantri* were borne by the same person, as were *nāyaka* and *sēnāpati* by another man. Even if the status titles are not the actual labels of specific castes, however, they could be taken as indicators of caste allegiance. That is, one could argue that the various social types signified by status titles represented different castes or caste-clusters. This argument is strengthened by the nature of the three remaining widespread titles found in medieval Andhra inscriptions, *reḍḍi, seṭṭi*, and *bōya*.[42] None of these three are interchangeable with other titles, and both *reḍḍi* and *seṭṭi* are widely regarded as caste names today. In modern Andhra Pradesh, *reḍḍi* is a name associated with a powerful landowning cluster of subcastes, while *seṭṭi* forms part of the caste-name of many South Indian merchant communities. Additionally, although the term *bōya* is no longer in use, one of the synonyms for *bōya* in the inscriptions is *golla*, the name of a widespread caste-cluster of modem Andhra pastoralists.[43]

Whether the interpretation of status titles as signifying caste affiliation is accepted or not depends a great deal on how one defines caste. Clearly the status titles do not correspond to the four *varṇas* of the classical Sanskrit tradition. Nor do modern scholars generally mean *jāti* when they speak of caste. Caste is often used to refer rather to a level of social organization at least one step above that of the *jāti* or subcaste. Some castes are said to be aggregations of just a few subcastes who know about each other and sometimes act in concert.[44] Members of this type of caste have substantial social interaction, in forms like the sharing of food or possibly even the exchanging of daughters in marriage, because they reside in a fairly compact territory. In this restricted definition of caste, there would commonly be a sense of shared origin—that is, a belief that the constituent subcastes were somehow related. It is evident that the status titles do not refer to communities of such limited character because of the diversity of people using any given title.

The breadth of social groups encompassed by a status title is particularly well illustrated in the case of the term *seṭṭi*. In medieval times this title was used by the Teliki community of oilmongers in Andhra and by various artisan groups throughout South India, as well as by purely mercantile communities.[45] Even today we find that *seṭṭi* and its Tamil equivalent *cetti* are utilized by a whole series of merchant, moneylending, and trading groups.[46] For instance, Kathleen Gough reports the presence of the Telugu Komati Chettiars in Tanjavur, along with the Nattukottai Chettiar caste of Madurai.[47] Because this title is used by communities of different geographical origin and linguistic background, *seṭṭi* cannot be interpreted as specifying a caste. It should be understood instead as the label of an entire social class, designating any person involved in the production and sale of commercial goods. Similarly, *reḍḍi* was a title originally held by village headmen regardless of their hereditary background.[48] Hence, although it had associations with agriculture, *reḍḍi* did not signify a specific hereditary group of peasants in medieval times. And the fact that the words *gōpa* (the Sanskrit word for 'cattle herder') and *golla* (the Telugu equivalent of *gōpa*) are used as synonyms of *bōya* underlines the term's significance.[49] The title *bōya* referred to the occupation of herding, rather than to a particular community.[50]

Status titles thus indicated membership in an overall occupational class rather than a localized community. Some scholars might still assert that the status classes represented castes, if they define caste broadly as a sociocultural category rather than more narrowly as an organized and interrelated group. The various endogamous subcastes that form a caste, in this broader definition, typically share no more than a name and occupation and perhaps some customs.[51] (The term 'caste-cluster' is sometimes used to designate this level of social grouping.) The reality of a caste exists more in the mind of the outside observer than in actuality, even though members of similar subcastes usually accept the assertion of common caste affiliation.[52] Since there are generally no attributions of kinship ties nor even any social interaction between the several subcastes in the larger caste unit, the main factor by which others identify them as a single social group is their shared occupation. In the words of Louis Dumont, 'One may conclude that profession is one of the differences, perhaps the most indicative difference, whereby a group seen from the outside, a caste, is designated'.[53]

If a similar occupation is the primary criterion for the inclusion of *jātis* in a caste, the second, broader, definition of caste (or caste-cluster) would seem to greatly resemble that of *varṇa.* Since the various subcastes that are combined under a common caste name might have no hereditary or kin link, surely a genealogical connection cannot be considered the defining feature of a caste. The entire system may be predicated on the principle of membership by birth in the constituent subcaste units, but caste identity derives from perceived similarities among subcastes based primarily on a shared societal function or occupational identity (such as potter, weaver, merchant, and so on). The four *varṇas* of Sanskrit literature are also social classes defined by occupational function. If caste merely denotes a grouping of social units that share a similar profession and status, then a caste (cluster) resembles a *varṇa* as a functional rather than genealogical classification.

Of course, much of the difficulty in defining caste occurs because there is no exact equivalent in indigenous languages. This is not to deny the existence of marriage-circles or hierarchical relations in Indian society. But well into the colonial period, if not even now, people in India had complex social identities in which, depending on the situation, one or another element would take the foreground. When colonial censuses attempted to ascertain caste affiliations, therefore, the responses ranged from names designating endogamous groups or occupations to titles and surnames. No single category to which people claimed affiliation corresponded to the Western construct 'caste.' But the colonial classificatory systems assumed that castes were coherent and homogeneous entities whose populations could be enumerated and whose characteristics could be specified. As Rashmi Pant astutely observes, the large mass of details accumulated about caste through the censuses and similar surveys were considered as confirmation of its existence, and so 'the theoretical question "what is caste" was increasingly hidden by the substantiality of caste beings'.[54]

The modern sociological discourse on caste derives from colonial practices and conceptualizations. Caste, in the sense of a large bounded community composed of interrelated subcaste units, is increasingly viewed as a theoretical construct (particularly for the precolonial period) rather than an observable reality.[55] This explains why anthropologists have disagreed on how to define a caste *grouping*, as distinct from the caste *system*. As we have seen, many scholars have now fallen back on occupation as the main criterion in establishing caste affiliation. In fact, European visitors of the seventeenth and early eighteenth centuries also classified Indian social groups primarily on the basis of occupation, as well as region of origin.[56] And, indeed, occupation appears to be the key factor in attributions of group identity among Indians themselves. The peoples known as gollas in Andhra today, for instance, comprise a heterogeneous conglomeration of endogamous groups linked only by the similarity of their traditional livelihood.[57] S. Westphal-Hellbusch[58] describes several instances of name shifts among pastoral groups occurring through assimilation. When segments of the cattle-breeding Rabaris of Saurashtra and northern Gujarat moved to eastern Gujarat and switched to sheepherding, they were no longer known as Rabari but instead were named for the local shepherd community, Bharvad. Conversely, another camel-breeding group that moved into Rabari territory has now been absorbed by the Rabaris and lost their distinctive name. In both cases, the critical criterion for classification was the type of animal husbandry practised. Along similar lines, G.D. Sontheimer has shown how both the occupation and name of the Gavli pastoralists of Maharashtra were assumed by another group that adopted the Gavli lifestyle.[59]

In other words, indigenous thought does differentiate broad categories of people even though concrete social entities corresponding to what we now call castes may not have existed. Often these social types are signified by the use of the same title. Dirks points out that titles associated with specific subcaste groups in Tamil Nadu were often adopted by other subcastes with similar occupations because of their prestige.[60] The Vellalar title 'Pillai' was usurped by other communities in Tanjavur including the Kallars, Maravars, and Agambadiyars.[61] Likewise, in north India many unrelated groups have adopted the names or titles of locally prominent ones. Hence, no common ethnic identity, kin relation, or social interaction necessarily motivated the use of the same title, which essentially identified a social category formed through the coming together of diverse groups that perceived commonalities between themselves or aspired to the prestige of an already-established group.[62]

I would argue that the status titles of medieval Andhra similarly reveal the existence of broad social categories based primarily on occupation. Although each particular title did not necessarily designate a distinct class, much less a bounded community or a hereditary grouping, various sets of these titles differentiated social types marked by a common status and shared occupation. The inscriptional status titles can be grouped into the following seven categories:

| | | |
|---|---|---|
| *bhaṭṭa/paṇḍita* | = | Vedic brāhmaṇa |
| *amātya/mantri/pregaḍa/rāju* | = | secular brāhmaṇa |
| *cakravarti/mahārāja/rāju* | = | royalty or nobility |
| *seṭṭi* | = | merchant, trader, artisan |
| *bōya* | = | herder, pastoralist |
| *reḍḍi* | = | village headman, warrior-peasant |
| *nāyaka/camūpati/sāhiṇi/ sēnāpati/rautu/leṅka* | = | military leader, local chief |

Taken as a whole, the status titles should be understood as a medieval Andhra form of social typology. They do not, of course, reflect all the multiple social identities that a single individual might embody, whether sectarian, linguistic, and kin-related or territorial and political. Nonetheless, since the titles appear in the same context, that of a publicly displayed inscription, there must be some consistency in what they signify. The social typology inherent in the status titles does not encompass all existing social groups. Those of inferior status and occupation do not appear in this scheme, for the simple reason that almost all medieval inscriptions document transfers of property to Hindu temples and hence only record the names of persons who owned something of value. Obviously, other classes besides those enumerated above existed. The issue is not to describe every existing social group but rather to note the salient fact of the medieval Telugu social universe's conceptual division into discrete functional orders or estates.[63] The significant point for our discussion here is the centrality of occupation in determining how people were classified.

[...]

## SUMMARY: THE FLUIDITY OF SOCIAL IDENTITIES

In the many debates over the true nature of precolonial Indian society, information drawn from inscriptional sources has been conspicuously lacking. The long dominance of structuralist approaches is certainly partially to blame. The messy details of actual behaviour seemed irrelevant to those searching for the underlying structures that were thought to generate practice, just as grammar generated speech activity. Behaviour that deviated from the ideal paradigm was no more than a lapse, an absence of culture. Inscriptional evidence of variation in cultural practice was thus no more significant than the linguistic divergences of epigraphic Sanskrit, which was similarly regarded as substandard. No allowance was made for regional variation, since it was assumed that the subcontinent constituted a single unified cultural zone. Nor have current, post-Orientalist approaches much improved our understanding of the precolonial past. Reconstructions of India before the British arrived are still often derived from colonial data, albeit from the early colonial period, and the many centuries of prior history collapsed into a monolithic and changeless traditional India.

I reiterate the point I have made before—inscriptions are not the optimal source material. They tell us what kinds of resources the privileged people of the period possessed, but not how they got them nor from whom. As a form of discourse, inscriptions are similarly limited in the range of their producers and consumers, for few people were literate or had recourse to the literate. The social identities inscribed in this form did not constitute the totality of existing identities, nor did they necessarily correspond to concrete social entities. The representations of the self offered in inscriptions might very well have differed from representations in other contexts. With all these limitations, inscriptions can never assume the role of sole informants on past life. To the extent that it is available, other information should certainly be used in conjunction with inscriptions. At the same time, we cannot deny that inscriptions give us access to a small slice of the past. If we are sincere in wanting to reconstruct precolonial society without the distorting effects of colonial constructs or of hegemonic brāhmaṇa discourse, how else can we possibly proceed?

What we learn from Kakatiya Andhra inscriptions is that social identities, at least within this context, were not expressed in terms of *varṇa* or *jāti*. Instead, we find a social typology embedded in the use of titles appended to male names. Specific sets of titles were associated with particular occupations. Not all men possessed these titles nor did they necessarily assume the same titles as their fathers. On this basis I believe that the titles represent earned statuses rather than ascribed rank. The emphasis in inscriptions on individual achievements reinforces my contention that social standing was not based solely on hereditary attributes but could be considerably altered by an individual's accomplishments. Success in a military career may have been the easiest way for a man to move upward in the world, and the number of men with military skills and experience in Kakatiya Andhra was substantial. The opportunities for social mobility were reinforced by the considerable physical mobility of the medieval Andhra population. Furthermore, although individuals—including many women who had independent rights over property—generally acted on their own in patronizing temples, they could also come together out of collective interests beyond that of kinship or locality. The Andhra that one sees in inscriptions thus bears little resemblance to the rigid, tradition-bound society implied by the common model of a social system composed of hierarchically ranked and hereditary *jātis*. Indeed, the reputed centrality of caste in precolonial India is undermined by the inscriptional evidence.

[...]

The transformation of occupational identities such as *kā(m)pu* and *reḍḍi* into hereditary 'caste' labels did not occur in Andhra until at least the late Vijayanagara period (ca. seventeenth century), if even then. Throughout much of the medieval period, the abundance of land and the ever-changing patterns of agrarian settlement fostered flexibility in social relations and mutability in definitions of community.

## NOTES

1 Among the leading revisionist works are Susan Bayly, *Saints, Goddesses and Kings: Muslims and Christians in South Indian Society, 1700–1900*, Cambridge, 1989; Nicholas B. Dirks, *The Hollow Crown: Ethnohistory of an Indian Kingdom*, Cambridge, 1987, and 'The Original Caste: Power, History and Hierarchy in South Asia', *Contributions to Indian Sociology*, vol. 23, no. 1, 1989, pp. 59–78; Christopher J. Fuller, 'British India or Traditional India? An Anthropological Problem', *Ethnos*, vols. 3–4, 1977, pp. 95–121; Paul Pederson, 'Khatri: Vaishya or Kshatriya, an Essay on Colonial Administration and Cultural Identity', *Folk*, vol. 28, 1986, pp. 19–31; D.A. Washbrook, 'Law, State and Agrarian Society in Colonial India', *Modern Asian Studies*, vol. 15, no. 3, 1981, pp. 649–721; Washbrook, 'Progress and Problems: South Asian Economic and Social History c. 1720–1860', *Modern Asian Studies*, vol. 22, no.1, 1988, pp. 57–96.

2 Romila Thapar, 'Social Mobility in Ancient India with Special Reference to Elite Groups', in R.S. Sharma (ed.) *Indian Society: Historical Probings in Memory of D.D. Kosambi*, New Delhi, 1974, pp. 103, 117, and 120.

3 A.L. Basham, *The Wonder That Was India*, New York, 1959. However, note that there are a few instances in Sanskrit literature where the word 'jāti' is used to signify 'varṇa' and vice versa (Suvira Jaiswal, 'Studies in Early Indian Social History: Trends and Possibilities', in R.S. Sharma (ed.), *Survey of Research in Economic and Social History of India*, Delhi, 1986, p. 47; Arvind Sharma, 'The Purusasukta: Its Relation to the Caste System', *Journal of the Economic and Social History of the Orient*, vol. 21, no. 3, 1978, p. 296.

4 Families claiming descent from the Eastern Chalukyas of Vengi traced their ancestry to the lunar grouping (for example, *SII* 4.735, *SII* 5.61, *SII* 6.96), while minor Telugu branches of the Pallava and Chola dynasties belonged to the solar division of the kṣatriya order (for example, *IAP*-C 1.137; *Andhra Pradesh Archaeological Series*, hereafter *APAS* 31.15; *HAS* 19 Mn.26).

5 Śūdra origin continued to be a source of pride in the émigré Telugu culture of later centuries (Velcheru Narayana Rao, David Shulman, and Sanjay Subrahmanyam, *Symbols of Substance: Court and State in Nayaka Period Tamilnadu*, New Delhi, 1992, pp. 7–8).

6 For example, *CPIHM* 1.10; *EA* 1.7; *EI* 5.17; *EI* 12.22, *EI* 18.41; *HAS* 4, *HAS* 13.25; *SII* 10.395. Copper-plate inscriptions are usually longer and stylistically more elaborate than stone inscriptions. Since the language used in them is typically Sanskrit, it is not surprising that they should contain references to pan-Indic concepts and status claims. Copper plates most often record land grants to brāhmaṇas, although this is not always the case in thirteenth-century Andhra.

7 See George W. Spencer, 'Sons of the Sun: The Solar Geneology of a Chola King', *Asian Profile*, vol. 10, no. 1, 1982, pp. 81–95.

8 Bernard S. Cohn, 'The Census, Social Structure and Objectification in South Asia', *Folk*, vol. 26, 1984, pp. 25–49, Pederson, 'Khatri: Vaishya or Kshatriya'.

9 A similar phrase is also found in Kannada inscriptions (Burton Stein, *Peasant State and Society in Medieval South India*, Delhi, 1980, p. 219).

10 M. Somasekhara Sarma, *History of the Reddi Kingdoms*, Waltair, 1948.

11 The notion of eighteen social units is widespread in Telugu popular literature of the medieval period (V. Narayana Rao, *Siva's Warriors: The Basava Purana of Palkuriki Somanatha*, Princeton, 1990, p. 304, n. 3). The number eighteen is also found in Tamil traditions relating to the Vellalars (Nicholas B. Dirks, *The Hollow Crown: Ethnohistory of an Indian Kingdom*, Cambridge, 1987, p. 140).

12 Pauline Kolenda, *Caste in Contemporary India: Beyond Organic Solidarity*, Menlo Park, California, 1978, pp. 18, 20; Kathleen Gough, *Rural Society in Southeast India*, Cambridge, 1981, p. 21.

13 Declan Quigley, *The Interpretation of Caste*, Oxford, 1993, p. 165.

14 Brenda Beck, *Peasant Society in Konku: A Study of Right and Left Subcastes in South India*, Vancouver, 1972, pp. 72, 87, 90; Dirks, *The Hollow Crown*, pp. 267–9.

15 Burton Stein, *Vijayanagara*. Cambridge, 1989, p. 106.

16 We get references to a Manma kula (for example, *HAS* 13.27; *IAP*-W.53; *SII* 6.602), Ayya kula (*EI* 3.15), Matturu kula (*APAS* 38.15), Durjaya kula (for example, *SII* 4.743 and 1333, *SII* 10.269), Matsya kula (*SII* 4.1368), Kayastha kula (*SII* 10.346), and Karikala kula (*SII* 10.409 and 417).

17 Brāhmaṇa gōtras are cited by lineages of chiefs in *APAS* 31.15; *ARE* 26 of 1953–4; *SII* 6.588 and *SII* 10.278. Non-brāhmaṇa gōtras are mentioned in *ARE*

349 of 1937–8; *NDI* Rapur 20; *SII* 5.183, 216 and 217; *SII* 6.99; *SII* 10.264, 293, 299, 357, 446, and 456.

18 K. Sundaram, *Studies in Economic and Social Conditions of Medieval Andhra*, Machilipatnam and Madras, 1968, pp. 57–64.

19 Kolenda, *Caste in Contemporary India*, p. 18; Richard G. Fox, *Kin, Clan, Raja and Rule*, Berkeley, 1971, p. 71.

20 Laurence W. Preston, *The Devs of Cincvad: A Lineage and the State in Maharashtra*, Cambridge, 1989, p. 69.

21 Fox, *Kin, Clan, Raja and Rule*, pp. 70, 75.

22 Dirks, *The Hollow Crown*, pp. 222, 224.

23 According to Stein, this is the conclusion reached by B. Suresh in his doctoral dissertation on the geography and ethnology of the Chola period (Stein, *Peasant State and Society*, pp. 102–3). Y. Subbarayalu, on the other hand, enumerates sixteen different castes figuring in the inscriptions of Chola Tamil Nadu. Although the term jāti was often used in reference to them, Subbarayalu admits that 'many of the so called castes were found rather as professional groups than as kinship groups' (Y. Subbarayalu, 'The Cola State', *Studies in History*, vol. 4, no. 2, 1982, pp. 265–306).

24 Ronald Inden, *Imagining India*, London, 1990, p. 82.

25 P.V. Kane, 'Naming a Child or Person', *Indian Historical Quarterly*, vol. 14, 1938, pp. 224–44; Gregory Schopen, 'What's in a Name: The Religious Function of the Early Donative Inscriptions', in Vidya Dehejia (ed.) *Unseen Presence, The Buddha and Sanchi*, Mumbai, 1996, pp. 66–72.

26 *Uttarāyaṇa-saṅkrānti* was a very popular time to make endowments in Kakatiya Andhra. It marks the beginning of the six-month period when the sun is moving north of the equator and is the same as *makara-saṅkrānti*, or the day the sun moves into the zodiacal sign Capricorn. Hence I translate it elsewhere as 'winter solstice,' although the observance of uttarāyaṇa-saṅkrānti in this era had diverged from the actual winter solstice due to calendrical inaccuracies. This inscription is dated on 25 March, however, which corresponds to makara-saṅkrānti, the day the sun enters the sign Aries, rather than to makara-saṅkrānti.

27 Personal communication from Malathi Rao.

28 Sarma, *History of the Reddi Kingdoms*, p. 260.

29 For more on Telugu names, see Andre F. Sjoberg, 'Telugu Personal Names: A Structural Analysis', in Bhadriraju Krishnamurti (ed.), *Studies in Indian Linguistics: Professor M.B. Emeneau Sastipurti Volume*, Poona, 1968, pp. 313–21.

30 Cheraku Bolla Reddi is one such instance (*APRE* 133 of 1966; *SS*: 169–70).

31 The suffixes *-peddi* and *-manci* on a personal name appear to mark brāhmaṇas (personal communication, S.S. Ramachandra Murthy).

32 Bruce Tapper, *Rivalry and Tribute: Society and Ritual in a Telugu Village* in *South India*, Delhi, 1987, p. 30; Edgar Thurston, *Castes and Tribes of Southern India*, 7 vols, reprint, Delhi, 1975 [1909], vol. 3, p. 314.

33 Only those records with adequate information on the donors were considered in this chapter, comprising a corpus of 1,024 inscriptions. The majority of these inscriptions (892 records, or 87 per cent) were issued by individual donors rather than by groups. Because some inscriptions document multiple sets of endowments, individual donors were actually responsible for a total of 1,019 different acts of

religious gifting (that is, endowments), as enumerated in Table 6.1. The number of donors is smaller than the number of endowments because some donors made more than one gift.

34 Brāhmaṇa amātyas appear in *SII* 10.325 and 337; brāhmaṇa *mantris* are found in *APRE* 408 of 1967, *IAP-W*.69, *SII* 4.1366, and *SII* 10.406; and *pregaḍas* who are definitely brāhmaṇa are donors in *HAS* 19 Mn.46, *SII* 4–715, *SII* 5.146, *SII* 10.318 and 453. Brāhmaṇa *varṇa* status has been ascribed only when membership in pan-Indic brāhmaṇa *gōtras* is specified or when the donor explicitly states that he is a brāhmaṇa.

35 *ARE* 324 of 1930–1 and 293 of 1932–3; *SII* 4.718 and 728.

36 For example, the Telugu Pallava lineage of Guntur and Prakasam districts (NDI Darsi 69, Kanigiri 24, Kandukur 61; *SII* 6.588; *SII* 10.278 and 362); the Yadavas of Addanki in Prakasam district (NDI copper-plate 17, Darsi 72, and Ongole 28); several Telugu Choda lineages in Prakasam, Nellore, and Cuddapah Districts (*ARE* 285 of 1949–50 and 18 of 1968–9; *IAP*-C 1.159; NDI Atmakur 7, Darsi 28, Kandukur 60, and Ongole 17-B); and the Kanduri Chodas of Nalgonda and Mahbubnagar districts (*APAS* 31.15; *ARE* 224 of 1935–36; *HAS* 19 Mn.17 and 34; SS.162–3 and 167–8). The title usually appears in the honorific plural form *mahārājulu* in Telugu inscriptions.

37 Among the dynasties that preferred this status title are the Parichchhedis of Krishna and Guntur districts (*SII* 4.969 and 985; *SII* 6.120; *SII* 10.269, 282, and 426), the Chagis of Krishna district, the Kolani princes of West Godavari district, and the Kota dynasty of Guntur district.

38 For example, *SII* 5.111, 112, and 141; *HAS* 13.25; and *EI* 4.33.

39 N. Venkataramanayya and M. Somasekhara Sarma, 'The Kakatiyas of Warangal', in G. Yazdani (ed.), *Early History of the Deccan*, London, 1960, p. 670.

40 Stein, *Peasant State and Society*, p. 407.

41 Thurston, *Castes and Tribes of Southern India*, vol. 5, pp. 38–40. *Nayudu* is the singular form of nāyaka in Telugu, *nāyakulu* is the plural and/or honorific form.

42 Other miscellaneous status titles are *bhakta* (Shaiva sectarian allegiance), *dāsa* (indicating Vaishnava sectarian allegiance), *dēsaṭi* (possibly referring to a segment of the *reḍḍi* community), *ōju* (from the Sanskrit word *upādhyāya* and used by master artisans), and *vaidya* (Ayurvedic doctor).

43 The singular form in Telugu is *bōyuḍu*, individual *bōyas* do not typically use the honorific plural.

44 David G. Mandelbaum, *Society in India*, Berkeley, 1970, p. 20.

45 K. Sundaram, *Studies in Economic and Social Conditions of Medieval Andhra*, Machilipatnam and Madras, 1968, p. 39.

46 David W. Rudner, 'Religious Gifting and Inland Commerce in Seventeenth-Century South India', *Journal of Asian Studies*, vol. 46, no. 2, 1987, pp. 372 n. 11.

47 Gough, *Rural Society in Southeast India*, p. 30.

48 Thurston, *Castes and Tribes*, vol. 6, p. 230; Sarma, *History of the Reddi Kingdoms*, p. 75.

49 Certain *bōyas* are referred to as *gōpa* in *SII* 4-1370, *SII* 10.284 and 333; bōya and golla are equated in *SII* 5.197. Bōyas often appear in Kakatiya-period inscriptions as the persons who are entrusted with livestock endowed to temples.

50 The meaning of bōya has changed considerably over time. During the seventh century, it appears appended to village place-names as an alternative designation for brāhmaṇa recipients of religious grants (*EI* 8.24, 18.1, 31.12). It may have either meant 'resident' or denoted a particular village office. By the eighteenth century, the label bōya was used for a Telugu-speaking community in the Kurnool–Anantapur region, resembling the Kannada-speaking Bedars, who were associated with hunting and often served in local armies (Thurston, *Castes and Tribes*, vol. 1, pp. 180–93).
51 Kolenda, *Caste in Contemporary India*, p. 20; Bernard S. Cohn, *India: The Social Anthropology of a Civilization*, Englewood Cliffs, N. J., 1971, p. 116.
52 Louis Dumont, *Homo Hierarchicus: The Caste System and Its Implications*. Chicago, 1970, p. 63; Cohn, *India: The Social Anthropology of a Civilization*, p. 126.
53 Dumont, *Homo Hierarchicus*, p. 95.
54 Rashmi Pant, 'The Cognitive Status of Caste in Colonial Ethnography: A Review of Some Literature on the Northwest Provinces and Oudh', *Indian Economic* and *Social History Review*, vol. 24, no. 2, 1987, p. 161.
55 See the discussion in David W. Rudner, *Caste and Capitalism in Colonial India: The Nattukotai Chettiars*, Berkeley, 1994, pp. 17–25. Rudner himself disagrees, believing that castes, defined as 'corporate kin groups with enduring identities, a variety of rights over property, and crucial economic roles' have functioned at supralocal levels over the last few centuries (p. 25).
56 Gita Dharampal-Frick, 'Shifting Categories in the Discourse on Caste: Some Historical Observations', in Vasudha Dalmia and Heinrich von Stietoncron (eds), *Representing Hinduism*, New Delhi, 1995, pp. 89–94.
57 Gunther-Dietz Sontheimer, 'The Dhangars: A Nomadic Pastoral Community in a Developing Agricultural Environment' in L.S. Leshnik and G.D. Sontheimer (eds), *Pastoralists and Nomads in South Asia*, Wiesbaden, 1975, p. 142.
58 S. Westphal-Hellbusch, 'Changes in Meaning of Ethnic Names as Exemplified by the Jat, Rabari, Bharvad and Charan in Northwestern India', in L.S. Leshnik and G.D. Sontheimer (eds), *Pastoralists and Nomads* in *South Asia*, Wiesbaden, 1975, pp. 117–38.
59 G.D. Sontheimer, *Pastoral Deities in Western India*, Anne Feldhaus (trans.), New York, 1989, p. 105.
60 Dirks, *The Hollow Crown*, pp. 174, n. 17, 248.
61 Gough, *Rural* Society *in Southeast India*, p. 300.
62 Fox, *Kin, Clan, Raja and Rule*, pp. 12–22, 44–6.
63 My impression is that a similar social typology existed in medieval Karnataka, with, for instance, *gavuḍa* replacing the Telugu reḍḍi, and *heggaḍe* instead of pregaḍa.

# 7

# Women and Power in Early Medieval Kashmir*

Devika Rangachari

**Early medieval Kashmir constitutes a discursive space that has been comprehensively delineated in terms of 'relevant' factors like its politics and topography. Yet, one of its most cardinal aspects—that of gender—remains in relative obscurity, an obscurity that is deepened by limited attempts to analyse this issue and by a general indifference towards women and their role in this time-span. Ironically, the very sources that are used for this seemingly all-inclusive yet gender-blind outline are the ones that lend themselves to a fruitful gender analysis and point to the extensive power and public presence enjoyed by royal and non-royal women in early medieval Kashmir. This essay discusses the potential of some of these sources for an understanding of gender relations in Kashmir between the seventh and the twelfth century AD. The focus here is on three literary sources that represent different genres of work—Kalhaṇa's *Rājataraṅgiṇī*, Kṣemendra's *Samayamātṛkā*, and the *Nīlamatapurāṇa*. The epigraphic evidence for this period in Kashmir is very inadequate and can, at best, be used as limited corroboration for textual material.**

## KALHAṆA'S *RĀJATARAṄGIṆĪ*[1]

The selected time-span of this study roughly corresponds to the historical subject matter provided by Kalhaṇa's *Rājataraṅgiṇī*, the most

*** Previously published as 'Gender Relations in Early Medieval Kashmir' in Upinder Singh and Nayanjot Lahiri (eds), *Ancient India: New Research*, New Delhi, Oxford University Press, 2009, pp. 282–304.**

important and exhaustive source for this period. The text provides a sequential narrative of the rulers of Kashmir from the earliest period (for which only legendary traditions exist) till the date of Kalhaṇa's work (AD 1149–50) in the form of a *kāvya* of 7,826 verses divided into eight books/*taraṅgas* of differing length. It owes its pivotal position in reconstructing Kashmir's history to several factors. On the one hand, it is the fullest and most authentic account of early Kashmir and is seen as a singular example of the genre of historical chronicles. In his endeavour to provide an authentic account of the history of Kashmir, Kalhaṇa consulted other types of evidence as well, such as sculptural and architectural remains, inscriptions, and coinage. Additionally, his lucidity, coherence, and attempts towards chronological precision imbue this text with great significance.

On the other hand, the text's treatment of women as historically relevant figures and the depiction of the immense formal and informal power wielded by them in this period indicates its lesser-known yet equally meaningful potential in the realm of gender studies.[2] Kalhaṇa's text highlights the power and agency of women in royal court culture in two essential ways—as sovereign rulers in their own right and as powers behind the throne. Power is wrested and exercised by them in what is essentially a patriarchal edifice, thus causing a certain amount of tension and ambiguity, not only in specific phases of Kashmir's history, but also in Kalhaṇa's portrayal of them. The contrast between the narrative and didactic sections of Kalhaṇa's text, evident in his alternate glorification and denigration of women, not only stresses their agency, but also reveals the complex power equations in the royal domain. This deliberate narrative style, however, has either been ignored or misinterpreted in secondary writings on Kashmir.

## Women Rulers

The *Rājataraṅgiṇī* reveals female rulership in Kashmir as an aspect that cut across time-spans and dynasties, and, moreover, as culturally acceptable. The throne was a source of legitimate authority for both royal and non-royal women, either as direct rulers or as regents. This, naturally, posed a distinct challenge to prescriptive norms of succession that favoured the male and that denied women access to public roles of authority.

It may be pertinent to note here that the origin myths of Kashmir identify the land as Goddess Pārvatī's material manifestation. This is reiterated in the context of the definition of its rulership and is used, additionally, as justification for the rule of Yaśovatī (Gonanda dynasty, dates unknown), the first woman ruler of Kashmir.[3] Thus, although Yaśovatī herself has a shadowy presence, the rule of a woman is justified by Lord Kṛṣṇa's injunction that all occupants of the throne are portions of Śiva and, therefore, need to be obeyed, thereby providing a strong divine sanction to male and female rulership in Kashmir. The exercise of formal authority by women rulers of Kashmir is automatically validated by this comprehensive divine endorsement. A detailed description of Yaśovatī's reign is not available, but the paucity of details on her persona could be linked to the fact that her significance seems to lie in giving birth to the future heir, Gonanda II.

The reigns of Sugandhā and Diddā, the two most prominent women rulers of Kashmir, are based on much firmer historical ground. Sugandhā, daughter of King Svāmirāja of the northern region, appeared as a prominent figure in the last stages of the reign of her husband, Śaṁkaravarman, of the Utpala dynasty (AD 883–902). She accompanied him on a fatal military expedition, acquiesced in a bid to temporarily conceal the fact of his death for political reasons, and was spared from becoming a satī owing to the task of guardianship of their minor son, Gopālavarman, thrust upon her. Sugandhā eventually ascended the throne of Kashmir, backed by strong public approval, thereby testifying to her popularity. Thus, Kalhaṇa shows her role and influence to span Gopālavarman's reign (AD 902–4) and her own (AD 904–6).

Sugandhā's reign was marked by conflicts between rival military bodies, the *ekāṅgas* (royal bodyguards) and the *tantrins* (courtiers), interspersed with the growing influence of her lover, Prabhākaradeva, and her own forays into power politics, as, for instance, her determined attempt to crown her relative, Nirjitavarman, on the throne 'as he would follow her will'. Interestingly, Sugandhā was also implicated in Gopālavarman's death, apparently engineered by Prabhākaradeva. Subsequently thwarted by an open rebellion by the tantrins, who overruled her preference by crowning Nirjitavarman's minor son Pārtha instead, Sugandhā left the palace. Her abortive bid to regain power in AD 914 resulted in her imprisonment and eventual execution. Kalhaṇa's tone here is even-handed and he recounts the events of Sugandhā's reign in a largely objective manner.

Diddā, the third woman ruler of Kashmir, also commenced her pursuit of power as a regent. Daughter of Siṁharāja of Lohara and maternal granddaughter of the powerful Bhīma Śāhi of Udabhāṇḍa (who later built the magnificent Bhīmakeśava temple in Kashmir to underscore Diddā's power),[4] Diddā's formidable influence spanned the reigns of her husband, Kṣemagupta, of the Yaśaskara dynasty (AD 950–8), and that of their son and grandsons, until she herself ascended the throne in AD 980–1. Her influence on the largely ineffectual Kṣemagupta was amply proved by his coins where, unusually, the *di* prefixed to his name was intended as an abbreviation of hers.[5] Coins bearing Kṣemagupta's name alone are rare, whereas the other type with *di-kṣemagupta de(va)* are very common. Kalhaṇa provides corroborative information and reveals 'Diddākṣema' to have been Kṣemagupta's popular nickname. Kṣemagupta's death in AD 958 resulted in Diddā exercising total power as guardian during the reign of their son, Abhimanyu (AD 958–72), displaying great political sagacity and fortitude.

As with Sugandhā, her growth to political maturity involved confrontations with rebellious factions and contenders to the throne. However, it was here that Diddā emerged triumphant, quelling her opposition with a sure hand, and soon dismissing the help of male councillors in her solitary pursuit of power. Interestingly, Diddā was physically disabled and was carried around by a porter-woman, Valgā, but she did not let this deter her in her quest for authority.

Kalhaṇa provides an account of the ministerial rivalries that faced the regent Diddā, prompting her to take unsound and impulsive decisions. However, with time her potential to rule surfaced and the shrewdness of her schemes for safeguarding her power, as in her alternate bribe-and-placation policy, is noteworthy. On the one hand, she bribed the Brāhmaṇas to rectify the impasse between her and the rebel grandsons of Parvagupta (Kṣemagupta's father), and bestowed offices on other malcontents. On the other hand, she destroyed the more intractable rebels by 'witchcraft', thereby exhibiting a ruthless streak that subsequently came to the fore. Minister Naravāhana, who gave Diddā sound advice and defended her against rebel forces, was of great help to her initially. However, she soon shook off his support and managed to get rid of her enemies in a systematic and ruthless purge.

After Abhimanyu's death, Diddā speedily disposed off her three grandsons, Nandigupta, Tribhuvana, and Bhīmagupta, in quick succession. She then assumed formal power and continued to rule Kashmir in a competent manner, providing peace and stability as well as a strong and effective administration. It is, perhaps, in Diddā's case alone that epigraphic evidence is of some relevance. Thus, the Srinagar Buddhist image inscription of AD 989 and the Srinagar inscription of AD 992 refer to her by the masculine epithets of *deva* and *rājan*, respectively, rather than *devī* and *rājñī*, an interesting gender reversion.[6]

Interestingly, both Sugandhā and Diddā formed part of a succession of women who precipitated important dynastic changes in Kashmir's history. Thus, Sugandhā enabled her lover, Prabhākaradeva's family to gain prominence in that Yaśaskara, his son, was later able to start his dynastic line. Likewise, Diddā bequeathed the throne to her maternal family from Lohara after a shrewd selection contest that her nephew Saṁgrāmarāja, won. Consequently, on her death in AD 1003, the rule of Kashmir passed to the house of Lohara in undisputed succession, the latter holding sway until and beyond the date of the *Rājataraṅgiṇī*'s completion. Interestingly, Kalhaṇa lauds this 'third wonderful change' of dynasties caused 'by association with women'.[7]

Female rulership, therefore, was a strikingly significant feature of early medieval Kashmir, attesting the agency of its women in a very emphatic manner. Yet the evidence of the *Rājataraṅgiṇī* in this regard is routinely ignored or trivialized in secondary writings. Accounts of Sugandhā and Diddā are rife with uncritical portrayals. For instance, M.L. Kapur's endeavour to mould Sugandhā into a feminine stereotype of political ignorance, helplessness, and passivity militates against Kalhaṇa's deliberately ambivalent portrayal that portrays her as a puppet of various political factions on the one hand, but clearly indicates her ambition, shrewdness, and desire for power on the other.[8]

Kapur exonerates Sugandhā of any real desire for the throne. Nevertheless, the circumstances leading to her assumption of power and the cooperation of rival groups of ekāṇgas and tantrins in her reign, among other factors, are clear indicators of her diplomatic talents and ability to rule. Kapur further invests Sugandhā with a halo of martyrdom, noting that her comeback bid was due to her love for the people and her desire to free them from tantrin misrule. This, again, flies in the face of Kalhaṇa's evidence. The queen's reluctance to abandon the palace the first time around implies her reluctance to relinquish power. She was obviously not burdened by royal power, as Kapur believes, and was clearly interested in staking her claim to it more than once.

Kapur similarly tries to conventionalize Diddā's figure, although her rule is shown to parallel and even overshadow the impact of various male rulers.[9] Stressing her 'first impulse' to immolate herself on Kṣemagupta's death, he notes her intelligence and political talents but hastens to add that she was 'uncommonly voluptuous, profligate and dissolute' with a 'limitless' lust for power.[10]

Similarly, several historians like S.C. Banerjee, U.N. Ghoshal, and P.V. Kane focus on Didda's cruelty and ambition—in short, her temerity in desiring total power. Epithets like 'dissolute', 'notorious', and 'self-indulgent' freely abound, while, ironically, male rulers who display the same ambition or cruelty are accepted as strong political figures who clearly did not vitiate the political atmosphere in the way these transgressive women figures did.[11] Ironically, Aurel Stein, the principal translator of the *Rājataraṅgiṇī*, is himself guilty of minimizing the text's potential by completely ignoring the presence of Kashmir's women rulers in the genealogical tables in his introductory preface.[12] Here, Yaśovatī, Sugandhā, and Diddā appear only as spouses, and not as rulers in their own right.

Interestingly, although the coinage of the women rulers of Kashmir can also be used as an entry point to study their power and presence, there is hardly any information or analysis available on this aspect in secondary works on Kashmir.[13] Both Sugandhā and Diddā issued coins in their capacity as sovereigns that refer to them by masculine epithets—as *śrī sugandhā deva* and *śrī diddā deva*, respectively. This is an important attestation of their power, raising the issue of the popular association of political authority with maleness, and whether women rulers needed to conform to this to gain acceptance. It is also notable that the copper issues of Sugandhā and Diddā (and those of their spouses) were common in Kashmir for several centuries. However, this is a fact that evokes very little interest.

Incidentally, this attitude of indifference not only permeates works dealing specifically with early medieval Kashmir, but also those that deal with royal life or social/political conditions in north India in this period. The overweening male focus, the factual errors, ambiguous references and dismissive statements with regard to women, and the desire to view them only within the parameters of 'social conditions' seem alarmingly consensual.[14] This is an offshoot of the overall tendency to view women as a peripheral, non-reactive, non-participatory group, whose 'status' or 'position' mechanically changes to reflect larger changes around them, rather than envisaging a certain degree of agency for women vis-à-vis historical processes.

M.K. Dhar's *Royal Life in Ancient India* is an illustrative case where women rulers form a part of 'social conditions', and Diddā's motives for ruling are completely distorted.[15] She is referred to as a queen (unnamed, with no mention of Kashmir) who killed her three grandsons for power. Dhar then makes the inexplicable observation that this was the result of Diddā's frustration with the king for neglecting her and bestowing favours on the principal queen and her children instead! As noted earlier,

Diddā was Kṣemagupta's chief and most desired queen, and, in fact, was a widow by the time she felt the need to dispose off her grandsons. Likewise, Saroj Gulati who attempts a 'critical appraisal' of different social institutions/customs in north India and 'their influence on the position of women' dismisses Sugandhā and Diddā in a obscure reference and trivializes facts relating to women rulers in general.[16] B.N.S. Yadava, too, blames Kashmir's 'ambitious queens' rather than ambitious kings for ruining the political atmosphere, and is similarly dismissive of their rule and contributions.[17]

Vina Mathur's *The Role and Position of Women in the Social, Cultural and Political Life of Kashmir* that purports to undertake a pioneering study of the position of women in Kashmir and then proceeds to lambast Kalhaṇa's 'chauvinistic' attitude is another illuminating example.[18] What is missed in Mathur's intensely critical view is the fact of Kalhaṇa treating women as historically relevant figures and charting their rise to power with objectivity.

It should be noted that the examples cited here are only a few of the many inadequate analyses available on the women rulers of Kashmir. Works that appreciate their role and contributions are, predictably, minimal. Kumkum Roy's analysis, however, forms a welcome and notable exception to the trend of ignoring or explaining away the masterful presence of women in Kashmir.[19] Roy notes the existence 'of alternative socio-political norms' here and of the tension in the *Rājataraṅgiṇī* inherent in reconciling Śāstric norms with a situation that clearly did not conform to them.[20] She observes that the patrilineal (and patriarchal) ideal was only one among several contending power sources in Kashmir.

Another rare avowal is Ashvini Agrawal's work that notes the 'significant role' played by women in the political life of Kashmir 'from time to time'. The role of Sugandhā, Diddā, and other prominent queens 'as king-makers, sovereigns, mediators and diplomats' is conceded. However, Agrawal's work is more a straightforward rendition of details than an analytical exercise.[21]

Very few works, however, actually focus on the pertinent question of how the women of Kashmir were able to bypass ideological stipulations that associated political authority with maleness and emerge as powerful political figures. There are two ways of examining this problem. On the one hand, the prescriptions contained in the *Dharmaśāstras* and other texts can be juxtaposed with the actual exercise of political authority. A general survey of prescriptive and normative literature shows a distinct hostility to the idea of formal female authority. However, the prescriptions were clearly not inflexible/hegemonic, and could be subverted on occasion. The divergence of views among lawgivers itself strengthens this contention.[22] Female power in Kashmir can be traced to this gap between theory and practice.

What may also be kept in mind is that Sugandhā and Diddā are not entirely unrepresentative of the situation in early medieval India. Interesting parallels can be drawn with the Bhaumakara queens of Orissa, and other notable dowagers like Prabhāvatīguptā of the Vākāṭaka family (fourth century AD), and Vijayabhaṭṭārikā of the Cālukya house (seventh century AD) The evidence would indicate that women in ruling families, including the women rulers of Kashmir, had some familiarity with politics and administration.

On the other hand, Cynthia Talbot's study of early medieval India and Europe can be examined for its relevance.[23] Talbot considers women political leaders from three regions between the ninth and thirteenth century AD—Sugandhā and Diddā of Kashmir, the women rulers of the Orissan Bhaumakara dynasty (Gaurīmahādevī, Daṇḍimahādevī, Vakulamahādevī, and Dharmamahādevī), and the four women rulers of Andhra (Rudramadevī, Gaṇapamadevī, Muppaladevī, and Vīryālā Nāgasānī). She then draws a parallel with medieval European women who possessed greatest political power in roughly the same period, pointing to the decentralized nature of the medieval European polity that associated political authority with particular families, thereby blurring the distinction between public and private spheres.

Claiming that medieval Kashmir, Andhra, and Orissa all resembled early medieval Europe in their lack of centralization, Talbot notes that women occupied a pivotal role in this decentralized situation where political power was personalized and could be embodied through marriage relations. Women were allowed to exercise political authority on several occasions to ensure the retention of a throne within the immediate kin group. Sugandhā's reign is a case in point. Thus, the centrality of the family in certain political cultures of the time could explain the phenomenon of ruling queens.

In addition, regency provided a justification for female authority. Talbot notes that the regent queen is shown as foregoing the 'attractive' option of self-immolation in order to fulfil her responsibilities towards her family and kingdom. Yet it is crucial to note here that both Sugandhā and Diddā used their regency as a stepping-stone towards acquiring power, and, hence, were not passive regents in the conventional sense.

The phenomenon of women exercising power in Kashmir, therefore, served to indicate constantly fluctuating social processes. Talbot stresses the flexibility of the prevalent gender ideology and construction of identity as well, whereby the gap between theory and practice could be reconciled through manipulation of gender imagery and privileging of maternal obligations. However, unlike rulers such as Rudramadevī and Raziya Sultan who deliberately adopted masculine clothing, styles, and titles to gain public acceptance, Kalhaṇa does not indicate any such attempt by the women rulers of Kashmir, except for the masculine titles on their coins. This indicates that women were tacitly accepted as legitimate wielders of power in the area.

One should also note that Talbot's theory cannot be rigidly applied to Kashmir. For instance, Diddā's bestowal of the throne to the Loharas was unorthodox in that the rights of her maternal family triumphed over that of the Yaśaskaras, her husband's family with whom the sovereignty was associated. Thus, her natal ties were given precedence over her husband's family. The formation of another dynasty, the Kārkoṭas, was similarly unusual in that the sovereignty was vested in the descendants of a king's daughter.[24] The specific conjunction of social and political circumstances that allowed women to exercise authority in Kashmir still remains a largely unexplored issue. One could, however, speculate that the strong tribal roots of this region, as also its geographical location that isolated it from the other kingdoms of north India, combined to produce a political and social climate that was conducive to the public presence of women with relatively unstructured gender roles.

## THE POWER BEHIND THE THRONE

The *Rājataraṅgiṇī* shows power being exercised by royal and non-royal women of Kashmir in a range of situations as queens, courtesans, court participants, mediators, dynasty makers and destroyers, and other capacities, thereby stressing their access to the public domain of politics. Prominent among the powerful queens was Sūryamatī, daughter of Inducandra of Jālaṁdhara and wife of Anantavarman of the Lohara dynasty (AD 1028–63). She acquired supremacy by solving a financial crisis with her independent resources and acumen. Thereafter, she took over the administration, dictated orders to Ananta, and eventually forced him to abdicate in favour of their son, Kalaśa. Despite Kalaśa's subsequent wayward behaviour, Sūryamatī restrained Ananta from punishing him, thereby prompting Ananta to kill himself. Sūryamatī's definitive political role was discernible even after her death in that Kalaśa's son, Harṣa's initial survival in politics was due to her sage advice.

Another prominent queen was Kalhaṇikā, wife of Jayasiṁha of the Lohara dynasty (AD 1128–49), who dispelled a rebel threat by her mediation. Having become chief queen with public approval, Kalhaṇikā underscored her importance through her influential role as mediator, successfully effecting a reconciliation between Jayasiṁha and his rebel cousin, Bhoja, and preventing an incipient *ḍāmara* rebellion.[25] Raḍḍādevī, Jayasiṁha's other wife, played an equally pivotal role in independently devising politically strategic marriages for her daughters. Other powerful queens included Śrīlekhā, Ananta's mother, who made an abortive bid for the throne, Śāradā, wife of Sussala, who legitimized a rebel scheme, and Sugalā, wife of Harṣa, who failed to kill him, but later boldly staked her claim as chief queen.

The vigorous participation of non-royal women in court politics was another striking feature of early medieval Kashmir. The diverse origin of queens was a clear indication that political power was a legitimate quest for non-royal women as well. In this context, the influence of courtesans and prostitutes on the throne was particularly noteworthy. For instance, Jayamatī, a temple dancer's ward 'of unknown origin' (VII.1460—...*kvāpi jātāṁ*...) and chief queen of Uccala of the Lohara dynasty (AD 1101–11), deliberately flouted his orders to kill Bhikṣācara, a future contender to the throne. She masterminded Bhikṣācara's escape and was, therefore, instrumental in enabling his accession to the throne at a later stage. Sāmbavatī, a courtesan and skilful mediator between political groups, and Kamalā, a temple dancer who was indirectly instrumental in the exiled Jayāpīḍa's resumption of power, were other stellar examples. So, too, was Jayādevī, a spirit distiller's daughter, whose hold over Lalitāpīḍa was used by her brothers to seize power, crown a series of puppet-kings, and eventually establish their own dynasty. There were numerous courtesans who appeared in the roles of dynasty makers/destroyers, power aspirants, court participants, and builders. Clearly, low origin was no barrier to their exercise of power in the public domain.

The *Rājataraṅgiṇī* provides other examples of prominent non-royal women in early medieval Kashmir. The role of the powerful ḍāmara-woman Chuḍḍā in charting political equations, challenging the reigning king, Sussala's might, and consolidating her son's power by becoming his guardian and protecting his interests was particularly noteworthy. So, too, was the role of Āsamatī, a relative of the Śāhi princesses, who changed the course of royal politics by thwarting Uccala's murderous designs, actively aiding Jayamatī in Bhikṣācara's escape, and at points seeming to be the more conniving of the two. In addition, one can consider Nonā, the rebel Bhoja's nurse, who played an important part in the reconciliation between him and Jayasiṁha by initially broaching the issue to the king. Sahajā, who mediated between Jayasiṁha and her rebel son, Mallārjuna's forces, and Sillā, who commanded her son's troops in his absence, were other illustrative cases. Obviously, therefore, non-royal widows were not relegated to passive roles in the contemporary socio-political scenario, thereby indicating an important point of convergence with some of their royal counterparts.

Nevertheless, the familiar bias against female figures in secondary sources is once more in evidence. This finds expression in, for instance, attempts to conventionalize Sūryamatī's figure, grudging mentions of Kalhaṇikā's role, and summary dismissals of the intervention of royal and non-royal women in politics in general.[26] Corroborative details of Sūryamatī's power in Bilhaṇa's *Vikramāṅkadevacaritam* (twelfth century AD) have been generally ignored, with the possible exception of the translators of the text who note that she was conversant with state policy.[27] Any attempt at a gender analysis or an acknowledgement of the light thrown on the contemporary socio-political scene is predictably missing.

## WOMEN BUILDERS AND DONORS

The building activities of men and women—as revealed by the *Rājataraṅgiṇī*—have important implications for a gender analysis of the politics and society of early medieval Kashmir. Royal and non-royal women are shown to parallel their male counterparts in this regard, indulging in building and donations not just for piety, but for other impelling motives as well. The power of women was made obvious in the physical landscape itself—in terms of the various towns, shrines, and buildings that usually bore their names (as, for instance, Kalyāṇadevī's Kalyāṇapura town and Diddā's Diddāsvāmin temple), and would have served as reminders to the people about their role and agency in a qualitatively visible sense. Although there is a clear linkage of power with the buildings of kings, this seemed to have been a driving factor for women too. The buildings of Sugandhā, Diddā, Sūryamatī, and other powerful queens like Ratnādevī (such as towns, *maṭhas*, temples, and *vihāras*) are a case in point. Prominent non-royal women builders included Sussala, the minister Rilhaṇa's wife, Valgā, Diddā's porter-woman, and the politically powerful courtesan, Sāmbavatī.

Thus, there were interesting variations in the social identities of builders and donors. Equally, there were disparate motives of donation. On the one hand, there were instances of women perpetuating their name through their towns/buildings, as in Diddā's Diddāpura town. On the other hand, there were women like Śrīlekha, an eager aspirant for the throne, who built maṭhas in honour of her husband and son against whom she was, simultaneously, plotting treason. Predictably, however, this well-documented sphere of female agency is either ignored or misconstrued by most writers on Kashmir. M.L. Kapur's attempt to associate piety and grief with the buildings of Sugandhā is a case in point.[28] The buildings of Diddā, the most prolific woman builder (the Diddāsvāmin temple, Diddāpura town and maṭha, the Siṁhasvāmin shrine, and her vihāra for foreigners being notable examples, in this regard), are summarily dismissed. So, too, are the *gokula*, maṭha, and town built by Ratnādevī, Jayasiṁha's wife, which outranked others of the same type in size and splendour.

Women's donations are closely linked with the control and extent of resources. Women donors in Kashmir were clearly not constrained by the norms of *Dharmaśāstra* texts in which their limited property rights and dependant religious identity precluded the possibility of their extensive/independent gift-giving. The Kashmir queens obviously had access to large amounts of money/resources that enabled them to finance constructions and make monetary donations towards buildings. Likewise, the possession of resources by non-royal women argues some amount of access and control in economic affairs.

Once again, one can draw attention to Talbot's study of thirteenth-century Andhra inscriptions wherein she concludes that royal women indulged in donations as this was the only socially sanctioned public activity and prestige-enhancing opportunity open to them.[29] This view is largely untenable in the case of women in early medieval Kashmir who had manifold opportunities for public and political activity, and did not need building/donative activities to register their presence. Their involvement in it was, in fact, a mere affirmation of their status.

The immense potential of the *Rājataraṅgiṇī* for a gender analysis of early medieval Kashmir is, therefore, obvious. On the one hand, Kalhaṇa conveys a sense of the interaction and tension between male rulers and female consorts, ruling queens and male advisers, and other protagonists in the royal court culture. On the other hand, one also gets a sense of the potentials and pressures in the world of non-royal women as they sought to negotiate for their sons and husbands in the political arena, as also an idea of the common social ground occupied by royal and non-royal women. An appreciation of the text's gendered potential is vital owing to the fact that it is used almost exclusively as a source for this period in Kashmir.

## KṢEMENDRA'S *SAMAYAMĀTṚKĀ*[30]

Although the *Rājataraṅgiṇī* provides significant examples of the role of prostitutes in early medieval Kashmir, it is Kṣemendra's *Samayamātṛkā* (eleventh century AD), a kāvya of 635 *śloka*s, which can be specifically related to Kashmir, that foregrounds their position and influence in a very effective manner. While its central idea of stressing the rapacity of the prostitute is reminiscent of Dāmodaragupta's *Kuṭṭanīmatam* (eighth century AD), its intrinsic potential for a gender analysis is greater—both in terms of the development of the story and in its overall characterization. The *Samayamātṛkā* essentially deals with a prostitute, Kaṅkālī's ingenious means of survival and her timely adoption as a mother by a young prostitute, Kalāvatī, whom she was instrumental in making wealthy by her judicious schemes. The numerous references to places in Kashmir as a part of Kaṅkālī's travels indicate a familiarity with its landscape and impart a tone of authenticity to the text.

The text traces the intelligent and resourceful Kaṇkalī's bid to survive by changing names, locales, and occupations, and simultaneously duping and controlling men with consummate ease. Sold at a tender age by her mother, Kaṅkālī (initially named Gargatikā) embarked on a trail littered with assumed names and pretended professions involving, among other things, fomenting trouble in a rich man's household to get rid of him and acquire his wealth, seizing the business of a horse-owner, bribing magistrates to fraudulently acquire property, cutting a jailor's tongue to escape imprisonment, pretending to be a businesswoman, a chief minister's daughter, and a spiritual adviser in turn, bearing a son and abandoning him after appropriating his jewels, assuming the identity of an ace gambler and astrologer, and duping and robbing kings, ministers, and fellow travellers. Her final successful endeavour was in helping Kalāvatī to ensnare a rich client, Śaṅkha, with clockwork precision, thereby justifying her selection as Kalāvatī's 'timely mother' (*Samayamātṛkā*).

As Kṣemendra's purpose was clearly to expose the cold-blooded aspects of prostitution, his stress is not so much on Kaṅkālī's resourcefulness and grit as on her deviousness and unscrupulousness. This translates into his harsh, and often exaggerated, portrayal of her character that is stripped of any redeeming feature. Her complete repudiation of motherhood underscores this. This makes an immediate point of contrast with the *Rājataraṅgiṇī* where the destructive potential of prostitutes is evoked along with their role as saviours and protectors, in a largely impartial manner.

Yet, ironically, Kṣemendra's stress on Kaṅkālī's rapacity actually underlines her strength, showing her to be a completely pragmatic survivor, and also indicating the possibilities and options open to a woman who was compelled by circumstances to live by her wits alone. Kaṅkālī's fluid adoption of various professions—most of which appear to be male prerogatives—further underscores the choices open to women who desired to lead unconventional lifestyles. Thus, she was alternately a businesswoman, manager of horses, astrologer, gambler, and maker of metal. The fact that people accepted her in these roles is an important comment on the contemporary social scene and corroborates Kalhaṇa's evidence on the public presence of women in early Kashmir. One might argue that prostitutes usually command a greater degree of freedom/licence than other women. However, Kaṅkālī always managed to conceal her actual trade from most of her associates. To them she was only an ordinary woman endeavouring to make a living.

Interestingly, Kṣemendra offers two varied motives for writing the *Samayamātṛkā*. He states at the outset that the text was intended to teach prostitutes the secret of their trade—a sarcastically worded intention, as his aim was clearly to teach the people about the threat posed by prostitutes.[31] The second motive, contained in the epilogue, was to provide the newly-crowned Ananta with ideas on the deployment of women in the enemy camp to effect the latter's downfall.[32] This is strongly reminiscent of Kalhaṇa's evidence of the destructive power of women and their potential to effect changes in rulership as, for instance, Cakravarman being murdered for his involvement with low-caste women, and Harṣa whose Śāhi wives egg him on to a self-destructive path. Ironically, while Kṣemendra strove to educate Ananta on the value of women as a political weapon, Ananta himself needed to be educated on political and other matters by his wife Sūryamatī, who took over the reins of administration from him.

Most secondary sources, once again, fail to exploit the *Samayamātṛkā*'s potential in revealing the specifics of a prostitute's status, and in indicating interesting points of convergence and divergence with Kalhaṇa's work among other things.[33] The bitterness of Kṣemendra's tone, viewed in conjunction with his intimate knowledge of prostitution, leads one to speculate whether it stemmed from some kind of personal experience and whether Kāṇkalī, one of the strongest female protagonists of contemporary literature, was based on an actual prostitute of his acquaintance. A more definite assessment cannot be made due to the lack of corroborative evidence. Nevertheless, the importance of prostitutes and their power, as attested by both the *Samayamātṛkā* and the *Rājataraṅgiṇī*, was a pivotal ingredient of the social and political history of early medieval Kashmir and, therefore, of a gender analysis of the time.

## THE *NĪLAMATAPURĀṆA*

The *Nīlamatapurāṇa* (seventh/eighth century AD), a Purāṇa of unknown authorship that provides information on the legendary lore, topography, and customs of Kashmir, is another important source for this period, and is the earliest indigenous text for the history of Kashmir. It provides the 'social background' to Kalhaṇa's 'dynastic and political history', and also corroborates the *Samayamātṛkā* in certain aspects.[34] Written in the Purāṇic style of interwoven dialogues, it is the only source that provides an account of Kashmir's formation, the details of which Kalhaṇa borrowed in his work. It also talks of the identification of the land of Kashmir and its sovereign with Goddess Pārvatī (Umā), as part of Lord Kṛṣṇa's justification for crowning its first woman ruler, Yaśovatī.

The importance of this text lies in the fact that it corroborates on a social level Kalhaṇa's indications of the power wielded by non-royal women in the political sphere. Of particular note was the participatory nature of their involvement in socio-political functions. Ranging from the king's coronation ceremonies to pilgrimages and annual festivals marking the land's birth, the participation of men and women on a more or less equal plane is implied. Furthermore, there are interesting indications of the intermingling of both sexes at various levels. Women were enjoined to accept gifts from their husbands' friends, and wine and dine with them, as part of the ritual worship of certain deities. This suggests a degree of freedom and liberality in society at obvious divergence from prescribed norms that dictated regulation of contact between the sexes.

Not only are women shown as enjoying themselves in a relatively uninhibited manner in indoor and outdoor festivals with men, as in the worship of Goddess Śyāmā that involved a festival of singing and dancing, but they also participated in and performed certain rites along with them, as in the worship of Goddess Kaśmīrā. There are several other indications of their status as, for instance, the stress laid on honouring maternal relatives and those by marriage. Of equal weight is the specific prescription of *śrāddha* (death ceremony) days for women along with men, an indication of the importance accorded to each sex.[35] Likewise, there are repeated references to 'happy women—well-fed, well-dressed, well-scented, well-anointed and decorated with ornaments', to be 'pleased' on particular days and 'honoured', as on the day of the first snow.[36] The significance of these injunctions lies in the fact that they form a part of the 'good customs' laid down by Nīla, the patron snake deity of Kashmir, for the acquisition of prosperity and peace by the people.[37] Hence, the enjoining of respect towards women and their participation in contemporary affairs in this list is noteworthy.

Significantly, the *Nīlamatapurāṇa* corroborates Kalhaṇa's picture of the power wielded by courtesans. They are equated with prominent citizens and are enjoined to play important roles in royal ceremonies as well as ordinary festivals. Interestingly, if the text apparently reflects the attempt to combat Buddhism and restore Brahmanical practices in Kashmir,[38] this then raises the question of how to reconcile the space accorded to prostitutes who are otherwise condemned in Brahmanical prescriptive works.

At the same time, the *Nīlamatapurāṇa* indicates that the position of women may not have been so remarkably exalted. The worship of (married) women on various occasions—as in the Īramañjarī festival or on the full-moon night of *mārgaśīrśā*—which is a notable refrain of the text, and its eventual linkage with fertility, is a case in point. Such a stipulation does not necessarily imply that women had a powerful position, but often the reverse. Moreover, the preconditions for this worship indicate that widows and single women are proscribed categories. Clearly, ambiguous signals of the agency of non-royal women can be recovered from the *Nīlamatapurāṇa*. And yet the perception of women as a relevant and participatory category stresses their role in the contemporary socio-political milieu. Questions can be raised on the authorial stance, on whether this was a reflection of reality and, if so, whether this could have laid the ground for the assumption of power by various categories of women in subsequent ages and the general acceptance thereof. There are no clear answers, but the mere fact that such questions can be raised exemplifies the potential of these sources for constructing a gender-sensitive history of Kashmir.

Yet, the *Nīlamatapurāṇa*'s potential in this regard has not been fully appreciated. The views of Ved Kumari, the principal translator of the text, are an illustrative example. For instance, although she acknowledges the 'somewhat different and unconventional picture' of female life in this text, she completely trivializes Yaśovatī's rule, of which the text gives important evidence. The queen is mentioned in passing at the end of a discussion on 'Women in the Family' as a part of the 'Position of Women'.[39] Yaśovatī does not even find a place in Kumari's discussion of the 'King and his Functions', despite being the first woman ruler of Kashmir and enabling the comprehensive definition of rulership in the kingdom. The potential of the text for a gender study is thereby effectively minimized.

Thus, that the same set of sources can be critically analysed to reveal a gendered perspective of early medieval Kashmir is undeniable. They reveal that royal and non-royal women of Kashmir seem to have wrested a distinct space for themselves within the contemporary society and polity. Their ability to subsume the patriarchal edifice in certain contexts and situations necessitates a rethinking of the negotiation of female identities within a patriarchal set-up.

As Roy notes, the rulers of Kashmir were evidently located within a social context that was less closely structured in hierarchical terms than the Śāstric ideal. Affinal kinsfolk could intervene to support/oppose rulers just as effectively as members of the patrilineage—and this was open to even relatively lower social categories like the *ḍomba*s and *cāṇḍāla*s. In such a situation, Roy opines that the rulers' conformity to Śāstric ideals would be superficial and their household would have contrasted with Śāstric norms at several levels. Domestic relations among non-royal groups would have been similarly loosely structured and divergent from the patrilineal model, thereby pointing to alternative forms of household organization in this region.

Women in Kashmir, therefore, clearly enjoyed a more equal status vis-à-vis men than those elsewhere and the assertion of their power seems to have been a fairly constant factor. One can contrast this with other parts of contemporary north India as, for instance, the kingdoms of Kanauj and Bengal-Bihar, where explorations of a similar nature reveal an intermittent expression of the role and influence of women over this time-span.[40] The question of woman's power is, consequently, a contextual one, calling for a careful analysis of available sources to glean pertinent information. The apparent irrelevance of women to the political and social order needs to be questioned and analysed, for this is often merely an erroneous projection by historical scholarship. In addition, it is necessary to explore the agency of different classes of women in any analysis rather than treating them as one amorphous whole. Thus, this essay has hopefully demonstrated the centrality of gender and its related explorations of female agency in any investigation of the society and polity of early medieval Kashmir.

## NOTES

1 M.A. Stein (ed.), *Kalhaṇa's Rājataraṅgiṇī*, vol. III, Bombay, 1988 (rpt); M.A. Stein (trans.), *Kalhaṇa's Rājataraṅgiṇī*, vols I and II, Delhi, 1989 (3rd rpt).

2 For more information on this theme, see Devika Rangachari, 'Gender and the Historical Chronicle: A Study of Kalhaṇa's *Rājataraṅgiṇī*', unpublished MPhil Dissertation, Delhi, 1997. See also Devika Rangachari, 'Kalhana's *Rājataraṅgiṇī*: A Gender Perspective', *Medieval History Journal*, vol. 5, no. I, 2002, pp. 37–75.

3 Ved Kumari (trans.), *The Nīlamata Purāṇa*, vol. II, Srinagar, 1973, verse 246. Kalhaṇa does not provide dates for this period of Kashmir's history, but Gonanda III can be presumed to have ruled around 1182 BC. The Gonandas were apparently the first dynasty to rule Kashmir.

4 Bhīma Śāhi is mentioned in Alberuni's list of Hindu Shahiyas of Kabul as the successor of Kamalu. He is also known from his coins.

5 Stein, *Kalhaṇa's Rājataraṅgiṇī*, vol. I, VI.177. Also A. Cunningham, *Coins of Medieval India*, Varanasi, 1967, p. 45, for details.

6 B.K. Kaul Deambi, *Corpus of Śāradā Inscriptions of Kashmir*, Delhi, 1982, pp. 97–8; K.N. Sastri, 'Srinagar Inscription of Queen Diddā', *Epigraphia Indica*, vol. XXVII, 1985 (rpt), pp.153–5. The first inscription records the consecration of a bronze statuette of the *bodhisattva* Padmapāṇi by Rājānaka Bhīmaṭa, a Buddhist devotee and son of Cāvata, and by the four brothers of Gaṇgā Devī. The second one mentions a certain Dharmāṇika honouring his mother by dedicating some religious institution or charitable work in her name.

7 Stein, *Kalhaṇa's Rājataraṅgiṇī*, vol. I, VI.366. Kalhaṇa's words are: *strī-saṁbandhena bhūpāla-vaṁśyānāṁ bhuvanādbhutaha, tritīya parivartoyaṁ vartate-mutra maṇḍale.*

8 M.L. Kapur, *Eminent Rulers of Ancient Kashmir*, Delhi, 1975; M.L. Kapur, *The History and Culture of Kashmir*, Delhi, 1992 (2nd edn).

9 Kapur, *History and Culture of Kashmir*, p. 45.

10 Ibid., pp. 50, 53, 59–60. Also Kapur, *Eminent Rulers*, p. 68.

11 S.C. Banerji, *Cultural Heritage of Kashmir*, Calcutta, 1965, p. 51; U.N. Ghoshal, 'The Dynastic Chronicles of Kashmir', *The Indian Historical Quarterly*, vol. XVIII, 1985 (rpt), p. 323; P.V. Kane, *History of Dharmaśāstra*, vol. III, Poona, 1946, p. 40.

12 Stein, *Kalhaṇa's Rājataraṅgiṇī*, vol. I, 'Introduction', Appendix II, pp. 139–44. Note that R.S. Pandit's translation of the *Rājataraṅgiṇī* is very literal and has an abundance of French terms. Moreover, his analysis of the text is sketchy, unlike Stein's well-structured and comprehensive one. See R.S. Pandit (trans.), *Rājataraṅgiṇī*, Delhi, 1935.

13 For instance, a seminal work on numismatics like P.L. Gupta's *Coins*, New Delhi, 1969, has a pronounced male bias and only fleetingly mentions associations of women with coins in early Indian history. For more information on the queens' coins, see Cunningham, *Coins of Medieval India*, p. 45; Devika Rangachari,

'Coinage and Gender: Early Medieval Kashmir', in H.P. Ray (ed.), *Coins in India: Power and Communication*, Mumbai, 2006, pp. 46–55.

14 For a critique of this, see Uma Chakravarti and Kumkum Roy, 'In Search of Our Past: A Review of the Limitations and Possibilities of the Historiography of Women in Early India', *Economic and Political Weekly*, vol. XXIII, no. 18, 1988, p. 2. See also B.D. Chattopadhyaya, 'General Editor's Preface', in Kumkum Roy (ed.), *Women in Early Indian Societies*, New Delhi, 1999, p. ix; Kumkum Roy, 'Introduction', in Kumkum Roy (ed.), *Women in Early Indian Societies*, New Delhi, 1999, p. 4.

15 M.K. Dhar, *Royal Life in Ancient India*, Delhi, 1991, pp. 9, 44–5, 58–9.

16 Saroj Gulati, *Women and Society: Northern India in the 11th and 12th Centuries*, Delhi, 1985, p. 28, where she mentions women rulers in one line. Also pp. 3, 39, 42.

17 B.N.S. Yadava, *Society and Culture in Northern India in the Twelfth Century*, Allahabad, 1973, p. 9.

18 Vina Mathur, *The Role and Position of Women in the Social, Cultural and Political Life of Kashmir: 7th century–16th century AD*, Jammu, 1985.

19 For more information on the consistent attempt to 'invisibilize' women in history, see Chakravarti and Roy, 'In Search of Our Past', pp. 2–10.

20 Kumkum Roy, 'Defining the Household: Some Aspects of Prescription and Practice in Early India', *Social Scientist*, vol. 22, nos 1–2, 1994, pp. 3–18.

21 Ashvini Agrawal, 'Women in the Political Life of Kashmir (c. AD 650–1150)', in C.M. Agrawal (ed.), *Dimensions of Indian Womanhood*, vol. I, Almora, 1993, pp. 87–8.

22 For instance, while the *Majjhima Nikāya*, the *Arthaśāstra*, and the *Jātakas* stress the complete unsuitability of a woman for rulership and administration, the Śāntiparva of the *Mahābhārata* authorizes the coronation of a vanquished ruler's daughter in the absence of suitable male candidates. See A.S. Altekar, *State and Government in Ancient India*, Delhi, 1958 (3rd edn), p. 87; A.K. Majumdar, *Concise History of Ancient India*, vol. 2, Delhi, 1980, p. 55; Beni Prasad and R.C. Majumdar, 'Political Theory and Administrative System', in R.C. Majumdar (ed.), *The Age of Imperial Unity*, Bombay, 1968 (4th edn), p. 303.

23 Cynthia Talbot, 'Rudrama-devī, the Female King: Gender and Political Authority in Medieval India', in David Shulman (ed.), *Syllables of Sky: Studies in South Indian Civilization in Honour of Velcheru Narayana Rao*, New Delhi, 1995, pp. 391–430.

24 For instance, Stein, *Kalhaṇa's Rājataraṅgiṇī*, vol. I, III.530.

25 Ḍāmaras were a class of feudal landholders that played an important part in the politics of Kashmir.

26 For instance, Ghoshal, 'Dynastic Chronicles of Kashmir', pp. 235–6; and Beni Prasad, *The State in Ancient India*, Allahabad, 1974, pp. 327–8, for an inadequate and cursory treatment of Sūryamatī's role. Also B.P. Mazumdar, 'Role of the Dāmaras in Medieval Kashmir', in K.M. Shrimali (ed.), *Essays in Indian Art, Religion and Society*, New Delhi, 1987, pp. 27–36, where there is no mention of Chuḍḍā and her role in the discussion on the ḍāmaras.

27 S.C. Banerji and A.K. Gupta (trans.), *Bilhaṇa's Vikramāṅkadevacaritaṁ*, Calcutta, 1965, p. 11.

28 Kapur, *History and Culture of Kashmir*, p. 43.

29 Cynthia Talbot, 'Temples, Donors, and Gifts: Patterns of Patronage in Thirteenth-century South India', *Journal of Asian Studies*, vol. 50, no. 2, 1991, p. 328.
30 R.S. Tripathi (ed. and trans.), *Samayamātṛkā of Mahākavi Kṣemendra*, Varanasi, 1967. Note that Kṣemendra's father was from a well-connected family in Kashmir and that his grandfather Narendra was a minister.
31 Ibid., I.3.
32 Ibid., 4.
33 For instance, Sukumari Bhattacharji, 'Prostitution in Ancient India', in Kumkum Roy (ed.), *Women in Early Indian Societies*, New Delhi, 1999, pp. 211–12, where she points to Kaṅkālī's 'lack of proficiency' in any other profession (a statement that is directly contradicted by the text), and ignores the indications of her grit and intelligence.
34 Ved Kumari, *The Nīlamata Purāṇa*, vol. I, Srinagar-Jammu, 1968, p. v.
35 Kumari, *Nīlamata Purāṇa*, vol. II, verses 485–6.
36 For instance, ibid., verses 548, 557, 483–4.
37 Ibid., verses 225, 900–1.
38 Deambi, *Corpus of Śāradā Inscriptions*, p. 263.
39 Kumari, *Nīlamata Purāṇa*, vol. I, pp. 94–5, 131–4.
40 For more information on gender in early medieval north India, see Devika Rangachari, *Invisible Women, Visible Histories; Gender, Society and Polity in North India (Seventh to Twelfth Century AD)*, New Delhi, 2009.

# Part III

## Religion and Culture, Within and Across Regions

# 8

# Domesticity and Difference/ Women and Men

## *Religious Life in Medieval Tamil Nadu**

Leslie C. Orr**

In recent scholarly examinations of women's ritual activity, there has been an increasing appreciation and valorization of the 'domestic'. This analytic category, which has been utilized with particular success by Susan Starr Sered in her research on elderly Jewish women's religious lives, has afforded investigators the opportunity to explore new contexts, to abandon an exclusive focus on formal and public expressions of religiosity, and to consider also the religious activities that take place outside of these frameworks and in arenas where women are more likely to be found.[1] But the conception of 'domesticity' implies not only a rethinking of the location of religion; even more important is the fact that it prompts us to pay attention to the interpretation of religious activities by those who engage in them. As Sered says, domesticity 'is not an inherent

* Previously published in Tracy Pintchman (ed.), *Women's Lives, Women's Rituals in the Hindu Tradition*, New York, Oxford University Press, 2007, pp. 109–29. By permission of Oxford University Press, New York.

** I am very grateful to Tracy Pintchman for her patience and perseverance as editor of this volume, to Norma Baumel Joseph for much conversation about and insight into women's ritual lives, to S. Swaminathan for invaluable aid in my work with the inscriptional material, to Padma Kaimal for delightful discussions about kings, queens, goddesses, and temples, to Anne Monius for sound advice on Tamil literary matters, to Katherine Young with whom I first read the *pavai* poems, to Uma Narayan for questions that helped clarify the issues at stake in this chapter, and to Michelle Bakker for her bibliographic assistance.

characteristic of any particular ritual, place, or event,' but is above all a matter of intent, in which 'the ultimate concerns of life, suffering, and death are *personalized*—domestic religion has to do with the lives, sufferings, and deaths of *particular*, usually well-loved, individuals'.[2] The acknowledgment of the validity and significance of such an orientation seems particularly helpful in the study of women's religious lives within the Hindu tradition, whose institutional structures generally exclude women from publicly recognized roles as renunciants or ritual specialists and whose textual traditions focus largely on men as the central religious actors and on transcending attachment as the primary goal of religious activity.

I propose in the present essay to explore whether a domestic religious orientation, engaged with the personal and the particular, can be discerned in the context of precolonial South India. My focus is on the period of the ninth to thirteenth centuries in that part of India today known as Tamil Nadu, and I draw on the resources provided by the thousands of inscriptions composed in the Tamil language and engraved in stone on the walls of Hindu and Jain temples during this period. These inscriptions record actions, particularly the making of gifts to temples, that were undertaken by a wide variety of people. These people—who sponsored building projects and gave land, money, livestock, ornaments, and images to the temple—included kings and queens, merchants and shepherds, Brahmins and temple women, and local 'lords' and their wives and daughters. There is, of course, a great deal that the inscriptions do not tell us; religious activities carried out in the home and in other contexts apart from the temple were rarely documented. Further, the inscriptions' accounts are restricted to the undertakings of people who had both the means to commission the engraving of such records and the desire that their actions should be known to posterity. But despite these limitations, the inscriptional corpus represents a discursive and social space in which both men and women participated, and it gives voice to particular individuals whose goals and motivations in undertaking various religious activities can be glimpsed in the records they have left.

## VOWS AND SELF-OFFERING

Perhaps the quintessentially domestic religious activity with which contemporary Hindu women are engaged, and which is attracting increasing scholarly attention, is the 'vow' or, in Sanskrit, *vrata*.[3] Women's observance of vratas typically involves worship, the creation of ritual designs, fasting, or other austerities, and the recitation of stories concerning the origin and power of the vow. These rituals are usually undertaken annually, on days sacred to the particular deity whose blessings are sought, and almost invariably have as their overt aim the well-being of children, brothers, or husbands. Hindu women throughout India observe such vows, and in contemporary Tamil Nadu, they are referred to by the term *nonpu.* It is therefore a matter of great interest to discover this word in the medieval Tamil inscriptions in the context of women's religious activities. Three stones set up in front of the temple dedicated to the goddess Mariyamman in Kandachipuram (a small place in South Arcot district), with short inscriptions in tenth-century characters, record the observance (*nol*) of *nonpu* by three women, all of them identified with reference to their fathers (*Annual Reports on [South Indian] Epigraphy,* hereafter *ARE* 57, 58, 59 of 1935–36); another stone found in a field in the nearby village of Ariyur documents the *nonpu* in the Durga temple of a woman who is nameless but is identified as someone's wife (*ARE* 234 of 1936–37).[4] Another four stones from Gangayanur, in the same area and evidently inscribed in the same period, bear very similar inscriptions; here the term *parani* is used instead of *nonpu,* but the verb *nol,* which is related to *nonpu* and means 'to endure, suffer, do penance,' is applied to the action of the four women—each of whom is identified both as a daughter and as a wife (*ARE* 458, 459, 460, 461 of 1937–38).[5] As these eight inscriptions are so few and so terse, we may find it useful to turn to Tamil literary sources for a greater understanding of the meaning of the term *nonpu* and the possible contexts for women's votive practices a thousand years ago.

An obvious starting point for such an examination is with two ninth-century devotional works, *Tiruppavai* and *Tiruvempavai*, the first composed by the female poet-saint Andal, a devotee of Vishnu, and the second by Manikkavachakar, whose poems praise Lord Shiva. Both of these hymns frame their expressions of praise and self-dedication within the context of a women's ritual in which a group of young women wake up early in the morning during the month of Markali in the cold season and go together to bathe in a pond or river, with the object of being granted a good husband. Andal's *Tiruppavai* is particularly detailed and informs us of the terms of the vow: the girls refrain from consuming ghee and milk, they bathe in the cold water and keep themselves unadorned, and they distribute alms. Following this period of self-denial, the girls dress up, feast on rich milk-rice, and take part in a procession featuring music, drums, singing, lamps, flags, and banners (*Tiruppavai* 2, 26, 27).

The *pavai* rituals outlined in these two ninth-century devotional hymns may possibly be linked to the temple festivals in the month of Markali that are described in inscriptions of the eleventh to thirteenth centuries. Although the inscriptions do not mention any special observances undertaken by women, or austerities as part of the proceedings, there are processions and feasting and even, at the temple of Tirupampuram (Tanjavur district), arrangements made for the singing of *Tiruvempavai*.[6] It is difficult, however, to see any connections between the pavai observances of the poems and the practices commemorated by the tenth-century *nonpu* and *parani* stones. For one thing, Andal and Manikkavachakar do not use the term *nonpu* to refer to the girls' ritual, which is called simply *pavai* or *markali niratal*, 'Markali bathing', in the poems. When we do encounter this term in the Tamil devotional literature—for example, in the hymns praising Shiva (composed in the sixth to ninth centuries) that are collected in *Tevaram*—it consistently refers to severe ascetic practices. In fact, those who most often perform *nonpu* in these texts are Jain monks, who are castigated by the Shaiva poets for their excesses (for example, *Tevaram* 2:121.10; 3:103.10; 5:32.9). In the sixth-century Buddhist text *Manimekalai*, the word also refers to austerities, which, again, are presented in negative terms, as selfish and vain, when undertaken by Jains (3.75, 90, 120; 21.98), although the text displays admiration for others who practise nonpu—including the Buddha himself (3.60; 5.99) and other sages and ascetics.[7] Twice in the *Manimekalai*, nonpu refers specifically to fasting, and in one case this is a fast to death; neither of these fasts is disparaged, nor identified as a Jain observance (T4.95; 17.4a).[8]

In light of the literary evidence, the tenth-century *nonpu/parani* stones would seem to commemorate the achievement of women who had carried out rather extraordinary acts of self-discipline—more along the lines of the *nonpu* of renunciants than the votive ritual of the young women in the *pavai* poems. In contrast to those who observed the *pavai* ritual, hoping to attain the auspicious state of marriage, the women who undertook severe ascetic practices would have done so with intentions similar to those of renunciants, seeking detachment from the realm of relationship and desire—a manifestly non-domestic goal. The inscribed stones, perhaps set up by their fathers or their husbands, may have honoured them for having completed an especially lengthy and rigorous fast, of the sort that is undertaken by Jain women today and celebrated by their families at its conclusion.[9] Or perhaps these women died in consequence of their austerities—since this is what is usually implied by the existence of a commemorative stone, in medieval South India as in contemporary North America.

For example, what is called in Tamil a *nicitikai* memorial was established in honour of Jains, both laypeople and renunciants, who undertook a fast to death *(sallekhana)*. In contrast to the many such inscriptions from the medieval period that one finds to the west, in what is today the state of Karnataka,[10] there are only a handful of these in Tamil Nadu. Of the Tamil records, there is only one (from Coimbatore district, in the western part of Tamil Nadu) that commemorates the fast to death of a woman, and her name, Pullappai, indicates that she was originally from Karnataka (*ARE* 597 of 1905). It appears that the practice of fasting to death as a means of purification—avoiding harmful behaviour and the accumulation of bad karma, striving for transcendence of one's physical state and liberation from this world—was less common, or in any case less commonly commemorated, by Jains in Tamil Nadu as compared to their cousins to the west. But in the Tamil country, these observances may not have been exclusive to the Jain community: it is possible that such practices and such motives are precisely those celebrated in the *nonpul/parani* stones.[11]

Another type of memorial that, again, is more commonly found in Karnataka[12]—and, even farther to the west, in Maharashtra[13]—is the *sati* stone. Indeed I know of no inscribed sati stones in Tamil Nadu.[14] There are, however, at least four inscriptions of the medieval period that have been engraved on temple walls in various parts of the Tamil country that record women's self-immolation: a tenth-century inscription from Allur, in Tiruchirappalli district, that records the gift of gold to the temple by a woman named Gangamadeviyar 'who was entering the fire' (*South Indian Inscriptions SII* 8.690); an inscription from Dharmapuri district, dated AD 1017, in which a wife is said to have 'entered the fire' following her husband's death (*Avanam* 12, 21);[15] the grant of land, recorded at Cheydunganallur in Tirunelveli district in the mid-twelfth century, for the merit of Puricanti, who 'entered the fire' (*ARE* 363 of 1959–60); and the gift of lamps by Vikrama Kampan for the merit of two persons who had died as a result of his attack—a warrior whose home had been ambushed and his wife, Vampu, who had subsequently 'entered the fire'—the donor having been ordered by the elders of the community to make this gift to the temple at Tirukalakkunram (Chingleput district) so that the brother of the dead man should desist from further vengeance (*ARE* 162 of 1932–33).[16] What is interesting is that two of these four inscriptions make no reference to the woman's status as a wife or a widow. In the absence of the mention of a husband, we may question whether these acts of self-immolation were satis at all, and I suggest that these women's self-sacrifice was not motivated by the desire to be reborn again with the bond of marriage preserved and to maintain the web of personal and particular familial ties even after death. That the first of these inscriptions records the woman's own gift to the temple, rather than arrangements made by others to honour her or make expiation for her death, indicates that the relationship being solemnized by her renunciation of life was that with God rather than with man. Thus this act of self-giving appears to be inspired by an impulse to transcend one's specific human and social condition.

In the Tamil country, and especially in the northwest parts of this region, the type of memorial we encounter most frequently is the hero stone. It is clear from the Tamil 'Sangam' literature of the early centuries of the first millennium that the setting up of hero stones for men who had fallen in battle or in cattle raids was a long-standing tradition.[17] The hero stones from the period we are considering—the ninth to thirteenth centuries—generally bear an image of an armed man and a Shiva linga, and about half of them are inscribed with a short statement telling how the hero met with death. Often he was engaged in combat on behalf of a lord and is referred to as his servant (*cevakan*); sometimes the person or group who erected the stone will also be mentioned (see, for example, *Cenkam Natukarkal CN* hereafter 56). As is the case for *nicitikai* and sati memorials, hero stones are much more abundant in Karnataka than in Tamil Nadu, and there they are adorned with more elaborate relief sculptures, including images of the hero ascending heavenward in the embrace of celestial maidens.[18] Although the hero stones found in Tamil Nadu lack such narrative depictions of the hero's postmortem destiny, the sculpting of the Shiva linga on many of these memorials suggests that the hero in death is consecrated to Lord Shiva, and will attain his divine abode—or, perhaps, that the hero's courageous protection of his community and loyalty to his chief are equated with the acts of self-sacrificing devotion performed by the worshipper.[19]

Another kind of self-offering recorded in the medieval Tamil inscriptions—and one with which women as well as men were involved—is the vow of the servant (fem. *velaikkari*, masc. *velaikkaran*) not to survive her or his master. There is a group of more than thirty records of such oaths of fealty by both women and men inscribed on the temple walls of Arakandanallur, in South Arcot district—a place very near to the sites where the *nonpu/parani* stones have been found (*ARE* 122–126, 136–150, 153–160, 162, 187, 188 of 1934–35). Another such record is found in the temple at nearby Elvanasur (*SII* 22.156): here we read of the vow made by the *velaikkari* Tevapperumal that she die together with her lord. Although these vows express the same values of faithfulness and self-dedication that are manifest in the hero stone inscriptions, they lack any explicit reference to religious motivations and expectations, devotion to a deity or anticipation of a heavenly reward; these records resemble other oaths engraved on temple walls in this part of South Arcot district, which solemnize political alliances among clans and agreements of mutual defence.[20]

Although we do not hear of any cases where the *velaikkari* or *velaikkaran's* promise of self-sacrifice in allegiance to a human lord was actually effected, devotion to the cause of a divine lord did result in acts of self-immolation. There is an inscription of the twelfth century from Punjai, to the south, in the Kaveri delta region, where we see a group of servants (*velaikkarar*) loyal to the trident of Shiva, who gave up their lives—by entering the fire—in support of the temple's contention of ownership of certain properties. The rival claimants to the land had to concede to the temple and were required by the local assembly to set up metal images of those who had died and to make a donation to provide for worship of these images (*ARE* 188 of 1925). At Paiyanur in Chingleput district, an inscription of uncertain date records another land dispute, evidently between the temple and the Brahmin assembly, in which two ascetics gave up their lives (*ARE* 108 of 1932–33). Finally, we might add to these examples of self-sacrifice a couple of cases in which the interests of the temple deity were furthered by the offering of one's head. At the temples of Jambai and Arakandanallur—in precisely the same area of South Arcot district where we find the *nonpulparani* stones and the *velaikkarar* oaths of fealty discussed above—inscriptions of the thirteenth and fourteenth centuries record land grants to the families of men who had cut off their heads in order that the temple *maṇḍapa* might be completed (*SII* 12.178; *ARE* 197 of 1934–35). It may be significant that, in both cases, these men were the relatives of temple women, but such extreme acts of self-dedication do not seem to have been undertaken by temple women themselves. It is unclear how precisely such acts were efficacious in advancing temple-building projects; perhaps the self-sacrifice exerted moral pressure on the people of the community who were in a position to provide financial support to the temple, in the same way that the deaths of Shiva's servants at Punjai forced local landowners to submit to the temple's demands. A further possibility, however, is suggested by the wording of another memorial of a head offering: this is a stone, with a representation of a man having decapitated himself with a sword, which bears a tenth-century inscription recording the man's offering of his head to the goddess and the granting of land to his relative, in recognition of this superior asceticism (*me tavam*) (*SII* 12.106).[21] The use of the term *tavam*, equivalent to the Sanskrit *tapas*, suggests that this act is equivalent to the austerities of sages and renunciants—performers of *nonpu*—and generative of a spiritual energy capable of bringing about a desired goal.

In the case of the *nonpu/parani* stones and several of the records of women entering the fire, the aims of the performers remain obscure, yet all of the self-sacrificing acts we have considered here seem to have a similar quality: the virtues displayed by women cannot be distinguished from those of the men whose deaths are commemorated in medieval Tamil inscriptions. These extraordinary acts and the fashion in which they were recognized and celebrated reflect the value placed on valour and self-sacrifice, whether that of women or of men. Within this group of activities, the undertaking of austerities is apparently the focus for some of the observances, while elsewhere loyalty and allegiance are stressed. In most cases, both aspects are present, as are both domestic and transcendent elements. Ironically, perhaps, women's acts of self-discipline and self-offering, documented in the records of *nonpus* and satis, point less consistently toward a domestic orientation, with their lack of reference to beneficiaries of the observance and their suggestion that it is the woman herself who attains her religious goal by renouncing her connection with the world. The self-sacrifices represented in the hero stones, in the *velaikkarar* oaths of fealty, and in the self-immolations and self-decapitations performed for the sake of the temple deity are motivated by this-worldly goals and are highly personalized, and thus domestic. The sense of relationship with and service to one's community, lord, or local deity—concern for '*particular*, usually well-loved, individuals', in Sered's words—is much more vividly presented in these cases, which refer for the most part to men's actions, than in the records of *nonpus* and satis carried out by women. But even here, in the absence of an explicit reference to a divine power or to a future existence after death, a transcendent dimension is invoked—by the celebration of the devotion, mastery of the self, and fearlessness that have allowed those whose acts are commemorated to rise above the ordinary sphere of human conduct.

## GIFTS TO GODS AND GODDESSES

The vast majority of medieval inscriptions concern much more mundane activities, but they do have another type of connection to the transcendent inasmuch as they record gifts to the divine beings enshrined in the temple. Overall, the lands of gifts that women and men made were identical in substance and in purpose. But closer examination reveals subtle differences, in terms of preferences and emphases in donative activity. To get a more precise sense of what these differences are, I surveyed a group of more than 2,000 inscriptions, of the ninth to thirteenth centuries, from six study areas in different parts of the Tamil country.[22] About 1,200 of these inscriptions are the records of gifts from individuals where it is possible to determine the sex of the donor: 161, or a seventh of these, concern the gifts of women. Most of the gifts of both men and women were for lamps to be burned in the temple (42 per cent of women's gifts; 35 per cent of men's); or for various worship services and festival observances (16 per cent of women's gifts; 25 per cent of men's).[23] But a number of the inscriptions record the setting up of images of deities—and this is a type of endowment that was apparently of considerable interest to women. While overall only one-seventh of the inscriptions recording gifts by individuals present women as donors, nearly a quarter of the 100 or so inscriptions documenting the establishment of new images in the temple identify women as their sponsors. Of the twenty-five goddess images newly consecrated, a third had been set up by women. This pattern seems to indicate a special affinity of women for the patronage of goddesses, and this is borne out in other ways: in the case of the forty inscriptions recording arrangements for worship and special gifts for goddesses already established in the temple, a quarter identify women as sponsors, a proportion that is about twice what one would expect given the number of female donors. Women's visibility in the establishment of images and the patronage of goddesses is all the more impressive when we consider that in inscriptions of the ninth to thirteenth centuries, half of all the images were sponsored and half of all the goddess-related donations were made during the thirteenth century—a period when the proportion of all gifts that were made by women had dropped to its lowest point, just over 10 per cent.[24]

Apart from the quantitative patterns that this survey of study areas reveals, we find in inscriptions recording women's donations from all parts of Tamil Nadu certain predilections with respect to the kinds of gifts they chose to offer goddesses. Very often they donated jewellery to adorn the goddesses' images. We see this even in the case of a Jain religious woman, identified as the disciple of a male sage, who presented gold ornaments to a Jain goddess at Chitaral in Kanniyakumari district at the end of the ninth century (*TAS* 1.194–5). Around the year 1000, there are many records of gifts of ornaments made by women of the royal court to goddesses enshrined in the temples of the Kaveri delta.[25] Among these donations, it is interesting to find in several instances the gift of an adornment referred to as a *tali*. Judging from the Tamil literature of the period, the word *tali* could simply mean a particular type of necklace, but beginning in the eleventh century, it began also to designate the emblem of marriage worn by women so long as their husbands remained alive.[26] In AD 981, a *tali* was presented by the Chola queen Cempiyan Mahadevi to the goddess Uma at Vrddhachalam (*SII* 19.302); a decade later, a palace woman in the service of one of Rajaraja's queens gave to the goddess Uma at Tiruvidaimarudur a gold *tali* set with a double row of gems and a pearl necklace (*SII* 23.278); and, in 1015 at Tiruvisalur, the daughter of a chief from northern Tamil Nadu who had married the Pandya king of the south similarly presented the goddess with a jewel-encrusted gold *tali* and other valuable ornaments (*SII* 2346). Later, toward the end of the thirteenth century, we find the wife of a temple Brahmin giving her own tali to the goddess of the temple at Tiruvattatturai in South Arcot district (*ARE* 227 of 1928–29). The gift of this special ornament, in the case of at least some of these women, would seem to express a particularly feminine concern that the goddess—in all of these cases, the consort of Shiva—be appropriately adorned as a wife. Further, the auspiciousness associated with the tali would be greatly enhanced when worn by the goddess (whose husband is immortal), and she who had presented the tali would have shared in that heightened auspiciousness, although she would not have received a *tali* in return, as do the *matammas* of Tirupati [...]. On the other hand, the Tamil inscriptions rarely record male gifts to the goddess of jewellery of any kind, and I have come across only one instance where a *tali* was offered by someone other than an individual woman; this is in an inscription of the late tenth century which records the granting of a *tali* to the goddess by the Brahmin assembly at Tiruvallam in North Arcot district (*ARE* 210 of 1921).

Another dimension of the feminine solidarity expressed through women's adornment of female deities emerges in inscriptions that indicate that a woman's gift to the goddess was a means of linking her with her female kin and of connecting them with the goddess. For example, a gift for the merit of her mother was made by a woman of the Malaiyaman chief's family, who, in 1133, built a shrine and installed an image of the 'bedroom goddess' (*tirupalliyarai nacciyar*), the form of the goddess whom the god Shiva would join every evening, at the temple of Siddhalingamadam in South Arcot district (*SII* 26.422). An inscription of the late twelfth century from Viravanallur in the far south of Tamil Nadu (Tirunelveli district) records that a woman serving in the palace of the Pandya kings at Madurai set up an image of the goddess, in the name of her daughter and named after her daughter, to which she presented jewels and other gifts to support worship (*ARE* 720 of 1916). And a hundred years later, in 1300, a dancing woman (*cantikkutti*) of the temple at Tiruvanaikkaval built a goddess shrine in the town of Valliyur, again in Tirunelveli district and far to the south of her hometown, where she set up images of the goddess and of her granddaughter (*ARE* 364 of 1929–30).[27]

Sometimes the network of female relations and feminine concerns is expressed in terms of a familial relationship between female donors and the goddesses themselves. In two inscriptions of the late tenth century from Tanjavur district, we find women referring to the goddess Uma, whom they had endowed with land, as their daughter (*SII* X9.404; *Varalaru* 1, 33–34).[28] But in another inscription of precisely the same period, from a temple farther up the Kaveri river, it is a male donor who claims the goddess Uma as his daughter, provides her with land to support daily worship and offerings, and gives her in marriage to the lord of the temple (*ARE* 151 of 1936–37). And several other inscriptions, somewhat later and from farther north, record land grants to goddesses given—by individual men or local assemblies—as *stridhana* (dowry) on the occasion of the goddess's marriage, again expressing a parental role and demonstrating that it was not only women who adopted a highly personal approach to temple patronage.[29]

There are two ways in which this concept of connection with a deity resonates with the Tamil devotional literature of the centuries immediately preceding the time in which the inscriptions were engraved. First, the sense of intimacy is present in both contexts, within the framework of a variety of possible close relationships, including—especially in the cases of the poems of the Alvars dedicated to Vishnu and in the inscriptions at which we have just looked—that of the role of parent to the divine child.[30] Even where a familial connection is not explicitly evoked, the poems and the inscriptions express—each in their own fashion—a familiar personal relationship between the devotee and the divine. Second, the particularity of place is emphasized: the deity being praised by the poet-saints or granted gifts by the worshipper is not represented primarily as an abstract and universal power—although his or her transcendent nature is of course acknowledged—but is recognized as the lord or mistress of a particular locality. The deity's distinctive site-specific personality is far more manifest in the inscriptions than is his or her sectarian or iconographic identity. These qualities of intimacy and local particularity found among worshippers in medieval South India—and the perspective in which the goddess is regarded as a daughter—prompt a comparison with the ritual activities of women in the contemporary celebrations of Durga *puja* in Bengal analysed by Sandra Robinson. As an example of women's ritual activities that 'are separate from but coordinate with brahmanic festivals,' Robinson describes what takes place after the priest's conclusion of the formal worship:

> [Women] approach the image of the goddess Durga to place food on her lips as a gesture of farewell before the image is taken away for immersion in a pond or tank. A psychodrama of reluctant departure accompanies this activity, inasmuch as the goddess has come only to go home again; there are wailing laments which explicitly replicate and anticipate the farewells of young brides as they leave their own families to return to their husbands' family homes.[31]

In Robinson's analysis of the temple setting of modern Bengal, there is a definite division between the official observances of the male priest, mandated by the Brahminical tradition, and the activities of female worshippers, which are clearly marked as domestic because of their personalized character and which are treated as marginal or supplementary rituals, however essential they seem to the women who perform them. There are two aspects of this dichotomy—the split between formal male ritual and domestic female ritual, and that between the role of the specially qualified ritualist and the role of the 'lay' worshipper—and, in each case, the first of the two activities or roles is acknowledged as fundamental, and the second is generally viewed as auxiliary or derivative. In the context of the medieval South Indian temple, on the other hand, at least from the perspective offered to us by the inscriptions, I would argue that there was a recognition of the value of the domestic orientation as expressed through the public religious activities of both women and men, and that lay religious activity—particularly temple patronage—by both women and men had an authority and impact that was not overshadowed by the prestige and expertise of priests and other temple servants.

If we consider the corps of temple personnel as the main actors, and their ritual duties as the crucial functions, we will perceive in the medieval South Indian temple a situation that is more complex but not dissimilar to the picture of the temple in modern Bengal that Robinson has sketched for us, with respect to the recognition of the relative value of male and female roles. While the temple in medieval Tamil Nadu presented more possibilities for female ritual participation than is the case today, women's presence and activities in temple ritual were regarded as optional and incidental.[32] Temple women were vastly outnumbered by their male counterparts and were entirely excluded from many of the roles that men fulfilled, including that of priest. The increasing visibility, in the thirteenth century, of temple women as singers and dancers at festivals—displacing, to some extent, the male performers who had earlier had these roles—seems to have been significant more as a manifestation of the privileges accorded to temple women (often in consequence of their gifts to the temple), than as the provision of a necessary service to the temple.[33] But if we shift our gaze from the temple servants to the temple's patrons, we see that women were far from marginal and that the religious activity of gift giving had a profound impact on the shaping of ritual life in the temple, giving form to new services and establishing new deities to be worshipped.

Donors were, of course, not only motivated by the desire to make their mark—both by effecting changes in the temple through their gifts and by documenting their piety and generosity for posterity on the temple walls—but had other objects in view. The expression of purpose that is most commonly encountered in the inscriptions is related to the creation and transfer of the merit that accompanies the making of a religious gift. In the medieval Tamil inscriptions, we do not find the explicit mention of *punya* or other terms denoting 'merit,' but the transfer of merit is indicated by the statement that a gift was made 'for' another or was 'connected to' (*cartti*) the recipient of the benefit of the donation. Although both men and women transferred merit at the same rate—in about 5 per cent of their gifts—there were clear differences in the identities of the beneficiaries.[34] Merit produced by the gifts of women was almost invariably transferred to relatives, while this was the pattern for men's gifts only about a third of the time; the merit more often went to men unrelated to the donor, including the king or local notables. Of the relatives to whom merit was transferred, by both women and men, male kinsfolk predominated—but the relative most likely to be mentioned by a male donor, his father, was scarcely ever mentioned by women. Here we see women locating themselves through their gift giving within a familial network in a pattern that is familiar from studies of contemporary Hindu women's votive behaviour—where vows are undertaken for the benefit of husband and children (and particularly, perhaps, sons)—and it seems that this is more characteristic of medieval women's donative behaviour than it is of their male counterparts. But it cannot be said that men's purposes in making gifts were radically different: they too had domestic motives and used temple patronage as a means of expressing connection with their kinsmen—as well as their mothers, sisters, and wives. That men may, in some ways, have had a *greater* stake than women in domestic goals, at least as these were made public in temple inscriptions, is suggested by the fact that several of the donations by men to temples are said in the inscriptions to be gifts of thanksgiving for having been granted a son (*SII* 26.516; *ARE* 366 of 1959–60). There is nothing equivalent among female donors.

Apart from such donations, made in gratitude, what kinds of future consequences were anticipated as the result of making gifts on behalf of oneself or another? The inscriptions tell us almost nothing about the benefits for the living. But a hint about the goal of gifts made for the merit of those who had left this world appears in an early twelfth-century inscription that records the gift of land for one who was deceased, 'praying [that he attain] Shivaloka' (*civalokaprarttam*) (*SII* S.460). Other possibilities are suggested by the *pallipatai*, or 'sepulcher temple,' erected in medieval Tamil Nadu over the remains of a prominent person and named after him or her.[35] Amid the obscurity that surrounds the meaning of these shrines, several authors maintain that their primary function was to legitimate the claim to rule by Chola kings descended from the deceased, who was glorified as a hero and king.[36] But the fact that more than half of those interred within the *pallipatais* were women seems to suggest rather different motives.[37] Meanwhile, in religious terms, it is not clear whether gifts for the merit of the departed, or the setting up of *nonpu* stones, hero stones, or *pallipatais*, had to do with fame and the honouring—or even 'deifying'—of a person of the past, or whether instead they were a matter of supporting the departed in an ongoing existence in the afterlife, where benefits would flow from the continuing worship carried out in his or her name.

Some further clues come from the inscriptions that record the arrangements made after someone had met a violent death. We have already had occasion to consider the inscription (*ARE* 162 of 1932–33) that describes the gift made by Vikrama Kampan in expiation of his murderous attack on a man and the subsequent act of sati by that man's wife: in this case, we learn that the two lamps were given for the merit of the two dead and as a means of averting the vengeance of the living. There are a few other such records where violence was purposefully done, either in battle or in rage—there is, for example, the case of the Brahmin who had beaten a man to death and who was required to give a perpetual lamp in expiation of this crime (*ARE* 528 of 1937–38). But, according to the inscriptions, most gifts of expiation were made after having inadvertently caused another's death. There were a large number of hunting accidents—described in inscriptions from Chingleput, North Arcot, and South Arcot districts—that prompted such gifts. In one such case, the motive for making the gift seems to have been to placate the spirit of the dead: the local council determined that the man who had accidentally killed another while hunting should donate a perpetual lamp to the temple in order to 'remove enmity' (*pakai ara*) (*SII* 7.85). This is also suggested by the case in which an intruder was stabbed to death by a merchant as the intruder attempted to rape the merchant's concubine; both the merchant and a relative of the deceased were together held responsible for donating gold for a lamp in the temple. Here the resolution does not so much reflect culpability or the need for the merchant to atone for wrongdoing but rather the necessity for there to be a memorial for the deceased (*SII* 22.77).

Women as well as men figure in these records, both as victims and as perpetrators. We have two inscriptions that order a gift of expiation for having caused the death of a woman—one of whom took poison because her husband was marrying another woman (*SII* 17.389), and another who killed herself after she had been put through an ordeal to get her to pay taxes she claimed she did not owe (*SII* 22.80). A chilling inscription of the twelfth century describes an act of violence carried out by a woman: Koccattan Kaman's wife threw a stick at her daughter, which accidentally hit another girl; the girl died twenty days later. It was agreed that a lamp should be donated to the temple by Koccattan Kaman, the husband of the murderous mother (*SII* 22.148). The inscription provides neither the name of his wife, nor that of the dead girl, who is identified simply as the daughter of Tappi Mintan Kaman. It is unlikely, therefore, that the lamp was being offered for the merit of the nameless girl. In fact, although women are the main actors in this unhappy drama, they seem to be entirely off-stage in the sequel. The gift of expiation was not made by the perpetrator of the violent act, but rather by her husband, who seems to bear responsibility for his wife's action.

If religious activity is regarded as domestic when it is undertaken for personal and individualized motives and for the benefit of family members or other well-loved individuals, it is difficult to make the case that medieval South Indian women's engagement with temple patronage indicates such an orientation to a greater degree than that of their male counterparts. It is true that women were more likely than men to transfer the merit arising from their gift giving to their kinfolk, especially their sons and husbands. But women refrained from making gifts for expiation or thanksgiving, which were the types of gifts that frequently expressed involvement on the part of men in a familial network and that made men the representatives for their family's culpability and its interests. Donations were also the means by which individuals forged links with the divinity enshrined in the temple. On the one hand, women's attention to, and special gifts of jewellery for, consort goddesses suggest a connection to these deities made more intimate by the sharing of the status of wife. On the other, records of men's gifts to the goddess as daughter express the closeness and tenderness of their relationship with the deity whom they worshipped. And both men and women, through their donations to gods and goddesses alike, participated in a realm of religious activity that was—in terms of its expression (and constitution) of a personal relationship with a deity and its focus on the identity of the particular god of a specific place—highly domestic in character.

## CONCLUDING REFLECTIONS

The category of the domestic is dearly a useful one in expanding our sense of what can properly and seriously be regarded as a religious context, a religious role, or a religious motive. Religion is not just what yogis and priests do. But the characterization of women's engagement with religion as pre-eminently domestic—personal, particular, and familial—and distinct from men's frameworks of religious undertaking cannot be maintained in the face of the evidence from medieval Tamil Nadu. Women's and men's religious lives were of course dissimilar in many ways. But the spheres of activity in which they found themselves were in large part congruent. If we want to differentiate male and female religious behaviours and purposes, it seems that we can best do this by thinking in terms of different colourings and shadings, rather than different positions or different perspectives on the meanings of their religious activities.

The inscriptions show us that renunciatory and self-sacrificial observances, undertaken by born women and men, had significance both in terms of ultimate, transcendent aims and as expressions of highly specific relationships and this-worldly goals. The devotional activities that were a part of temple life, including making gifts to gods and goddesses, similarly had both feminine and masculine manifestations and simultaneously engaged abstract conceptions of devotion and divinity, on the one hand, and personal connections with the local and particular, on the other. Finally, our exploration of the contexts and roles in which medieval South Indian women functioned suggests that the category of the 'religious' itself is in the end less helpful than we might have expected in an analysis of these acts of renunciation and devotion. The inscriptions demonstrate again and again that the religious act has antecedents, meanings, and consequences that spill over into other realms. The records of women's gifts portray them as participants in networks of property transactions, as sponsors of land improvement projects, and as parties to contracts and compacts. The epigraphs, although engraved on the walls of temples, speak to issues of identity, position, and power—and not only mark the special gestures and achievements of individuals but are themselves constitutive of the shifts in status that accompany these acts. The boundary between the religious and the political, or the religious and the economic, is as indistinct as that between women's domestic rituals and men's 'high' religion. In other words, what yogis and priests—and women—do is not just religion.

## NOTES

1 Susan Starr Sered, *Women as Ritual Experts: The Religious Lives of Elderly Jewish Women in Jerusalem*, New York, 1992, pp. 139–40.

2 Ibid., p. 32.

3 Holly Baker Reynolds, 'The Auspicious Married Woman', in Susan S. Wadley (ed.), *The Powers of Tamil Women*, Syracuse, New York, 1980, pp. 35–60; Sandra P. Robinson, 'Hindu Paradigms of Women: Images and Values,' in Y.Y. Haddad and E.B. Findly (eds), *Women, Religion, and Social Change*, Albany, 1985, pp. 181–215; I.V. Peterson, 'The Tie That Binds: Brothers and Sisters in North and South India,' *South Asian Social Scientist*, vol. 4, no. 1, 1988, pp. 25–52; Mary McGee, 'Desired Fruits: Motive and Intention in the Votive Rites of Hindu Women,' in Julia Leslie (ed.), *Roles and Rituals for Hindu Women*, Teaneck, NJ, 1991, pp. 71–88; Laxmi G. Tewari, *A Splendor of Worship: Women's Fasts, Rituals, Stories and Art*, New Delhi, 1991; Anne MacKenzie Pearson, *Because It Gives Me Peace of Mind: Ritual Fasts in the Religious Lives of Hindu Women*, Albany, 1996; June McDaniel, *Making Virtuous Daughters and Wives: An Introduction to Women's Brata Rituals in Bengali Folk Religion*, Albany, 2003.

4 That three of the *nonpu* stones are placed in proximity to a goddess temple, and that one explicitly mentions the observance taking place in a goddess temple also suggests a possible link to contemporary women's votive ritual, which is often dedicated to female deities (Reynolds, 'The Auspicious Married Woman', p. 50; McDaniel, *Making Virtuous Daughters and Wives*, pp. 111–12).

5 One of the four *parani* stones records the fact that a pillar (*tari*—evidently the stone itself which bears the inscription) has been erected in recognition of the

observance of the parani. In general, in inscriptional usage, the term parani refers to a division of time (a *nakshatra* or asterism) which occurs every month. That the practice of austerities, or the observance of a vow, should have a specific calendrical referent is not surprising, although I know of no other examples where the nakshatra parani has these associations.

6 A temple woman (*tevaratiyal*) was granted the privilege of singing part of the hymn at Tirupampuram's Markali festival in exchange for her gift of several images to the temple, according to an inscription of the early thirteenth century (*Nannilam Kalvettukal*, hereafter *NK* 139). Other references to Markali festivals come from Chidambaram (*SII* 4–223), from Kudumiyamalai, in Tiruchirappalli district (*Inscriptions (Texts) of the Pudukkottai State Arranged according to Dynasties*, hereafter *IPS* 291 and 301), and from Tirumogur, in Madurai district, where it was the occasion for the celebration of the marriage of Vishnu to the goddess (*ARE* 334 of 1918). For further discussion of festival observances, see Leslie C. Orr, 'Processions in the Medieval South Indian Temple: Sociology, Sovereignty and Soteriology,' in Jean-Luc Chevillard and Eva Wilden (eds), *South Indian Horizons: Felicitation Volume for François Gros on the Occasion of His 70th Birthday*, Pondichéry, 2004, pp. 437–70.

7 Anne Monius ('The *Manimekalai's* Buddhist Audience', in *Proceedings of the Eighth International Conference – Seminar on Tamil Studies*, Madras, forthcoming) suggests that the *Manimekalai*'s emphasis on nonpu indicates that this text is affiliated especially with Hinayana or Theravada Buddhist teachings. Not surprisingly, in *Cilappatikaram*, a Jain text written at around the same time as the *Manimekalai*, we find the word 'nonpu' utilized with quite positive connotations, generally with reference to the austerities of Jain renunciants and lay people (10.24, 47; 15.153, 164; 16.18; 26.226), but also applied to the rites of marriage observed by the hero (1.53).

8 We also find 'nonpu' referring to the fast to death in *Cilappatikaram* (17.83).

9 Josephine Reynell, 'Prestige, Honour and the Family: Laywomen's Religiosity amongst the Svatambar Murtipujak Jains in Jaipur', *Bulletin d'Etudes Indiennes*, vol. 5, 1987. The fasts carried out by contemporary Jain women have different aims and different effects from those undertaken by Hindu women as an aspect of the observance of votive rituals. Jain women's austerities bring about a withdrawal from the world and are a means of self-purification; the power generated by fasting (*tapas*) is understood as 'cooling' female sexuality (Reynell, 'Prestige, Honour and the Family', pp. 343–51). On the other hand, while the ascetic component of Hindu women's *vratas* equally generates power, this is utilized in the context of engagement with the world, allowing women to influence the welfare of their families: their *tapas*, viewed as 'heat,' has a beneficent effect because it is channelled toward such ends (Reynolds, 'The Auspicious Married Woman', pp. 46–50; McDaniel, *Making Virtuous Daughters and Wives*, pp. 108–09; cf. Pearson, *Because It Gives Me Peace of Mind*, pp. 211–17).

10 S. Settar, and Ravi K. Korisettar, 'Nisidhis in Karnataka: A Survey', in S. Settar and Günther D. Sontheimer (eds), *Memorial Stones: A Study of Their Origin, Significance and Variety*, Dharwar, 1982, pp. 283–93; Leslie Orr, 'Jain Worship in Medieval Tamilnadu', in N.K. Wagle and Olle Qvarnstrom (eds), *Approaches to Jaina Studies: Philosophy, Logic, Rituals and Symbols*, Toronto, 1999, pp. 250–74.

11 Three of the eight women whose observance of nonpu/parani was commemorated are described only as daughters and not as wives. These may have been very

young women carrying out this practice, or it is possible that they were renunciant women, similar to the Jain 'religious women' identified in medieval Tamil inscriptions as teachers (Leslie, C. Orr, 'Jain and Hindu "Religious Women" in Early Medieval Tamilnadu', in John E. Cort (ed.), *Open Boundaries: Jain Communities and Cultures in Indian History,* Albany, 1998, pp. 187–212). There are very few inscriptional references to ascetics among women whom we would classify as 'Hindu'—terms like *tapasyar* are almost invariably applied to men rather than women—but those few that exist (for example, *SII* 8.225; *ARE* 120 of 1912), as well as the intriguing references to 'pilgrim mothers' (*paradeshi ammaimar*—for example, *SII* 5.748; *ARE* 271 of 1927–8), point to the potential for alternative ways of life for women.

12 S. Settar, 'Memorial Stones in South India', in Settar and Sontheimer (eds), *Memorial Stones,* p. 196.

13 Günther D. Sontheimer, 'Hero and Sati-stones of Maharashtra', in Settar and Sontheimer (eds), *Memorial Stones,* p. 277–81.

14 K.R. Srinivasan, *Some Aspects of Religion as Revealed by Early Monuments and Literature of the South,* Madras, 1960, pp. 6–7.

15 I am indebted to S. Swaminathan for calling my attention to this inscription, and for providing me with the text, published in the Tamil journal *Avanam.*

16 None of these four records commemorates the death of a royal woman. There is an inscription at the temple of Brahmadesam, in North Arcot district, dating from the middle of the eleventh century, that records the gift of a water shed by the brother of the Chola queen Viramahadeviyar, to quench the thirst of his sister who, having arisen to Shiva's heaven and joined the feet of Brahma, was interred in the *pallipatai* (sepulchre temple) of her deceased husband Rajendra I (*ARE* 260 of 1915). This inscription has often been considered evidence of the Chola queen's act of sati, and it is dated in the same year as Rajendra's death, but, unlike the four inscriptions we have just considered, there is no direct reference to Viramahadeviyar taking her own life. A more explicit indication of such an act by a woman of the Chola royal family—although it is found in a record dating a half century later than the event itself—is found in the lengthy *prashasti* of Rajendra I that prefaces the Tiravalangadu copperplate inscription (*SII* 3.205). Here, in verses 65–6, the queen Vanavanmahadevi is depicted as following her husband Sundara Chola (Rajendra's grandfather) to heaven, jealous of the attentions that the celestial maidens would bestow upon him.

17 Srinivasan, *Some Aspects of Religion,* pp. 3–6; K.V. Soundara Rajan, 'Origin and Spread of Memorial Stones in Tamil Nadu', in Settar and Sontheimer (eds), *Memorial Stones,* pp. 59–75; Settar, 'Memorial Stones in South India', pp. 184, 187.

18 Settar, 'Memorial Stones in South India'; S. Rajasekhara, 'Rastrakuta Hero-stones: A Study', In Settar and Sontheimer (eds), *Memorial Stones,* pp. 227–30.

19 Padma Kaimal, 'The Problem of Portraiture in South India, circa 870–970 AD', *Artibus Asiae,* vol. 59, nos. 1–2, 1999, p. 132) points out that the portrait sculptures of donors in early Chola period temples are stylistically similar to the images carved on hero stones, and suggests that this reflects a similarity in the valuation of the worthiness of the acts that are commemorated in the two contexts—both of which involve loyalty, submission, and offering of the self. It is interesting to note that after AD 970, portrait sculptures of female donors virtually disappear (despite the major activities of women as temple patrons), while they were more in evidence in the preceding hundred-year period (Kaimal, 'The Problem of Portraiture in South India, p. 179).

20 Leslie C. Orr, 'Tracing Women's Lives in Medieval Tamil Inscriptions', paper presented at the annual meeting of the American Academy of Religion, November 21–24, 1998, Orlando, Florida.

21 On head-offerings to goddesses in South Indian sculpture and literature, see J.P. Vogel, 'The Head-offering to the Goddess in Pallava Sculpture', *Bulletin of the School of Oriental and African Studies,* vol. 6, 1930–2, pp. 539–43; Srinivasan, *Some Aspects of Religion,* pp. 29–30); and J. Filliozat, 'L'Abandon de la vie par le sage et les suicides du criminel et du héros dans la tradition indienne', *Arts Asiatiques,* vol. 15, 1967, pp. 65–88.

22 These six study areas are—from the northern to the southern part of Tamil Nadu—Chingleput taluk in Chingleput district, Cheyyar taluk in North Arcot district, Cuddalore taluk in South Arcot district, Mayavaram taluk in Tanjavur district, Tiruppattur taluk in Ramnad district, and Ambasamudram taluk in Tirunelveli district. For this survey, I relied on the abstracts of the published and unpublished inscriptions (drawn for the most part from the *ARE* publications) in the volumes of T.V. Mahalingam, *A Topographical List of the Inscriptions in the Tamil Nadu and Kerala States,* 8 vols, New Delhi, 1985.

23 Women were much less likely than men to sponsor arrangements for the offering of food to Brahmins, ascetics, and devotees in the temple. This may be because the institutionalization of such feeding eclipsed a sphere of religious activity that had belonged to 'the housemistress at the door' (Ellison Banks Findly, 'The Housemistress at the Door: Vedic and Buddhist Perspectives on the Mendicant Encounter', in Laurie Patton (ed.), *Jewels of Authority: Women, Tact, and the Hindu Tradition,* New York, 2002, pp. 13–31; see also Nalini Balbir, 'Jainism', in Arvind Sharma (ed.), *Religion and Women,* Albany, 1994, pp. 121–38). The giving of alms to mendicants probably continued to be largely a private, informal, individual, and home-based affair, rather than taking place in the public, permanent, and formal contexts described in the inscriptions, especially the *maṭha* ('mutt'), which was predominantly a feeding-house in this period. But as feeding came to be a means through which the temple, or the sectarian community, could confer honour and recognition for patronage, service, and leadership, there may have been a diminution of women's importance with respect to this religious activity.

24 Leslie C. Orr, 'Women's Wealth and Worship: Female Patronage of Hinduism, Jainism, and Buddhism in Medieval Tamilnadu', in Mandakranta Bose (ed.), *Faces of the Feminine in Ancient, Medieval, and Modern India,* New York, 2000, pp. 124–47.

25 B. Venkataraman, *Temple Art under the Chola Queens,* Faridabad, 1976, pp. 52–8, 66–71, 130–6.

26 C.J. Jayadev, 'Literary and Ethnographic References to the Tali and the Tali Rite', in *Archaeological Society of South India: Transactions for the Year 1959–60,* Madras, 1960, pp. 50–1.

27 Women's gifts to the male deity enshrined in the temple, in support of various offerings and services, could equally serve to create links with female kin—or, for that matter, with the men of their families.

28 Again, I thank S. Swaminathan for alerting me to the existence of the inscription published in the Tamil journal *Varalaru,* and for kindly supplying me with the text.

29 In AD 1037, a gift of land for a garden was given by a Brahmin man as *stridhana* to the goddess Sita who was to be married to Lord Rama, at Vadamadurai in

Chingleput district (*ARE* 26a of 1952–3); in 1100 at the Shiva temple in Brahmadesam in South Arcot district, the Brahmin assembly (*mahasabhaiyar*) provided land as *stridhana* for the goddess who had been established in the temple by a local man (*ARE* 192 of 1918); and in 1137, the village assembly (*urar*) gave land as stridhana to the 'bedroom goddess' at the Shiva temple of Seyyur, in Chingleput district (*SII* 8.30). On stridhana in medieval Tamil Nadu—which meant not only the transfer of property to a daughter, but could involve the transfer from a man to his son-in-law or a woman to her daughter-in-law—see Orr, 'Tracing Women's Lives in Medieval Tamil Inscriptions' and *Donors, Devotees and Daughters of God: Temple Women in Medieval Tamilnadu,* New York, 2000, pp. 72–3, 77–8, 226.

30 Despite the theological precedent in Tamil devotional literature, worshippers do not take a parental role in the inscriptions recording their gifts to male deities. The god enshrined in the temple is not addressed as 'son'; instead we find the reverse—that records issued in the name of the Lord refer to devotees as 'our children.' Perhaps this discrepancy can be explained by the fact that the majority of temples providing inscriptions in our period were dedicated to Shiva, a deity who is rarely if ever envisioned as a child—in contrast to his son Murugan, his consort Uma, and various manifestations of Vishnu (see Paula Richman, *Extraordinary Child: Poems from a South Indian Devotional Genre,* Honolulu, 1997).

31 Robinson, 'Hindu Paradigms of Women: Images and Values', pp. 196–8.

32 Leslie C. Orr, 'Women of Medieval South India in Hindu Temple Ritual: Text and Practice', *Annual Review of Women in World Religions* vol. 3, 1993, pp. 107–41; Orr, *Donors, Devotees and Daughters of God,* 2000.

33 See note 6 above for an example of a temple woman's 'deal,' in which her right to participate in ritual resulted from a donation. I have discussed at length temple women's activities—both as temple servants and as temple patrons—in Orr, 'Women's Wealth and Worship'.

34 This discussion is based on Orr, 'Women's Wealth and Worship'.

35 Srinivasan, *Some Aspects of Religion,* pp. 12–13; N. Sethuraman, 'Crusade against Guhai (Monastery)', *Journal of the Epigraphical Society of India* (*Purabhilekha Patrika*) vol. 17, 1991, pp. 29–37.

36 Venkata Raghotham, 'Kinship, Politics and Memory in Early Medieval Tamil Country: A Study of the Funerary Shrines of the Cholas', in L.K. Srinivasan and S. Nagaraju (eds), *Sri Nagabhinanda-nam: Dr. M.S. Nagaraja Rao Festschrift,* Bangalore, 1995, pp. 593–608; Yasushi Ogura, 'The Changing Concept of Kingship in the Cola Period: Royal Temple Constructions, c. A.D. 850–1279', in Noboru Karashima (ed.), *Kingship in Indian History,* New Delhi, 1999, pp. 119–41.

37 In the seven inscriptions where there is an explicit indication of the character of the temple as a *pallipatai,* and a clear identification of the person in whose honour it was built, we find mention of four pallipatais constructed for men (of whom three are Chola kings), and six for women (including five Chola queens). In chronological order, from the ninth to the thirteenth centuries, these inscriptions are: *EI,* 192*ff*; *SII* 8.529; *SII* 3.15; *ARE* 271 of 1927; *ARE* 260 of 1915; *EI* 41.10B; and *ARE* 124 of 1936–7. N. Sethuraman ('Crusade against Guhai (Monastery)', *Journal of the Epigraphical Society of India* (*Purabhilekha Patrika*) 17, 1991, pp. 29–37) and Ogura ('The Changing Concept of Kingship in the Cola Period', in Karashima (ed.), *Kingship in Indian History,* pp. 119–41) emphasize the role of Pashupata Shaiva

preceptors as officiants at the pallipaṭais, and Sethuraman considers that those interred in the pallipatais would have been those initiated into the Pashupata tradition. The tradition of building royal memorial temples, widespread in the Deccan during this same period, was evidently more deeply rooted and of a different character from the practice found in the Tamil country, to the south and east (see Phillip B. Wagoner, 'From "Pampa's Crossing" to "The Place of Lord Virupaksha": Architecture, Cult and Patronage at Hampi before the Founding of Vijayanagara', in D.V. Devaraj and C.S. Patil (eds), *Vijayanagara: Progress of Research 1958–51*, Mysore, 1996, pp. 141–74).

# 9

# Cult Region

## *The* Purāṇas *and the Making of the Cultural Territory of Bengal**

Kunal Chakrabarti

### I

For a long time, South Asia has been viewed as a single cultural area. This holistic approach is now at a discount and the so-called 'middle-run history' is increasingly receiving greater attention from historians and social anthropologists alike. In a sharp critique of cultural holism in the anthropology of South Asia, John Leavitt has argued recently that such an approach seeks to explain the variety of data available from different parts of India in terms of a relatively small and simple set of underlying cultural or ideological patterns. While Robert Redfield's model of great and little traditions freezes and perpetuates the view of the nineteenth-century British observers that Indian culture consists of 'an ideal-typical "real" pan-Indian civilization' and a number of 'survivals' from earlier, locally represented and semi-civilized stages, Louis Dumont replaces this dualism with a monism which claims that the two traditions are no more different than 'a general idea and the local working out of that idea'. This conception, elaborated by McKim Marriott among others, tends to reduce all particularities in Indian cultural traditions to just variations of a broader pattern, which 'radically underestimates the reality and importance of regional and historical specificity in South Asia'.[1]

*Previously published in *Studies in History*, vol. 16, no. 1, ns, 2000, pp. 1–16. 

Social scientists' interest in the question of the formation of regional identity, based on a set of specific cultural characteristics, is therefore of comparatively recent origin. Predictably, there is no consensus on the definition of a region. After examining forty such definitions, Beajeau-Garnier, for example, was able to detect only one point of unanimity among them: a region is a spatial unit distinct from the space that surrounds it.[2] This fundamental and rather obvious constituent of a region is of little use to me, for I am concerned with the process of how the socially bound space designated Bengal (corresponding roughly to the present West Bengal and Bangladesh) came to acquire the distinctive characteristics that mark it off as a cultural unit at a certain level of generalization. The expression 'cultural unit' also requires some clarification. Without getting into the controversy on yet another definition, let me state simply that by culture here I understand a persistent arrangement of those aspects of material conditions, social organization, language, religious systems, behavioural patterns, symbolic codes, moral visions, and interpretive practices which a group of people share in common.

Identity on the other hand, is largely a mental construct. It is a consciousness of participating in a culture which endows a group of people with a sense of belonging to a community. This consciousness is elusive and unquantifiable, because the recognition of a common culture is often implicit. Obviously, I am speaking not of that assertive identity hastily forged in response to a perceived threat or contemporary aspiration, but of a popular awareness developed inexorably, but almost imperceptibly, over the centuries through a process of natural selection of intrinsic and fundamental elements in the culture, recognized by people all over the region. If identity is the self-description of a person or a group which outlines defining characteristics, this description was seldom articulated in pre-modern times. Identity formation, therefore, refers to a process, occurring over a period of time under a given set of conditions. The processual aspect needs to be emphasized, because I will be looking at the brahmanical initiative in reorganizing the social structure, and particularly the religious mores, of the indigenous people of Bengal through the codification of a set of texts called the *Upapurāṇas* during the early medieval period, which may be considered to be the first systematic attempt to create a cultural tradition in Bengal transcending purely local boundaries.

## II

The corpus of literature called the *Purāṇas* was composed with a view to revitalizing the brahmanical social order which was undermined seriously during the early centuries of the Christian era by the widespread popularity of Buddhism, the beliefs and practices of Tantra and such other factors. The *brāhmaṇas* perceived that it was necessary to widen the social base of brahmanism in order to meet this challenge. They, therefore, attempted to draw people from the non-brahmanical fold into their sphere of influence and earn their trust in brahmanical leadership. The result was the creation of a composite, syncretic religious system which incorporated diverse rituals and beliefs without endangering the social supremacy of the *brāhmaṇas*.[3] Thus the *Purāṇas* evolved out of an interaction between the brahmanical tradition and many local traditions. However, by the time the first phase of the composition of the *Purāṇas* was complete, it had already acquired an identity independent of its Vedic moorings and the various assimilated local traditions. Consequently, when from the post-Gupta period, large-scale *brāhmaṇa* migrations started reaching areas which had hitherto been peripheral to their influence such as Bengal they brought with them a Purāṇic worldview which was now a recognized part of the brahmanical tradition. But the level of assimilation achieved by these *Purāṇas* must have proved inadequate to the needs of a particular region, for now a new genre of religious literature came into being—the *Upapurāṇas*—which offered a balance between the Purāṇic brahmanical tradition and the exclusively regional local traditions, but with the same end in view.[4] The largest number of the extant *Upapurāṇas* were written in Bengal, approximately between the eighth and the thirteenth centuries AD.

Assimilation of local customs in some form was one of the prime endeavours of these texts. Indeed, in the epics, which are justly considered proto-Purāṇic, the tendency to acknowledge and uphold *lokadharma* (religious duties of the common people) was already discernible.[5] What is called *lokadharma* in the *Mahābhārata* was transformed into *ācāra* in the more explicit Bengal *Purāṇas*. *Ācāra* is a difficult term to translate, but it corresponds roughly to the custom, practice, and usage of a specific region at a given time, in consonance with one's stage and order of life. The Bengal *Purāṇas* declare that one must perform the duties prescribed by the Vedas and demonstrate allegiance to the 'Purāṇic high gods, because these are inescapable preconditions of *dharma*. But even such acts of merit are rendered ineffective if one deviates from the locally prevailing custom, for in all sacred scriptures, ācāra has the first consideration. *Dharma* arises from *ācāra*.'[6]

In these instances the term *ācāra* has been used in its widest possible sense. But it also has specific implications. These text recommend that 'all the *varṇas* should perform the practices of the village (*grāmācāra*) prevailing at the time, in keeping with the ways of the *Smṛtis*'[7] or, 'the practice of different places (*deśācāra*) should be followed by the people born in those places'.[8] The *Bṛhannāradīya Purāṇa* further proclaims: 'Correct statement is truth. Those who are committed to *dharma* will tell the truth which is not contrary to *dharma*. Therefore statements wise men make after proper consideration of time and space (*deśakālādivijñānāt*), which are in conformity with their own *dharma*, are truth.'[9] Thus it does not hesitate to designate even truth as context specific and hence conditional, such is the magnitude of importance placed on local customs. It is obvious that *deśa* (place) here refers to small localities inhabited by little communities and not to the wider regional unit.

Apart from *ācarā*, the other expression that the Bengal *Purāṇas* use frequently is *laukika*—literally popular. The *Bṛhaddharma Purāṇa* apportions dharma into two fundamental categories—*vaidika* and *laukika*.[10] At times they seem to be independent of and yet consistent with each other,[11] and at other times they form a continuum.[12] Significantly, the *Brahmavaivarta Purāṇa* asserts that in case of a conflict between these two sources of *dharma*, popular custom must prevail.[13]

## III

Before Purāṇic brahmanism reached Bengal, it was already under the pervasive influence of Tantra, with its emphasis on low castes and on women in religious performances. Moreover, Bengal was one of the last strongholds of Buddhism in India. Thus, it was a difficult terrain for the imposition of the brahmanical worldview. In such situations, the usual Purāṇic technique is to isolate the single major pre-existing factor within the local cultural traditions, to transform and legitimize it, and them to use the same factor to promote and transmit its own ideas. In Bengal the *Purāṇas* chose the goddess, presumably because of her pervasive presence among the local people,[14] and constructed a regional cult which later became one of the major symbols of Bengal's cultural tradition.

By regional cult, I refer to the 'cults of the middle-range—more far-reaching than any parochial cult of the little community, yet less inclusive in belief and membership than a world religion in its most universal from'.[15] John Leavitt has identified at least three major features of a regional cult: annual, seasonal, and calendrical cycles of regional rituals; social patterning within which such rituals take place; and people's background knowledge of the divinities who are a part of the myths and songs invoked in these rituals.[16] All these attributes can be observed in the cult of the regional goddesses of Bengal that the *Purāṇas* created and helped to promote.

Let me discuss one example of the process of creation of a goddess of regional dimension from the locally available material. The presiding goddess of a very popular non-brahmanical women's *vrata* (vowed observance) in Bengal is Maṅgalacaṇḍī. Maṅgalacaṇḍī is not mentioned in any of the high-profile Sanskrit texts written outside of Bengal, but she is fairly prominent among the less important goddesses in the Bengal *Purāṇas*. A major long vernacular poem (*Maṅgalakāvya*), was composed in sixteenth-century Bengal in her honour,[17] and printed collections of *vratakathās* and *pāñcālīs* of Maṅgalacaṇḍī are produced in large numbers even today. When these apparently disparate accounts of the goddess are matched, they reveal an intricate complex of interpretation of traditions, and of survivals and transformations in the brahmanical assimilative process, spread over nearly a millennium.

The *Devī Purāṇa* refers to a goddess called Maṅgalā who, it says, should be worshipped to ward off evil and to attain happiness.[18] Shashibhushan Dasgupta believes that Maṅgalā is the precursor of the later Maṅgalacaṇḍī. He cites a verse from *Śabdakalpadruma* which mentions Maṅgalā as one of the eight *yoginīs*.[19] Of these, Maṅgalā and Saṁkaṭā are worshipped through *vratas* by Bengali women.[20] The Sanskrit texts, however, neither recommend nor lay down the procedure for a formal worship of these *yoginīs* in the brahmanical way. Dasgupta conjectures that they were non-brahmanical goddesses venerated by women. Therefore brahmanism was willing to accommodate them up to a point but was not prepared to accept them within the brahmanical pantheon.[21]

That the eventual inclusion of this presiding goddess of a women's *vrata* into the brahmanical pantheon was an afterthought on the part of the authors of the Bengal *Purāṇas* is attested to by the possibility that they were evidently uncertain about her antecedents. The following passage from the *Brahmavaivarta* and the *Devībhāgavata Purāṇas* shows how a Purāṇic deity was fashioned. Śiva addresses her thus:

> You bestow delight and good fortune, you bestow bliss and auspiciousness (*maṅgala*)—that is why you are called Maṅgalacaṇḍikā. You are the most auspicious of all that is auspicious.... You are worshipped on Tuesday (*maṅgalavāra*), desired by all. The king Maṅgala, born of the family of Manu, always worships you.... You are the bestower of auspicious salvation.... People worship you on every Tuesday; you bestow abundance of bliss on all. Thus, after praising Maṅgalacaṇḍikā and worshipping her on Tuesday, Śiva departed. The goddess Sarvamaṅgalā was first worshipped by Śiva, next by the planet Maṅgalā (Mars), then by the king Maṅgala, and then on every Tuesday by the women of every household. Finally she was worshipped by all men desirous of their welfare.[22]

Thus, all conceivable *maṅgalās* have been heaped on her and the original passage reads like an insensitively overdone example of alliteration.

We have seen that the precursor of the Purāṇic Maṅgalacaṇḍī was in all likelihood known as Maṅgalā. Although the goddess Caṇḍī, later to be known as the generic name for nearly all goddesses of non-Vaiṣṇavite affiliation, had already been described as *sarvamaṅgala-maṅgalye* (repository of all auspiciousness) in the *Devī-Māhātmya* section of the *Mārkaṇḍeya Purāṇa*,[23] this had noting to do with the local goddess Maṅgalā of non-brahmanical origin. Besides, proper names are often non-connotative, and the fact that auspiciousness is a desirable quality in a goddess is an entirely coincidental occurrence in this case. Yet the Bengal *Purāṇas* accepted the literal meaning of the word and proposed a simple equation between the name and the meaning in order to justify the Purāṇic reconstruction of the deity. Either they were unaware of the popularity of the independent goddess Maṅgalā or they chose to ignore it.

The latter seems to be the more reasonable explanation, since the internal evidence of the *Purāṇas* indicates that their authors were familiar with the popular stories associated with Maṅgalacaṇḍī, which came to acquire their poetical form much later in the various *Caṇḍīmaṅgalakāvyas* of medieval Bengal. The *Bṛhaddharma Purāṇa* contains a verse which says:

> You tricked Kālaketu by assuming the form of a lizard and granted him a boon. You are the auspicious Maṅgalacaṇḍī; you saved a merchant and his son from the king Śrīśālivāhana by devouring and throwing up an elephant, sitting on a lotus.[24]

These are, in a nutshell, the two stories narrated in the *Caṇḍīmaṅgalakāvyas*. The vernacular poets of Bengal also knew of this verse. Indeed, Lālā Jayanārāyaṇa, a Bengali poet of the eighteenth century, has referred to the *Uttarakhaṇḍa* of the *Bṛhaddharma Purāṇa* where the verse is in fact located, and has included a translation of this verse in his *Caṇḍikā-maṅgalakāvya*.[25] In the Dhaka University collection, there is a Bengali manuscript of a *Caṇḍikā-khaṇḍa* claiming to be a part of the *Devī Purāṇa*, which deals in sixteen chapters with these stories of Maṅgalacaṇḍī.[26] The vernacular *pāñcālīs*, which are read on the occasion of the observance of her *vrata*, also tell the same stories,[27] and there are allusions to them even in the doggerel verses (*chaḍā*) that young girls recite during the performance of a typical *kumārī vrata* (meant for unmarried women). In one such *chaḍā* the goddess is asked, 'Mother, why are you so late today?' She replies that she had a lot of work to attend to, one of her tasks being to free the king from the prison.[28] This, I suspect, is a corruption of the original, or, at any rate, the popular story, where the merchant was freed from the prison by the king through the grace of the goddess. Thus Maṅgalacaṇḍī is a unique example in which the different layers of her story are traceable, layers which correspond to and resonate with one another.

And yet the *Purāṇas* ignored these stories, even though they were available to them. In the chapters in the *Brahmavaivarta* and the *Devībhāgavata*, where they sought to establish the credentials of Maṅgalacaṇḍī with a suitable anecedote, the authors narrate the rather bald and ingenuous story of Śiva's battle with Tripurāsura (the demon Tripura) whom he defeated with the help of the goddess Maṅgalacaṇḍī.[29] That they chose to succumb to such an unimaginative stereotype in preference to the much more complex and exciting stories in circulation, is a clear reflection of the fact that they deliberately rejected the local popular goddess. But she was important enough to take note of. Hence, brahmanism constructed a synthetic story, in line with the archetypal brahmanical story to assimilate the goddess and claim her as its own. Hence the rather transparent and laboured attempt to collect all the *maṅgalās* (auspiciousness) so that the popular Maṅgalā is substituted by the new Purāṇic Maṅgalacaṇḍī. The Bengal *Purāṇas* failed miserably in this attempt, but their primary purpose was served. Maṅgalacaṇḍī was raised to the rank of one of the approved brahmanical goddesses.

This elevation was accomplished by employing the vintage strategy of brahmanism, namely, by demonstrating identification with Caṇḍikā, the *mūlaprakṛtirīśvarī* (goddess of primordial nature). Maṅgalacaṇḍī has been described repeatedly as the primary aspect of *prakṛti* and is said to have been born out of her mouth.[30] She is merely another manifestation of Durgā.[31] Maṅgalacaṇḍī is then equated with the high-profile goddess who had already been established in the upper echelons of the brahmanical hierarchy of divinities. Thus, Lakṣmī, Sarasvatī, Durgā, Sāvitrī and Rādhikā pre-date the creation of the universe. Those who emanate from them are their manifested selves, and Maṅgalacaṇḍī is one of them.[32] The identification is so complete that Maṅgalacaṇḍī has been assigned a *Śākta-pīṭha* (the most sacred centres of pilgrimage for the worshippers of the goddess). In the *Bṛhaddharma Purāṇa*, Durgā proclaims that she exists as Maṅgalacaṇḍī at the Maṅgakoṣṭhapīṭha in Ujjayini.[33] R.C. Hazra points out that this Ujjayinī is the same as the ancient city popularly known as Ujānī, which comprises the modern villages of Kogram, Mangalkot (Sanskrit Maṅgakoṣṭhaka), and Aral, situated on the bank of the river Ajay in the Burdwan district of West Bengal.[34] Both the *Pīṭhanirṇaya* and the *Śivacarita*, two important treatises on the subject, mention Ujjayinī/Ujānī as a *mahāpīṭha*.[35] In the long list of *Śākta-tīrtha*s in the *Devībhāgavata*, Ujjayinī is referred to as Mahākāla, the seat of Śaṁkarī,[36] and in the *pīṭhamālā* section of Bhāratacandra's *Annadāmaṅgala* (the last of the major *Maṅgalakāvya*s in Bengal, composed in the eighteenth century) Maṅgalacaṇḍī is said to reside at Ujānī, served by a Bhairava.[37] It is important to remember that Dhanapati, the merchant protagonist of the second story of the *Caṇḍīmàngalakāvya*s, belonged to Ujānī.

At the end of this process, brahmanism succeeded in turning Maṅgalacaṇḍī into something of a Purāṇic celebrity. As a result, the vernacular *pañcālī*s of Maṅgalacaṇḍī—which are the authentic carriers of her popular story—in an attempt to emulate the heavy pontifical style of the *Purāṇas*, presumably for the sake of credibility, rather incongruously include a note on the procedure of her worship, complete with *sāmānyārghya*, *bhūtaśuddhi*, *prāṇāyāma*, *karāṅganyāsa* and the like, as well as a *dhyāna* (meditative reflection on the nature of the goddess).[38] This dhyāna is an exact quote of the three verses of the *Kālikā Purāṇa*, describing the goddess Maṅgalacaṇḍī.[39] It also mentions a Sanskrit *mantra* (sacred hymn):

*nārāyaṇyai vidmahe tvāṁ caṇḍikāyai tu dhīmahi* I
*tanno lalitakānteti tataḥ paścāt pracodayāt* II

This is claimed to be the *gāyatrī* of Maṅgalacaṇḍī, and has once again been lifted straight from the *Kālikā Purāṇa*.[40] Thus, Maṅgalacaṇḍī was turned upside down.

It is virtually impossible to try and establish a chronology of such overlapping developments, simultaneously operative at many levels. For example, was Maṅgalacaṇḍī a goddess with a distinct personal profile in pre-Purāṇic Bengal, merely ratified by brahmanism, or were there many local goddesses with similar characteristics who coalesced into the synthetic figure of Maṅgalacaṇḍī through brahmanical meditation? If so, was the name Maṅgalacaṇḍī—a very Sanskritic name with no Sanskritic antecedent—already in existence, or was it the creation of the Bengal *Purāṇas* which the authors of the vernacular *Caṇḍīmaṅgalakāvya*s borrowed as a convenient medium of authentic credentials to arrange a sprawling mass of folk materials into a structured narrative? These questions cannot be answered with certainty. What is known for sure, however, is that the authors of the Bengal *Purāṇas* were evidently familiar with the folk stories associated with Maṅgalacaṇḍī which they chose to ignore, and that the various *Caṇḍīmaṅgalakāvyas* reflect an awareness of the brahmanical worldview which they appropriated without acknowledging the source. Through this complex interaction, a deity with an elaborate baggage came into its own, and eventually became one of the widely recognized symbols of Bengal's cultural identity. The contribution of the vernacular literature in the making of this tradition is obvious. As a result, the constitutive role of the Bengal *Purāṇas* in this process is often marginalized.

## IV

Bengal, however, is not an isolated example. There are several other regions in India where brahmanism acted as a catalytic agent in the process of crystallization of their respective regional traditions, even though the mode of brahmanical intervention, and consequently the manner in which these traditions took shape, might have varied from one region to another. Comparison with two other cultural regions may help illustrate this point.

The history of Bengal's neighbouring state Orissa closely parallels the developments in Bengal in many respects. Perhaps the most important similarity between them is the fact that brahmanism arrived late in both regions. Thus, all that follows from it in the case of Orissa—the existence of a number of fairly well-developed indigenous traditions, the brahmanical attempt to establish cultural hegemony through socio-religious reorganization (including the composition of a *Purāṇa*)[41] and the transformation of a local tribal deity into a prime brahmanical godhead—have their variants in Bengal.

The regional tradition of Orissa, however, derives its cultural identity primarily from a far more tangible object than the mere recognition of a common cult form, namely a firmly located cult centre. It was the temple of Jagannātha at Puri that came to symbolize the regional consciousness of an entire people. Hermann Kulke has shown that the resolve of Anantavarman Coḍagaṅga, who was personally a Śaiva all his life, to build a temple for Jagannātha at Puri around the middle of the twelfth century was a political decision. By the eleventh century, Vaiṣṇavism had begun to exercise considerable influence on Orissa. Anantavarman was keenly aware of this religious trend and he decided to erect a temple for Puruṣottama in order to base his power on a rising movement. Thus, from the beginning, the religious complex at Puri was conceived as a legitimating agency for the rulers of Orissa. Eventually, King Anaṅgabhīma III adopted the god Puruṣottama at Puri as the official state deity in AD 1230/31, dedicated the Orissan empire to Jagannātha, and proclaimed himself to be merely the 'deputy' (*rautta*) of the god.[42]

As the temple gained in importance as a prime centre of pilgrimage both within Orissa and throughout north India, its legitimizing authority increased in scope and intensity. By the late sixteenth century, temple records began to describe Jagannātha as 'the overlord of the kingdom of Orissa', and no ruler of Orissa, whether Oriya or not in origin, could hope to establish hegemonic control over the territory of Orissa without, at least notionally, acknowledging this supra-temporal seat of power. Except Sultan Sulaiman of Bengal, who during his brief occupation of Cuttack in the third quarter of the sixteenth century destroyed the image of Jagannātha and desecrated the temple, all the other invaders of Orissa, including the Mughals, the Marathas, and even the English East India Company, sought legitimation for their rule by attempting to gain control over the temple.[43] When the kingdom disappeared, Jagannātha began to symbolize a growing secular force, the language-centred Oriya nationalism in its formative phase'.[44] This undisputed regional pre-emergence of Jagannātha is due primarily to the deity's physical location in a monumental temple which received sustained state patronage for a considerable period of time. The temple of Jagannātha thus became the living image and the point of convergence of the pride and aspirations of a people, which together comprise the core constituents of any regional consciousness.

Bengal did not have any such temple of major regional significance. Indeed, although contrary arguments have been posed, Bengal never developed the culture of temple building as a part of premeditated state policy. Borrowing from Ronald Inden, Richard Eaton has argued in his monograph on medieval Bengal that like several other ruling dynasties of early medieval India, such as the Pratihāras and the Rāṣṭrakūṭas, the Sena rulers of Bengal also established centralized state cults, physically expressed in massive and elaborately carved temples.[45]

It is true that there are references to a number of temples in the Bengal epigraphs from the Gupta period onwards, and excavations have unearthed the ruins of several temples, a few of which were fairly large and impressive.[46] Even the *Rāmacarita* mentions that opulent tempoles were being used for worship in different parts of Varendrī, while Rāmapāla has been credited with the construction of three rows of temples dedicated to Śiva in his newly founded capital Rāmāvatī.[47] Thus, there was obviously no dearth of temples in early medieval Bengal, but none of these was built on the assumptions on which the Jagannātha temple was predicated from the beginning, nor did they compare with the Jagannātha temple in dimension or significance. It is possible that the

Senas had internalized the political culture of the other contemporary ruling dynasties, but the fact remains that they did not construct a grand temple which would legitimize their rule and make their subjects identify themselves with the temple as the pre-eminent cultural symbol of the region. From the available evidence it seems that the temples of early Bengal were local centres of worship which eventually decayed due to lack of patronage or were destroyed by Muslim invaders. By the time the core of the Bengal *Purāṇas* was codified, state power had passed into the hands of Muslim rulers. Without the necessary political support, brahmanism in Bengal failed to encourage the construction of a 'goddess temple' of comparable scale around which the process of regional state formation or the organization of a priesthood into a clearly defined hierarchy would revolve, as it did in Orissa.

In the absence of an overarching temple integrating diverse local elements into a common bond of loyalty, a cult centre, insignificant to begin with but gradually gaining in importance over a period of time, can perform the same social function. The anthropologist Victor Turner has drawn attention to two spatially distinguishable kinds of cult forms—one representing crucial power divisions and classificatory distinctions within and among socially and politically discrete groups, and the other representing ritual linkages between these groups. The first emphasizes exclusiveness, while the second emphasizes inclusiveness. It is in cults of the second kind, Turner argues, that individual responsibility is extended from the domain of immediate kin and neighbourhood relations in localized normative systems to that of wider and more diffuse communities sharing common ideas and values. He refers to pilgrimages and the organization of pilgrimage centres in complex large-scale societies and 'historical religions', such as Hinduism, as examples of inclusive cults, and to localized religious activities focused on local shrines which are themselves parts of bounded social fields as examples of exclusive cults.[48] It is this inclusive cult centre, which has the potential to draw on a large catchment area and to transform itself eventually into a major pilgrimage site, which can submerge the affiliations of small communities to the purely local parochial cults and impart to them a sense of belonging to a wider socio-religious network, encompassing what has been termed a 'cult region'.[49] Unlike the monumental temple, instituted and supported by the regional kingdom from above, such cult centres become inclusive through a historical process, as people themselves define and organize their cult regions over time.

Cult regions may develop in a variety of ways, and we have a fascinating account of the evolution of the cult of Viṭhobā at Pandharpur in western Maharashtra from the sixth century, AD to the present day.[50] Pandharpur is an inclusive cult centre *par excellence*. It presents the story of the successive layers of transformation of a local deity in a peripheral area, a process begun through brahmanical mediation but later reclaimed by the lower castes, till its final incarnation as Viṭhobā, in which form it straddled many differences to emerge as a common cultural inheritance of the Maharashtrians. Pandharpur attracts pilgrims from almost all over Maharashtra, but scarcely from outside, which is the hallmark of an inclusive cult region.

The parallels that Pandharpur offers to developments in Bengal are obvious but the departures are no less conspicuous. While the importance of Viṭhobā rests primarily on its being at the centre of a pilgrimage site, Bengal never produced a centre of pilgrimage of comparable regional dimension. Gaṅgāsāgara (the confluence of Gaṅgā and the Bay of Bengal) is perhaps the only major pilgrimage site of early medieval Bengal, and it has been promoted systematically in the Bengal *Purāṇas*.[51] But there is no firm evidence to suggest that it took off as a significant centre of religious congregation before the early nineteenth century. Besides, the site remains deserted throughout the year except on the day of *Pauṣa-saṁkrānti* in the month of January, when a fair is organized in honour of Kapiḷa, who is reputed to have been the founder of the *Sāṁkhya* philosophy. But neither the river Gaṅgā nor the sage Kapila invoke typically Bengali associations, and the pilgrims who come from all over the country (especially neighbouring Bihar) to attend the fair and obtain piety, far exceed the number of Bengali participants.[52] The popularity of the *Śākta-pīṭhas*, a few of which are mentioned in the Bengal *Purāṇas*[53] (though these do not necessarily correspond to the sites now in worship), is also a late medieval phenomenon and is not unique to Bengal. The success of the Gauḍīya Vaiṣṇava movement had resulted in the emergence of some sacred sites in the sixteenth-seventeenth centuries, such as Navadvīpa, the birthplace of Śrī-Caitanyadeva. But its religious appeal, which remained confined largely to south-western Bengal, declined over the years. Moreover, both the *Śākta-pīṭhas* and the Vaiṣṇava sites retained their essentially sectarian character and therefore cannot claim ubiquitous acceptability. The bhakti movement itself, despite its professed egalitarianism, was initiated by a brāhmaṇa in Bengal. The subsequent theological debates were conducted partly in Sanskrit, and even though it was fairly broad-based and encouraged the development of vernacular literature, bhakti in Bengal never assumed the aspects of an overwhelmingly low-caste protest movement, as had happened at Pandharpur. Thus, Bengal cannot be described as a cult region in terms of a universally recognized pilgrimage site.

## V

However, I argue that Bengal does qualify to be considered as a cult region. Indeed, it was on the shared understanding of a variously represented common cult form that the earliest, and still inarticulate, foundation of Bengal's regional tradition was laid. In the absence of a central monitoring agency such as the temple of Jagannātha or an inclusive pilgrimage site such as Pandharpur, the cult of the regional goddesses, conceived and promoted by the Bengal *Purāṇas*, helped to create a common focus and to integrate the highly stratified rural society in Bengal. The annual worship of Durgā, also mentioned repeatedly in the Bengal *Purāṇas*[54] but not popularized before the late medieval period, now functions as the supreme signifier of Bengal's religious culture to the 'outsider'. However, in this essay I have traced the evolution of Maṅgalacaṇḍī in preference to Durgā order to highlight the processes by which the local goddesses were universalized within the cultural space of, in Deryck Lodrick's words, an 'experienced region',[55] and to show how the newly acquired syncretic identity of these goddesses in turn helped to reinforce the regional identity of Bengal. Anthropological studies reveal that there exists an unstated agreement among the various caste groups of rural Bengal from the brāhmaṇas to the very lowly placed in the hierarchy, that the worship of these regional goddesses is a shared responsibility of the entire village community.[56] The religious culture of Bengal is embedded in this larger system of social practice. The practice is kept going by a busy sacred calendar which, in my opinion, has contributed more to the construction of the internal perspective than the spectacular annual worship of Durgā. There are minor subregional variations in the procedures of worship or in the nature of caste participation, but a common orientation towards the regional goddesses makes Bengal a cult region, even though almost by default. Those local goddesses who, due to the absence of brahmanical recognition, could not make it to the regional grade, continue to be an integral feature of the religious culture of Bengal. However, their exclusive character barred them from providing an active input into the growth of Bengal's regional consciousness.

This scenario is not unique to Bengal, but nowhere else did a set of texts play such a crucial role in the cultural transformation of a region.

brahmanism in Bengal, through the codification and transmission of the *Purāṇas*, succeeded in creating a public realm in which diverse local elements could converge on a common core through the mediation of a supra-local agency. This common core had set the terms for a larger community consciousness. By community, I refer to a process of social interaction which gives rise to a more extensive attitude and practice of interdependence among its constituents. Community is often viewed as a structure of institutions capable of objective definition. But I have used the term in the sense of an internal perception of a cultural identity, a common way of thinking and behaving. According to this approach, community is an aggregative device in which commonality is not necessarily uniformity:

> It is a commonality of forms (ways of behaving) whose content (meanings) may vary considerably among its members. The triumph of community is to so contain this variety that its inherent discordance does not subvert the apparent coherence which is expressed by its boundaries.[57]

Thus, although the members of a community may recognize important differences among themselves and the meanings they attach to cultural symbols may also vary, they nevertheless share the symbols. Symbols are by definition multivalent and part of their meaning is subjective. But the common form of the symbol helps to aggregate the various meanings assigned to it, just as the symbolic repertoire of a community aggregates the individual and the group differences that exist within the community. The process of aggregation so transforms the differences into an appearance of similarity that people tend to invest the community with ideological integrity.[58] This integrity derives from the self-definition of the community as bearers of the same culture. Hence, culture rather than structure is the point of departure in my understanding of community.

In Bengal, brahmanism performed the role of combining the small parochial communities with the dominant symbol of the regional goddess which became one of the enduring features of its regional tradition. brahmanical culture, in creative interplay with the diverse local cultures of Bengal, transformed itself into a regional brahmanical culture, characterized by a range of common cultural denominators and a shared vocabulary of values that later proved to be typical of Bengal. In the process, brahmanism helped local cultures to transcend their purely local boundaries, and encouraged them to participate in, and eventually to develop a sense of belonging to, a larger cultural system.

The system was flexible enough to continue to accommodate new elements and yet sufficiently firm to soften discord and maintain a commonality of forms. In other words, brahmanism was instrumental in creating a wider cultural community by extending the frontiers of recognition of the local cultures.

This does not mean that the boundaries of local cultures were completely obliterated. Instead, the process of cultural transaction created an altered conception of cultural space in which the region became another unit of identification. In the hierarchy of cultural units, the region stands halfway between the pan-Indian level, represented by brahmanism and described by Hitesranjan Sanyal as *mārga* (literally the path, and by implication classical) culture, and the local level, represented by ethnic groups and described by Sanyal as *jana* (literally people and by implication indigenous) culture.[59] The interaction between these two levels resulted in the inauguration of a trend of cultural growth through elaboration and modification at both levels which helped the local society to overcome the limitations inherent in it and allowed the new cultural pattern to assume a broader significance.

> New idioms emerged in the process of cultural growth. These idioms may be local in origin but they cut across the boundaries of localized ethnic group identities and spread over a larger territory with common cultural characteristics and aspirations, that is to say, *deś* [*deśa*] (in the traditioinal sense of the term, as against its modern meaning of the nation state).... The growth of the intermediate level of culture is an effective force in consolidating the concept of *deś* as a cultural phenomenon, as also in defining the boundaries of the physical space covered by a *deś*.[60]

Indeed, I am referring to a period when neither the national identity of India nor the provincial identity of Bengal as politico-administrative units had developed. Therefore, these nomenclatures are being applied only in retrospect. However, from the cultural imbroglio caused by the intervention of brahmanism in the existing order to fragmented little communities, an inchoate idea of a cultural territory larger than the purely local, and consequently the first imperfect awareness of a cultural community wider than those of parochial ethnic groups, had begun to emerge. At least, the Purāṇic testimony points to that direction and the vernacular literature of the medieval period confirms this supposition. Surely, the indigenous local cultures, involved in this process of cultural transformation, did not give up all their internal differences and become one homogenous cultural community. Not all of them comprehended the implications of the transformative process in exactly the same way, not did they relate to the ideological underpinnings of the process or to the cultural objects created in the process with equal intensity. Needless to say, there were instances of imperfect integration and also of dissent. But to the extent that a large majority of them accepted the newly emerging cultural symbols in one way or another, a different order of cultural identity was established.

Cultural identities evolve over a period of time and are subject to continuous renewal and change. Cult regions are also created through historical transformations. I have looked merely at the beginning of this process. It is true that much emphasis on the origin of cultural identity may exert a backward drag and make one oblivious to future developments. I nevertheless submit that the Purāṇic synthesis in Bengal should be considered seriously as the point of departure which generated, for the first time, that necessary cultural resource which enabled little communities to transform themselves into a regional community which could be culturally identified and territorially demarcated.

## NOTES

1 John Leavitt, 'Cultural Holism in the Anthropology of South Asia: The Challenge of Regional Traditions', *Contributions to Indian Sociology*, vol. 26, no. 1, January–June 1992, pp. 3–33. However, it should be mentioned that even though I sympathize with Leavitt's critique of the pan-Indian brahmanical model which often disregards the particularity of regional traditions, the role of brahmanism in the making of these regional cultures cannot be ignored. While it is obvious that each regional tradition must be endowed with unique cultural characteristics to distinguish it from other similar traditions, I argue that the common factor of brahmanical presence in different degrees in each of these does not necessarily undermine their uniqueness. Indeed, I will go a little further and assert that it was as a result of the brahmanical intervention, especially in peripheral areas such as Bengal, that clusters of fragmented but interrelated indigenous local cultures could converge on a common core and acquire a wider identity which both included and transcended the local specificities. In other words, it is not so much in content as in agency that I acknowledge the role of brahmanism in the formation of regional traditions in India. Leavitt's critique does not take into account the heuristic value of the generalizations of such scholars as Redfield. For a detailed discussion on this subject, see Kunal Chakrabarti, 'Anthropological models of cultural interaction and the study of religious process', *Studies in History*, vol. 3, no. 1 (n.s.), 1992, pp. 123–49.

2 Cited in Deryck O. Lodrick, 'Rajasthan as a Region: Myth or Reality', in Karine Schomer, Joan L. Erdman, Deryck O. Lodrick and Lloyd I. Rudolph (eds), *The Idea of Rajasthan: Explorations in Regional Identity*, vol. 1: *Constructions*, New Delhi, 1994, p. 2.

3 For a discussion on the social backdrop and the process of codification of the *Purāṇas*, see R.C. Hazra, *Studies in the Purāṇic Records on Hindu Rites and Customs*, Delhi, 1975, pp. 193–264.

4 R.C. Hazra, *Studies in the Upapurāṇas*, vol. I, Calcutta, 1958, pp. 1–28.

5 Cited in R.C. Hazra, *Studies in the Upapurāṇas*, vol. II, Calcutta, 1963, pp. 162–3.

6 *Bṛhannaradīya Purāṇa*, 4, 20–7; 14.210.

7 Ibid., 22.11.

8 Ibid., 22.17.

9 Ibid., 15.24–25.

10 *Bṛhaddharma Purāṇa*, III.4.15.

11 *Brahmavaivarta Purāṇa*, IV.32.25.

12 Ibid., IV.92.87–88.

13 Ibid., III.7.49–50. For a detailed discussion on the manner in which the Bengal *Purāṇas* attempt to integrate local customs and practices with brahmanism, see Kunal Chakrabarti. 'Texts and Traditions: The Making of the Bengal *Purāṇas*', in R. Champakalakshmi and S. Gopal (eds), *Tradition, Dissent and Ideology: Essays in Honour of Romila Thapar*, New Delhi, 1996, pp. 73–77.

14 Very little is known about the pre-history of Bengal. Bengal's continuous association with the non-brahmanical goddesses is attested to by vernacular evidence as far back as it goes. But it cannot take us beyond the beginning of the second millennium AD. Despite the absence of archaeological evidence or written records, however, it is still possible to infer the centrality of the goddesses in the religious practice of the indigenous population of pre-Purāṇic Bengal from ethnographic studies of the tribes and low castes of Bengal, made during the late nineteenth century. See, for example, the exhaustive survey of H.H. Risley, *The Tribes and Castes of Bengal: Ethnographic Glossary*, vols I and II, Calcutta, 1981 [1891].

15 Richard P. Werbner, 'Introduction', in Richard P. Werbner (ed.) *Regional Cults*, London, 1977, p. ix.

16 Leavitt, 'Cultural Holism', p. 4.

17 Although Mukundaram Chakrabarti, the sixteenth-century poet, is the best-known author of *Caṇḍimaṅgalakāvyam*, several versions of this poem are available, composed by different authors both before and after Mukundaram. There can be little doubt that the stories that these texts narrate were borrowed from an oral core and were in wide circulation before their codification. For a detailed discussion, see Ashutosh Bhattacharya, *Bāṅglā Maṅgalakāvyer Itihāsa*, Calcutta, 1975, pp. 473–585.

18 *Devī Purāṇa*, 45.19.

19 Shashibhushan Dasgupta, *Bhārater Śakti Sādhanā O Śākta Sāhitya*, Calcutta, 1367 B.S. p. 175.

20 'Saṁkaṭā Maṅgalacaṇḍī vrata', in Gopalchandra Bhattacharya (ed.), *Bāromāser Meyeder Vratakathā*, Calcutta, n.d. pp. 200–3.

21 Dasgupta, *Bhārater Śakti Sādhanā*, p. 175. However, one need not look for fragments of elusive evidence to establish a connection between Maṅgalacaṇḍī and women. Both the *Brahmavaivarta* (II.44.6 and II.I.86) and the *Devībhāgavata Purāṇa* (IX.47.6 and IX.1.86) state that Maṅgalacaṇḍī is the tutelary deity of women, who

grants them all their wishes. The *Brahmavaivarta* (II.1.84 and II.16.64–72) adds that women worship her with five kinds of offerings, and that Maṅgalacaṇḍī herself, along with Ṣaṣṭhī, Manasā and a few others, is a manifested woman (*vāstavā strī*), who appears in every age as the best of them. Hence it is reasonable to assume that Maṅgalacaṇḍī or her prototype was a local deity of tribal origin who was adopted by the womenfolk of brahmanical homes, perhaps as the deity presiding over their vratas.

22 *Brahmavaivarta Purāṇa*, II.44.30–38; *Devībhāgavata Purāṇa*, IX, 47.27–35.

23 *Mārkaṇḍeya Purāṇa*, 91.9.

24 *Bṛhaddharma Purāṇa*, III.16.45.

25 Hazra, *Studies in the Upapurāṇas*, vol. II, pp. 458–9.

26 Ibid., p. 189.

27 Krishnachandra Gupta (ed.), *Śri Śri Maṅgalacaṇḍīr Pāñcālī*, Calcutta, 1391, B.S.

28 *'kena mā tomār āj eta velā'?*
*'hāste, khelte, pāter dolāy dulte.*
*nirdhanīke dhan dite, aputrakke putro dite.*
*kānāke cakṣudān karte, khoḍāke kāmadev karte,*
*rājāke kārāgāre khālās karte, tāi āj āmār eta velā'*,
(This was told to me by Rupamanjari Sen.)

29 *Brahmavaivarta Purāṇa*, II.44; *Devībhāgavata Purāṇa*, IX. 1.83–84.

30 *Brahmavaivarta Purāṇa*, II.82; *Devībhāgavata Purāṇa*, IX. 1.83–84.

31 *Brahmavaivarta Purāṇa*, II.44.5–6; *Devībhāgavata Purāṇa*, IX. 1.47.5–5.

32 *Brahmavaivarta Purāṇa*, II.16.65–66 and 70.

33 *Bṛhaddharma Purāṇa*, I.14.14.

34 Hazra, *Studies in the Upapurāṇas*, vol. II, pp. 48–9, fn. 123.

35 D.C. Sircar, 'The Śākta Pīṭhas', *The Journal of the Royal Asiatic Society of Bengal, Letters*, vol. XIV, 1948, Delhi, pp. 35 and 41.

36 *Devībhāgavata Purāṇa*, VII.38.23.

37 *Annadāmaṅgala, pīṭhamālā* section: verse 22, *Rāmaprasāda Bhāratacandra Rachanāsamagra*, Calcutta, 1986, p. 260.

38 Gupta, *Śrī Śrī Maṅgalacaṇḍir Pāñcālī*, p. 2.

39 *Kālikā Purāṇa*, 80.51–4.

40 Ibid., 80.56.

41 *Skanda Purāṇa, Utkalakhaṇḍa.*

42 Hermann Kulke, 'Early Patronage of the Jagannātha Cult', in A. Eschmann, Hermann Kulke, and G.C. Tripathi (eds), *The Cult of Jagannāth and the Regional Tradition of Orissa*, New Delhi, 1978, pp. 139–55.

43 For details, see Hermann Kulke, 'The Struggle between the Rajas of Khurda and the Jagannātha Temple': and, '"Juggenaut" under British supremacy and the Resurgence of the Khurda Rajas as "Rajas of Puri"' in Eschmann *et al.* (eds), *The Cult of Jagannāth*, pp. 321–9, 337–8, 345–8; Prabhat K. Mukherjee, *History of the Jagannātha Temple*, Calcutta, 1977, pp. 17–18, 30.

44 G.N. Dash, 'Jagannātha and the Oriya nationalism', in Eschmann *et al.* (eds), *The Cult of Jagannāth*, p. 362.

45 Richard M. Eaton, *The Rise of Islam and the Bengal Frontier, 1204–1760*, New Delhi, 1994, pp. 14–15.

46 R.C. Majumdar, *History of Ancient Bengal*, Calcutta, 1971, pp. 510–11, 603–4, 612–21.

47 *Rāmacarita*, III.10, 30, 33–4, 39–41.

48 Victor Turner, 'Pilgrimages as social process', in *Dramas, Fields, and Metaphors: Symbolic Action in Human Society*, Ithaca and London, 1974, pp. 185–6.

49 Werbner, 'Introduction', in Werbner (ed.), *Regional Cults*, pp. ix–xii. Werbner disagrees with Turner on a few minor matters, but those are irrelevant for our purpose.

50 G.A. Deleury, *The Cult of Viṭhobā*, Poona, 1960, see particularly pp. 193–203.

51 See, for example, *Mahābhāgavata Purāṇa*, 73.37; 75.28; *Devī Purāṇa*, 66.10; *Kriyāyogasāra*, 4.112; *Brahmavaivarta Purāṇa*, III.30.215; *Bṛhaddharma Purāṇa*, 1.6.34.

52 Tarundev Bhattacharyya, *Ganga Sagar Mela*, Calcutta, 1976.

53 See, for example, *Devībhāgavata Purāṇa*, VII.30.65; *Kālikā Purāṇa*, 18.42–5.

54 *Mahābhāgavata Purāṇa*, 36.71–2, 45.33–42, 48.13. *Devībhāgavata Purāṇa*, III.24.19–20; *Devī Purāṇa*, Chapter 22.59.16; *Brahmavaivarta Purāṇa*, 1.6.60; *Kālikā Purāṇa*, 60.1–44.

55 According to Lodrick, an experienced region has an internal perspective and represents 'a people's shared reaction to their particular segment of space, or specific features associated with that space, that leads to an awareness of its distinctiveness'. Lodrick, 'Rajasthan as a region', p. 4.

56 See, for instance, R.M. Sarkar, *Regional Cults and Rural Traditions: An Interacting Pattern of Divinity and Humanity in Rural Bengal*, New Delhi, 1985, pp. 182–3, 285–91, 305–16.

57 Anthony P. Cohen, *The Symbolic Construction of Community*, Chichester, 1985, p. 20.

58 Ibid., p. 21.

59 Hitesranjan Sanyal, 'The nature of peasant culture in India: A study of the Paṭ painting and clay sculpture in Bengal', *Folk* (Copenhagen), vol. 26, 1984, pp. 148–73.

60 Ibid., p. 168.

# 10

# The Flying Messenger*

Kapila Vatsyayan

Amongst the 108 cadences of movements known as the *karaṇas* described in chapter IV of the *Nāṭyaśāstra* is a variety which may be classified as the *Vṛścika*. Literally speaking, this means the scorpion or '*scorpion-legged*'.

The most important feature of this *karaṇa* is an extension of one leg, either sideways or to back or front, extended forward or crossing. The cadence takes its name from this important feature, and all the cadences belonging to this category arrive in a moment of time at a pose, which gives the impression of kneeling in static positions and flying in dynamic movements.

The *Nāṭyaśāstra* lists nearly ten *karaṇas* of this variety, such as the *Nikuñcita*, the *Vṛścika kuṭṭila*, the *Latā Vṛścika*, the *Vṛścika recita*, *Vṛścika*, the *Mayūralalita Siṁharakṣita*, and the *Lalāṭatilaka*. To these could be added the three *karaṇas* which derive their movement from the *cari* [*Cari* refers to different types of gait or movement in dance: Parul Pandya Dhar] positions and which may be roughly grouped as the *Bhujaṅgatrāsita* variety, namely the *Bhujaṅgatrāsita*, the *Bhujaṅgatrāsita recita*, and the *Bhujaṅgāñcita;* one more *karaṇa* called the *Vidyudhbhrāntā* could be included. These four form a distinct separate group, which is characterized by a crossing.

In terms of kinetics, one has to understand this as a movement of the lower limb, either by using the whole leg as a unit or as two sections—of the thigh and the calf—with a break in line by an extension or flexion

* Previously published in H.P. Ray (ed.), *Sacred Landscapes in Asia: Shared Traditions, Multiple Histories*, New Delhi, India International Center and Manohar, 2007, pp. 225–38.

of the knee resulting in an acute or obtuse angle. The static leg is usually bent with the knee turned outward sideways, termed in the *Nāṭyaśāstra* as the *kṣipta* position in some contexts, and *naṭa* in others. The torso, the lower waist and upper chest can be treated in a variety of ways, so can the upper limbs, to complement the lower limb position: mainly it can be frontal or profile or a posterior view or an anterior view of the upper torso and a posterior view of the lower limbs. The close connection between dance and sculpture in the Asian and Indian artistic traditions needs no restatement. Any lay-observer is aware of the similarity of approach and treatment of the human form in the twin arts. From the earliest times, the dancing figure inspired the sculptor and the sculpturesque beauty of line and form inspired the dancer; the connection was not just on the level of spirit and content but also concrete form. Indonesian, Cambodian, Laotian, Thai, Burmese, and Ceylonese dance and sculpture leave the same impression. There is an awareness immediately of an intimate connection between the two art forms in a region and amongst traditions of dance and sculpture in different regions. A closer scrutiny reveals that this overwhelming impression is created on account of a proximity of content and a similarity of techniques of stylization employed in sculpture and dance.

While it is not possible to go into the fascinating and complex history of interaction between Indian and Asian artistic traditions, it would be worthwhile to understand the nature of this similarity and distinctiveness in the context of some specific motifs, such as the *Vṛścika karaṇa* on account of its extraordinary popularity in dance technique and its continued depiction and portrayal in the sculptural mural and fresco traditions of South-East Asia.

In India, one of the first portrayals of this occurs in the context of the motif of the flying *vidyādharas*, *gandharvas*, *mithunas*, dancing *kinnaras*, and other miscellaneous niche and corner figures. While it is true that most of them do not depict dance poses and very many of them have not been modelled with dance in view, many of them can be classified as dance poses even if they occur on arches, niches, and corners and fulfil a purely architectural function.

The sculptural representation of *gandharvas* and *apsarā* and of male and female forms flying are found in Indian art from the earliest times. Actually by the time Bharata codified movements of dance, a high degree of stylization must have already taken place to enable him to prescribe the rules for movement suggestive of flying, leaping, and kneeling in many chapters of his work. The sculptural representation may well have preceded Bharata's codification.

Movements of flying could have been suggested in a variety of ways and an obvious one could be to take a leap in the air by losing or suggesting a loss of contact with the ground. In sculpture also, the suggestion of flying could be communicated through a pair of wings as is common in the European tradition. Although wings have been used in some sculptural representations in Sanchi and Bharhut and in a few examples of Indonesian sculpture and some frescoes in Pagan, by and large this has been avoided in the Asian and Indian artistic traditions. In these traditions the movement is suggested through a stance which is not realistic but is stylized and symbolic even if giving the impression of natural ease. The principle uniformly followed allows movement only of one leg and at no time is the forking of the legs permitted. This is adhered to, without exception, in all representations of the motif throughout the sculptural and dance tradition of the region covering the Indian subcontinent and many countries of South-East Asia, extending over a period of ten centuries and more.

The *vidyādhara* from Ranigumpha Udaygiri caves (Fig. 10.1) is perhaps the earliest example of the historical period. A celestial figure carrying a tray of garlands is seen with one knee bent in front and the other leg extended at the back in an arch. The weight of the body is on the foot of the bent knee in front and the tray of flowers in one hand helps the forward thrust of the figure. Although the pose cannot be

Figure 10.1: *Vidyādhara*, Ranigumpha, Udayagiri

clearly identified as a position of the *Vṛścika karaṇa* it is a very definite precursor of the motif. Such precursors can also be seen in the poses of the flying figures and the couples seen on the arches of Bharhut, Sanchi, and Karli. In Sanchi we also come across one- or two-winged figures.

By the time we come to Mathura, Amaravati, and Nagarjunakonda, the motif shows remarkable development. Slabs, *toraṇas*, pillars, and medallions depict a variety of poses in which flying or kneeling for adoration of the Buddha is depicted by a knee bent in front either touching the ground or the whole calf resting on the ground with the thigh resting on it or just the foot touching the ground and the knee in line with the torso; the other leg is extended, thrown backwards or sideways with the thigh either at the level of the ground or below the torso; the calf and foot are sometimes at the level of the waist or even the shoulders. In the latter case, an outward flexion results in a raising of the free extended calf and foot. These poses can be identified as the *Kuñcita karaṇa* or *Vṛścika recita karaṇa.* Sometimes an impression of dynamism is created in limited space through the grace, elegance, and flow of the released extended leg. In the *stūpas* of Amaravati and Nagarjunakonda there are innumerable examples and variations of these, specially when they occur in limited space on a semi-circular *toraṇa* arch/*stūpa*.

In a terracotta from Sonkh, Mathura, excavated recently, the same *karaṇa* has been portrayed in a circular disc with remarkable ingenuity. A detailed analysis of the relief makes it clear that the artist was fully conversant with earlier techniques and that he surpassed them in using the motif in a limited circular space. In a medallion from Amaravati we have the first depiction of the *Bhujaṅgāñcita* variety in a court scene. This is without doubt a precursor of a pose which culminated ultimately in the *Naṭarāja* pose of the *Bhujaṅgatrāsita* variety, seen in all parts of India specially of the Pallava, Chola and Vijayanagaram schools. But the consideration of the *Bhujaṅgātrāsita* is not our chief concern here. Multiple examples of the *Vṛścika* pose can be seen in Gupta sculptures from Deogarh, Nalanda, and finally Elura (Fig. 10.2) where we find some outstanding examples of the flying motif. Unlike Amaravati and Nagarjunakonda, in the Kailāśa temple the flying figures occur on walls, freed in space without fulfilling any architectural function. Instead of the *Ūrdhvalatā* arch of the leg being taken to the high head region, the extended leg is taken to a much lower level of the flexed knees. A sense of release from gravity is created by this seemingly careless extension. The *siddhas* of Mamallapuram are close seconds to the dynamic flying figures of Elura; it is this pose which gives the impression of space in spite of the crowded multiplicity of figures. It should be noted that until

Figure 10.2: Flying figure, Elura

the seventh and eighth centuries no twisting of the torso or turning around the sacrum (*trika*) is noticed. The torso is frontal or in profile, but never screwed or spiral. In medieval sculpture a significant development takes place—most of the flying figures from the eighth-century onwards have a *naṭa* or *kṣipta* position of the knee, as also a *naṭa* bend of the side (*pārśva*) and this becomes increasingly accentuated. The trend culminates in the sculptures of Khajuraho and Konaraka where the waist is screwed or spiralled completely thus meeting the description in dance texts of a *vivartita* or *nivṛta* movement. In the temples of Khajuraho these dancing and singing *kinnara*, *gandharva*, and *yaksha* attain complex poses which tax our credulity. A variety of rhythmic lines and curves together leave an impression of difficult turns, twists, and even contortions. Their figures occur in niches, or corners on walls everywhere and even on the reliefs on the back of *Varâha*. Many of them can be identified as the *Vṛṣcika kuttika* or the *Vṛścika recita karaṇas* (Fig. 10.3a & b) and the variations of the *Lalāṭatilaka*.

In Indian dance also, this movement is seen in practically all styles of dance ranging from the tribal and folk to the sophisticated chiselled classical forms. In Himachal Pradesh, the collective dances of the hill regions use a movement which is reminiscent of the kneeling positions seen in the scenes depicting the adoration of the Buddha in Amaravati sculpture. In Mayurbhanj Chhau and in the Seraikella Chhau there are a series of movements which use the *Vṛṣcika* leg extension. The leaps and jumps so characteristic of Mayurbhanj Chhau dancing are characterized by these extensions and elevations. In Bharatanatyam one witnesses these in the *adavus* [*adavu* refers to a unit or phrase of abstract dance; a dance step, done to rhythmic syllables: Parul Pandya Dhar] of the *Tat Tai Tam* variety where both a side leg extension as also a twisting of the torso around the sacrum is noticed. They are also seen in the *pui adavu*. In the *abhinaya* [*abhinaya*, lit. 'to carry forward or to take forward', refers to the expression of sentiments and emotions with the help of facial, hand and body gestures and movements in response to lyrics, usually set to music: Parul Pandya Dhar] portions, Hanuman is depicted by the dancer by suddenly sitting on the ground with one bent knee in front and the other leg extended backwards on the ground: here the pose suggests Hanuman, the son of Pavana. The symbolism of content and form is complete. For the idea of the omnipresent Kṛṣṇa playing the flute, the same pose is used.

In the sculpture of Indonesia (Fig. 10.4) Cambodia, Thailand, and of Yapahuwa of Sri Lanka and the murals of Pagan (Myanmar) there are innumerable examples of the *Vṛṣcika karaṇa*, with the *kuṭṭila* and the *Ūrdhvalatā* movements.

Figure 10.3a: Duladeo Temple, Khajuraho

In this brief survey we can take only one or two examples from each sculptural tradition as illustrations of the pervasive popularity of the pose in the sculptural and dance traditions of South-East Asia. In Chandi Mendut (Indonesia) in the northern wing of the flight of stairs there

Figure 10.3b: Duladeo Temple, Khajuraho

occur two scenes in which the *Vṛṣcika karaṇa* is noticed. In one, the extended leg is at the same level as the bent knee in front and the torso is seen in profile: the balance of the figure is perfect. In Borobudur there is a prolific use of the motif in many contexts. An outstanding example is seen in the panel depicting the Buddha bathing in the Nairanjana river. The *gandharvas* surround the Buddha and are seen in varying movements of the *Vṛṣcika karaṇa*. One is in a simple *Vṛṣcika*, the other is

Figure 10.4: Varying movements of the *Vṛṣcika karana*, Borobudur

*Vṛṣcika kuñcita* and the third in a *Vṛṣcika recita*. Practically every flying celestial being is seen in a chiselled pose of this category.

In the Lara Djnonggrang group in Prambanan [in Java] there is a continuation of the tradition. Here one witnesses the pose not only in flying figures in the *Ramāyaṇa* panels but also in the dancing figures from the balustrade of the Śiva temple. In the context of Indonesian art one must mention that these flying figures without wings and in the *Vṛścika* pose occur side by side with the innumerable *kinnaras* and *kinnaris* with wings. Most important amongst the Indonesian figures is the *garuḍa* figure seen in relief, stone, and bronze. The *kuñcita karaṇa* is his characteristic pose. In Chandi Djago and other temples of the Majhapahita period, Hanuman is often shown traversing lands and seas in this pose. This is repeated in Panataran (Fig. 10.5), Chandi Tigawangi where it is seen in the depiction of the scenes from the story of Sri Tanjung. The amazing continuity of the motif in low bas-relief and subsequently in the Wayang figures is as puzzling as impressive.

In Angkor Wat and Angkor Thom, in the context of the *Rāmāyaṇa* and the *Mahābhārata*, as also other scenes, there is a recurrence of the motif. Here also the arch determines the pose. The Khmer group has many walls and panels of such figures. Indonesian dancing, whether Javanese or Balinese, and Khmer dancing frequently embodies this movement to show flying, moving in the sky, and so on. In detail there are many definite differences and distinctions, but the principle first enunciated by Bharata, of one knee bent or the unfolded leg and the other extended leg is universal. Illustrations will make the point clear, of proximity in

Figure 10.5: Demon in flight before Hanuman, Panataran, Indonesia

art forms and consanguinity of approach in different regions. Examples of the motif are found in Thai sculpture (Figs. 10.6–7) of varying periods (Dvaravati, Lopburi, or Ayodhya periods). It occurs frequently in Thai dancing, both Nang and Khon. The highly picturesque stylized stances of the fighting scenes in the *Rāmāyaṇa,* the flight of Sītā, are all executed through a beautifully controlled *Vṛşcika karaṇa.* The particular movement is known as *Kinnari* in Thai dancing. It is an essential part of the training of Thai dancers, both male and female, specially in the salutation of the celestials known as *Thrp-Pranom.*

One would have thought that Burma [Myanmar] may have discarded this sensuous motif. But no, here in the frescoes and murals of Pagan

Figure 10.6: Decoration, Sukhotai period, Thailand

Figure 10.7: Couple in flying posture, woodcarving, medieval Thailand

(Fig. 10.8), the motif occurs often. The *gandharvas* fly, the *vidyādharas* wear boots and have wings, but the pose is *Vṛścika kuṭṭila*. In Burmese dancing, there is a high degree of articulation at the knee, just so that this sculpturesque effect can be created (Fig. 10.9).

The motif is seen in Sri Lanka, on the walls of Yapahuwa and in the murals of Sigiriya. The movement seems to have gone out of vogue, however, in Kandyan dancing, as it has become extinct in many styles of Indian dancing particularly Manipuri, Kathak, and Kathakali.

Figure 10.8: Scene from Payathon-Zu, Pagan

Figure 10.9: *Vṛścika kuṭṭila* movement in dance, Myanmar

Figure 10.10: Flying *gandharvas* from Durga Temple, Aihole

This survey will make it clear that these countries shared a self-conscious tradition of stylization. Within the large common base there was a continuous give and take, not only of literary themes, philosophic and aesthetic ideas, but also of specific aspects of artistic form and technique, each contributing to the other to evolve a distinct regional form.

The *Vṛṣcika karaṇa* is one amongst several motifs, which are awaiting a detailed comparative study by scholars so that points of similarity and distinction can be identified.

# Part IV

## Mapping Language, Ideas, and Attitudes

# 11

# The Sanskrit Cosmopolis and the Vernacular Revolution*

Sheldon Pollock

[...]

## THE COSMOPOLITAN IN THEORY AND PRACTICE

The intensifying interactions today between local and translocal forms of culture and ways of political being, which have become truly global for the first time, have generated renewed scholarly interest in the idea of the 'cosmopolitan.'[1] As many have recognized, the processes at work in contemporary globalization are not altogether unprecedented. But our understanding of what exactly is new and different about them, beyond the sheer fact of their temporal speed and spatial reach, depends on our capacity to grasp the character of the earlier processes of globalization—of a smaller globe, to be sure—and the cosmopolitan identities that have characterized other historical epochs.[2]

The labels by which we typically refer to these earlier processes—Hellenization, Indianization, Romanization, Sinicization, Christianization, Islamization, Russification, and the like—are often used crudely and imprecisely. Yet they do serve to signal the historically significant ways in the past of being translocal, of participating—and knowing one was participating—in cultural and political networks that transcended the

*Previously published as 'Introduction' in Sheldon Pollock, *The Language of the Gods in the World of Men: Sanskrit, Culture, and Power in Premodern India*, Berkeley, University of California Press, 2006, pp. 10–30; New Delhi, Permanent Black, 2007. This is an extract from the chapter. In the present version some portion of the text and notes have been removed. For the complete text see the original version.

immediate community. These ways varied widely. In Hellenization, the dominant commitment was to a language, a culture, and even an aesthetic; in Christianization, by contrast, to a certain set of beliefs, in Islamization, to a certain set of practices, and in Romanization, to a particular political order—or so one might speculate, and speculation is all one can do for the moment. The comparative study of pre-modern processes of cosmopolitan transculturation—of how and why people may have been induced to adopt languages or life ways or modes of political belonging that affiliated them with the distant rather than the near, the unfamiliar rather than the customary—is very much in its infancy, even for a phenomenon as significant in the creation, or construction, of the west as Romanization. And when these earlier processes do come under scholarly scrutiny, they are typically not seen as processes at all, ones through whose dialectical interaction the global and the local are brought into being simultaneously and continuously. Rather, they tend to be thought of as pregiven, stable, and sharply defined—the global or cosmopolitan as the exogenous, great tradition over against the local or vernacular as the indigenous, little tradition. They have taken on the character of stable entities that interact in thing-like ways, rather than being seen as constantly changing repertories of practices.

[...] The quasi-global formation that characterized early southern Asia—one that came into being around the start of the Common Era and at its height a thousand years later extended across all of South and much of Southeast Asia—and the problems that must be addressed to make some sense of it need to be analysed. The story of how this formation arose—how Sanskrit travelled the vast distance it did and came to be used for literary and political texts, and what such texts meant to the worlds of power in which they were produced—has never been told in the historical detail it merits. Indeed, it is unclear whether the fact that there is a story to tell has been fully recognized.

A number of factors account for this neglect. The temporal and spatial magnitude of the Sanskrit cultural and political order: the conceptual otherness of the subject matter; the apparent anomalousness vis-à-vis peer formations such as Confucian China or Latinate Europe, which has served to make the South Asia case almost invisible; the difficulty of the languages involved; the risk of provoking specialists of the particular regions where such study has always been parceled out; the almost immediate discovery of counter cases to any tendency one believes to have discerned—all these obstacles have combined to induce a powerful resistance to generalization and large-scale interpretation.[3] In addition, Sanskrit studies, heir to a brilliant and imperious intellectual tradition that had set its own agenda in the important issues of the human sciences, has had grounds to rest content with addressing the questions predefined by this tradition—and the historical expansion of the realm of Sanskrit culture was not one of them.

Symptomatic of the many problems of understanding this realm and its history is the question of how even to refer to it. The phrase adopted here, 'Sanskrit cosmopolis', is not without its drawbacks. Besides being hybrid and ahistorical, it is actually uncosmopolitan in the cultural specificity of the form of citizenship implicit in it: membership in the *polis*, or the community of free males. But the very need for such a coinage reveals a social fact of some theoretical importance. Other great globalizing processes of the past found epic formulation and conceptualization, whether in terms of a cultural particularity (Hellenismos or Arabīya or Fārsīyat) or a political form (*imperium romanum* or *guo*, the Sinitic 'fatherland'). But for neither the political nor the cultural sphere that Sanskrit created and inhabited was there an adequate self-generated descriptor. Even the word *saṃskṛti*, the classicizing term adopted for translating 'culture' in many modern South Asian languages, is itself unattested in pre-modern Sanskrit in this sense. We will find Indian theory distinguishing the great Way, *mārga*, from Place, *deśī*, but both terms refer, significantly, only to cultural practices and never to communities of sentiment. If we are therefore obliged to invent our own expression for the transregional culture-power sphere of Sanskrit, the fact that Sanskrit never sought to theorize its own universality should not be seen as lack or failure. On the contrary, it points to something central about the character and existence of the Sanskrit cosmopolis itself: a universalism that never objectified, let alone enforced its universalism.

The phrase 'Sanskrit cosmopolis' carries three additional implications that make it especially useful here. The first is its supraregional dimension ('cosmo-'), which directs attention toward the expansive nature of the formation. The second is the prominence given to the political dimension ('-polis'), which was of particular importance in this form of global identification. Last, the qualification provided by 'Sanskrit' affirms the role of this particular language in producing the forms of culture and political expression that underwrote this cosmopolitan order.

The history of the Sanskrit language and its social sphere has long been an object of interest to Sanskritists, for this is a curious history that holds considerable theoretical interest. The Sanskrit cosmopolis did not come into being simultaneously with the appearance of the Sanskrit language. Its development was slow and tentative, and for it to come about at all the very self-understanding of the nature and function of the 'language of the gods,' as Sanskrit was known, had to be transformed. I have delineated the circumscribed domain of usage and access that characterized the language from its earliest appearance in history to the moment when this field was dramatically expanded around the beginning of the Common Era. Ritualization (the restriction of Sanskrit to liturgical and related scholastic practices) and monopolization (the restriction of the language community, by and large, to the ritual community) gave way to a new sociology and politicization of the language just around the time that western Asian and central Asian peoples were entering into the ambit of Sanskrit culture. Whether these new comers, the Śakas (Indo-Scythians) in particular, initiated these processes or simply reinforced those already under way cannot be determined from the available evidence. What is not in doubt is that it was then that a new era—a cosmopolitan era—began.

Two key inventions, the second a subspecies of the first, marked the commencement of the cosmopolitan era in the literary-cultural domain and would continue to mark its expansion: *kāvya*, or written literature, and *praśasti*, or inscriptional royal panegyric. I have set out the grounds for thinking of Sanskrit *kāvya*—a category ... that was clear and distinct in premodern South Asia—as a new phenomenon in Indian cultural history when it first appeared a little before the beginning of the Common Era. From the first, *kāvya* was almost certainly composed and circulated (though not typically experienced) in writing; it was this-worldly (*laukika*) in its themes, even when these concerned the divine (no *kāvya* was incorporated into temple liturgy until the waning centuries of the cosmopolitan order): it was directed above all toward investigating the elementary forms of human emotional experience; at the same time (and for the same reason) it was centrally concerned with the nature of language itself, with its primary phonic and semantic capacities. In all these features *kāvya* was demonstrably something new in the historical record—something startlingly new to the participants in Sanskrit culture. Its novelty was thematized in the Sanskrit tradition itself with the story of the invention of *kāvya* told in the prelude to what came to be called the 'first poem,' the *Vālmīki Rāmāyaṇa*. In reflexively framing its own morality in away that would be impossible in a preliterate world, and in doing so around the narrative of human response to problems of a human scale, the *Rāmāyaṇa* account captures some central features of the new expressive form that was *kāvya*.

Central to the theorization of *kāvya* in the cosmopolitan epoch was the restriction on the languages capable of producing it. The literary conquest of cosmopolitan space by Sanskrit produced a conception of literature as something able to be embodied only in language that was itself cosmopolitan. This was, of course, pre-eminently Sanskrit, though two other closely related idioms—Prakrit, the 'natural' or informal language, and Apabhramsha, the dialectal (literally, decayed)—were counted as legitimate vehicles for *kāvya* from the first appearance of literary–theoretical reflection in the seventh century. Both Prakrit and Apabhramsha were in fact constituted as transregional *koinés.* [A koine is a regional dialect or language that becomes the standard language of a larger area] through the production of literary tests and grammatical descriptions, and they were used for literary production (almost exclusively so) across the subcontinent, the former from about the second or third century, the latter from about the fifth or sixth. (Since neither was spatially circumscribed, or reflexively understood to be so circumscribed, in the production of literary and political texts, neither qualifies as an instance of vernacularization.) But both languages occupy a much more subordinate position in literary history than Sanskrit, having never achieved anything like Sanskrit's density of textual production or its spatial spread—neither was ever used for the production of literary texts outside the subcontinent. Sanskrit was the transregional code that filled the domain of the literary. The closed set of literary languages meant in principle that *kāvya* could not be made in other localized languages; in this thought world, the very idea of *deśī kāvya*, 'vernacular literature', would have constituted a contradiction in terms. And in practice it was never produced—until the vernacular moment came, when it was. [...]

Once Sanskrit emerged from the sacerdotal environment to which it was originally confined, it spread with breathtaking rapidity across southern Asia. Within three centuries Sanskrit became the sole medium by which ruling elites expressed their power from as far west as Puruṣapura in Gandhāra (Peshawar, in today's northwest Pakistan) to Pāṇḍurāṅga in Champa (central Vietnam), and Prambanan on the plains of Java. Sanskrit probably never functioned as an everyday medium of communication anywhere in the cosmopolis—not in South Asia itself, let alone Southeast Asia—nor was it ever used (except among the literati) as a bridge- or link- or trade-language like other cosmopolitan codes such as Greek, Latin, Arabic, and Chinese. And aside from the inscriptions which have larger purposes, there is little evidence that it was ever used as the language of practical rule: tasks such as chancery communication or revenue accounting seem to have been accomplished by informal uses of local language. The work Sanskrit did do was beyond the quotidian and the instrumental: it was directed above all toward articulating a form of political consciousness and culture, politics not as transaction of material power—the power of recording deeds, contracts, tax records, and the like—but as celebration of aesthetic power. This it did in large part through the new cultural-political practices that came to expression in the *praśasti*, which not only arose coevally with Sanskrit *kāvya* but from the first exploited the full range of resources of the language-centered aesthetic of literature. Inscribed on rock faces or copper-plates or, at a later date, temple walls, and thus to varying degrees publicly availably, the *praśasti* was the literary expression of political selfhood. To a large extent, the Sanskrit cosmopolis consisted of precisely this common aesthetics of political culture, a kind of poetry of polity in the service of what was in some measure an aesthetic state. An examination of the semantics of inscriptional discourse aims to illuminate these concerns and illustrate its procedures. To foreground aesthetics, however, is not to argue with Weber (or Clifford Geertz) that culture is all that constituted polity in the non-modern non-West and that other core isssues of power were never addressed. A case study of the pragmatics of inscriptional discourse among the Kalyāṇa Cālukya dynasty is meant to show how seriously matters of real power were taken and how carefully memory was manufactured in its interests.

Even in such cases, however, we must be cautious about reducing the relationship between culture and power in the Sanskrit world to one of simple instrumentality. Things are much more complicated, and more interesting, than that. A vision of grammatical and political correctness—where care of language and care of political community were mutually constitutive—was basic to the cosmopolitan ethos from the very beginning. Something of the character of this linkage will have become apparent already in the history of the inscriptional habit, and further dimensions are brought to light by an examination of royal practices in the domain of grammar and literature. Sanskrit philology was a social form as well as a conceptual form, and it was inextricably tied to the practices of power. Overlords were keen to ensure the cultivation of the language through patronage awarded to grammarians, lexicographers, metricians, and other custodians of purity, and through endowments to schools for the purpose of grammatical studies. They were also responsible for commissioning many of the most important grammars. For a polity to possess a grammar of its own was to ensure its proper functioning and even completeness, so much so that a competitive grammaticality, even grammar envy, can be perceived among kings in the Sanskrit cosmopolis, as the narrative of Jayasiṃha Siddharāja of

Gujarat illustrates. Kings also evinced consuming interest in demonstrating their Sanskrit virtuosity in literary matters. An encyclopedia of royal conduct from early twelfth-century Karnataka, the *Mānasollāsa*, demonstrates how literary–theoretical competence (*śāstravinoda*) was as central to kingliness as military competence (*śāstravinoda*). Episodes of grammatical and literary correctness such as these are not idiosyncratic tendencies of the persons or places in question. They point toward an ideal of proper rule and proper culture being complementary—an ideal in evidence throughout the cosmopolitan age, from the earliest recorded evidence in the second century, and beyond into the vernacular epoch, when so many cosmopolitan values of culture and power came to find local habitations and names.

Even if the transregional formation for which Sanskrit was the communicative medium was never named in the language, the transregionality of both culture and power decisively manifested itself in shaping Sanskrit discourse. The analytical matrices employed in much Sanskrit systematic thought—from the typology of females in the *scientia sexualis* to instrumental and vocal music and dance—are effectively geocultural maps of this vast space. The basic geographical template by which culture was conceptualized was, for its part, established only in the early centuries of the cosmopolitan era, reaching its final form in a mid sixth-century work on astral science [Varāhamihira's *Bṛhatsaṃhitā*], and was transmitted more or less invariantly for the next ten centuries. Of particular interest is the spatialization of Sanskrit literature itself, through the discourse on the 'Ways' of literature, modes of literariness conceived of as regional styles within a cosmopolitan space. The regionality of the cosmopolitan language was qualified, however. It was the same Sanskrit everywhere—an elementary aspect of the language ideology of Sanskrit is its invariability across time and space—though differently realized in terms of phonological, semantic, or syntactic registers. But these regional differences were in fact part of the repertoire of a global Sanskrit, with writers everywhere using them to achieve different aesthetic ends (the southern style for erotic verse, for example, or the northern for martial), and thus they constituted a sign precisely of Sanskrit's ubiquity. This idea is beautifully captured in a tenth-century tale of the origins of literary culture: Poetry Man [*Kāvyapuruṣa*] is pursued by his wife-to-be, Poetics Woman [*Sāhityavidyā*], and in the process creates literature across South Asia—and only there. Literature is decidedly transregional if not quite universal.

But where was this 'South Asia'? As represented in such treatises, the Sanskrit cosmopolitan order appears smaller than the cosmopolis was in actuality, for aside from the very occasional mention in Sanskrit texts of Suvarṇabhūmi (Malaysia), Yavadvīpa (probably Java), Śrīvijaya (Palembang), and the like, Southeast Asia never formed part of the representation (the same holds true of Tibet and parts of central Asia, which participated in a more limited fashion in the Sanskrit cosmopolitan order). The conceptual space of Sanskrit texts was slow to adjust, or so one might think, to the new and larger circulatory spaces through which people had increasingly begun to move. Indeed, these actual spaces were vast, and so was the spread of Sanskrit culture, enabled by the diffusion of *kāvya* and *praśasti* on the part of peripatetic literati and the cultivation everywhere of a literarily uniform Sanskrit. Accordingly, in the first millennium it makes hardly more sense to distinguish between South and Southeast Asia than between north India and south India, despite what present-day area studies may tell us. Everywhere similar processes of cosmopolitan transculturation were under way, with the source and target of change always shifting, since there was no single point of production for cosmopolitan culture. Yet just as Southeast Asia was included in the circulatory space of the cosmopolitan order, so it came to be included in its conceptual space thanks to the transportability, so to speak, of that space. In their own geographical imagination the imperial polities of Southeast Asia—Angkor around 1000 is exemplary here—made themselves part of the cosmopolitan order by a wholesale appropriation of its toponymy. With Mount Meru and the Gaṅgā river locatable everywhere, there was no spatial centre from which one could be excluded; the Sanskrit cosmopolis was wherever home was. There is nothing in the least mystical about this replicability; it is a function of a different, plural, pre-modern logic of space.

While modern-day equivalents to places mentioned in these spatializations are often provided here so that some geographical image will form in the mind's eye of the reader, establishing positive concordances is not the objective. The goal instead is learning to understand how people conceptualized macrospaces in the past, and what work in the spheres of culture and power such conceptualization was meant, or not meant, to do. To explore this topic is not to presuppose a seamless continuity from the sixth century to today's representations of Akhaṇḍ Bhārat, 'Undivided India', that have produced the 'cartographic anxiety' behind so much of contemporary Indian political action.[4] The very appropriation and concretization of a sometimes imaginary and often vague geographical past in a precise and factual present constitute one of the deadly weapons of nationalism and a source of the misery of modernity. Pre-modern space, whether cosmopolitan or vernacular, is not the nation-space—and yet it was no less filled with political content than it was with cultural content. The attempt to recover knowledge of this space is not fatally distorted by the discourse of nationalism. Far from disabling a history of the pre-modern politics of space, the distortion of national narratives is precisely the condition that makes it necessary. Such a history need not be crippled by teleology; it can instead be seen as a history of the teleological. The national narrative is a second-generation representation only made possible by the existence of a first-generation representation—one informed, however, by a very different logic that nationalism often seeks to elide.

That the space promulgated by Sanskrit analytical matrices was conceived of not just as a cultural-space but also as a power-space is demonstrated by the Sanskrit *Mahābhārata*. In this *itihāsa* (narrative of 'the way it once was'), or 'epic' in Western parlance (genre identity is no trivial matter, given the modern discourse on 'nation,' 'epic,' and 'novel'), the transregional frame of reference structures the entire work. Moreover, the dissemination of its manuscripts and the distribution of royal endowments for its continual recitation actualized literary spatiality, turning representations into components of popular consciousness: people recited and listened to the *Mahābhārata*'s story of a macrospace of power even while they inhabited that very space. The evidence assembled to demonstrate this claim aims to correct errors old and new: for instance, that it was only on mountain-tops that the language of the gods touched the earth, or that it was nationalist modernity that invented the cultural-political salience of Indian epic discourse.[5]

Whatever else the *Mahābhārata* may be, it is also and pre-eminently a work of political theory—the single most important literary reflection on the problem of the political in southern Asian history and in some ways the deepest meditation in all antiquity on the desperate realities of political life—and to mention it with reference to the ecumenical culture of the Sanskrit cosmopolis naturally raises the question of how the cultural order articulated with political practice. As noted earlier, understanding the character of polity in pre-modern South Asia is far more difficult than describing its cosmopolitan culture, and scholars have generated wildly discrepant accounts of what polity meant. While some of these are examined briefly, more attention is given to the modes and character of political imagination. This is not, however, a *pis aller* [last resort]. Almost as important as what polities did—and just as real—is what they aspired to do. In its aspirations the imperial polity of the Sanskrit cosmopolis was marked by several consistent if elusive features.

It was territorially expansive, though territoriality in pre-modern South Asia remains an underdefined concept. It was politically universalistic, though what political governance actually meant is hard to pin down. It was ethnically non-particularized, if the term 'ethnic' may be used when it is not even certain that ethnies in the political-science sense actually existed. The fact that these aspirations were embedded in a set of cultural practices like *kāvya* and *praśasti* suggests that the practice of polity was to some degree also an aesthetic practice. *Kāvya* and *rājya* were mutually constitutive; every man who came to rule sought the distinction of self-presentation in Sanskrit literature, typically in the permanent public form of the *praśasti*. This constitutive relationship, however, presents interpretive challenges. The single available explanation of the social function of Sanskrit cosmopolitan culture is legitimation theory and its logic of instrumental reason: elites in command of new forms of social power are understood to have deployed the mystifying symbols and codes of Sanskrit to secure popular consent. Absolute dogma though this explanatory framework may be, it is not only anachronistic but intellectually mechanical, culturally homogenizing, theoretically naïve, empirically false, and tediously predictable [...].

The peculiar character of the Sanskrit cosmopolis as a cultural and political order becomes clear only through comparative analysis. 'Beware of arriving at conclusions without comparisons,' said George Eliot. I agree, though perhaps not for her reasons. Comparison always implicitly informs historical analysis, given that the individual subjectivity of the historian inevitably shapes his research question. And these questions can be more sharply formulated and better answered if the comparison behind them is explicit.[6] Moreover, there is a natural proclivity to generalize familiar forms of life as universal tendencies and common sense, and comparison serves to point up the actual particularity, even peculiarity, of such supposed universalisms.

[...] If some similarities link the Roman and the Sanskrit cultural-political orders, the differences are such that the one presents itself as a kind of countercosmopolis to the other. In both worlds, literature, after making a more or less sudden irruption into history, became a fundamental instrument for the creation of a cosmopolitan culture, with literati across immense space being trained according to comparable standards and producing literature that circulated across this space. But Latin interacted with local idioms in a way radically different from that of Sanskrit. Radically different, too, were the origin and character of the empire form, as well as the modalities of affiliation to Roman culture, or Romanization.

The Sanskrit cosmopolis was characterized by a largely homogeneous language of political poetry along with a range of comparable cultural-political practices. Constituted by no imperial state or church and consisting to a large degree in the communicative system itself and its political aesthetic, this order was characterized by a transregional consensus about the presuppositions, nature, and practices of a common culture, as well as a shared set of assumptions about the elements of power—or at least about the ways in which power is reproduced at the level of representation in language. For a millennium or more, it constituted the most compelling model of culture-power for a quarter or more of the inhabitants of the globe. And it only ended, at various times and places in the course of the first five centuries of the second millennium, under pressure from a new model. If the Sanskrit cosmopolis raises hard questions for political and cultural theory, so do the forms of life that superseded it. The fact that this later transformation occurred at all, however, has been of scarcely more interest to historical research than the Sanskrit cosmopolis itself.

## THE VERNACULAR IN THEORY AND PRACTICE

The problem of the vernacular claims some attention, for without this contrastive category, and the contrastive reality of both cultural and political self-understanding toward which it points, the cosmopolitan has no conceptual purchase. Like 'cosmopolitan,' 'vernacular' is not something that goes without saying, and not only because of its own scalar ambiguities (how small qualifies as vernacular?). A range of conceptual and historical problems have combined to effectively conceal the very process of people knowledgeably becoming vernacular—what is here termed 'vernacularization'—leaving it largely unhistoricized and even unconceptualized in scholarship. And until these problems are clarified and some reasonable working hypotheses framed, vernacularization itself cannot even be perceived, to say nothing of its cultural and political ramifications. The problems here are in fact not all that different from those presented by cosmopolitanism, though they are perhaps denser. Besides considering the pertinent relational boundaries, we need to be clear about what the process of vernacularization entails, in particular what role to assign to writing and to the creation of expressive texts. Only when we gain some clarity about the intelligibility and reality of the object of analysis, and how this object exists in time, can we begin to ask why it has the particular history it does.

Simply to define the vernacular over against the cosmopolitan and leave it at that—even to make unqualified use of any of the kindred terms or phrases adopted here, like 'regional' and 'transregional'—elides some important aspects of their relativity. An obvious one is the potential of a local language to become translocal, and the consequences this can have for codes that are yet more local, so to say. The extreme case is offered by the cosmopolitan languages themselves. All of them began their careers as vernaculars: Latin in the third century BCE was firmly rooted in Latium (central Italy) before setting out on its world conquest in lockstep with the advance of Roman arms. Sanskrit is the great anomaly here, since long before the onset of the cosmopolitan era it had become transregional—though not yet cosmopolitan—through the spread of Vedic culture.[7]

An expansion of the vernaculars in the post-cosmopolitan era occurred, too, but of an altogether different order of magnitude. Take the language now called Old Kannada. This developed from the prestige dialect of an area in northwest Karnataka into a unified medium for literary and political communication over a limited zone of southern India late in the first millennium. The intellectuals who cultivated the language clearly understood these spatial limitations and harboured no illusions about or aspirations toward its universalization. They defined a literary culture, and along with it a political order, in conscious opposition to some larger world, in relationship to which they chose to speak more locally. And they were fully aware they were doing so. And yet Kannada in fact became transregional—sometimes domineeringly transregional—for writers in still smaller zones marked by other idioms, such as Tamil Nadu and the southern Konkan on the west coast; as a result neither Tulu nor Konkani was committed to writing, let alone elaborated for literature, until the colonial era. A precisely similar dynamic reveals itself in the history of vernacularization in western Europe. The vernacular that came to be called French first acknowledged spatial limits as compared with the limitless Latin, and later evinced an expansiveness into narrower spaces—or what were thereby transformed into narrower spaces—such as Brittany or Provence.[8]

If a certain transregionality thus characterized the vernaculars that attained cultural-political salience, this was on an entirely different scale from the cosmopolitan codes they displaced. This difference can be plotted along both the axis of material practice and that of subjective understanding. Sanskrit literary texts came to circulate from Sri Lanka to Sorcuq in central Asia, and from Afghanistan to Annam in South east Asia (just as Latin literary texts circulated from Iberia to Romania and Britain to Tunisia). They filled all the available cultural space, their expansion as literary-political media limited only by other cosmopolitan cultural formations; in northern Vietnam, for example, from the fifth century on, Sanskrit's advance was arrested by Chinese, as that of Latin was arrested by Greek in the eastern Mediterranean a few centuries earlier. The vernaculars inhabited much smaller zones; the limits they confronted, or rather helped to produce, were certain cultural-political isoglosses, [isogloss refers to the geographical boundary of a feature of a language], so to speak [...].

The objective dimensions of vernacular place over against those of cosmopolitan space were also registered within the subjective universes of the vernacular intellectuals. To participate in Sanskrit literary culture was to participate in a vast world; to produce a regional alternative to it was to effect a profound break—one the agents themselves understood to be a break—in cultural communication and self-understanding. It was in conscious opposition to this larger sphere that these intellectuals defined their regional worlds. They chose to write in a language that did not travel—and that they knew did not travel—as easily and as far as the well-travelled language of the older cosmopolitan order. The new culture-power places they projected, which were the conceptual correlates of the isoglosses just mentioned, fully testify to this sense of limit and contrast sharply with the spatial matrices at work in Sanskrit culture.

The localization in question is reflected in the South Asian term for the vernacular. If 'Sanskrit cosmopolis' is a phrase hobbled by its hybridity, its adoption is an adversity that cannot be avoided and that anyway has uses in foregrounding the quasi-global, the political, and the cultural 'Vernacular' has similar liabilities and benefits. To be sure, a pejorative connotation haunts the Latin etymon—it refers to the language of the *verna*, or house-born slave, of Republican Rome—which has little political-cultural relevance to pre-modern South Asia. However, in a more common, indeed classical, sense the Latin *vernacularis* is 'local,' 'native', 'inborn,' even 'Roman' (in contrast to *peregrinus*, 'foreign'). Apart from the fact that the cosmopolitan culture of Rome could be conceived of as native (another of its radical differences from the Sanskrit order, deriving from Latin's very different history), the sense of local does map well against the South Asian idiom. In many South Asian languages the conceptual counterpart to the cosmopolitan is *deśī*, the 'placed', or '[a practice] of place'. Yet it is critical to register at once the paradox that what was deśī was not often thought of as native, inborn, or sometimes even local [...]. Not only was the creation of local places a cultural process consequent upon literary vernacularisation, but the very ubiquity of the self-same term *deśī* across South Asia is a sign of the *cosmopolitan* origins of the literary vernacular itself.

Finding vernacularization in history presupposes not just a sense of relevant orders of magnitude but also a clear conceptualization of the vernacularizing process and of the very idea that this process can begin. The question of beginnings raises a range of cognitive, conceptual, and ideological problems. A postmodern anxiety now attaches to the question of beginnings, the ominous phrase 'quest for origins' conjuring up intellectual failings ranging from theoretical innocence to fundamentalism. There are older anxieties, too. The possibility of vernacular beginnings is often denied since, in a positivist historical sense, a beginning is always hostage to the fortune of historical preservation. Beginnings are held as suspect, produced by the machinations of modern (or pre-modern) inventors of tradition. They are historically unintelligible, since producers of culture often think they are beginning the new when they are continuing the old, or (more often in India) the reverse. They are undefinable, since boundaries between new and old, especially language boundaries, can be very blurry. And they are illogical because they cannot escape circularity: an absolute historiographical beginning has already organized the evidence required for its own justification.

Such problems might seem fatal, but far from weakening a historical account of the vernacularization process, they can strengthen it if they form part of the substance of that account. Beginnings are not only a *pāramārthika sat* according to some absolute historiography but a *vyāvahārika sat* according to the actors' understanding of their own life experiences[9]. Thus, many vernacular literary cultures acknowledge and commemorate beginning (as the cosmopolitan Sanskrit tradition does), and the memories developed around that beginning are themselves significant. Traditional accounts have certain vested interests, of course, and will often misrepresent what seems to us the truth of the matter. Yet misrepresentation is real and falsification is true, in the sense that both have a historical reality. And for many literary cultures in South Asia evidence is available, far richer than that for Europe, in fact, that allows us to see vernacularization actually taking place—one of the few great historical changes in pre-modern India that we can actually document with some precision.

Vernacularization is here understood—not a priori or stipulatively but from tendencies visible in the empirical record—as the historical process of choosing to create a written literature, along with its complement, a political discourse, in local languages according to models supplied by a superordinate, usually cosmopolitan, literary culture. The process can thus be broken down into three connected components.

Two have already been introduced: literization, and literarization.[10] The third, closely related to the latter, is 'superposition,' or the presence of dominant language and literary formation. While literarization and superposition can be briskly reviewed, literization needs additional attention.

Gaining access to writing, the resulting symbolic elevation of what is written, and the transformations to which the written text becomes subject by the very fact of its being written—such literization is the component without which vernacularization cannot be perceived as historical fact. Local languages of course existed in oral prehistory but only in a phenomenological rather than a conceptual sense, as 'Language' or language continua rather than as defined languages. One such continuum, Kannada—or what in later literized discourse was named Kannada—merged imperceptibly into what in later discourse was named Marathi and Telugu, just as preliterate French merged into preliterate Spanish and Italian. In such a lifeworld, Kannada and the other languages should not even be regarded as pregiven points on a spectrum: the division of that continuum is an effect of, among other things, the cognitive revolution of writing that was part of the vernacularization process itself.

Although the materials assembled here will often be seen to contradict the views of Mikhail Bakhtin, they confirm his argument that 'unified' or 'unitary' language is 'not something given' but something 'posited' in opposition to 'the realities of heteroglossia'. [In Bakhtin's writings, heteroglossia refers to the existence of multiple voices and conflicting discourses in a language or text.] it 'constitutes the theoretical expression of the historical processes of linguistic unification and centralization.' What enables this positing, unification, and centralization to begin is literization and the processes of literary elaboration (Nietzsche's *objektive Schriftsprache,* [*objective written language*]). Writing 'creates' a language discursively as well as factually, promoting its regularization and, above all, its conceptual differentiation.[11] These are processes of which, again, pre-modern South Asian vernacular writers were fully aware, as the great monuments of vernacular unification demonstrate. In this sense, vernacularity is not a natural state of being but a willed act of becoming. When cultural actors 'choose a vernacular language' for literature and so inaugurate the vernacularization process, it is important to understand that they are choosing something that doesn't exist yet as a fully formed, stable totality: instead, Language is constituted as *a language*, as a conceptual object, in part by the very production of texts. Choosing at the inaugural moment means to begin to create such a totality out of the continuum of patois that constitutes language in a preliterate world.

To write at all in pre-modernity, let alone to write literarily, always meant writing in a language that was both learned and learned, endowing it with new norms and constraints and, inevitably, the new social status associated with constraint and normativity. Thus one definition of vernacular found in sociolinguistics, the 'unstandardized native language of a speech community,' is not relevant here, for in many cases the creation of a literary vernacular carried with it a powerful imperative toward standardization, often accompanied by formal grammaticization. It is the technology of writing that first began to unify the vernaculars, a process only intensified and not inaugurated by print. Historically speaking, what counted in the history of vernacular literary culture—what made history not only for us, by providing historical objects, but for the primary agents themselves, by marking a rupture in the continuum of history—was the committing of local language to written form.[12] Yet central to understanding the history of vernacularization is the fact that more than inscription was required for its achievement. Also essential was the creation of a vision of power and culture made possible only by the elaboration of a literary corpus. This rarely occurred at the inaugural moment of literization: as the South Asian materials show unequivocally, that moment was always *documentary*, non-literary. Contrary to what we commonly assume, the history of a language and its literature are not coextensive.

The claim that literary vernacularization can begin and thereby become historically meaningful as a category of cultural analysis would indeed be unintelligible if either of two assumptions dealt with earlier were true—that the oral can be literature or that literature can be anything that is written. Neither proposition was historically the case for the societies under consideration here. Writing was constitutive of the process that made the vernacular literary, because the 'literary' in these societies was the written production of expressive forms of language use, for the most part the sort prescribed in the dominant cultural formation against which the regional was defining itself. Accordingly, literization, the development of a written form of the vernacular, may have been a necessary condition for vernacularization but it was not a sufficient one; also required was literization, the development of imaginative, workly discourse.

The fundamental differentiation between documentary and workly literization, as well as the gulf that eventually arose between orality and written literature, are made manifest in a range of South Asian narratives of vernacular self-assertion and risk. When the cultural notables of his town punished a seventeenth-century Marathi poet [Tukarām] by throwing his texts in a river, it was because what he had written in the language of Place was no mere document but *kāvya*. And his anguish that his work may have been lost was not misplaced: literature *could now be lost* since it was something written and impermanent rather than something oral and stored lastingly in the memory: When the text-artifact was gone, the text was gone.

A prevalent feature in the vernacularization process is the time lag between literization and literarization. Many languages, from Marathi to Khmer, reveal long histories prior to their literary transformation. In all cases literization was mediated by Sanskrit. Sometimes this happened simultaneously with the introduction of cosmopolitan literary culture, sometimes centuries later; inscriptions in Khmer are found from as early as the seventh century, within a few generations of the appearance of Sanskrit in Cambodia, those in Marathi from only at the end of the tenth century, after a millennium of Sanskrit literary culture in the region. Yet it was only much later—for Marathi, around the fourteenth century, for Khmer, around the sixteenth or seventeenth—that those languages came to be used for literary forms of writing. The possibility that languages could be speciated through initial documentary elaboration and yet remain indefinitely restricted to nonliterary functions by a firm division of linguistic labour was the norm in the Sanskrit cosmopolitan world. Four hundred years of Marathi literature, and a thousand of Khmer; did not disappear without trace. Rather, until Khmer and Marathi vernacular newness entered their worlds, Sanskrit occupied the entire space of literate literature and literate political expression, a fact we see registered in the Sanskrit theory of literary language as a closed set. Some of the earliest textualizations of the languages of Place are found in the twelfth-century encyclopedia mentioned earlier [Mānasollāsa]: these are presented not in the section on literature, however, but in that on song; the author is clear that 'literature' is a cosmopolitan practice; all the rest is just music. Only once we have established the fact that vernacular literature did begin, by reason of newfound literariness wedded to literacy, can we ask the all-important questions why it began when it did and why at this or that particular social site.

If naturalists and other indigenists are predisposed to discover an ever-deeper history for the literature of the Folk, reaching back to a golden moment of pure autochthony, historical analysis shows that literatures typically arise in response to other literature *superposed* to them in a relation of unequal cultural power. In pre-modern India this other literature was preeminently Sanskrit, but also to some degree Prakrit and Apabhramsha (which were particularly rich sources of metrical forms for the vernaculars to appropriate), Tamil in some areas of south India, and much later, Persian in some areas of the north. Conformity with the superposed matrix and its norms was the goal of those vernacular textbooks meant to 'ornament' the language. Indeed, they were part of a literary apparatus that was adopted wholesale during the crystallizing moments of many vernacular literary cultures and formed a core component in the creation of what is here named the 'cosmopolitan vernacular,' that register of the emergent vernacular that aims to localize the full spectrum of literary qualities of the superposed cosmopolitan code.[13]

[...] Few literary cultures anywhere permit the degree of historicization we can achieve for Kannada, due to the density of inscriptions and of texts recopied with singular devotion for more than ten centuries. Whereas Kannada was first literized as early as the fifth century, it did not come to be used for the production of *praśasti* until the ninth, when the elaboration also began of what, by the end of the thirteenth, would be a complete array of the elements of a literary culture. When the process of literarization was inaugurated, it occurred in one place only: the royal court. The first literary text in Kannada, and one of the great documents in the history of South Asian vernacularization, the *Kavirājamārgam* (Way of the King of Poets), was produced at the court of the ruling dynasty in ninth-century Karnataka. It adopts and adapts a cosmopolitan poetics, the great Way of writing, from an earlier Sanskrit treatise and makes it serve as the framework for a theory of the literary practices of Place, creating in the process one of the earliest examples of the cosmopolitan vernacular that in many regions would become the pre-eminent register of regional literary expression until the coming of colonialism.

To speak of a cosmopolitan vernacular is not just to acknowledge that 'different languages are penetrated by each other, thus revealing every language's intimate discord with itself, the bilingualism implicit in all human speech': nor even to try to update the idea of 'vernacular humanism,' of 'using the ancient languages as models and so making the vernacular languages into worthy vehicles for literature and culture.'[14] It is to point to the historical creation of a medium of culture that was not only new in itself but appropriate to a new vision of power—a medium of Place for a political vision of Place, but fashioned according to the time-honored model of *kāvya* and *rājya* of the great Way, which had been tied to no one place but were inclusive of them all. The existence of such a vision, and the fact that political power was centrally interested in sustaining a vernacular literary culture to produce it, find repeated corroboration in Kannada. Just as the *Kavirājamārgam* particularizes a global aesthetic, so the Kannada *Mahābhārata* of Pampa (*c.* 950) localizes a translocal narrative in the service of a new (or newly self-conscious) regional power formation, shrinking the space of the Sanskrit epic and its political vision to a narrower place, Kannaḍanāḍu, the culture-land of Kannada, which had already been announced in the *Kavirājamārgam*. The philological impulse of the *Kavirājamārgam* was also elaborated in a whole new set of vernacular subdisciplines, above all, grammar, which found its supreme expression at the Hoysaḷa court in the thirteenth century with the composition of one of the greatest regional-language grammars of India, the *Śabdamaṇidarpaṇam* (Jewelled Mirror of Language). Especially important here is the new cultural consciousness, unknown to the Sanskrit world, exhibited in the claims of the vernacular grammarian to legislate literary norms.

Virtually all of the traits explored in the Kannada world—the time lag between literization and literarization, the place of the court in the creation of literary culture, the epicization of regional political space, the character of vernacular philology—mark the histories of vernacularization across southern Asia and their conceptualization, the rationalizations of rationality. The historical material itself presents few serious challenges of interpretation. More difficult to explain is the transformation that was concurrently under way in the political sphere and the nature of its relationship to developments in literary culture. Choosing a language for literary and political text production implies affiliating with an existing sociotextual community or summoning such a community into being. For it is in part from acts of reading, hearing, performing, reproducing, and circulating literary and political texts that social groups come to produce themselves and understand themselves as groups. This is especially the case when a notable feature of the texts in question, what might be termed an indexical rather than referential feature, is the very use of vernacular language for producing literary and political discourse. Whatever else it may be, the vernacularization of literature and political discourse is a social act, and one that typically bears major geocultural and political entailments.

While it is no easier to understand the practices of power in the second millennium than in the first, it is clear that during the period 1000–1500 these practices took on far more distinctively regionalized traits than ever before. Whether crystallizing culture spheres were the cause or consequence of crystallizing power spheres, or whether the two arose through a kind of dialectical dynamic, a new symmetry between the domains was patently being created. Functional regions began to coincide with formal regions—those new and coherent representations of place in vernacular literature that superseded the vast geocultural spaces prevalent during the preceding millennium. Understanding the nature of the new political order that arose with vernacularization is as difficult as understanding the nature of 'empire' in the cosmopolitan epoch, and it has seemed preferable, therefore, to name this new political form neutrally as the 'vernacular polity' rather than try to shoehorn it into some given European conceptual category (such as 'protonation'). But one thing is certain: however much the fact may conflict with dominant social-science theory, especially of nationalism, power and culture had indeed a very considerable, if sometimes obscure, inclination for each other in premodern South Asia.

That the context of power fundamentally shaped the process of vernacularization in South Asia sits awkwardly with the unchallenged scholarly consensus regarding its origins as essentially religious, a kind of Indian Reformation. This view is as erroneous as is the one that locates the origins of European vernacularization in the real Reformation (sometimes Protestant presuppositions do not even work for Europe). Virtually all the reasons adduced for explaining vernacularization in South Asia as originating in a socioreligious rebellion are dubious. The presumed concomitance between Sanskrit and Brahmanism on the one hand and vernacularity and non-Brahmanism on the other does not hold for much of the period under discussion. The vision of Sanskrit as a sacred language 'jealously preserved by the Brahmans in their schools' may not be the pure illusion of the colonial officer who gave it expression, yet it is undoubtedly something that developed late in this history of the language, when, for reasons very likely having to do with vernacularization itself, language options shrank for many communities and Brahmanical society reasserted its archaic monopolization over the language (the Catholic Church's eventual monopolization of Latin is an instructive parallel both historically and structurally).[15] In most cases, vernacular beginnings occurred independently of religious stimuli strictly construed, and the greater portion of the literature thereby created was produced not at the monastery but at the court. Only after vernacularization had been consolidated, and in reaction to an already-existing courtly literary and political culture, did a more demotic and often more religiously insurgent *second* vernacular revolution take place (as in twelfth-century Karnataka, fifteenth-century Gujarat, sixteenth-century Assam, and elsewhere). Here the cosmopolitan vernacular was challenged and in some cases displaced by a regional vernacular, a register far more localized in everything from lexicon to metrics to themes. The present account, by foregrounding the role of power in creating both the Sanskrit cosmopolis and the various regional worlds that succeeded it, aims to redress an interpretive balance that for too long has been skewed toward the religious.

In the nexus of poetry and polity we also encounter what is most salient and most neglected for a cross-cultural historical analysis of vernacularization. [...] Temporal, spatial, and other synchronies and symmetries abound. The tempo and structure of Dravidian and Germanic vernacularization, for example, form a striking contrast with those of north Indian and Romance languages. Many of the textual components in European vernacularization are comparable to those found in South Asia, such as the localization of superposed literary forms, genres, and themes. The social milieus are similar, too. The European vernaculars achieved literary expressivity—and often did so with astonishing abruptness—through the agency of courtly elites: whereas vernacular culture was undoubtedly in some sense popular culture in its origins, the process of full vernacularization was decidedly not. Yet there are important differences, too. In Europe the vernacular's admission to literacy was more contested, both linguistically and ideologically; the cosmopolitan formation was more stubborn in its claim to primacy. A far more significant divergence is found in the development of polity. In both areas the political order that emerged in conjunction with vernacularization offered a regional alternative to the transregional imperial formation. But the specific character of the European form, and its endpoint, the nation-state, was unlike anything found in South Asia. The cultural and political theory designed to make sense of the European nation-state is often, and too facilely, applied to the pre-modern world outside of Europe, distorting thinking about language and identity, and identity and polity, and thereby occluding the specificity of the Indian case and its misfit with models designed to explain the European. The comparative turn is therefore imperative for a history and theory of vernacularity in southern Asia.

The transformations in culture and power that began concurrently in India and Europe around the start of the second millennium were consolidated by its midway point. The rules of the new vernacular game of polity and poetry had largely been drawn up; the cosmopolitan order in both worlds was almost completely supplanted by the seventeenth century. If it is becoming possible to recognize vernacularization as a key historical problem only now that it is ending, the recognition is the easy part. Far more difficult is understanding the hard history of its origins, why across much of Eurasia the world abandoned cosmopolitanism and empire in favor of vernacularity and regional polities, and why this happened when it did. Whereas we can identify some factors that clearly contributed—reinvigorated trading networks in the early second millennium concentrated wealth in local power centres, the expansion of Islam on its western and eastern frontiers offered new cultural stimuli—a unified explanation of the historical origins of vernacularism is as improbable as a unified explanation of the cosmopolitanism that preceded. Yet the lack does not preclude learning lessons from these events, both for the theory of culture and power and for their practice.

To study the history of vernacularization is to study not the history of the emergence of primeval and natural communities of peoples and cultures but the historical inauguration of the naturalization of peoples and cultures through new conceptual and discursive practices. This naturalization took place by a double procedure of reduction and differentiation: as unmarked dialect was turned into unifying standard, heterogeneous practice into culture, and undifferentiated space into place, new regional worlds were created. What was inside these worlds would eventually be seen as the indigenous and natural; what was outside, as the exogenous and artificial. This did not happen everywhere in a similar manner; not all ways of the cultural production of vernacular sameness and difference have been the same, any more than all cosmopolitanisms have been the same. Figuring out what may have been distinctive about these vernacular and cosmopolitan practices is a precious if elusive prize.

## NOTES

1 See, for example, Sheldon Pollock, 'Introduction: Cosmopolitanisms,' in Carol Breckenridge *et. al.* (eds), *Cosmopolitanism*, Durham, 2002.

2 Arjun Appadurai has rightly cautioned against a 'rush to history' meant to neutralize the 'special anxiety about its own not-newness' that contemporary globalization seems to provoke (Appadurai, 'Globalization and the Rush to History', Sawyer Seminar Lecture, New York, 1999). An example is A.G. Hopkins (ed.), *Globalization in World History*, New York, 2002.

3 Heine had a sense of this resistance 150 years ago: 'Es ist zu wünschen, dass sich das Genie des Sanskritstudiums bemächtige; tut es der Notizengelehrte, so bekommen wir bloss—ein gutes Kompendium'. Heinrich Heine, 'Aphorismen und Fragmente', *Sämtliche Werk*, vol. 14, Munich, 1964, p. 113.

4 The phrase is that of Sankaran Krishna, 'Cartographic Anxiety: Mapping the Body Politic in India', *Alternatives*, vol. 19, no. 4, 1994, pp. 507–21.

5 The first is Sylvain Levi's assessment (cited in Jules Bloch, *Indo-Aryan from the Vedas to Modern Times*, Paris, 1965: 14–15): the second is standard-issue postcolonial theory.

6 Curiously, little good theoretical work seems to be available on cultural and political comparison. See for now John Bowen and Roger Peterson (eds), *Critical Comparisons in Politics and Culture*, Cambridge, 1999, pp. 1–19 and especially Urban's essay in that volume, pp. 90–109.

7 On the early history of the transregionality of this culture, the work of Michael Witzel is central; see for example, Michael Witzel, 'On the Localization of Vedic Texts and Schools', in G. Pollet (ed.), *India and the Ancient World: History, Trade and Culture before AD 650*, Leuven, 1987.

8 An impatience not unlike that sometimes felt by Kannadigas (and Kannada scholars) toward Tamilians (and Tamilists) who pretend to represent 'south India' (see B.R. Gopal, 'Two Dominant Societies of South India—Karnataka and Tamil Nadu: A Study in Contrast', in Albrecht Wezlar and Ernest Hammerschmidt (eds), *Proceedings of the Thirty-Second International Congress for Asian and North African Studies*, Hamburg, 25–30 August 1986, Stuttgart, 1986 and 'Dakṣiṇa Bhāratada Eraḍu Pramukha Vībhinna Samājagaḷu,' in S.L. Bhyrappa *et al.* (eds), *Māna. H.M. Nayaka Abhinandana Grantha*, Mysore 1992, and cf. for example, Hermann Kulke (ed.), *The State in India, 1000–1700*, Delhi, 1995, p. 169) is found among Tulavas (and specialists in Tulu) toward the Kannadigas who pretend to represent 'Karnataka'. See Lauri Honko *Textualising the Siri Epic*, Folklore Fellows Communications, vol. 118, no. 264, Helsinki, 1998, pp 245*ff.* Comparable responses in Provence and Brittany are well known; a memorable account is Pierre Jakez Helias, *The Horse of Pride: Life in a Breton Village*, New Haven, 1978.

9 [Indian philosophers distinguish between two kinds of truth. "The prior term [*pāramārthika sat*] points toward the absolute truth of philosophical reason, the second [*vyāvahārika sat*], toward the certitudes people have at different stages of their history that provide the grounds for their beliefs and actions." (Pollock, *The Language of the Gods in the World of Men*, pp. 2–3)]

10 [For Pollock, 'literization' refers to the development of a written form of a language; 'Literization' refers to the development of 'imaginative workly discourse'; 'workly' refers to that which is 'imaginative, performative, expressive'. See ibid., pp. 4–5, 23, 283.]

11 This is sometimes referred to in sociolinguistics as Ausbau (elaboration) after Heinz Kloss, '"Abstand Languages" and "Ausbau Languages"', *AL*, 9.7: 29–71, 1967, which Kloss himself conceived of as the process whereby language differentiation is created, as between Swedish and Danish, which are therefore Ausbausprachen, or 'languages by design', as opposed to Abstandsprachen, or 'languages by distance', such as English and French. Bakhtin's observation is found in M.M. Bakhtin, *The Dialogic Imagination: Four Essays*, Austin, 1981, p. 270.

12 Two scholars who have rethought technologies and beginnings in European literature are Paul Zumthor, *La lettre et la voix: De la 'littérature' Médieval*, Paris, 1987, who locates the critical moment in script culture, and Hans Ulrich Gumbrecht, 'Beginn von "Literatur"/'Abschied vom Kōrper?', in Gisela Smolka-Koerdt *et al.* (eds), *Der Ursprung von Literatur: Medien, Rollen, Kommunikationssituationen Zwischen*

*1450 und 1650*, Munich 1988, who finds it in print culture, each technology possessing its particular textual and performative consequences. On writing and language naming see Tore Janson, 'Language Change and Metalinguistic Change: Latin to Romance and Other Cases', in Roger Wright and Rosamund Mekitterick (eds), *Latin and the Romance Languages in the Early Middle Ages*, London, 1991, pp. 23–8. The sociolinguistic definition is that of Ralph Fasold, *The Sociolinguistics of Society*, Oxford, 1984, p. 62 (following Charles Ferguson).

13 Texts that 'adorn' the South Asian vernaculars by framing grammatical and rhetorical norms (the *Siyabaslakara* of ninth-century Sri Lanka, the *Kannadabhāṣābhūṣaṇam* of eleventh-century Karnataka, the [*Braj*] *Bhāṣābhūṣaṇ* of seventeenth-century Jodhpur) are precisely equivalent to those meant to 'illustrate' the European vernaculars.

14 Giorgio Agamben, *The End of the Poem*, Stanford, 1999, p. 59; Erich Auerbach, *Literary Language and its Public in Latin Antiquity and in the Middle Ages*, Princeton, 1965, p. 319.

15 See George Grierson, *Linguistic Survey of India*, vol. I, pt. I, Introductory Calcutta, 1927, p. 1129 for the quote. The gradual decrease in language options in early-modern South Asia is touched on in Sheldon Pollock, *Literary Cultures in History: Reconstructions from South Asia*, Berkeley, 2003, pp. 73*ff*.

# 12

# Politics, Violence, and War in Kāmandaka's *Nītisāra**

Upinder Singh**

The historiography of early medieval India (*c.* 600–1300 CE) has been dominated by the question of whether this period should be understood within the frameworks of the integrative, feudal, or segmentary state models.[1] Initially enlightening, the half century or so of this debate has reached an impasse, and the debate itself has become an obstacle to fresh thinking. Clearly, it is time to frame new questions and re-think the ways in which we can think about the early medieval.

A comprehensive, historically grounded intellectual history of this age does not exist, a fact that is especially surprising considering that these centuries were marked by exceptional intellectual vitality. One of the many issues that have received inadequate scholarly attention is the reciprocal relationship between early medieval political processes and the intellectual engagement with these processes in texts of the time. The most important intervention against this indifference has been

* Previously published in *The Indian Economic and Social History Review*, vol. 47, no. 1, 2010.  This is an extract from the chapter. In the present version, some portions of the texts and notes have been removed. For the complete text see the original.

** I would like to thank the anonymous referee for many extremely valuable suggestions which have been incorporated into the final version of this article. I would also like to thank Vijay Tankha, Dilip Simeon, Nayanjot Lahiri, Suryanarayana Nanda, and Seema Alavi for various kinds of help rendered.

made by Sheldon Pollock, who has emphasized the fact that the cognitive production of political orders is a significant and integral constituent of these orders and that it is, therefore, essential to explore the 'political imagination,' which includes ideas and aspirations of rule.[2] Ronald Inden has analysed the representations of the concepts of mastery, lordship, and political hierarchy in early medieval India in literary and epigraphic sources.[3] And Daud Ali has offered a very thought-provoking, though homogenized, analysis of the representations of courtly culture in texts, inscriptions, and art of the first millennium.[4]

While drawing on the insights of these scholars, my own perspective differs in several respects. While I am interested in analysing the political discourse (I prefer this term to Pollock's 'political imagination') represented in texts, I think it is important that such an analysis must be very carefully calibrated with respect to chronology and spatial context and should not end up presenting an over-homogenized picture of either the discourse or the politics of the time. Further, while identifying shared ideas, and those with an exceptional longevity, it must be equally sensitive to differences in perspective, emphasis, and argument within texts of a particular genre and across texts belonging to different genres produced at different points of time.

The focus of this article—a close analysis of the *Nītisāra* ('The Essence of Politics') of Kāmandaka—is part of a larger study of political ideas. Comparisons with the *Arthaśāstra* provide a useful basis for identifying this text's perspective. Apart from *Nītisāra's* representation of the morphology of monarchical power, I also examine how the text engaged with an important political problem, namely the interface between kingship and violence, with special reference to punishment, hunting, and war. The issue of violence in Indian intellectual traditions and history has many facets, and there are some illuminating works on the subject.[5] Violence and non-violence have especially been discussed in the context of sacrifice, religion (Vedic religion, Hinduism, Buddhism, and Jainism), asceticism, vegetarianism, and Buddhist and Jaina environmental ethics. War has often been discussed by scholars in the context of the Buddhist tradition and works such as the *Bhagavad Gītā* and *Mahābhārata.* More off the beaten track is Daud Ali's analysis of the social meanings of violence, gastronomy, and war in the *Kaliṅkattupparaṇi,* a riveting twelfth-century text composed in the Cōla court.[6] There is, nevertheless, a need for a more comprehensive, diachronic study of the ways in which the issue of violence was dealt with in ancient and early medieval India. The focus of such a study must not only be on understanding representations of violence, but also on arguments and attitudes towards its various forms.

Historicizing normative texts raises a fundamental question about the relationship between theory and practice. Pollock has pointed out that in the Indian intellectual tradition, *śāstra* ('theory') is generally held to precede and govern *prayoga* ('practical activity'), and suggests that the ideas that came to be associated with the nature of *śāstra* may be connected with the belief in the transcendent character of the Vedas.[7] However, he himself points to the fact that there were exceptions to this position, significantly enough in works on politics and medicine. A further necessary caveat to this argument is that *śāstric* self-representation should not be conflated with the way in which *śāstric* knowledge was actually produced in early India. The discipline of history assumes that the creation of a textual tradition involved an interface with its historical context, and it can be demonstrated that historical reality intruded into many a 'normative' text. However, the biggest challenge in historicizing ancient and early medieval political treatises is to meaningfully anchor their political discourses (the plural is deliberately used to underline their diversity in type and perspective) in the peculiarities and demands of their genre, and in their evolving and changing political contexts, without slipping into the error of presenting these discourses as either insulated from or direct reflections of those contexts.

## KĀMANDAKA'S *NĪTISĀRA* AND KAUṬILYA'S *ARTHAŚĀSTRA*

Kāmandaka's *Nītisāra* is a treatise on politics written in Sanskrit verse, consisting of twenty *sargas* (cantos) subdivided into thirty-six *prakaraṇas* (sections).[8] It discusses the principles according to which a king should rule his kingdom and how he could attain political paramountcy and prosperity for himself and his subjects. As is the case with many early Indian texts, it is difficult to ascertain when and where the *Nītisāra* was written. Estimates of its age generally range between the first and seventh centuries CE.[9] The evidence recently cited to suggest the contemporaneity of the *Nītisāra* with the Gupta emperor Candragupta II (*c.* 375–415 CE) is not convincing.[10] A more cautious approach, placing the text between *c.* 500–700 CE is better, and the *Nītisāra* can thus be situated at the threshold or the advent of the early medieval.

Among the ancient Indian political treatises, it is Kauṭilya's *Arthaśāstra* that has naturally attracted the maximum attention of scholars, being the first surviving text on the subject and also because of its masterly coverage of an enormous range of issues related to statecraft. The *Arthaśāstra* has often been treated simplistically by historians as a direct description of the Maurya state and administration. Such a treatment is problematic because it is a theoretical treatise, not a descriptive work, and although its core probably dates to the Maurya period, it has interpolations belonging to later centuries.[11]

As for the *Nītisāra,* historians have cited stray references from the text to illustrate aspects of Gupta or post-Gupta polity, administration, and revenue systems, but the text as a whole has not received the attention it deserves. This, in spite of the fact that it acquired an authoritative reputation, being cited in many later Indian works and also travelling to Southeast Asia.[12] The scholarly neglect of the work may have been in part because of problems of dating, but the most important reason why it has not been taken seriously enough is that Kāmandaka has been viewed as a derivative, unoriginal thinker who tried to simply parrot Kauṭilya's ideas, sometimes incorrectly.[13] This essay seeks to prove that a close reading of the *Nītisāra* does not support such an assessment. It is also emphasized that political treatises of this kind have to be recognized as important sources for and, in fact, as important constituent elements of, ancient and early medieval polities.

Because of its śāstric nature, the *Nītisāra* should certainly not be read as a direct description of how states were actually governed or royal policies formulated during the time of the Gupta and Vākāṭaka empires and their immediate aftermath. And yet, it offers a perceptive, graphic morphology—often abstract rather than literal—of the structure and relationships of monarchical power politics of its time. This morphology was rooted in various things: the genre and scholarly tradition within which the text situated itself, the specific historical and political context in which it was produced, and the ideas and perspective of the author, including his philosophical moorings.

Beyond the question of what such texts can tell us about the times in which they were written, it is also necessary to recognize their great influence. The authors of such treatises were learned Brāhmaṇas, at least some of whom were closely associated with royal courts. The presumed audience—and also, in large part, the subject—of these works was the 'political class': people associated with the exercise of political power in various ways. This included kings (more specifically the *vijigīṣu*—the king desirous of extensive conquest), royal officials, counsellors, courtiers,[14] military commanders, ambassadors, and others. Texts like the *Nītisāra* are, therefore, not only representative of a political discourse rooted in the political realities of their time, but also made an impact on those realities. It should also be noted that the ideas of the political theorists were known, absorbed and expressed in poetry, drama, didactic stories and sayings, and reached wider audiences through written, oral, and performative traditions.

## TRADITION, AUTHORITY, AND DEBATE

Before entering into an analysis of the political discourse of the *Nītisāra*, it is necessary to look carefully at certain general issues related to the production of knowledge in ancient and early medieval India. Ancient *śāstric* discourse on politics was part of an intellectual milieu marked by continuous and wide-ranging debate, a fact often masked by the constant invoking of tradition. [...] In fact, it can be argued—and this point is borne out by the *Arthaśāstra*—that in spite of the great premium placed on tradition, disagreement with earlier authorities ultimately contributed to a scholar's reputation.[15]

[...]

While Bṛhaspati is the most frequently cited authority in the *Nītisāra*, it is Viṣṇugupta, alias Kauṭilya, the author of the *Arthaśāstra*—referred to on two occasions as 'our guru'[16]—who holds the pre-eminent position for Kāmandaka. The text opens with a salutation to the god Gaṇeśa, the king,[17] and Viṣṇugupta, in that order. The eulogy of Viṣṇugupta (*NS* 1.1.2–6) describes him as one who was born in a great lineage with descendants famous all over the world for their *ṛṣi*-like conduct in not accepting gifts of any kind; who was as effulgent as the sacrificial fire; who was so well-versed in the Vedas that he had mastered through his intellect all four of them as though they were one; who through his powers, as irresistible as furious thunder, had uprooted the great and powerful Nandas. [...]The precise identity and background of the author or authors of many ancient Indian texts is often elusive. But this description of Viṣṇugupta can be read as a portrait of the political Brāhmaṇa—the kind of advisor considered by Kāmandaka to be most suited (and most likely) to deliver the teaching on politics. This may well have been a self-portrait of Kāmandaka himself. The connection with Viṣṇugupta was also important for establishing the bona fides and boundaries of the discipline that the *Nītisāra* dealt with, and that is probably why Kāmandaka ascribes the invention of *nītiśāstra* to his famous predecessor.

[...]

In the many-faceted and vibrant intellectual milieu of ancient and early medieval India, disciplinary boundaries were understood and the political treatises self-consciously situate themselves within a larger knowledge universe. But knowledge and ideas also readily flowed across disciplinary boundaries. The texts on polity share with the *Dharmaśāstra* and philosophical texts ideas related to *karma* (the consequences of action), rebirth, *caturvarga/trivarga* (the four or three goals of human life), and *varṇāśrama dharma* (*dharma* based on *varṇa* and *āśrama*). [...]

[...]

The inter-disciplinary dialogue of which the political treatises were a part extended to other realms of specialized scholarship as well. In fact, the organic theory of the *saptāṅga rājya* may have more connections with medical knowledge than hitherto suspected. It seems to be more than a coincidence that *āyurveda* talks of seven elements of the body and the political treatises talk of the seven elements or limbs of the state.[18] The discussion of the *vyasanas* (calamities) and concerns for purification (*śuddhi*) of the various elements of the body politic (for instance, of the *maṇḍalas*) in texts such as the *Nītisāra* also resonate with issues of health, disease, and cure with which the medical treatises grappled, albeit in the context of the body politic rather than the human body.[19]

[...]

## THE VIJIGĪṢU'S QUEST FOR POWER

The prime subject as well as audience for the *Nītisāra* was the king (*rājan*), whose various epithets announce him as lord of the earth, of all men, and of the *maṇḍalas* (*mahipati, pārthiva, pṛthvīpati, mahibhuja, bhūpati, kṣitibhuja, nṛpa, narapati, nareśvara, maṇḍalādhipa*). Monarchy (*rājya*) is the only kind of state mentioned by Kāmandaka, as his work post-dates the annihilation of the major oligarchies (*gaṇas* and *saṅghas*) by the Gupta emperor Samudragupta (*c.* 350–70). This is in contrast to the *Arthaśāstra,* which discusses oligarchies, although it too considers monarchy as the norm and addresses its teaching to the king.

The king is not defined by what he is but what he aspires to become. The kind of monarch that the *Nītisāra* (and the *Arthaśāstra*) has in mind is one who is ambitious and upwardly-mobile, a vijigīṣu—a king desirous of attaining political paramountcy, one who seeks dominion over the whole earth washed by the ocean (*samudraprakṣālitā dhāritrī*) (*NS* 16.24.35). The graphic image—one which endures in texts and inscriptions over several centuries—of the paramount king is that of one who plants his foot on the heads of enemies adorned with excellent helmets and bejewelled crowns (*NS* 14.20.12).

While the *Nītisāra* has a strong sense of the past, the past it invokes is not one that modern historians would regard as 'historical.' In fact, the deliberate avoidance or erasure of the latter is because the text's discourse (like that of other *śāstras*) speaks of universals, not particulars.[20] It is not surprising that a work that claimed to lay down the principles of polity for all time to come ignored the inconsequential kings of mundane petty power politics and drew its illustrations from the gods, demons, and men of the epic-*Purāṇic* tradition, whose fame or notoriety transcended time and space. Apart from analogies between the king and the elements of nature,[21] the *Nītisāra* frequently compares him with the gods, especially Indra, Yama, and Prajāpati. The text abounds in references to Paraśurāma, Ambarīṣa, Yudhiṣṭhira, Bhīma, Nala, Janamejaya, and Rāma, leaving no doubt that the *Mahābhārata* and *Rāmāyaṇa* were pivotal to Kāmandaka's political discourse, in fact more so than to that of the *Arthaśāstra*.[22]

The *Nītisāra*, like many texts of ancient and early medieval India, talks of the intimate connection between kingship—*rājatā* (*NS* 20.34.16)—and the prosperity of the king, his realm, and his subjects. Śrī and Lakṣmī represent fortune and prosperity as well as goddesses personifying these things, and many of the references to them are clustered in the *Utsāhapraśaṁsā* ('in praise of energy') *prakaraṇa* (*NS* 14.20). The feminine deification of fortune lent itself well to the use of gendered imagery, one that is overtly sexual, even violent; this is found frequently not only in the political treatises but also in Sanskrit *kāvya*.[...]

## THE MORPHOLOGY OF MONARCHICAL POWER

The emphasis on the power and ambitions of the *vijigīṣu* should not obscure the fact that the polity of ancient Indian political treatises such as the *Arthaśāstra* and *Nītisāra* is an organic one, where the king is embedded in a web of complex, reciprocal relationships with the other *prakṛtis* (elements of the state), listed by Kāmandaka as *svāmin* (lord, king), *amātya* (counsellor), *rāṣṭra* (domain), *durga* (fort), *koṣa* (treasury), *bala* (military might), and *suhṛt* (ally).[23] This interconnectedness should not be lost sight of in discussions of the structure of the polities of early medieval India. [...]

The *Nītisāra* underlines the fragility of power and the inherent instability of all political and personal relationships and offers a graphic morphology of the political world of its time [...] the king and his court were the epicentre of a complex and far-reaching web of political relationships, manoeuvres, and intrigues, one which extended far beyond the court into the domains and courts of neighbouring and distant kings and chieftains, as well as into the forest.

The fundamental premise that underlies Kāmandaka's entire discussion of politics is the view that human nature is essentially selfish and that all people are *arthārthin*, that is, seek to further their personal interest. The challenge for the *vijigīṣu* was to harness other people's desire to further their self-interest to ensure the satisfaction of his own ambition and desire for political aggrandizement.

From the point of view of the king, the world was a treacherous but challenging place. Fate was definitely a factor (*NS* 12.17.20) to be reckoned with, but political success required many inherent and cultivated positive qualities (*guṇas*) and a great deal of deliberate effort. Kāmandaka's long list of *guṇas* that the king should possess (there are similarities with the *Arthaśāstra* in this discussion) reveals an important aim of the political theorists—to temper brute power with virtue.[24] According to the *Nītisāra*, the many *guṇas* necessary to become a successful *vijigīṣu* included nobility of ancestry, intelligence, truthfulness, and powers of endurance. The most important quality, however, was *pratāpa* (prowess). Energy (*utsāha*) and constant vigilance were also required to safeguard and extend political power. The maintenance and extension of this power did not only involve coercive power and conquest. It was essential to skillfully use force (*daṇḍa*) along with the other political expedients (*upāyas*), namely *sāma* (pacification), *dāna* (giving gifts), and *bheda* (creating dissension), in order to generate and maintain confidence (*viśvāsa*) in the various *prakṛtis*. Confidence, in turn, was an essential prerequisite for eliciting loyalty and love (*anurāga*) from subjects, soldiers and allies—the kind of loyalty and love that would extend over many generations. There is no separate word for loyalty in the text, but is subsumed in other terms such as *sevā* (service) and *bhakti* (devotion), and is emphasised by assertions that the king should not be forsaken by his courtiers.

The political importance of the royal household in the politics of the monarchical states of the time is amply evident in the *Nītisāra*'s detailed discussion of princes (*NS* 7.10) and the harem (*NS* 7.11). Members of the harem (*antaḥpura, avarodhana*) were the *abhyantara jana* (inner people) and included the king's mother, his wives, courtesans (*rūpajīvās*), and the many attendants who waited on all these women. The harem was a place of pleasure and sensual indulgence. It was also the locus of the serious business of producing heirs—an issue that the *Nītisāra* does not see as a problem, the virility of the king perhaps never being in doubt. And yet, as for Kauṭilya, it was also a place of danger and intrigue, one where the king was strongly advised never to completely lose his head in the pursuit of sexual pleasure or emotional engagement.

In the *Nītisāra* (16.24.28), there are seven types of people associated with the king—his own men, those of his allies, those who have taken refuge with him, those related to him, those associated with him for some specific purpose or action, his servants, and those won over by various services and gifts. The category of the king's own men (*nija*) included his courtiers (*anujīvīs*), to whom he was tied with complex ties of reciprocity. An entire *sarga* (*NS* 5.8) is devoted to the relationship between the *svāmin* and his *anujīvīs*. The latter are mentioned in the same breath as the *bandhu* (kinsmen) and *mitra* (friends), and the summary of their duties includes giving the king good counsel, dissuading him from inappropriate acts and implementing his desires (*NS* 5.8.50).[25] High-ranking royal officials such as *amātyas, mantrīs, sacivas, adhyakṣas, dūtas, mahāmātras,* the *purohita*, the *senāpati*, and astrologers appear to be included in the category of courtiers. There is a long list of the ideal qualities of an *anujīvin*, but it is interesting to note that the synopsis of the most essential qualities leave out high birth and proficiency in the Vedas (*NS* 5.8.12–15). The discussion of the relationship between the king and his courtiers was no doubt rooted in the contemporary political context—specifically in the need for the king to create around him a group of capable and loyal courtiers, and the latter's desire and ambition to move up in the courtly hierarchy. The relative status of an individual in this hierarchy was determined by the level of proximity, physical as well as affective, to the king.

[...]

The most evocative and most entertaining part of Kāmandaka's treatment of the king's relationship with his courtiers is his lengthy and very specific discussion of the protocol and decorum of the *rājasabhā* or *saṁsad* (court) (*NS* 5.8.17–34). The challenge for the courtier was to be counted among those who were cultured (*sabhya, ārya*). He was advised to meticulously tailor his deportment and behaviour to prevailing court protocol and propriety in accordance with his rank and position. And yet, he had to simultaneously strive to rise above others in the court milieu by making a strong, distinctive impression, especially on the king.

Kāmandaka's discussion of court protocol, broadly similar to that offered by Kauṭilya (*AS* 5.4), is general enough to be considered as fairly close to the basics of protocols actually existing in various royal courts of the subcontinent during the time. The intelligent (*medhāvin*) courtier had to be formally admitted into the royal assembly-hall. He was advised to be properly attired, to take his allotted seat and to wait patiently for his turn to pay respect to the king with due humility.

According to Kāmandaka, the *anujīvin* should be conversant with what was appropriate to place and time (*deśakālajña*) and should be an expert in interpreting the king's gestures, appearance, and movements (*iṅgitākāratattvavid*). He should be very careful about where and how he looked and how he spoke, and was advised to gaze intently at the king's face in order to observe his reactions and to listen very attentively to whatever the lord said.

Just as important as creating the right impression was avoiding creating an adverse one [...]

While attempting to move closer to the king and up the ladder of success (these two things were synonymous), the ambitious courtier had to reckon with those who shared these ambitions and those who had already achieved them. Apart from being deferential towards the king, he was advised to be respectful towards superiors and the king's sons, friends, companions, and favourites (*vallabhas*). Such people, it is pointed out, could pierce the heart of the courtier in the *saṁsad* by their ridicule (*NS* 5.8.19–20). The courtier was also advised to avoid meeting or interacting with women (presumably of the harem) and their supervisors, habitual sinners, messengers from hostile chiefs, and those who had been dismissed by the master (*NS* 5.8.32).

In its description of the overlap between the personal and the political, the *Nītisāra* offers an important insight into the polities of mid-first millennium India. Some insights can also be gleaned by noting what the text does *not* mention or highlight. The political elites of the time must have been internally divided into factions, and the inter-relationships among these factions must have had many complex strands, including alliance, competition, rivalry, and hostility. The *Nītisāra* is intriguingly reticent on this important issue and this reticence may have been deliberate.[26] Kāmandaka's aim may have been to deliberately mask elements of factionalism and conflict within the political elite and to emphasize and thereby try to inculcate within that elite a certain cohesion that did not exist in actuality. [...]

Emotions were an important part of Kāmandaka's political discourse, and political success was considered to be considerably dependent on the ability to create in oneself and in others certain desirable emotional states and dispositions.[27] In his interactions with his courtiers, the king's aim was to secure their devotion (*bhakti*), loyalty, and affection. For courtiers, a crucial objective was to obtain royal affection (*anurāga*), and to regain it if it was lost for some reason or another. There was also the more pragmatic aim of acquiring permanence (*sthāne sthairya*) of position (*NS* 5.8.5), something no doubt difficult in a polity where everything was always in a state of flux.

In terms broadly similar to those of the *Arthaśāstra* (*AS* 5.5), but in greater detail, the *Nītisāra* explains how the *anujīvin* could gauge the success or failure of his attempts to worm his way into his master's affections. Kāmandaka lists the visible signs of a king who was attached (*anurakta*) and one who was indifferent or hostile (*virakta*) (*NS* 5.8.35–38). [...]

The description of the signs of a king displeased with his *anujīvin* are more graphic and are also dilated upon (*NS* 5.839–46). [...]

The *Nītisāra* (like the *Arthaśāstra*) indicates the great importance of the king's kinsfolk in the world of political power. Apart from their place within the royal household, allies included those related by blood (*aurasam*) (*NS* 4.7.74). But in a situation where feigning and double-dealing were intrinsic parts of political culture, the king could never rely on their loyalty or allegiance, and the danger of betrayal was not a possibility, it was a very likely probability. A king supported by his brothers was invincible (*NS* 9.14.46), but a king could not trust even his father for seeking shelter (*NS* 11.16.35), let alone his sons and wives. The latter were, in fact, among the greatest sources of danger to him.

Personal friendship too had a place in political discourse and in the political world.[28] Kings had to win over friends through kindness (*NS* 3.6.33) and they were the king's companions during his leisure-time pursuits (*NS* 7.11.34). The killing of friends was one of the various possible causes of war (*NS* 10.15.4), along with other causes including dishonour, the killing of kin, and the abduction of women. The king's friends seem to be distinct from the *vallabhas* or favourites, although one can imagine that there must have been some overlap between the two categories. The *vallabhas* seem to have been considered especially problematic characters by Kāmandaka. In fact, they are the only group singled out for specific mention in the *kaṇṭakaśodhana* ('removal of thorns') section (*NS* 6.9.9) and are also mentioned as one of several sources of fear to the subjects (*NS* 5.8.82). It may be noted that the phrase *vallabha-durlabha* ('not to be entered by royal favourites') in numerous land grant inscriptions of the early medieval period suggests that the *vallabhas* were identified as potential trouble-makers for the donees, villagers, or both.

The terms denoting friendship and cordiality had many different nuances, and the vocabulary of kinship and friendship extended to many political relationships. The familial term *parivāra* is used synonymously for *sacivas* (counsellors) (*NS* 4.7.10). The ally is referred to as *mitra* or *suhṛt.* Cordiality had to be cultivated with the *maṇḍalikas* (governors) of distant regions and with governors of forts. Attachment, estrangement, love, loyalty, confidence, and friendship are sentiments that are invoked to describe relations between king, courtiers, subjects, and other rulers. Disposition and sentiment were clearly important ingredients in the *Nītisāra*'s political discourse and, presumably, in the monarchical power politics of its time. Of course, revealing as the basic morphology of monarchical power and courtly life that is represented in the *Nītisāra* is, it is essential to keep in mind that it is an idealized and aestheticized morphology.[29]

## DANGERS TO KING AND KINGDOM

Like his counterpart of the *Arthaśāstra,* the king of the *Nītisāra* too inhabits a very dangerous world, and his foremost challenge (and indeed duty) is to protect himself. The detailed description of the king as a figure assailed at all times and from all sides by the threat of assassination, especially through poison, may have been realistic. And even if it is exaggerated, it suggests that this was considered a very real threat and a source of anxiety for kings and political theorists alike. It was because of the ever-present danger to his person that the king was advised to be well protected, ever-vigilant, and to sleep lightly like a *yogin* (*NS* 16.24.44).

Going by the lengthiness of the discussion, the most dangerous place for the king was the harem (*NS* 7.11.41–50). This was a space where there was much coming and going, and all these movements required careful regulation. Members of the *antaḥpura* were to be watched over by officers known as *antaḥpurāmātyas.* Spies in various disguises were also to keep a strict watch over everyone.[30][...]

The *antaḥpura* was a place of pleasure where the king engaged in sexual activity with wives and courtesans (*rūpajīvās*), but Kāmandaka seems to recommend that the king should not sleep there, as no matter how beloved she might be, too much confidence must never be placed in a woman. To hammer home the point, numerous examples are given of treacherous queens who had killed their husbands. Sons too were a source of serious trouble, and had to be both protected and protected from (Kauṭilya too warns of these problems). The first verse of the *Rājaputrarakṣana prakaraṇa* (*NS* 7.10) suggests that this section is concerned with the protection *of* princes. But the subsequent discussion makes it abundantly clear that it is really about protection of the king *from* princes. Whether descriptive or exaggerated, the entire discussion indicates that these issues were considered central to the safety and survival of the king.

Political success did not only involve the king keeping his own house in order, it also required effective management and manipulation of many other relationships. Beyond his own household and court, the king interacted with those of other kings. Allies, neutral parties, and enemies could be identified according to certain principles and could be dealt with effectively in various ways. The enemy (*ari*) was a potent source of danger to the king and to his sovereignty. What complicated matters was the fact that in the circle of kings, relationships were ever-changing—at one stroke, allies could become enemies and vice versa (*NS* 8.13.72–73).

Potential trouble-makers included those only partially integrated into the circle of kings—*sāmantas* (bordering chiefs or rulers) and *āṭavikas* (forest dwellers), frequently mentioned in the same breath (*NS* 14.21.29; 15.23.22). In the *Nītisāra,* as in the *Arthaśāstra*, the term *sāmanta* does not yet have the connotations of a subordinate feudatory, which it acquired in later times.[31] The category of subordinate rulers in fact seems to be represented in the discussion of types of alliances rather than of the *sāmantas.* For instance, there is a discussion of the various kinds of treaties or agreements that could be concluded with a weaker or defeated power. Among these, the *puruṣāntara sandhi* carried the express obligation that the army chiefs (*yodhamukhyas*) of the ally would serve the *vijigīṣu*'s interests (*NS* 9.14.13). But there is no detailed description of the elaborate protocols that involved an ostentatious display of the hierarchy of power between paramount and subordinate kings, of the sort that are found in texts of later centuries.

Ancient Indian political theorists were tuned in to the dangers of political crisis and collapse. In several places, Kauṭilya alludes to the danger of an insurrection by disaffected subjects (*prakṛtikopa*) (for example, *AS* 1.19.28). Kāmandaka classifies disturbances that could assail the kingdom into two categories—internal (*antaḥprakopa*) and external (*bāhyaprakopa*) (*NS* 16.24.19–21). The former, described as potentially more harmful, included disaffection among the royal *purohita, amātyas,* princes, members of the royal family, commanders and chiefs of army contingents. *Bāhyaprakopa* included disaffection among provincial governors, frontier guards, forest people, and those compelled to surrender.[32]

But the king's most dangerous enemy was the king himself. The *Nītisāra* talks at great length about the problems that a kingdom faces due to the king's own character and dispositions. These include *vyasanas* emanating out of vanity (*mada*), anger (*krodha*), and attachment to sensual pleasures (*kāma*) (*NS* 15.23). A kingdom in which the king is afflicted by *vyasanas* is in deep trouble, even if the other *prakṛtis* are functioning well. The king was also implicated in a number of problems arising out of the fact that the exercise of power invariably involved violence of various kinds, and it is to this that we now turn.

## THE PROBLEM OF POLITICAL VIOLENCE

There are many problems in correlating the connotations of the value-loaded term English word 'violence' with what is often taken as its closest Indian counterpart—the Sanskrit word *hiṁsā*. Although violence has been a perennial feature of human history, its definition, the difference between legitimate and illegitimate infliction of injury or use of force, and the grounds of justification for or condemnation of these are very culture-specific.[33] War forms a central event in the two great Sanskrit epics and the dilemmas and problems associated with large-scale military conflict are more graphically revealed in the *Mahābhārata* rather than the *Rāmāyaṇa*.[34] But it also looms large or lurks on the fringes of many an ancient and early medieval text. In the political treatises, it is centre stage.

Without going into the intricacies of semantic issues related to violence, the focus here is on certain specific activities associated with kingship that, according to our contemporary notions of violence, inevitably involved a measure of violence towards humans or animals—the punishment of criminals, war, and hunting. The *Nītisāra,* like the Indian tradition in general, distinguishes between legitimate and illegitimate force. It is evident that the political theorists were concerned with theorizing the limits of force and violence perpetrated by the state in these spheres. The fact that *daṇḍa* means both force and justice directs our attention to the insistence that the use of force must never be impulsive or random but must always be tempered by reflection and calculation, involving a judicious compromise between the demands of political expediency and justice.

As for Kauṭilya, for Kāmandaka too, the goals of kingship were the attainment of enduring political paramountcy and the prosperity of the king and his subjects. Attaining these goals often involved using violent and what would ordinarily be considered deceitful means, and the political theorists were not squeamish about such matters. *Daṇḍa* involves suppression (*'damo daṇḍa iti khyāta',* *NS* 2.3.15) and as mentioned above, it means both coercive power as well as justice. The opening verse of the *Nītisāra* refers to the king as the wielder of daṇḍa (*daṇḍadhara*, *NS* 1.1.1). He maintains *varṇāśrama dharma* through *daṇḍaśakti* (the power of *daṇḍa*) (*NS* 2.3.34). Daṇḍa must be exercised to ensure the protection and promotion of the prosperity of the *prajā* (subjects), and there was a reciprocal relationship between the prosperity of the *prajā* and the *rājan* (*NS* 1.1.14).

Kāmandaka offers various justifications for violence, referred to in one place as *siṁhavṛtti* ('the policy of a lion') (*NS* 12.17.25). The most important of these is the attainment of desired ends, specifically the expansion and consolidation of political power. Violence is also justified on the grounds of what would result from its absence. In this world, according to Kāmandaka (*NS* 2.3.40), people move about in different directions, trying to pursue their own interests by devouring others, as though out of greed for the latters' flesh. *Daṇḍa* is necessary, otherwise *mastyanyāya* ('the law of the fish', that is, the big fish eating the smaller fish), the much favoured, enduring trope for disorder par excellence in many ancient Indian texts, prevails.

The discussion of *upāṁśudaṇḍa* (secret killing) includes advice on the modus operandi to kill adversaries, and the section on *māyā* describes various sly tactics to defeat enemies (*NS* 6.9.10–13). Enemies can be legitimately killed by the secret administration of poison or by enlisting the services of estranged court physicians (*NS* 9.14.70). Harshness or violence may also be necessary to deal with dishonest and impious people (*NS* 6.9.5), those who obstruct the course of *dharma*, or *rājavallabhas* who create trouble, individually or collectively (*NS* 6.9.10). Kāmandaka recommends that royal favourites (*nṛpavallabhas*) should be killed through *upāṁśudaṇḍa* if they cause loss of lives and become a source of anxiety to the people (*NS* 18.27.11).

Justice is another important justification for violence. However, the king must be careful to blend the use of coercive power (*daṇḍa*) with *naya* (legal procedure) in order to be praised as a *yuktadaṇḍa* (*NS* 15.23.12). He is urged to use *daṇḍa* as firmly as *Daṇḍin* (that is, Yama), but blended with the impartiality of the nature of the earth and compassion similar to that shown by the creator Prajāpati towards his own created beings (*NS* 3.6.1). Coercion must be tempered with justice and a sense of proportion, for excessively harsh punishment terrifies the people, just as leniency makes the king worthy of contempt (*NS* 6.9.15; p. 131). So far, all this is in conformity with the attitude of many ancient Indian texts.

A difference in perspective emerges when Kāmandaka speaks of three types of *daṇḍa*—capital punishment, fines, and rigorous punishment causing bodily and mental suffering. There are two types of execution: open (*prakāśadaṇḍa*) and secret (*upāṁśudaṇḍa*). An intelligent ruler desirous of religious merit should not inflict capital punishment on Brāhmaṇas and men of *dhārmika* disposition or on *antyajas* ('outsiders' or outcastes); the reason for excluding the latter is not made explicit (*NS* 18.27.13). In fact, according to the *Nītisāra,* capital punishment (*prāṇāntika daṇḍa*) should be avoided even for the gravest offence, with the exception of the most serious one, namely *rājyāpahāra* (usurpation) (*NS* 15.23.16). Kāmandaka's disapproval of capital punishment is in sharp contrast to Kauṭilya, who recommends the death penalty for several offences apart from those that are treasonable, from robbing the treasury to stealing or killing or inciting someone to steal or kill an animal belonging to the royal herd.[35]

Embedded in a political discourse that is peppered with disquisitions on violence, there is also mention of the virtue of *ahiṁsā* (non-injury). *Ahiṁsa,* refined speech (*sunṛtā vāṇī*), truthfulness (*satya*), purity (*śauca*), pity (*dayā*), and forgiveness (*kṣamā*) constitute the *sāmānya dharma,* the *dharma* which is applicable to all people, irrespective of *varṇa* and gender (*NS* 2.4.32). The code of conduct of the *vijigīṣu* includes avoiding the company of dishonest and unrighteous folk, offering support to honest people and observing *ahiṁsā* towards all beings (*NS* 14.21.51). This is in tune with the *Arthaśāstra,* which expresses similar views (1.3.13; 1.7.2). But Kāmandaka's distinctive stance on violence, already hinted at in his position on capital punishment, is reflected more clearly in discussions of specific issues such as the royal hunt and war.

## THE KING, THE FOREST, AND THE HUNT

In many cultures, in many chronological contexts, the royal hunt has been seen as a natural activity for kings, and in fact as an important expression of the king's sovereignty. The importance of the royal hunt has been recognized by scholars in the context of the Mughal emperors,[36] but not so in the context of earlier rulers of the subcontinent. The hunting expeditions of the Mughals are described in the Persian chronicles and represented in miniature paintings, and the authors of these chronicles did not consider hunting a problematic activity from either a pragmatic or an ethical point of view.[37] The ancient Indian political theorists, on the other hand, had much to say on the matter. And one of the most significant aspects of the *Nītisāra* is its opposition to the royal hunt, an activity that was considered by Kauṭilya as integral to the king's way of life.

The forest and forest people loom large in the writings of political theorists. For Kāmandaka (as for Kauṭilya and the Sanskrit poets), the forest was a place associated with renunciants and ascetics. But more importantly, the political theorists recognized it as a place exceptionally rich in economic and military resources—especially elephants, which were greatly prized for their role in war—and where kings build forts (*vanadurga*). Elephant enclosures (that is, forests) and regular forests were two of the eight sources of income (*aṣṭavarga*) of the state (*NS* 5.8.78–79). Forest dwellers (*āṭavikas*) were by nature *adhārmika* (impious), *lubdha* (greedy), *anārya* (uncultured), and *satyabhedin* (untrustworthy) (*NS* 19.28.8). Forest troops (*āraṇyaka/āṭavika bala*) had to be used by the king in his military campaigns, but they were even more unreliable than troops alienated from the enemy camp (*NS* 19.28.9–10). From the king's point of view, the forest was, at the end of the day, a lucrative, but problematic space.

The forest was also a place where the king hunted, but Kāmandaka had strong reservations about this activity. The dangers of the *yānavyasana* (the calamity of the march), described in the *Nītisāra* just before those of *mṛgayāvyasana* (the calamity of the hunt), appear to apply to both (*NS* 15.23.19–22).[38] These include the physical strain resulting from prolonged riding, accidental fall or injury, and the loss of horses or chariots. Further, there is the suffering caused by hunger, thirst, exhaustion, severe cold, storm, heat, and wastage of resources. Travelling through areas that are very hot, sandy or thorny, or dense forests infested with prickly creepers and shrubs, or hilly areas prone to falling boulders, or tracks that are uneven due to stones, earthen mounds, and ant hills—all this causes much distress. Enemies may be lurking among rocks, rivers, or forests, and there is the possibility of sudden capture or death at the hands of *sāmantas, āṭavikas*, and others. The other dangers specifically arising out of the *mṛgayāvyasana* include the possibility of the king being attacked by his own followers or kinsmen, captured by enemies, or mauled by bears, pythons, wild elephants, lions, or tigers. He may lose his way in the forest, with the path obscured due to smoke arising from forest fires, and may be reduced to wandering around helplessly (*NS* 15.23.23–24).

According to Kāmandaka, these potential dangers can to some extent be neutralized by ensuring that the king rides on the back of a swift but easily controllable animal, by having the outskirts of the forest carefully examined and protected against all dangers, and ensuring that their interiors are well lit and rendered free of ferocious animals (*NS* 2.3.36). But this does not fully settle matters. For Kāmandaka, as for Kauṭilya, hunting, along with women, drinking and gambling, is a royal vice. But while Kāmandaka is willing to accept moderate levels of indulgence in women and drink, gambling and hunting are to be shunned as far as is possible.

Apart from the physical dangers it entails for the king, Kāmandaka's objection to hunting is also based on the fact that this activity could lead to the king wasting his time, and also that any kind of addiction weakens character. But his most important argument is that hunting is a great *vyasana* (*mahat vyasana*) because of the inherent evils of taking life (*doṣāḥ prāṇaharāḥ*) (*NS* 15.23.23).

To make sure that he has covered all the ground concerning this issue, Kāmandaka lists the various supposed benefits of hunting (*NS* 15.23.25). He cites the view that hunting provides the king with physical exercise which, in turn, results in his developing endurance, immunity from indigestion, heaviness, and susceptibility to catching cold. Another argument proferred by some in favour of hunting is that it develops skill and excellence in hitting stationary or moving targets with arrows. These are, in fact, precisely the arguments made by Kauṭilya in the *Arthaśāstra* (8.3.46). But Kāmandaka firmly refutes them by asserting that all these benefits can be obtained through other means. For instance, maladies such as indigestion can be remedied through regular physical exercise, and marksmanship in archery by practising with artificial targets (MS 15.23.27). This is in sharp contrast to Kauṭilya, who describes hunting as the least harmful and gambling as the most harmful of the *vyasanas* (*AS* 8.3).

Kāmandaka also suggests another interesting alternative (*NS* 15.23.28–40) to the regular royal hunt. Kauṭilya too refers to this option, though very briefly. For a king who is unable to give up hunting, an artificial, sanitized game forest should be created (*mṛgāraṇya*), where he could hunt for sport (*krīḍā*) alone.[39] The features of this game forest are then specified: It should be located just outside the town (presumably the capital city), should be over half a *yojanā* in length and breadth, and should be surrounded by a ditch and ramparts so that the animals cannot escape. It should be situated at the foot of a hill or next to a river, and should have plentiful supplies of water and grass. It should not have thorny creepers, shrubs, or poisonous plants. Any crevices in the ground should be filled up with earth and gravel, and the surface should be levelled by removing stumps of trees, mounds of earth, and rocks. It should be made attractive with well-known flower-bearing and fruit-bearing trees providing pleasing, thick, and cool shade. The pools in this park should be shallow, abounding in flowers and birds of different species, and cleared of ferocious aquatic animals. The park should have beautiful creepers laden with flowers and leaves inside and on the sides of the surrounding ditch. It should be provided with animals such as she-elephants and their young ones, tigers and other big game with their teeth and nails removed, and horned animals whose horns have been broken. A space outside the park should be cleared of trees and pillars, and the ground should be levelled, so that it is inaccessible to enemy forces and enhances the feeling of comfort for the king. The park should be guarded by trustworthy forest people who are resolute, hardy, pains-taking, and conversant with the moods of wild animals. The king's own men, of boundless energy and experienced in hunting, should introduce various wild animals into the park. The king may then enter it for sport, accompanied by a select group of trusted attendants, without detriment to his other duties. As he enters, fully armed soldiers should carefully stand guard outside, vigilant for signs of danger to their royal master.

In his detailed description of an artificial, sanitized game forest for the royal hunt, Kāmandaka offers a compromise between the royal predilection for hunting and the dangers and problems that this activity entailed.[40] In spite of describing this option, it is noteworthy that Kāmandaka disapproves of hunting not only on pragmatic grounds, that is, the physical danger to the king and the possibility of it entailing a neglect of royal duties. He also objects to it on two moral grounds—that is, it harms the king by weakening his character, and it involves violence against animals. The second argument indicates that it is not *excessive* hunting alone that is considered a problem; hunting itself is problematic because of the fact that it does violence to animals. This stand against an activity conventionally associated with kingship can be further connected with Kāmandaka's stand on the most violent of all political activities—war.

## THE PROBLEM OF WAR

In ancient and early medieval India, battles were fought (as they are now as well), for a variety of reasons including the control of land and resources and as an assertion of political hegemony, and given the endemic nature of war, it is not surprising that disquisitions on the subject abound in texts. In the context of ancient India, the Maurya emperor

Aśoka is considered the foremost exemplar and proponent of the principle of non-violence at the political as well as personal level. His thirteenth rock edict is, in fact, a remarkable document, giving a strong, reasoned critique of war, raising the discourse of kingship and conquest to a completely new level. However, although the political theorists recognized war as a necessary instrument of state policy, they also recognized its dangers and problematic nature. Moreover, attitudes towards war could and did differ.

Ali briefly refers to the complex and ambivalent connection between courtly manners and violence, arguing that while military prowess and ritualized and honourable violence were important parts of courtly culture, they came to be tempered by irenic values and an emphasis on compassion, kindness, and gentility.[41] My own perspective on the issue of violence is different. The focus here is not the relationship between violence and courtly manners and culture, but on violence as a politico-ethical problem, and the ways in which the political theorists addressed this problem.

General disquisitions on war (*vigraha, yuddha*) can be distinguished from the strategies to be adopted in military expeditions (*yāna*), and Kāmandaka, like Kauṭilya, discusses both. As mentioned earlier, the key player whose interests are central to the *Nītisāra* is the *vijigīṣu*, and there are detailed discussions of military strategies and formations. In fact, the text culminates in a description of a successful military campaign. However, within all this, it also makes a strong case for the exercise of extreme caution in waging war, and the case it makes is not simply one of expediency. Thus, while there is much that is in common between the *Arthaśāstra*'s and *Nītisāra*'s discussion of the conduct of inter-state relations, for instance in the idea of twelve elements in the *rājamaṇḍala* (circle of kings) and the six strategies (*guṇas*), there is also much that is significantly different.[42]

Various aspects of war are discussed in the *Vigrahavikalpa prakaraṇa* (*NS* 10.15) and in other sections as well. The typology of war in the *Nītisāra* includes the basic distinction between *kūṭayuddha* (secret war) and *prakāśayuddha* (open war) (*NS* 19.31.54). *Kūṭayuddha* includes duping and enticing the enemy, nocturnal raids, and setting up camouflaged encampments. Kāmandaka asserts that the king does not transgress *dharma* by killing the enemy through the tactics of *kūṭayuddha*. The example given is that of Aśvatthāman killing the sons of the Pāṇḍavas while they were asleep. Kāmandaka also gives a detailed listing of the causes of war (*NS* 10.15.3–5) such as the usurpation of the kingdom, the abduction of women, the luring away of learned men and soldiers, the killing of friends and political rivalry. He also mentions a third kind of war—*mantrayuddha* (diplomatic warfare) (19.28.15–17).[43] It may be noted that Kāmandaka does not use Kauṭilya's well-known typology of the types of conquerors—the *dharmavijayin* (who conquers for the sake of glory and is satisfied with the mere submission of the defeated king), *lobhavijayin* (who conquers out of greed and wants to obtain land, money, or both), and *asuravijayin* (who makes conquests like a demon, seizing the land, money, sons, and wives of the conquered king and kills him) (*AS* 12.1.10). In the *Nītisāra,* war is no longer graded according to a hierarchy of honour and propriety. The only relevant issues are its cost and chances of success.

What is most significant from the point of view of political theory, especially when seen in the context of the endemic warfare of the time, is the fact that the *Nītisāra* contains many different kinds of very specific arguments against war. Objections to war on pragmatic grounds are to be expected in the political treatises. The basic point on which the experts on politics agreed was that it was essential for the *vijigīṣu* to carefully assess the likely costs and consequences of war. The potential gains of war are territory (this is the most important), allies and wealth, and the king should embark on war only if there was a clear prospect of attaining these (*NS* 10.15.31). The *Nītisāra* also recommends a long-term perspective on pragmatism, pointing out that political success does not hinge on a single victory. Like Paraśurāma, the king who commands respect from all through his prowess is the one who has to his credit many victories on different battlefields (*NS* 9.14.51).

Kāmandaka lists sixteen types of war (*vigraha*) that should not be fought (*NS* 10.15. 19–23). Although there were those who thought otherwise, for Kāmandaka, there was no point in embarking on war if the enemy was much more powerful and the chances of victory bleak.[44] There was no justification for fighting a more powerful enemy, for clouds can never move in a direction opposite to that of the wind. Even if the enemy equalled the *vijigīṣu* in terms of resources, war could lead to death and destruction, sometimes of both parties. Both would perish like two unbaked pitchers striking against each other, like the demons Suṇḍa and Upasuṇḍạ destroyed each other. Other wars that should not be fought included those for the sake of others or for the sake of women, those against venerable Brāhmaṇas, those that promised to be long drawn out, and those undertaken in times when troop movement was difficult.

The risks of war were enhanced by the uncertainties it entailed, and there was no point risking what could be seen for unseen gains (*NS* 16.24.14). This is why a prudent king should avoid war, even when it was thrust on him. 'As victory in war is always uncertain, it should not be launched without careful deliberation' (*NS* 10.15.24). The policy of reeds (*vaitasī vṛtti*) rather than that of snakes (*bhaujaṅgī vṛtti*) should be followed, that it, it was better to be flexible rather than attack at the slightest provocation (*NS* 10.15.35–36).

Kauṭilya too briefly refers to the fact that war entails losses, expenses, marches away from home, and hindrances (*AS* 7.2.2), but Kāmandaka dwells on this issue in greater detail. Apart from the arguments against war based on expediency and the uncertainty of gains, the *Nītisāra*, has many verses dilating on the inevitably disastrous results of war, especially one launched hastily without due consideration and consultation. If a ruler acts in a way contrary to the *śāstra* and suddenly falls on an enemy, it is unlikely that he will be able to get out of this situation without feeling the impact of the enemy's sword (*NS* 12.17.6). In the course of war, the king could, in a single instant, suffer the loss of wives, friends, allies, wealth, kingdom, fame, and even his own life (*NS* 19.14.75). In view of the fact that war necessarily entails loss of men and resources, various difficulties, and the death of principal officers, an intelligent ruler should not continue war, even if he has to willingly accept hardship, for war has inherently disastrous consequences (*doṣas*) (*NS* 19.14.72). Considering the constant anxiety and mental suffering resulting from war, the intelligent ruler should not indulge in frequent warfare (*NS* 19.14.74). Thus, Kāmandaka argues persuasively, recourse to war, especially frequent war, must be avoided.

Kāmandaka also points to the fact that wars often served the selfish interests of members of the political class other than the king. For instance, *mantrīs* (ministers) may desire a prolongation of war due to their self-interest, and a ruler who acts on their counsel may simply play into their hands (*NS* 12.17.41). The idea of setting his house in order before launching on fresh military campaigns is also emphasized when Kāmandaka states that the *vyasanas* of state should be remedied before a ruler launches an attack against the enemy (*NS* 14.21.18).

The text further points out that war was neither the only nor the best expedient (*upāya*) that could be used by the *vijigīṣu* to achieve his ends. *Sāma* (conciliation), *dāna* (gifts), *bheda* (sowing dissension) were the well-known list of political expedients mentioned by Kauṭilya. Kāmandaka expands this list by adding three more—*māyā* (deceitful tactics), *upekṣā* (indifference), and *indrajāla* (conjuring tricks) (*NS* 18.27.3). He argues that conciliatory measures should always be adopted to prevent war.

The ancient political treatises refer to three types of power at the command of the king. Of these, Kāmandaka describes *mantraśakti* (the power of counsel) as superior to *prabhuśakti* (the power of lordship, that is, military might) and *utsāhaśakti* (the power of energy) (*NS* 12.17.7). In this, he is of the same opinion as Kauṭilya.[45] Only by the possession of *mantrabala* does a ruler, following the track of *naya*, become capable of subjugating the powerful enemies who are like vicious serpents (*NS* 12.17.58). Implicit here is the idea that brute force is not the best option for maximizing political gain. Kauṭilya too drives home the point when he asserts that if the *vijigīṣu* uses excessive force, the circle of kings may rise against him and he may be destroyed, or that force (*daṇḍa*) cannot be used against a multitude of people. The political theorists were obviously keenly aware of the limits of the efficacy of force.

The final, culminating *prakaraṇa* (*NS* 20.36) of the *Nītisāra* deals with *prakāśayuddha* (the conduct of open war), and everything in the text seems to be leading up to the crisp description of a successful military charge against the enemy. But before getting to this point, Kāmandaka has offered his audience abundant and diverse arguments to make his point that war must always be a last resort.

## CONTROLLING THE CONTROLLER

While the goal of the *Nītisāra*'s teaching is political success, an awareness of the possibilities of political malfunction through excess, imbalance, and tyranny is ever-present. In certain situations, for instance if the king is excessively attached to *dharma* or *artha*, or if he is mentally ill, the functions of the *vijigīṣu* should be discharged by *mantrīs* possessing the requisite qualities (*NS* 14.21.60). The ability of the king to achieve his political ambitions hinged on his ability to effectively control the various *prakṛtis* of the state. The *Nītisāra*, like many other texts, recommends that the king cultivate discipline, self control, and equanimity in himself, in princes, and among his subjects.[46]

The very first *prakaraṇa* of the *Nītisāra*, the *Indriyajaya prakaraṇa*, deals with the topic of the control of the senses.[47] The *Arthaśāstra* too emphasizes the importance of discipline and control of the senses (*AS* 1.6.3). Restraint of the passions and self-control are among the important qualities (*ātmasampad*) of the king (*NS* 4.7.15–19); in fact, these are his pre-eminent qualities, his *ātmasaṁskāra* (*NS* 4.7.4). These qualities were connected with a character trait that was greatly valorized by political theorists—*vinaya,* which was a cocktail of several things: discipline, good breeding, propriety, humility, modesty, mildness, and good behaviour. *Vinaya* is a quality that a king should possess, one that should be inculcated in princes, and a crucial factor in defeat or victory (*NS* 1.2.70).

Ali argues that that for members of the political class, control of the senses was considered a precondition for the enjoyment of sensual and worldly pleasures, and self-mastery and equanimity as essential for success in the courtly circle.[48] Even if, as he suggests, the emphasis on *vinaya* in the court context functioned as a powerful worldly idea, a kind of internalized self-regulating mechanism that helped people succeed in getting ahead and also helped maintain the courtly hierarchy, its origins still require explanation. The source of the emphasis on self-control seems to be two-fold. First, as mentioned earlier, the discourse of political theorists was embedded in a larger philosophical discourse. The emphasis on self-control and equanimity in the *Nītisāra* seems to have, in part, sprung from the philosophic underpinnings of the political discourse, the desirability of the control of the senses being a fairly widespread idea in ancient Indian philosophical systems.[49] Early in the text, Kāmandaka defines *anvīkṣikī* as that which develops the self-knowledge (*ātmavidyā*) that looks through happiness and sorrow, and asserts that it is by realizing the true nature of joy and sorrow that the king renounces them both (*NS* 2.3.11). Numerous examples are given to prove the transience of life and its pleasures, and great emphasis is placed on the control of the sense organs (*NS* 3.6.9). Striking in its Upaniṣadic ring is the assertion (*NS* 4.7.78) that just as the *antarātman,* residing in the midst of *prakṛti* (nature), permeates (*samaśnute*) the world consisting of moving and unmoving elements, similarly does the king, in the midst of the *prakṛtis* (elements of the state) permeate the world consisting of moving and unmoving elements.

As important as the text's *dārśanic* underpinnings for understanding the emphasis on royal self-control was its politico-historical context. In an age of political aggrandisement, political theorists must have not only been concerned with the question of how the power of the king could be increased but also with how it could be contained. Emphasizing the importance of *mantraśakti* (the power of counsel) could only go so far. Ultimately, in ancient monarchical states, the only agent of effective control on the ambitions and transgressions of the king was the king himself. This may have been the second important element explaining Kāmandaka's (and Kauṭilya's) emphasis on the king controlling himself and his passions. The contradiction that the *Nītisāra* offers—what may in fact be described as an important element in the classical Indian ideal of kingship—is that of a king who aspires to become a world conqueror but who is not moved by the lust for power, or for anything else, for that matter. Renunciation was built into the ideal prototype of the king, and this is reflected in the ideal of the *rājarṣi*, an ideal which is pervasive in the cultural traditions of ancient and early medieval India.[50]

## HISTORICIZING THE *NĪTISĀRA*

Historicizing the *Nītisāra* involves contextualizing it within the genre of ancient and early medieval Indian political treatises and within the realities of monarchical power politics at the advent of the early medieval. The perspective represented in this text is that of a Brāhmaṇa political theorist who was probably closely involved in contemporary politics, addressing members of the political class, including the king. While the text is broadly speaking 'normative' in nature, within this normative discourse, we can view a morphology of monarchical power politics and we can also see the author grappling with pressing issues of his time, including those related to unbridled and unsatiated royal ambitions and endemic war and violence.

The leading political theorists of ancient and early medieval India had a similar socio-political background and shared similar concerns and conceptual vocabulary, ones which extended beyond their circle to other members of the intelligentsia, including the poets. They participated in the creation of a basic common stock of ideas and metaphors that became part of a relatively stable classical Indian model of kingship which, with regional and chronological variations, spread beyond the confines of the subcontinent into Southeast Asia as well.[51]

Yet, within the parameters of this model, these thinkers had their distinct and distinctive positions and points of view as well. In fact, a close reading of the *Nītisāra* reveals that the usual description of this text as an unoriginal versified summary of the teaching of the *Arthaśāstra* is incorrect. Kāmandaka certainly drew on the Kauṭilya's ideas (and those of others as well), but he had his own point of view on several matters. His concerns and opinions can be gauged through a careful analysis of the issues he discusses, his arguments and emphases. Just as interesting as his assertions are his silences. There is only a hint of cleavages within the political elite, and it may be noted that apart from a brief reference to the crime of usurpation, Kāmandaka does not directly discuss issues which must have been of pressing practical import such as disputed succession, coups, and dynastic change.

The morphology of the state, royal court, and household in the *Nītisāra* corresponds broadly to that of the *Arthaśāstra*. And yet, in spite of shared rhetoric and imagery, Kāmandaka lacks Kauṭilya's confident, even audacious vision of political power and empire. This must have been at least in part due to the fact that the core of the *Arthaśāstra* was composed at least half a millennium, if not more, earlier, during a period of aggressive empire-building, while the *Nītisāra* was composed in a very different political scenario, against the backdrop of imperial decline (of the Guptas and Vākāṭakas). The political battles were now among monarchical states and the oligarchies no longer figured as contenders among the circle of kings. Compared with still later texts, although the ideal of political paramountcy is very important, in the *Nītisāra,* the *sāmantas* still seem to be bordering chiefs, and the discussion of the protocol between paramount and subordinate rulers is not as detailed or elaborate.

The *Nītisāra*'s ostensible aim was to reveal how the *vijigīṣu* could achieve his goal of political paramountcy and the text often has the ring of idealization and universalization, especially when it talks of the ideal virtues of the king. But there seems to be something more than banal idealization or pious platitude here. Although many of the virtues that are described as desirable in a king are presented as inborn, they are actually cultivable, and the idea that is implicit is that there is a difference between a king who becomes king and one who is worthy of being one. The entire discussion can be seen as an attempt of a political theorist to emphasize the ethical dimension of political discourse.[52]

A similar concern for building bridges between ethics and political realities can be seen in Kāmandaka's discussion of various forms of violence associated with kingship—punishment, hunting, and war. While he does justify violent means in order to justify certain ends (justice, the desire for exciting sport, and the goal of territorial expansion respectively), a careful reading of the text suggests a more complex and nuanced perspective. Along with advice, there is a great deal of admonition and warning of the calamities that will afflict the kingdom if a king lacks the necessary virtues or abilities, or if the balance of virtue that is necessary for the other human agents in the *saptāṅga rājya* is disturbed.

The long deliberative sections on war, advocating extreme caution, suggest the despondency of a political thinker who disapproved of the frequent destructive warfare that marked his time. That this disapproval was part of Kāmandaka's larger convictions related to violence and non-violence is evident from his view on capital punishment. It is also evident in his diatribe against the royal hunt, which, contrary to Kauṭilya's view on the matter, is viewed as the worst of the royal vices, and is disapproved of not only on the grounds of expediency but also on the grounds that it involves moral weakening of the king and death to the hunted animals. These radical points of view have, strangely enough, hitherto gone unnoticed in works on ancient Indian political thought, which have incorrectly presented the *Nītisāra* as a feeble versified echo of the *Arthaśāstra*.

Further, embedded in a text which seems to be a celebration of royal and political ambitions, is a strong insistence that the king exercise control over his senses. This insistence may have been a reaction to the disastrous results of the wanton, licentious lifestyle of many contemporary kings and/or a reflection of the most basic form of self-control that was advocated by many dārśanic schools of the time. The Upaniṣadic ring of *Nītisāra* 4.7.78, mentioned earlier in this essay, seems to betray a more specific philosophical orientation. But apart from the philosophical inspiration, the emphasis on self-control can also be seen as an attempt of the political theorists to deal with a very central problem: How was the power of the king to be controlled and checked in a polity which lacked any institutional checks? Virtue, caution and power of counsel were emphasized again and again. But theorists such as Kāmandaka recognized that ultimately, no external controls could be counted on, and the only real control on the king's power was the one that he had to be persuaded to exercise over himself.

## INCORPORATING PERSPECTIVES ON VIOLENCE INTO POLITICAL HISTORY

In spite of problems in dating their work precisely, it is essential to incorporate the ideas of the political theorists into historical writings on political processes in ancient and early medieval India. Such an exercise involves situating these texts within their historical context, a careful reading of their opinions and arguments on various issues, and a comparison between texts (and inscriptions) belonging to different periods of time. Comparison reveals much continuity in terms of concepts and vocabulary, but also indicates differences in perspective, and shifts in emphasis and nuance. We have seen that a comparison of the *Arthaśāstra* and *Nītisāra* reflects a refashioning of the political model. While the *Arthaśāstra* can be seen as a brilliant exposition of the dizzy heights of power to which a king could aspire, inspired by the vision of an omniscient, omnipotent and omnipresent state, the *Nītisāra's* tone is more cautious and restrained. Kāmandaka is certainly concerned with how a king could increase his power and dominion, but he is equally, if not more, concerned with how royal power, war, and violence could be contained and controlled. The *Arthaśāstra* reflects an earlier model of an arrogant, absolutist state; the *Nītisāra* represents a later, less exultant reflection on political power, one in which non-violence has significantly tempered the discussion of violence, especially with regard to punishment, the royal hunt, and war.

[...]

The question of how political violence was conceptualized, defined, justified, delimited, criticized, or condemned in texts belonging to different genres, languages, and periods needs to be analysed, and the results of such an analysis should be part of the historian's discourse on political processes in ancient and early medieval India. The sheer pervasiveness of political violence in human history, and the problem it presents in our own time, makes an engagement with this issue especially pertinent.

## NOTES

1 The literature on these frameworks is well known and enormous, and it is therefore neither possible nor necessary to give exhaustive references. A good sample of the various views is on display in Herman Kulke (ed.), *The State in India 1000–1700*, New Delhi, 1997.

2 Sheldon Pollock, *The Language of the Gods in the World of Men: Sanskrit, Culture and Power in Premodern India*, Berkeley, 2006.

3 Ronald Inden, *Text and Practice: Essays on South Asian Cultural History*, New Delhi, 2006, pp. 129–78.

4 Daud Ali, *Courtly Culture and Political Life in Early Medieval India*, New Delhi, 2006.

5 See for instance, Jan E.M. Houben and Karel R. van Kooij (eds), *Violence Denied: Violence, Non-violence and the Rationalization of Violence in South Asian Cultural History*, Leiden, 1999.

6 Daud Ali, 'Violence, Gastronomy and the Meanings of War in Medieval South India', *The Medieval History Journal*, vol. 3, no. 2, 2000, pp. 261–89.

7 Sheldon Pollock, 'The Theory of Practice and the Practice of Theory in Indian Intellectual History', *Journal of the American Oriental Society*, vol. 109, no. 4, 1989, pp. 499–519. He adds that this stance is diametrically opposite to that found in the West, and that adherence to this postulate had profound implications for the production of knowledge in Indian civilization.

8 The author's name has been read as Kāmandaki by some scholars. The text used for this article is Sisir Kumar Mitra's revised edition and translation, Calcutta, 1982, which is based on Rajendralala Mitra's *The Nītisāra, or The Elements of Polity by Kāmandaki*, which was published between 1849 and 1884. This uses an anonymous commentary called the *Upādhyāyanirapekṣā*. Although I have drawn on this edition, I have relied on my own translation of the text. In references hereafter, *Nītisāra* has been abbreviated to *NS*.

9 Bhaskar Anand Saletore, *Ancient Indian Political Thought and Institutions*, New York, 1963, p. 9.

10 Michael Willis, *The Archaeology of Hindu Ritual: Temples and the Establishment of the Gods*, New Delhi, 2009, pp. 62–3. Willis's hypothesis that the 'Deva' mentioned in the first verse of the *Nītisāra* is none other than Candragupta II, on the grounds that the latter is referred to as 'Deva' or 'Devagupta' in inscriptions, seems weak. So does his assertion that since Kāmandaka describes himself as a disciple of Viṣṇugupta, alias Kauṭilya, a generation, or thirty to forty years, must separate the two political theorists.

11 The date of the *Arthaśāstra* is an issue of continuing debate. Many Indian historians accept R.P. Kangle's argument that the core of the text was composed in the early Maurya period during the last quarter of the fourth century BCE (Kangle, *The Kauṭilīya Arthaśāstra*, Part III, Bombay, 1965, pp. 59–115); of course additions, interpolations, and recasting may have extended into the early centuries CE. Western scholars, on the other hand, are persuaded by the results of Thomas R. Trautmann's statistical analysis of word frequencies in the *Arthaśāstra* (Trautmann, *Kauṭilya and the Arthaśāstra: A Statistical Investigation of the Authorship and Evolution of the Text*, Leiden, 1971), on the basis of which he has made a case for several different authors. He suggests that Book 2 (which deals with internal administration) may have been completed by *c.* 150 CE, and the final compilation of the entire text was complete by *c.* 250 CE. References to the *Arthaśāstra* (abbreviated to *AS*) in this essay are to Kangle's critical edition (Kangle, *The Kauṭilīya Arthaśāstra*, Part I).

12 U.N. Ghoshal, *A History of Indian Political Ideas: The Ancient Period and the Period of Transition to the Middle Ages*, reprint edition, Oxford 1965 [1959], p. 395 n. 1.

13 See, for instance, Saletore, *Ancient India Political Thought and Institutions*, pp. 54, 289, 340; Ghoshal, *A History of Indian Political Ideas*, p. 383; K.V.R. Aiyangar, *Some Aspects of Ancient Indian Polity*, second edition, Patna 1998 [1935], pp. 24–5.

14 While the term *anujīvin* literally carries the connotations of dependence and has, therefore, been often translated as 'dependant,' in the context of the court, it is better to translate it as 'courtier'.

15 Ali's (*Courtly Culture and Political Life in Early Medieval India*, p. 276) argument that the *Arthaśāstra* marks a significant shift in the language of lordship, from agonistic to irenic kingship is thought-provoking. However, the shift does not seem to have been a complete one.

16 *NS* 2.3.6 and *NS* 11.16.42.

17 According to some scholars, the reference is to the god Viṣṇu, but the verse seems to refer to a generic king.
18 The seven elements are chyle, blood, flesh, fat, bone, marrow, and semen. The term *doṣa* also occurs in *āyurveda*, but has a different meaning than that in the political treatises. The three doṣas or humours are substances which circulate within the body—*vāta* (wind), *pitta* (choler), and *kapha* or *sleṣman* (phlegm). Disease arises when a humour collects in the wrong area of the body and becomes inflamed (Dominik Wujastyk, *The Roots of Ayurveda: Selections from Sanskrit Medical Writings*, New Delhi, 2001, pp. 4, 31). The terms *guṇa* and doṣa as indicative of positive qualities and faults occur in many different kinds of discourse, including as features of language in Indian literary theory.
19 For an interesting discussion of the connections between medicine and poetry, see Francis Zimmermann, 'Ṛtusātmya: The Seasonal Cycle and the Principle of Appropriateness', *Social Science and Medicine*, vol. 14B, no. 2, 1980, pp. 99–106.
20 Sheldon Pollock ('Mīmāṁsā and the Problem of History in Traditional India', *Journal of the American Oriental Society*, vol. 109, no. 4, 1989, pp. 603–10) has expressed this eloquently in a broader context, arguing that in Sanskritic India, history was not unknown but denied. His hypothesis, which merits careful consideration, is that this was because the authority of the Veda was considered by Mīmāṁsā as based on its timelessness, and that this became a model for all forms of knowledge.
21 He is compared with the sun, moon, Vindhyas, rain-bearing clouds, earth, blazing fire, lion, elephant, and snake. He is also compared with the *kalpavṛkṣa* (the wish-granting tree).
22 The Sanskrit epics were pivotal to many other discourses on politics and kingship in ancient and early medieval India. The full extent of this importance and influence—reflected in texts, inscriptions, and sculpture from many parts of the subcontinent and beyond—is something which has not yet been fully gauged.
23 The seven elements of the state in the *Arthaśāstra* are *svāmin, amātya, janapada, durga, koṣa, daṇḍa,* and *mitra*. The *Nītisāra* (*NS* 4.7.1) makes a slight modification in terminology, replacing *janapada* with *rāṣṭra, daṇḍa* with *bala,* and *mitra* with *suhṛt*. It is interesting to note that Bṛhaspati rather than Kauṭilya, is cited as the authority on the seven elements of the kingdom (*NS* 8.12.5).
24 In the context in which the word *guṇa* occurs here, it does not (as suggested by Ali, ibid., 90–1) have any connection with *sattva, rajas,* and *tamas*.
25 The text makes a distinction between servants (denoted by *bhṛtya* and *sevaka*) and dependants/courtiers of a higher socio-political standing (denoted by *anujīvin*).
26 There is passing reference to hierarchies within the court circle, for instance, in the mention of the honorific paraphernalia such as umbrella, fly-whisk, coachman, and grooms that the *mahāmātras* and certain other high-ranking officials enjoyed (*NS* 13.19.44). The dependant is advised to observe decorum in deference to other courtiers' rank and there is mention of his rivals (*vipakṣa*; 5.8.40). But there is no direct or detailed discussion of court factions and rivalries.
27 Ali has very effectively demonstrated (*Courtly Culture*, p. 183) the coincidence of the terminology of emotions and political dispositions in a variety of courtly literature of the first millennium.

28 Since the terms suhṛt and mitra are used in the text to refer to personal friends as well as political allies, in some cases it is not clear which of these meanings is intended.

29 One of the problems in Ali's discussion is that he occasionally slips from his stance of viewing the various discourses on courtly culture as representations to one where these representations are presented as descriptions of courtly life. He does, however, point out that the texts themselves mention the breach of court protocol.

30 *NS* 13.19.42–43 suggests that spies pretending to be idiots, dumb, blind and deaf persons, eunuchs, *kirātas* (hunters), dwarfs and hunchbacks, petty craftsmen, monks/mendicants, minstrels, slave women, garland-makers, and artists should keep a watch on members of the harem.

31 See Lallanji Gopal, 'Sāmanta: Its Varying Significance in Ancient India', *Journal of the Royal Asiatic Society*, vol. 5, nos 1–2, 1963, pp. 21–37, for a discussion of changes in the connotations of the term sāmanta.

32 *AS* 9.5 has a more general discussion of troubles emanating from the interior and the outer regions.

33 See, for instance, Houben and van Kooij (eds), *Violence Denied*, pp. 1–3.

34 Much has been written on this theme. For instance, Danielle Feller Jatavallabhula ('Raṇayajña: The Mahābhārata War as a Sacrifice' in Houben and van Kooij (eds), *Violence Denied*) examines the idea of war as sacrifice in the Mahābhārata, while Madeleine Biardeau ('Ancient Brahmanism, or Impossible Violence' in Denis Vidal, Gilles Tarabout, and Eric Meyer (eds), *Violence/Non-violence: Some Hindu Perspectives*, New Delhi, 2003, pp. 85–104) looks at issues related to violence in the *Manu Smṛti* and the Mahābhārata, especially at Arjuna's assertion of the impossibility of avoiding violence.

35 *AS* 4.11.11–12; 2.5.17; 2.5.20; 2.29.16.

36 See, for instance, Ebba Koch, *Mughal Art and Imperial Ideology: Collected Essays*, New Delhi, 2001.

37 Divyabhanusinh Chavda, personal communication.

38 Vyasana can mean vice, calamity, or affliction.

39 References to such a sanitized forest occur in *AS* 1.21.23; 2.20.3. *AS* 2.20.4 suggests that the king should in addition establish another kind of animal park where animals are welcomed as guests, presumably a sanctuary where they are given protection. Elsewhere (*AS* 2.26.1), Kauṭilya talks of fines that should be imposed on those who kill animals whose killing has been prohibited or which inhabit the king's reserved park.

40 That this idea was well known is evident in Kālidāsa's *Raghuvaṁśa* (9.53) where Daśaratha is described as going to hunt in a sanitized forest (described in much less detail). It is no coincidence that calamity befalls him there, when he inadvertently kills the son of a blind ascetic, resulting in the curse that leads to the subsequent tragic events. For what could be more graphic than this as an illustration of the calamities that would befall kings who fell prey to the vice of excessive hunting?

41 Ali, *Courtly Culture and Political Life in Early Medieval India*, pp. 99–102.

42 The six *guṇas* are *sandhi* (alliance), *vigraha* (war), *yāna* (marching on an expedition), *āsana* (staying in one place), *saṁśraya* (seeking shelter) and *dvaidhibhāva* (a double policy of sandhi with one king and *vigraha* with another).

43 Kauṭilya too uses the categories of *prakāśayuddha*, *kūṭayuddha*, and *mantrayuddha*, but he adds a fourth one—*tūṣṇīmyuddha* (silent war), which involves the use of secret practices and instigation through secret agents (*AS* 7.6.41).

44 Others differed on this point. For instance, Kāmandaka cites Bharadvāja as stating that a king should fight against the enemy with all his might, like a lion, and that it was possible for a weaker king to outmanoeuvre a stronger one through sheer courage (*NS* 9.14.56).

45 The *Arthaśātra* too gives primacy to mantraśakti (*AS* 9.1.29).

46 The king, through *daṇḍa*, has to restrain his subjects running after vices (*viṣayas*) (*NS* 2.5.43).

47 It should be noted that a very basic level of self-control is being advocated here. For instance, higher than control over the senses is *ātmajaya* (control over the self).

48 Ali, *Courtly Culture and Political Life in Early Medieval India*, pp. 138, 241, 245.

49 It features, for instance, in *sāṁkhya, yoga*, Upaniṣadic, Buddhist, and Jaina thought.

50 *AS* 1.7.3 in fact describes the life of such a *rājarṣi*.

51 The continuities and variations in the classical model of kingship can be seen clearly in studies of the imaging of kingship in inscriptions belonging to different centuries and to different regions and sub-regions. For an analysis of the details and patterns revealed in the inscriptions of ancient and early medieval Orissa, see Upinder Singh, *Kings, Brāhmaṇas and Temples in Orissa: An Epigraphic Study* AD *300–1147*, New Delhi, 1994, pp. 82–122.

52 I disagree completely with scholars who argue (for example, Ghoshal, *A History of Indian Political Ideas*, p. 385) that the politics of texts such as the *Arthaśāstra* and *Nītisāra* is devoid of ethics. In fact ethics was central to ancient Indian discourse on politics.

# 13

# Images of Raiders and Rulers*

B.D. Chattopadhyaya

## I

It is already well-known—but apparently needs to be reiterated—that written sources from about the eighth century do not use terms which are today used as generic terms to refer to the Muslims.[1] It is not altogether true, as seems to be suggested by some, that sources reveal lack of familiarity with specifics as regards terms and concepts connected with Islam.[2] At least in the middle of the thirteenth century, there is clear evidence of familiarity with the term *Musalamāna* (literally, 'one who submits to Allah'), and of concepts which relate to the practice of Islam.[3] But such evidence is extremely rare, whereas generic terms which were in use in earlier times to denote outsiders or others to the society, were grafted on to newcomers, without even partial modifications. The general absence of a term in written sources cannot by itself be a proof that it was unfamiliar. On the other hand, it may be interesting to speculate why, if a term was known, as *Musalamāna* was known in the thirteenth century, it was not used commonly. The use as well as non-use of particular words, in addition of course to ways they were used, may indeed be indicative of attitudes.

What were then the terms used commonly? And, do appropriate references, arranged in a chronological order, suggest any evolutionary

*Previously published in B.D. Chattopadhyaya, *Representing the Other? Sanskrit Sources and the Muslims*, New Delhi, Manohar, 1998. This is an extract from the chapter. In the present version, some portions of the text and notes have been removed. For complete text see the original version.

pattern? It can be noticed, when one wades through a substantial series of comparable epigraphic records, that terms found in these records (and literary texts as well) may be broadly grouped into four categories, the classification being based on how these terms were derived. I would consider the category of ethnic names as most important, as the majority of terms used—and most regularly—derive from tribal/community names. Ethnic names are, in general, specific references, not liable to inappropriate attribution, and included in this category, we shall find the following terms, in their specific contexts: *Tājika*, *Turuṣka*, *Gaurī*, *Mudgala*, *Turuti* (*Turbati*), *Paṭhāna*.

Terms delivered from country of origin are *Pārasīka* and *Garjaṇa/Garjaṇaka*. As we shall presently see, *Pārasīka* was originally distinctly pre-Islamic, and changed its connotation to move over to the category of generic terms, qualified to be used interchangeably with other generic terms. *Garjaṇa/Garjaṇaka* was derived from the placename Gazni, and referred to the ruler of Delhi. *Hammīra*, another term in common use, was derived from *āmir* and, unlike *Suratrāṇa*, which, having been derived from Sultān remained an honorific, could be a generic term, as suggested by the title of the play *Hammīramadamardana* and many references in the inscriptions. The other generic terms were: *Yavana*, *Mleccha*, and *Śaka*.[4] All these terms were in use in early historical times, but although *Yavana* and *Mleccha* were already generic terms with reference to 'outsiders' in the early historical context, the ethnic term *Śaka* came to acquire, or so it appears, a generic connotation only in early medieval times, perhaps through its continued association with the *Śaka* era.[5] Another instance of an ethnic term changing into a generic term in the early medieval period is *Turuṣka*; its use was too frequent to have been restricted to a single ethnic connotation alone.

This, admittedly, is a brief introduction to the range of terms used and to what they seem to have conveyed; what is required now is to make more detailed reference to their contextual occurrences.

## II

Two terms in early use were Pārasīka and Tājika. Pārasīka was definitely connected with pre-Islamic Persia, and for its early use, D.R. Bhandarkar's comments appear to be still pertinent: 'a Pārasīka is distinguished from a Pahlava in ancient Indian works and records. The latter is identical with Iranian Pahlav and is taken to denote a Parthian. Pārasīka, on the other hand, is the Pahlavi Parsik, denoting an inhabitant of Pars, the ancient Persis or modern Fars. It should further be remembered that the meaning which attaches to the word depends upon the period to which any particular reference to it belongs.'[6] Bhandarkar's precise identification of Pārasīkas of AD 300–700 with 'Iranians of the time of or connected with the Sassanian dynasty', and of a later period, with the 'Muhammadan inhabitants of Persia' may not apply uniformly to all Pārasīka references so neatly, but a shift in the connotation did definitely take place, making it a generic term interchangeable with Śāka, Mleccha, or Yavana, rather than with a fixed connotation in relation to 'Muhammadan inhabitants of Persia'.[7] Pārasīka, in fact, can be used to question a fixed relation between ethnicity and the connotation of a term. In the *Raghuvaṃśam* (iv) of Kālidāsa, King Raghu encountered the Pārasīkas, who were westerners (*pāścātya*), in his *digvijaya* undertaken on the land route. Kālidāsa tells us that Raghu 'could not bear the flush caused by wine in the lotus faces of the Yavana women; that a fierce battle took place between him and the westerners who had cavalry for their army; that he covered the earth with their bearded heads, severed by his arrows, that the survivors put off their helmets and sought his protection, and that his soldiers beguiled the fatigue of conquest with wine in vineyards covered with choicest skins'.[8] Other practices associated with the Pārasīkas are condemned in *Dharmaśāstra* texts and other genres of literature, *Vṛddha Yājñavalkya* duly dictating that on 'touching Caṇḍālas, Mlecchas, Bhillas, Pārasīkas and others and those that were guilty of the mortal sins, one should bathe together with the clothes worn'.[9] However, the references to the Pārasīkas in epigraphs and literature from the close of the seventh century were in all likelihood to Persian settlements on the western coast and such references are devoid of any ethnic attributes. It is not at all clear when Pārasīka came to denote a Muslim; possibly, by the close of the eleventh century, when Kulottuṅga Cōḻa claimed to have 'scattered (his) enemies (and) whose fame is spontaneously sung on the further shore of the ocean by the young women of the Persians (*Pārasī*)',[10] the term had acquired a new connotation.

The earliest occurrence of the term Tājika is in the Kavi plate from Broach (Bharoch) district, Gujarat. Dated 22 June 736, the plate[11] which records a gift of land to God Āśramadeva, mentions the Tājikas in order to highlight the military achievements of Jayabhaṭa IV, Gurjara feudatory of the contemporary Maitraka ruler of Valabhi, the actual raid having been undertaken at the city of the lord of Valabhi from Sind. The context of the grant is not military, but it is intended to convey the impression that by forcibly vanquishing the Tājikas, Jayabhaṭa was able, 'even as a cloud extinguishes with its showers the fire that troubles all people', to put an end to the unending misery of the people (*aśeṣa-loka-santāpa*).

The term Tājika, it has been suggested,[12] was derived from Pahlavi Tāzīg, in turn derived from the name of the Arab tribe Ṭayyi. However, a recent intensive probe into the various possibilities regarding the derivation of the term shows that it derived from Arabic tribal or tribal confederation of the Ṭaiyi, and, further, that 'an old Parthian formation of the name which by the third century must have been Tāžīg may be envisaged'.[13] In any case, the term in use in India was thus of West Asian origin, but it was indigenized, as were other terms of the categories listed above. The term, in a similar context, occurs in another near contemporary record from Navasari, also in Gujarat.[14] The feudatory who this time inflicted what is represented as a major defeat on the advancing Tājika army was Cālukya Pulakeśirāja. His overlord, the illustrious king Vallabha, rewarded the unique display of the feudatory's valour with such titles as *Dakṣiṇāpatha-sādhāra* (the pillar of *Dakṣiṇāpatha*), *Calukki-kul-ālaṁkāra* (ornament of the family of the Calukkis), *Pṛthivī-vallabha* (beloved of the earth), and *Anivartaka-nivartayitṛ* (repeller of the unrepellable). Dated 21 October 739, the Navasari plates of Pulakeśirāja provide a graphic description of the devastations caused by the Tājika army which had set out to cause more devastations:

When the army of the Tājikas,—which poured forth arrows, javelins and iron-headed clubs; which destroyed, with its rapidly brandished and glittering swords, the prosperous Saindhava, Kacchella, Saurāṣṭra, Cāvoṭaka, Maurya, Gurjara and other kings; which, desiring to enter Dakṣiṇāpatha ... with a view to vanquish all Southern kings, came, in the very first place, to conquer the *viṣaya* of Navasārika, which rendered the regions between the quarters dusky with the dust of the ground raised by the hard and noisy hoofs of its galloping horses; the bodies (of warriors) in which appeared dreadful as their armours, were reddened by very large streams of blood (gushing) from the intestines which came out of the cavities of their big bellies, as they impetuously rushed forth and were completely pierced by spear-heads; which had previously not been vanquished even by numerous eminent chiefs among hosts of kings, who offered their heads in return for high honour and gifts they had received from their lord; who opposed it, biting mercilessly both their lips with the tips of their teeth; who, though they were great warriors and had their sharp swords reddened by the mass of blood that flowed when the sides of their loins and trunks of hostile elephants were rent on several extensive battlefields, could not attain success; who cut off the necks of their enemies' heads, as if they were plucking the stalks of lotuses, hitting them with their horse-shoe-shaped sharp arrows which were quickly discharged for the destruction of their adversaries; whose bodies were covered with a coat of bristling hair on account of their martial spirit and excitement,—was defeated in the forefront of the battle in which headless trunks began a circular dance to the accompaniment of the loud noise of drums beaten continuously in joy caused, as it were, by the thought: 'Today at least we have, by laying down our heads, paid off the debt we owed to our lord in (this) one life.'

This extensive, involved passage, offering a glory description of the battle between Avanijanāśraya Pulakeśirāja and his loyal retainers on one side and the Tājikas on the other, is cited here as an appropriate text for the study of representation. The passage represents an actual battle fought, but uses various literary conventions to take the description beyond ordinary portrayal in order to project the loyal achievements of a feudatory, the loyalty of whose own subordinates contributes in making the imagery of the battle and the battlefield so vividly splashed with colour. The evidence of the Navasari plates is commonly cited to highlight successful national resistance in the face of threat to the integrity of the country,[15] but while analysing the evidence as bearing upon a historical event, it is necessary to remember that a description of this kind is rather unique, and, therefore, needs to be juxtaposed with other references to Tājika and other raids, and, secondly, that according to the evidence of the plates, the text was written by 'illustrious Bappabhaṭṭi, the *Mahāsāndhi-vigrahika* and *Sāmanta*, who has attained the *Pañcamahāśabda* and is the son of the *Mahābalādhikṛta* Haragaṇa'. The ancestry and the station of the author would surely have reflected on the vividness of the imagery. [...]

[...]

The point may perhaps be effectively stated by analysing another early, eighth-century inscription, referring to the Tājikas. The inscription of Pratīhāra Vatsarāja, dated AD 795, and of uncertain provenance,[16] was intended to record the construction of a temple of Caṇḍikā by a member of a subordinate family of the Pratīhāras. The record refers to the Pratīhāra rulers Nāgabhaṭa I and Vatsarāja, and attributes sovereign kingship (*sārvabhauma-nṛpatitva*) to Vatsarāja achieved through victories over Karnāṭa and Lāṭa in the south, which took his armies down to the southern ocean, his victory over Jayāpīḍa, which took his army to the Himalayan heights, his victory over the Lord of Gauḍa, as also by virtue of his victories over Mleccha and Kīra kings, respectively of the western and northern quarters. Vatsarāja's subordinate Śrīvarmaka too claimed several victories, including one on the Tājika ruler who was taken captive (*baddhaḥkṛta-sakala-jagajjāgaras-Tājikeśo*). Others defeated by him were: Keśari, who was forced to pay tribute; the ruler of hill tribes who were punished, and Vyāghra, the powerful Tomara king. Victories over enemies of Karṇāṭa and Gauḍa are claimed by feudatory Śrīvarmaka's son Gallaka as well in the record.

As can be seen from another record, also mentioning the Tājikas and belonging to the Rāṣṭrakūṭas of the Deccan, the terms of representation of victories achieved over enemies are in accordance with the convention which seeks to place the ruler, sometimes through the mediation of his subordinates, in a position of universal sovereignty.[17] The convention underlines the need for multiplicity of enemies who are vanquished; further, acknowledgement of defeat is opposed to the concerns of sovereignty. If at all defeat has to be acknowledged, it has to be couched in terms acceptable to the convention. The Rāṣṭrakūṭa grant, that of Kṛṣṇa III (939–67) from Chinchani in Thane and datable to the middle of the tenth century,[18] credits the ruler with victories over Pāṇḍya, Oḍra, Siṃhala, Cōḷa, Pārasīka, Āndhra, Draviḍa, Barbara, Tājika, Vaṃkina, Hūṇa, Khasa, Gurjjara, and Mālavīyaka. The list is impressive, as was the projected status of the Rāṣṭrakūṭas in their records, and the fact that the Tājikas and the Pārasīkas should be mentioned among those who were subdued by Kṛṣṇa III is additionally significant. The Pārasīkas were in all probability an important community of western India located within Rāṣṭrakūṭa territories; some representatives of the Tājikas were political subordinates of the Rāṣṭrakūṭas in western India. In fact, another Chinchani grant of an earlier date, of AD 926, belonging to the period of Rāṣṭrakūṭa Indra III, refers to Madhumatī of the Tājika community who had received the entire *maṇḍala* of Saṃyāna, on the western coast, from Kṛṣṇarāja II (878–915).[19] Madhumatī, obviously a Sanskritized form of Muhammad, was the son of Sāhiyarahāra (or Yarahara), and he had another name, Sugatipa. As a feudatory ruler of *Saṃyāna-maṇḍala*, appointed by the Rāṣṭrakūṭas, Sugatipa was involved in projects of a religious nature, but as a governor, his position was similar to that of a member of the family of Tājikas who were closely associated with the Kadambas of Candrapura and Goa. G.M. Moraes, on the basis of inscriptional evidence preserved in a later Portuguese version, suggests that this association dates to the time of Guhalladeva II (980–1005?). When Guhalladeva's pilgrimage to Somnath was interrupted, he had to make his way to Goa. 'A native of this city named Madummod, of Tāji origin, the wealthiest among all sea-faring traders, a person of great wisdom, rendered a great and public service to the above-mentioned king Guhaldev.'[20] The city of Goa which was made the capital of his kingdom by Kadamba Jayakeśi I (1050–80) 'owed a substantial part of its prosperity to the wise administration of Saḍano, a grandson of the merchant Muhammada who...had rendered valuable service to Guhalladeva. Jayakeśi appointed him governor of the Konkan. Prudent, just, and liberal, he was well-versed in mathematics and 'the fourteen arts, the four resources, and the seven solicitudes.'[21] According to sources used by Moraes, in 1053 Saḍano established in the capital a charitable institution which arranged food for the poor and the helpless and lodgings for the pilgrims; the resources for running the institution came from trading vessels and merchants from foreign countries.

Saḍano, the competent administrator, is obviously identical with Saḍhaṇa mentioned in the Panjim plates of Jayakeśi I dated AD 1059. [...]

[...]

The Tājika presence in western India was on a scale which may be considered not too insignificant for the formation of images about them; they would be considered as Mlecchas, despite the deliberate Sanskritization of their ethnic and personal names, and the reference to the Mlecchas and the Tājikas in the inscription of 795, of Pratīhāra Vatsarāja, need not be taken to relate to two separate communities. In fact, both Yavana and Mleccha were terms which, after having acquired a generic connotation suitable for application to outsiders, continued in use. The mention of the Yavanas in the Kharepatan (Ratnagiri district, Maharashtra) inscription of 1095[22] of the time of Śilāhāra ruler Anantadeva and of the Mlecchas in the Vadavali grant (Thane, Maharashtra) of 1127[23] of the time of Śilāhāra Aparāditya I would have related to the Tājikas who, as already pointed out, had a significant political presence in western India in early medieval times, to the extent of being listed among adversaries even when they could be appointed as governors and could be seen as contributors to the promotion of an ideal socio-religious order.

To return to the question of representation in terms of literary convention, it may be instructive to study the images which are projected about the Tājikas in the specific context of western India of early medieval times. Tājika raiders of the Navasari record of AD 739 were obviously considered capable of causing political devastations; the Yavanas of the Kharepatan plate, who overran the Konkan country as a result of a civil war after Mummuni, harassed the Gods and Brāhmaṇas (*devadvijāti-pramatha-vidhi*) and were 'violent and vile' (*ugra, pāparāśi*). These are traits which may be seen as conforming to what the Yavanas or Mlecchas would generally be associated with. However, the general is not necessarily universal, and what the Chinchani plates tell us about the activities of the Arab governor Sugatipa will, again, have to be understood, and in a specific context, of what is associable with the Tājikas/Yavanas/Mlecchas. The point about the general and the specific may also be explored by trying to see the relationship between the Tājikas/Mlecchas and the norms of the existing social order. Note, for example, the case of Chittukka, who according to the Vadavali plates (Thane, Maharashtra) of Śilāhāra Aparāditya I (AD 1127), was an *asura*—a demon—born to devastate the world (*jagad-dalayitum*).[24] 'All the feudatories gathered round him...the wealth of religious merit was destroyed, the elders perished, refugees were harassed, all townsmen and their servants were ruined and all prosperity of the kingdom came to an end.'[25] The calamity to the Śilāhāra kingdom, seen in general terms of devastation to the world, was caused by an individual who, when Aparāditya fought him single-handed, with only one horse, ran away and sought refuge with the Mlecchas. The inscription does associate, in the end, the Mlecchas with calamity, but not as its originator in this specific context. At the same time, as will be mentioned later, the Mlecchas are generators of calamity in other situations in which Mleccha domination causes total ruin of the existing political and social order. The general tenor of how the Tājikas as Mlecchas or as Yavanas would be perceived and represented, which would sometimes accord with representations of individuals from other social groups, would pose a contradiction with other types of representation. It will have to be seen whether contemporary conventions can in any way illuminate and resolve this contradiction.

## III

References to Tājikas in inscriptions appear to discontinue after the tenth century,[26] although, judging from the history of commercial and other contacts with the Arab world,[27] it is rather surprising that the term does not continue to figure with any importance in the epigraphic and other records of western India. The term which assumes increasing importance is Turuṣka, although this preliminary statement requires several qualifications. First, it is not that the term Turuṣka is of later usage than Tājika and replaces it. Second, it is not Turuṣka alone which comes to be in use. For example, the term Śaka can be seen to be in use where one could expect Turuṣka. Similarly, as can be seen from the Vilasa grant of Prolaya Nāyaka, of the first half of the fourteenth century from Āndhra Pradesh,[28] Turuṣka could be substituted not only by such terms as Yavana, but by another term initially of a different ethnic origin, Pārasīka, as well.

Probably mentioned as *Tu-Kiue* in the Chinese annals of Tang and other dynasties,[29] Turuṣka is mentioned in early Indian literary sources from about the seventh century onward: in the *Harṣa-Carita* of Bāṇa who distinguished them from the Pārasīkas; in the *Garuḍa*, *Vāmana*, and *Bhāgavata Purāṇas*; in *Amarakośa*; in the *Kāvya Jānakīharaṇa* of

Kumāradasā[30] and other texts. The *Rājataraṅgiṇī* reference to Kaṇiṣka and his successors as Turuṣka[31] is perhaps to be explained in terms of the manner in which the term Turuṣka was being used with reference to the Shahiyas of Kabul, to even the Tibetans, and to the rulers of the north in general in the *Kumārapāla-carita* which specifies Caulukya Kumārapāla's conquests by relating them to the cardinal directions in which they were undertaken: Gaṅgā on the east, Vindhyas on the south, Sindhu on the west, and Turuṣka country on the north. Before, however, the actual establishment of the Turkish Sultanate in Delhi, the Turuṣkas start figuring on the political horizons of rulers located in different parts of the subcontinent. Perhaps the earliest epigraphic document to refer to the Turuṣkas as political adversaries is a fragmentary Sarada inscription from Hund (Attock, Pakistan), assigned, on palaeographic grounds, to the second half of the eighth century.[32] K.V. Ramesh finds in this document reference to the routing of a Muslim army in the Sindhu country by the local ruler Anantadeva,[33] but with reference to the evidence of Al-Beruni and Kalhaṇa regarding the Turuṣkas, it has alternatively been suggested that it was the ethnic Turks before conversion, who are mentioned in documents of this period.[34]

Whatever be the religious affiliation of the ethnic Turks of the Hund record, the Sagar Tal (Gwalior) inscription of Pratīhāra king Vatsarāja of the ninth century[35] refers to the Turuṣkas in a manner which is similar to how they figure in other early medieval records before the establishment of the Delhi Sultanate: that is, by listing them among other enemies of the ruler. The extensive achievements of Pratīhāra Nāgabhaṭa II, which included victories over the countries of Āndhra, Sindhu, Vidarbha, and Kaliṅga, extended to the seizure of the hill forts of the kings of Ānartta, Mālava, Kirāta, Turuṣka, Vatsa, and Matsya. The Yavana king,[36] of the Khalimpur plate of Pāla ruler Dharmapāla, a formidable adversary of the Pratīhāras, approved, along with kings of Bhoja, Madra, Kuru, Yadu, Avanti, Gandhāra, and Kīra, the installation of the king of Kānyakubja by Dharmapāla; perhaps he too was a Turuṣka, and his inclusion, among a number of rulers of northern and central India, suggests a pattern which is similar to the inclusion of the Turuṣka among a number of political adversaries.

[...]

The Turuṣka was thus not the unique foe, and even the unparalleled valour of Vāghela Lavaṇaprasāda, crushing the Turuṣka king who had spattered the earth with the blood flowing from the cut-off heads of numerous kings' does not refer to the Turuṣka as his single adversary. The epigraphic document of 1253, referring to it, mentions also

Lavaṇaprasāda's victories over Raṇasiṃha who resembled Rāvaṇa, over the Cāhamāna king of Nadol, the Paramāra king of Dhar, and the kings of the Deccan and of Maru. Epigraphic documents of the period, taken collectively, are in fact replete with references to who could be perceived as political adversaries and to the metaphors of heroes: they point, not to singularity, but to multiplicity.

## IV

Sanskrit texts, which style themselves as *Mahākāvyas*, often refer to the Yavanas, Mlecchas, Turuṣkas interchangeably, and they too do not carry the impression of the emergence of a single foe, as a literary motif, posing threat to the military might of the central character of the *Mahākāvya*. One can assume that from the point of view of the literary idiom this would not have been desirable and in consonance with the intended status of the hero. A detailed examination of the texts from this perspective cannot be a part of the present study, but the point can be made by using one general study on Sanskrit 'Historical' *Mahākāvyas*[37] and by referring to at least one medieval *Mahākāvya*[38] in some detail.

*Pṛthvīrāja-vijaya* of Jayānaka,[39] one of the early texts of the genre of the historical *Mahākāvya*, centres around Cāhamāna Pṛthvīrāja who, as a hero, is characterized as *dhīrodātta*, and who, inexplicably, continues to be designated by modern historians as 'the last Hindu emperor of India'. Written possibly between 1191 and 1193, *Pṛthvīrāja-vijaya* begins with an account of the ancestry of Pṛthvīrāja, tracing his lineage to the Sun, and the narrative moves through generations of Cāhamāna rulers till it reaches Pṛthvīrāja. Among Pṛthvīrāja's predecessors, Ajayarāja and Arṇorāja are shown as having encountered and defeated the Muslims, and, of course, *Pṛthvīrāja-vijaya* is about Pṛthvīrāja's own victory over the Muslims. But in terms of his priority, when Pṛthvīrāja attained maturity to rule the kingdom, first was his campaign against Nāgārjuna, who had taken possession of Guḍapura. Pṛthvīrāja also resolved to vanquish beef-eating Mleccha Gaurī (that is, Ghuri), and bestowed gifts on a messenger who brought news from Gujarat of the routing of Gaurī (Ghuri) army, but then the narrative, in the penultimate canto of the text, moves off in a different direction: Pṛthvīrāja retires to a picture gallery and becomes absorbed in a painting portraying the beauty of Tilottamā.

*Pṛthvīrāja-vijaya*, in the form in which it is available now, is an incomplete text, and one is thus deprived of the text's detail of Pṛthvīrāja's victory over and representation of Gaurī in the last canto of the text. However, another text, *Hammīra-mahākāvya*,[40] written perhaps in the second half of the fifteenth century, around another Cāhamāna ruler

Hammīra of Raṇastambhapura also has many references to conflicts with the Turuṣkas, interspersed with references to conflicts and intrigues with other kings. To Siṃharāja, a predecessor of Hammīra, is attributed a victory over Hetima, a Mleccha general; but Siṃharāja's *digvijaya* (conquest of all quarters) is directed against Karṇāṭa, Lāṭa, Cōḷa, Gurjara, and Aṅga. In *Hammīra-mahākāvya's* continuous narration of events, of the period between the death of Pṛthvīrāja IV and Hammīra, conflict with the Mlecchas is a recurrent theme, but here too references to such conflicts are combined with references to conflicts with other kingdoms, court intrigues, and religious benefactions and other activities. The motif of digvijaya is also used for Hammīra (whose name as that of his brother Suratrāṇa are derived respectively from *āmir* and *sultān*) and covered, as mentioned in the text, Bhīmarasapura, Gaḍhamaṇḍala, Dhāra, Ujjayinī, Medāpata, and Acaleśvara. Hammīra's relation with Alauddin, Sultan of Delhi, is represented as one of high intrigues. Hammīra insults his own official; the official seeks refuge at the court of Delhi; to avenge his insult, Alauddin enlists support from Aṅga, Telaṅga, Magadha, Mahīśūra, and other regions. In the final encounter with Alauddin, Hammīra, frustrated by the treachery of his subordinates, kills himself; one of the few trusted subordinates who fight for Hammīra in his last encounter is Mahimasāhi, a Yavana.

Encounters with Turuṣka or Yavana rulers of the south figure prominently in some texts written in that region. *Madhurā-vijaya*,[41] which was written by Gaṅgādevī, in the second half of the fourteenth century, in celebration of Vijayanagara prince Kampana's victory over the Madura Sultans, uses motifs found in other texts as well. One of several descriptions of Bukka, father of Kampana and one of the founders of Vijayanagara, is that he was born to free the world of the Mlecchas. However, when Bukka advised Kampana on his plan of campaign, Kampana's adversaries were to be Camparāya, ruler of Taṇḍiramaṇḍala and of the city of Kāñcī, and several forest kings, before he was to proceed against the Sultan of Madura. Kampana's success in the south led to the establishment of Marataka as the capital of the new province, and, the text asserts, kings from Magadha, Mālava, Sevuṇa, Siṃhala, Ḍramila, Kerala, and Gauḍa waited at the gates for their turn to pay Kampana homage. Kampana, in the end, achieved success against the Yavanas of Madura through divine intervention.

*Sāluvābhyudaya*, written around 1480 by Rājanātha Diṇḍima[42] is about another Vijayanagara figure, Sāluva Narasiṃha. Sāluva Maṅgi, an ancestor of Narasiṃha, had, in his time, set out to defeat Mleccha *suratrāṇa* of the south and had, it is stated, removed fears of Kerala, Cōḷa, and Pāṇḍya kings. Cantos 3–13 of the text focus on the *Cakravartī* aspirations of Narasiṃha who fought against Kaliṅga, Cōḷa, and Pāṇḍya; marched down to the *setu* of Rāma, and then on to Anantaśayanam; achieved victory over Turuṣka; and then proceeded through Daśārṇa to the Himalayas. Kings of Aṅga, Koṅkaṇa, Kaliṅga, Khala, Tila, Kāruṣa, Gurjara, Lāṭa and so on acknowledged his suzerainty, and even after his anointment as a Cakravartī in front of God Viśveśvara of Kāśi, he went on to defeat Vaṅga, Kaliṅga, Gauḍa, Prāgjyotiṣa, and a host of other countries. He also defeated the Turuṣkas, who are stated to have been endowed with various weapons and who tortured the earth.

Another interesting text, from the point of view of representation of historical events, as also that of relation with the Yavanas is *Rāṣṭrauḍhavaṃśa-mahākāvyam*, written by Rudrakavi, a poet from the south (*dakṣiṇadig-bhava-kavi*), at the instance of his patron king Nārāyaṇa Śāha, Bagula ruler of Mayūragiri, in 1596.[43] The original seat of the Rāṣṭrauḍha family is traced in the text to Kānyakubja, and it is given both solar and lunar descent through divine intervention. The narrative moves through thirty-eight generations of the family, till it reaches the time of Nārāyaṇa Śāha's son Pratāpa Śāha. Gajamalladeva, twenty-sixth in descent from the earliest member of the lineage, is stated to have defeated the Gurjaras and the Mālavas, and after having killed Alauddin (*Alāvadinam Yavanādhināthsam*),[44] to have taken his kingdom. His son Malugi is stated to have captured Rāmarāja of Devagiri, but at the humble request of Rāmarāja's minister Hemādri, released him, after making him a feudatory (*sāmantamādhāya punar-mumoca*).[45] Nānadeva, twenty-eighth in descent, was a casualty at the hands of crores of Turuṣka soldiers of Dillīśvara (*Koṭi-Turuṣka-sainyair*),[46] who had conquered Karṇāṭa, Lāṭa, Utkala, Cōḷa, Gauḍa, Kaliṅga, Vaṅga, and other countries. However, Khaḍgasena, Nānadeva's grandson, is stated to have defeated eight thousand Mughal warriors along with their leader Mallikā (*Sa Mallikākhyam Yavanādhinātham jitv-āṣṭasahasra-Mugala-vīrān*).[47] Successes against the Yavanas, as also other rulers marked the times of Rāma, Nānadeva II, and Bhairavasena. In fact, Bhairavasena, while he offered protection to the ruler of Maṇḍapaparvata (Mandu) by defeating one Sulema Śāha, at the same time extended help to Bāhādura Śāha, the Sultan of Gujarat (*Gurjaradeśa-pātrisāha Sulatāna Bāhādura*) who was a *Turuṣka-narendra* and who was protecting his subjects with 'respectful adherence to the dharma appropriate to his own descent' (*nijavaṃśocita-dharma-saṃbhrameṇa*),[48] Bhairavasena's help extended to campaigns in the south, against Citrakūṭa and against the Mughal ruler Humayaun (*Humāyu Mugilādhirājaḥ*). Bhairavasena was regarded as a friend (*mitra*) by the Sultan of Gujarat and was generously rewarded by the latter for his friendship.

Amicable contact with the Mughal monarchy and court began with Akabbara, a *kṣoṇipati* and *avanipurandara*, when Vīrasena, Bhairavasena's son, spent some time at the Mughal court. Although Nārāyaṇa Śāha, son of Bhairavasena and patron of the author of this *mahākāvya*, lent initial support to the Ahmednagar ruler Burahāṇa Śāha, the arrival of Akbar's son Murāda Śāha in Broach, with orders for Nārāyaṇa Śāha to extend support to Murāda, made both Nārāyaṇa and his son Pratāpa to switch allegiance to the representative from Delhi.

Pratapa Śāha, depicted in the text as a great plunderer, was on the forefront of the assault on the capital of Nijāma Śāha of Ahmednagar, and in the concluding part of the *mahākāvya*, it is claimed that Pratāpa was loved by (*praṇayī*) *Śāha Murādarājaśrīkhānakhāna-kṣitipa*.[49]

Obviously, this selective gist of the text leaves out other details of claimed military achievements, against Yavanas, and non-Yavanas, religious benefactions which interspersed with campaigns of victory, and of conventional romance and intrigue. What emerges even from this selective gist—and from the *mahākāvyas* cited above—is that war against Turuṣka/Yavana (even when Yavanas may be depicted as allies) had by the medieval period become a part of the *digvijaya* lore, and the narrative world of the authors of the *mahākāvyas* had to be characterized by contestation for political authority by contestants of heterogeneous origin. In the *Rāṣtrauḍhavaṃśa-mahākāvya*, the undisputed authority of course lay with Śāha Śrīmad-Akabbara (Akbar), but that was not irreconciliable, till the end, with the 'sovereign' status of *Mayūragirikeśari-Śrī-mahārājādhirāja-Śrī Nārāyaṇa Śāha*.

## V

I have been trying to show, by citing epigraphic and literary sources, that as raiders and contestants for political power, the Tājikas and the Turuṣkas were depicted by contemporary authors as among many claimants in a situation of intense and constant competition. Whatever the political history of the period, even of the time of Akbar, this was what informed, through the use of literary convention, the narrative structure of the texts. The question to proceed to from this would be: how is Turuṣka rule perceived? What kind of break, if any, in the genealogy of rule, is perceived in the available documents, once the Sultanate came to be established in Delhi?

There is a cluster of interesting epigraphs of the thirteenth century from the Delhi region, which originated mostly from the merchant families of the area and to which we may turn for an initial answer to this query.

I start with the quite well-known Palam Baoli inscription of AD 1276,[50] almost the whole of which is in Sanskrit, written by Paṇḍita Yogīśvara. One notices that the inscription contains three genealogies. The genealogy of *ṭhakkura* Uḍaḍhara, a *purapati* in Śrīyoginīpura (Delhi), who had constructed numerous extensive *dharmaśālās* and was now constructing a well, to the east of Pālamba-grāma (Palam) and west of Kumumbapura, for religious merit, derived from a recorded *vaṃśāvalī* which incorporated the separate genealogies of his parents. The other genealogy was that of the recent and current rulers of Delhi, starting with Sāhavadina (Sihābuddin) and coming up to Śrī Hammīra Gayāsaṃdīna (Ghiyasuddin Balban). These rulers are listed as a part of a genealogy of rule. The *sāmrājya* (sovereign state corresponding to the universe) is represented as belonging to its emperor Śaṃkara (Śiva) whose *abhiṣeka* was performed by the celestial river Gaṅgā.

According to the Palam Baoli inscription, it was Lord Śaṃkara who was thus the emperor of the Universe, but in the kingdom of Hariyānaka, in which Śrīyoginīpura or Ḍhillī was located, it was a succession of royal families who enjoyed the earth: first the Tomaras, followed in succession by the Cauhāṇas and then, currently, by the Śakas.[51]

Similar genealogy is present in the Sarban stone inscription of AD 1378, found in the Raisina area of Delhi.[52] The object of this Sanskrit inscription too, is to record the construction of a well in the vicinity of the village Saravala (Sarban) in the *pratigaṇa* of Indraprastha in the country of Hariyānā, for attainment of heaven by deceased ancestors, by two merchant brothers. The record contains a short genealogy of this merchant family from Agrataka (*Vaṇijām-Agrotaka-nivāsinām*). The second genealogy, of succession of rule, also relates to the country (*deśa*) of Hariyānā which is comparable to heaven on earth. The city of Ḍhillī in that country, says the record, was built by the Tomaras: the Tomaras were succeeded by the Cāhamānas who were conscientious in looking after their subjects; 'then, Mleccha Sāhavadina, whose scorching might burnt the garden which was the family of his enemy, took the city by force. Since then the city has been enjoyed by the Turuṣkas, the current lord of the land being Śrī Maham-madaśāhi.'[53] The city was taken by force which the Naraina stone inscription, written a year earlier (1327), but also falling in the reign of Muhammad bin Tughlaq,[54] describes as *nijabāhuvīrya*, that is, 'might of his own arms'. The purpose of this epigraph too is to record the construction of a well, for the satisfaction of the ancestors, by a merchant of—as the *vaṃśavarṇanam* (genealogical) part of the record describes it—*Rohītaka-vaṃśa*,[55] at the village of Nāḍāyaṇa, located in the western direction of Indraprastha. This is in the great and virtuous province of Hariyānaka where Kṛṣṇa along with Pārtha wandered for the suppression of sin; in its city of Ḍhillī, sin is expelled through the chanting of the Vedas. And in this country, 'there is the famous king Mahamudasāhi, the crest jewel of all the rulers of the earth, who by the strength of his own arms, has crushed (his) enemies, and is the powerful Śaka Lord'.[56]

The representation of the succession of rule,[57] in the country of Hariyānā and in the city of Indraprastha or Ḍhillikā[58] uses symbols, similes, and motifs which are common in other Sanskrit inscriptions, including *praśastis*, of earlier and of the same period; the ruler of the Śaka, Turuṣka, or Mleccha descent may be seen to fit into the same convention, and if there is a new element or trait associated with his rule, it has to be so modified as to conform to this convention. One evidence of this is seen in the way the royalty of the Śaka/Turuṣka/ Mleccha ruler is expressed: as *nṛpa*, *nṛpati*, *nṛpati-vara*, *nāyaka*, *samrāṭ*, *pṛthvīndra*,[59] *bhūmipati*, *bhūpati*,[60] *mahārājādhirāja*,[61] and *paramabhaṭṭāraka*,[62] ruling over his *vijaya-rājya*.[63] Secondly, the ruler's sovereignty extends over the earth having the ocean as its girdle, and his conquests extend to all directions. Note, for example, how the kingdom of Śrī Hammīra Gayāsaṃdīna is described in the Palam Baoli inscription of 1276.[64]

> In his kingdom, abounding in benign rule, extending from Gauḍa to Gajjana, from the Draviḍa region and from the Setubandha (to the north) where the entire region was filled with inner content, the earth bore vernal floral charms produced by the rays of the innumerable precious stones and corals which dropped on it from the crowns of the bent heads of the rulers who came from every direction for his service ...
>
> The earth being now supported by this sovereign, Śesa, altogether forsaking his duty of supporting the weight of the globe, has betaken himself to the great bed of Viṣṇu; and Viṣṇu himself, for the sake of protection, taking Lakshmī on his breast, and relinquishing all worries, sleeps in peace on the ocean of milk.

Established metaphors are invoked to represent military exploits as well as the stability of the kingdom of the Śaka/Turuṣka ruler, much in the same way as they would be described in the records of the other ruling dynasties of the period. The point about this is that the inscriptions were not necessarily representing only empirical reality or concrete events; what is to be noted in this is the selection of terms for representation of what the rulers were seen as upholding. Thus, the wealth which was acquired, was seen, in an inscription of the time of Sikandar Shah Lodi, as having been acquired by adhering to the correct principle (*nyāyenopārjita*); the ruler was thus one 'who was beloved of his subjects (*prajā*) and giver of joy to them'.[65] The representation of Turuṣka/Śaka/Yavana rulers as adhering to norms which had been in existence earlier included other traits which they came to be endowed with. There was, apart from the usual Sanskritization of individual names and names of lineages,[66] the modification of the title Sultān to *Suratrāṇa*, which gave it the literal meaning 'Saviour of Gods'.[67] This pattern of representation also makes intelligible the search for a lunar, Pāṇḍava lineage for a medieval Muslim ruler of Kashmir, or the projection of Śāhi Śrīmad-Akabbara (Akbar), in the sixteenth century text *Bhānucandra-carita*, as Rāma.[68]

If these representations are seen as relevant for understanding one dimension of the culture and politics of the early medieval/medieval period, then reference may be made to some additional material, bearing on the process of internalization. The Sultan of Delhi, as we have seen, could be a *mahārājādhirāja* and *paramabhaṭṭāraka*; the Candella rulers, Paramārdideva, Trailokyavarmadeva, and Vīravarmmadeva, were called *paramabhaṭṭāraka*, *mahārājādhirāja*, *parameśvara*, *paramamāheśvara śāhi-mahārāja* in the Charkhari (Charkhari tahsil, Hamirpur district, Uttar Pradesh) copper-plate inscription of 1289.[69] The Arabic term *āmir*, modified to Hammīra or Hamvīra, could both denote the 'alien' who was an adversary, as also a local ruler, who could subdue the alien Hammīra.[70] Sultan, transformed into *Suratrāṇa* could thus be appropriated by rulers claiming to be sovereign among Hindu kings (*Hindurāya-suratrāṇa*), the term deriving its connotation not from its literal meaning, but from what its original (*Sultan*) signified. The term *Hindurāya-suratrāṇa* is of Vijayanagara origin; used, along with numerous other titles, it was intended to project the Vijayanagara rulers as chiefs among Hindu *rāyas* or kings;[71] the selection of the particular suffix '*suratrāṇa*' to *Hindurāya* makes it represent exactly what it is intended to oppose: the political might of the *sultan*. The title, like some other titles denoting political power such as *Śāha*,[72] was thus not essentialized but could remain open for use among royalty in general.

## VI

Turuṣkas/Śakas/Mlecchas, depicted as shouldering the great burden of the earth (*mahābhāra*)[73] to the extent of relieving Viṣṇu of his worries,[74] is one kind of representation. In another kind, they themselves become the great burden of the earth, and the ruler who subdues them becomes comparable to Viṣṇu: this is a complete reversal of the former representation. Note, for example, the following reference to Candella Trailokyavarman, father of Vīravarman, in the Ajaigarh Fort rock inscription of 1261 of the time of Vīravarman: 'Then Trailokyavarman, protector of the earth, who knew well how to provide for forts, ruled; like Viṣṇu he was, in lifting up the earth, immerged in the ocean formed by the streams of Turuṣkas.'[75]

The earth submerged by the Turuṣkas/Mlecchas is a regular motif, which is used to underline the significance of its rescue. The motif is related to the perception of a changed order, of departure from what is familiar and held valuable, and, at times, of surrender to current reality, and, at other times, of positive action. The attitude of surrender to what is perceived as a changed order is expressed, with great pathos and faith in miracle, in an inscription written towards the close of the twelfth century and found at Etawah fort in Uttar Pradesh.[76] The inscription is of *mahārāja* Ajayasiṃha who, the record claims, was a nephew of the Gāhaḍavāla ruler Jayaccandra. The inscription states that *mahārāja* Ajayasiṃha and his *ācārya* and priest performed a *mahāyoga* of Caṇḍikā. It also refers to the installation, made earlier, of an image of Durgā, but 'now, with great sorrow, touching her with my head, I place this Durgā, the dweller of the fort and destroyer of bad luck into this pit, till the God Skanda turns their (of the Mlecchas) glory (sun) to dust. When ill fate meets Yavanas, she might reappear, or manifest herself again amidst uproar'.[77]

It has been mentioned before that the perception of the violation of an existing order, by 'violent and vile' Yavanas who harassed gods and Brāhmaṇas, the most important symbols of that order, is present in the Kharepatan plate of 1095 of the Śilāhāras of Konkan. The perception, more vividly expressed, and sometimes using the motif of the submergence of the earth, because of Mleccha domination, is present in records from the thirteenth–fourteenth centuries. I shall give below excerpts from literary and epigraphic records of the period, both to illustrate how several images were made to converge in the literary idiom, and to make the point about counter-representation clearer.

The first reference I make is to *Madhurā-vijaya*, which, as mentioned earlier, was a *mahākāvya* written by Gaṅgādevī, in the second half of the fourteenth century, in celebration of the victory of her husband Kampana over the Turuṣkas of Madurai. The narration,[78] providing an elaborate commentary on the nature of Turuṣka rule in Madurai, is done by a mysterious lady, the gift of a sword by whom enables Kampana in the end to kill the Turuṣka ruler:

Vyāghrapurā had truly become the inhabitance of tigers where men lived formerly; the dome of the central shrine had become so dilapidated that it was only the hood of Ādiśeṣa that protected the image of Raṅganātha from falling. The Lord of Gajāraṇya, who is said to have killed an elephant to obtain its skin for a garment, was reduced to a similar condition because of its being deprived of clothes.[79]

The continuation of the narrative is in a similar vein:

The temples in the land have fallen into neglect as worship in them has been stopped. Within their walls the frightful howls of jackals have taken the place of the sweet reverberations of the *mridanga*. Like the Turushkas who know no limits, the Kaveri has forgotten her ancient boundaries and brings frequent destruction with her floods. The sweet odour of the sacrificial smoke and the chant of the Vedas have deserted the villages (*agrahāras*) which are now filled with the foul smell of roasted flesh and the fierce noises of the ruffianly Turushkas. The sub-urban gardens of Madura present a most painful sight; many of their beautiful coconut palms have been cut down; and on every side are seen rows of stakes from which swing strings of human skulls strung together. The Tamraparni is flowing red with the blood of the slaughtered cows. The Veda is forgotten and justice has gone into hiding; there is not left any trace of virtue or nobility in the land and despair is writ large on the faces of the unfortunate Draviḍas.[80]

The calamity, of which man and nature are both perceived to be agents, is made to be of cosmic proportions, and this is what links it up with the image of the recovery of the earth which became submerged in the ocean as a result of Mleccha rule, entitling its rescuer identity with the Primeval Boar (*Mahā-Varāha*). The Annavarappadu plates of 1385 and 1401, from the West Godavari district of Āndhra Pradesh, refer to king Vema of the Reḍḍi family as having been 'praised as the Primeval Boar (*Mahā-Varāha*) by all the learned for his act of lifting up the country that was submerged under the *Mleccha*... ocean; the land of the Āndhra shone brilliantly, and while this king was lawfully ruling (the earth), there flourished all the *śāstras* and Vedas and hundreds of sacrifices were performed'.[81]

'Blinding blackness, to which the earth passed' afflicted by the Turuṣkas, is another metaphor to underscore the calamity of Mleccha rule. It is used in another inscription from Āndhra, the Vilasa Grant of Prolaya Nāyaka, discovered near Pithapuram in East Godavari district and dated to about AD 1330.[82] [...]

[...]

The *Madhurā-vijaya* and the epigraphic records from Āndhra that I have cited all talk about calamity; in addition to other traits of disorder, the calamity takes the form of an end to the recitation of the Vedas, destruction and neglect of temples, decline of the settlements of the Brāhmaṇas and so on. The Vilasa Grant describes the collapse of an ideal social order in comprehensive terms, and the above traits are the chief traits of the order which is restored: this is a feat comparable to the lifting of the earth submerged in the ocean. It is a feat highlighted by portraying the magnitude of the calamity, of the total destruction of what is perceived as valuable in society, brought about by the rule of the Yavanas.

The description of the devastation, whether portrayed in the *Madhurā-vijaya* or the Vilasa Grant will be, and has been, commonly taken to represent the one and exclusive reality of Yavana rule; the return to the old order, similarly, is taken to represent the reality of a liberation. It needs to be seen, however, that the image of the Turuṣka/Yavana *suratrāṇa* and of his community as the destroyer of the existing social order is what may be called counter-representation of the *suratrāṇa* as the perpetuator of that social order, or vice versa. The event of Yavana victory and rule is a reality, but the reality, as the Palam Baoli inscription and the Vilasa Grant show, could be represented in two ways. In one representation, the destroyer of the Yavana who is a destroyer of social order is comparable to Viṣṇu; in another, the Yavana, as a benign ruler, gives succour to Viṣṇu who, leaving the burden of preservation to the ruler, retires to peaceful sleep in the ocean of milk. It cannot be argued that chronologically one representation replaces the other. The Yavanas of the Kharepatan plate (AD 1095) were 'violent and vile', so were the Yavanas of *Madhurā-vijaya* and the Vilasa Grant. But, if the Rāṣṭrakūṭa plates of the early tenth century from Chinchani wished that the rule of the Yavana ruler Śrī Sugatipa, of the prowess of the Sun (*Sūryatejāḥ*) continued (*praśastu*),[83] the Kangra Jwalamukhi praśasti from north India, written between 1433 and 1446, also wished the fame (*kīrtti*) of Śrimad-Śāhi-Mahammada, the ruler of Delhi, to be victorious.[84] The lord of Delhi (*Dillīśvara*) in the period of the Mughals could be seen as performing different roles: he could both be a support to what is described as a *Rāmarājya* (*varṇyate tasya rājyam hi Rāmarājyopamam śubham*)[85] as one comparable to Rāma, the lord of Delhi could himself be seen as a ruler of *Rāmarājya*.[86] The representations of Yavana rule can thus be seen to constitute a contradiction, the origin of which needs to be explained.

## NOTES

1 Romila Thapar, 'Imagined Religious Communities? Ancient History and the Modern Search for a Hindu Identity', in Romila Thapar, *Interpreting Early India*, Delhi, 1992, pp. 60–88; Anwar Hussain, 'The "Foreigners" and the Indian Society (Early Eighth Century to Thirteenth Century): A Study of Epigraphic Evidence from Northern and Western India', M. Phil dissertation, Centre for Historical Studies, Jawaharlal Nehru University, 1993.

2 Shashi Joshi and B.S. Josh, *Struggle for Hegemony in India 1920–47: Culture, Community and Power*, New Delhi, 1994, p. 190.

3 See D.C. Sircar, 'Veraval Inscription of Chaulukya-Vāghela Arjuna, 1264 AD', *Epigraphia India* (*EI* here after), vol. 34 (1961–2), Delhi, 1963, pp. 141–50; D.C. Sircar, *Select Inscriptions Bearing on Indian History and Civilization*, vol. 2, Delhi, 1983, pp. 402–8. The inscription was originally edited by E. Hultzsch, 'A Grant of Arjunadeva of Gujarat, Dated 1264 AD', *The Indian Antiquary* (hereafter *IA*), vol. 11, 1882, pp. 241–5.

4 See Aloka Parashar, *Mlecchas*; H.P. Ray, 'The Yavana Presence in Ancient India', *Journal of the Economic and Social History of the Orient*, vol. 31, 1988, pp. 311–25.

5 See D.C. Sircar, *Indian Epigraphy*, Delhi, 1965, pp. 258–66.

6 D.R. Bhandarkar, 'Pārasīka Dominion in Ancient India', *Annals of the Bhandarkar Oriental Research Institute*, vol. 8, 1926–7, pp. 133–41.

7 The term *Pārasika* came to be used for Indian Muslims as well. See Vilasa Grant from Āndhra cited later.

8 Bhandarkar, 'Pārasīka Dominion in Ancient India'.

9 P.V. Kane, 'The Pahlavas and Pārasīkas in Ancient Sanskrit Literature', in *Dr Modi Memorial Volume*, edited by Dr Modi Memorial Volume Editorial Board, Bombay, 1930, pp. 352–7.

10 E. Hultzsch, 'Four Inscriptions of Kulottuṅga Chola', *EI*, vol. 5, Delhi, rpt, 1984, p. 104.

11 V.V. Mirashi, *Inscriptions of the Kalachuri-Chedi Era*, pt. I Corpus Inscriptionum Indicarum, vol. 4, Ootacamund, 1955, pp. 96–102. The relevant passage in the inscription reads: *Asidhārājalena Śamitah prāsabham Valabhipateḥ pure yenāśeṣa-loka-santāpa—kalāpades—Tājik—ānalo Jayabhaṭajaladaḥ eṣaḥ* The same passage occurs, as a part of the long genealogical portion, in the Prince of Wales Museum Plates of Jayabhaṭa IV: AD 736 (lines 31–2); Mirashi, *Inscriptions of the Kalachuri-Chedi Era*, pt. I, p. 106.

12 D. Pingree, 'Sanskrit Evidence for the Presence of Arabs, Jews and Persians in Western India: c. 700–1300', *Journal of the Oriental Institute*, vol. 31.2, 1981–2, pp. 172–82.

13 W. Sundermann, 'An Early Attestation of the Name of the Tajiks', in W. Skalmowski and A.V. Tongerloo (eds), *Medioiranica* [Proceedings of the International Colloquium organized by the Katholieke Universiteit Leuven from 21 to 23 May 1990 (Leuven, 1990)], pp. 163–71. I am thankful to Ingo Strauch of Humboldt University, Berlin, for not only giving me this reference but also making a photocopy of the article available for my use.

14 Mirashi, *Inscriptions of the Kalachuri-Chedi Era*, pt. 1, pp. 137–45.

15 See, for example, the following comments on the Arab raids of the period: 'Either Śīluka or his successor was on the throne when the Arabs swept over the whole Rājputānā and Gujarāt, and advanced as far as Ujjayinī. The Gurjara kingdom of Jodhpur was overrun, but the Pratihāra king Nāgabhaṭa of Avantī withstood this terrible shock and hurled back the invaders. The credit of saving western India from the hands of the Arab invaders belongs to him, and he shares the glory with the Cālukya king Avanijanāśraya Pulakeśirāja who stopped their advance into southern India.'

'The Arab invasion must have brought about great changes in the political condition in western India by destroying or weakening numerous small states.' R.C. Majumdar, *The Classical Age* (vol. 3 of *The History and Culture of the Indian People*), Bombay, 4th edn., 1988, p. 155.

16 K.V. Ramesh and S.P. Tewari, 'An Inscription of Pratīhāra Vatsarāja. Śaka 717', *EI*, vol. 41, Delhi, 1989, pp. 49–57.

17 Apart from other qualities, the hero of a *mahākāvya* was to possess the urge for conquest. See David Smith, *Ratnākara's Haravijaya: An Introduction to the Sanskrit Court Epic*, Delhi, 1985, pp. 29–30.

18 D.C. Sircar, 'Rashtrakuta Charters from Chinchani', *EI*, vol. 32, Delhi, rpt, 1987, pp. 55–60.

19 Ibid.

20 G.M. Moraes, *The Kadamba Kula: A History of Ancient and Medieval Karnataka*, Bombay, 1931, pp. 171–2.

21 Ibid., pp. 185–6.

22 V.V. Mirashi, *Inscriptions of the Śilāhāras* (*Corpus Inscriptionum Indicarum*, vol. 6), Delhi, 1977, pp. 115–20.

23 Ibid., pp. 120–7.

24 Ibid., Verse 20 of the record reads:

*Āsīt—k'opyasuro—jagad-dalayituṃ Chittukka-nāmāntakas-tasyaivaṃ ca samastam-eva militaṃ sāmantacakraṃ tataḥ dhvaste dharmadhane gateṣu guruṣu kliṣṭe vibhāsaṃśraye sīrṇṇe jīrṇṇapuraprajāparijane naṣṭe ca rāṣṭrodaye.*

25 Later references to Tājikas seem to be found only in texts. See M. Monier-Williams, *A Sanskrit–English Dictionary*, Delhi, rpt, 1993, p. 441.

26 See V.K. Jain, *Trade and Traders in Western India (AD 1000–1300)*, Delhi, 1990, passim.

27 N. Venkataramanayya and M. Somasekhara Sharma, 'Vilasa Grant of Prolaya Nayaka', *EI*, vol. 32, 1957–8, Delhi, rpt, 1987, pp. 239–68.

28 P. Prasad, 'The Turushka or Turks in late Ancient Indian Documents', *Proceedings of the Indian History Congress*, 55th Session, Aligarh, 1994, Delhi, 1995, pp. 170–5. André Wink summarizes views on the nomenclature and origin of the Turks thus: 'The very word "Turk" or "Tüṙk" appears as the name of a Central-Asian nomad people only from the 6th century onwards, when in 552 the "Turk" Qaghanate was founded on the Orkhon river in Mongolia. The Chinese name for the Turks was *Tu-Kueh*. which was apparently derived from "*Türküt*", the Mongol plural of *Türk*. The Greeks called them *Tourkoi*. the Arabs *Atrak* (sg. *Turk*), while in new Persian they became known as *Turkan* (sg. *Turk*). Originally, *Türk* was an ethnonym which was associated with a small tribe headed by the Ashina clan; it meant "the strong one" and within the semantic range of a whole series of tribal names

which connoted "force", "violence", "ferociousness", and so on'; André Wink, 'India and Central Asia: The Coming of the Turks in the Eleventh Century', in A.W. Van Den Hoek, D.H.A. Kolff, and M.S. Oort (eds), *Ritual, State and History in South Asia: Essays in Honour of J.C. Heesterman*, Leiden, New York, Koln, 1992, p. 755. It is possible that some of the Sanskrit appellations such as *atibala* used with reference to the Turuṣkas were literal translations of tribal connotations mentioned by Wink.

29 Cited in G.R. Nandargikar, The *Raghuvanśa of Kālidāsa*, Bombay, 3rd revd, and enl. edn, 1897, pp. 123–4.

30 *Rājataraṅgiṇī*, I. 170.

31 K.V. Ramesh, 'A Fragmentary Sarada Inscription from Hund', *EI*, vol. 38, Delhi, 1971, pp. 94–8.

32 K.V. Ramesh, *Indian Epigraphy*, vol. I, Delhi, 1984, pp. 90–1.

33 P. Prasad, 'Turushkas'.

34 R.C. Majumdar, 'The Gwalior Prasasti of the Gurjara-Pratīhāra King Bhoja', *EI*, vol. 18, pp. 99–114; D.C. Sircar, 'Gwalior Stone Inscription of Bhoja I (*c.* 836–85 AD)', *Select Inscriptions*, vol. 2, pp. 242–6.

35 F. Kielhorn, 'Khalimpur Plate of Dharmapaladeva', *EI*, vol. 4, Delhi, rpt, 1979, pp. 243–54.

36 V.V. Mirashi, *Inscriptions of the Kalachuri-Chedi Era*, pt. 2, pp. 402, 404–5.

37 Chandra Prabha, *Historical Mahākāvyas in Sanskrit, Eleventh to Fifteenth Century AD*, Delhi, 1976.

38 *Rāṣṭrauḍhavaṃśa-mahākāvyam*, published as Embar Krishnamacharya (ed), *Rāshṭrauḍhavaṇśa Kāvya of Rudrakavi*, with an introduction by C.D. Dalal, Gaekwad's Oriental Series, no. 5, Baroda, 1917.

39 See the summary of the contents in Chandra Prabha, *Historical Mahākāvyas*, chap. 4.

40 Ibid., chap. 9.

41 Ibid., chap. 10.

42 Ibid., chap. 11.

43 E. Krishnamacharya, *Rāṣhṭrauḍhavaṃśa*, Introduction. The Bagula rulers were chiefs of Baglana, between Surat and Nandurbar, in the Mughal *Suba* of Gujarat. See A.R. Khan, *Chieftains in the Mughal Empire During the reign of Akbar*, Simla, 1977, pp. 86–7.

44 *Rāṣṭrauḍhavaṃśa-mahākāvyam*, 3.11.

45 Ibid., 3.13.

46 Ibid., 3.33.

47 Ibid., 3.39.

48 Ibid., 6.11.

49 Ibid., 20.84 and 20.87.

50 P. Prasad, *Sanskrit Inscriptions of Delhi Sultanate 1191–1526*, Delhi, 1990, pp. 3–15. For Palam Baoli and other Sanskrit inscriptions of the Sultanate period from Delhi and Uttar Pradesh, I have generally, though not solely, depended on this work.

51 The Palam Baoli inscription gives the following genealogy of the Delhi rulers: Sāhavadina (Sihābbuddin), Ṣuduvadīna (Qutbu'ddin Aibak), Samusadīna

(Shamsuddin Iltutmish), Pherūjasāhi (Ruknuddin Firūz), Jalāladīna (Jalāluddin Razia), Maujadīna (Muizuddin Bahram), Alāvadīna (Alauddin Masud), Nasaradīna (Nasiruddin Mahmud), Śrī Hammīra Gayāsadīna (Ghiyāsuddin Balban).

52 Prasad, *Sanskrit Inscriptions*, pp. 27–31; J. Eggeling, 'Sarban Inscription in the Delhi Museum', *EI*, vol. I, 1892, rpt, Delhi, 1983, pp. 93–5.

53 This is a rough translation of the following part of the text:

*Atha pratāpadahanadagdhāri-kula-kānanaḥ*
*Mlecchaḥ Sāhavadina-stāṃ Balena Jagrhe purīm*
*Tataḥ prabhṛti bhuktā sā Turuṣkair-yāvad-adya puḥ*
*Śrī Mahammadaśāhis-tāṃ pāti samprati bhūpatiḥ.*

P. Prasad's translation of this is somewhat unsatisfactory.

54 P. Prasad, *Sanskrit Inscriptions*, pp. 22–7.

55 *Rohītaka-vaṃśa*, obviously locating its origin in Rohitaka or Rohtak in Haryana, can possibly be identified with the merchant subcaste of the Rohatgis; P. Prasad, *Sanskrit Inscriptions*, p. 16.

56 *Tatr-āsīn Mahamudasāhir-akhila-kṣoṇiśa-cūḍamaṇir vikhyāto nija-bāhu-vīrya-dalit-ārātiḥ Śakendro Balī.*

57 The succession of rule from Tomara, through Cāhamāna, to Śakendra or the ruler of the Śakas figures also in another stone inscription, possibly from Sonepat; P. Prasad, *Sanskrit Inscriptions*, pp. 15–18.

58 Compare the evidence of Palam Baoli and other inscriptions from Delhi with that of *Vividha-tīrtha-kalpa* of Jinaprabhasūri, a Jaina text of the first half of the fourteenth century: 'Pattana was established by Vanarāja', the pearl of the Caukkada [Cāpotkaḍā, Cāvaḍā] dynasty in Vikarama 802 in Lāksārāma in the region under the rule of king Anahilla. Seven kings of the Cāvaḍā dynasty reigned: Vanarāja, Yogarāja, Kṣemarāja, Bhuyagaḍa, Vajrasiṃha, Ratnāditya, and Sāmantasiṃha. Then eleven kings of the Caulukya dynasty reigned in that town: Mūlarāja, Cāmuṇḍarāja, Vallabharāja, Durlabharāja, Bhīmadeva, Karṇa, Jayasiṃhadeva, Kumārapāladeva, Ajayadeva, the younger Mūlarāja, and Bhīmadeva. Then reigned the kings in the Vāghelā years: Lavaṇaprasāda, Vīradhavala, Vīsaladeva, Arjuna, Sāraṅgadeva, and Karṇadeva. Then in Gujarat came the rule of the Sultans: 'Ala-ud-dina, etc. But Ariṣṭanemi Svāmī is worshipped in the same way today.' John E. Cort (tr.) 'Twelve Chapters from the Guidebook to Various Pilgrimage Places, the *Vividhatīrthakalpa* of Jinaprabhasūri', in Phyllis Granoff (ed.), *The Clever Adulteress and Other Stories: A Treasury of Jain Literature*, Oakville, New York, and London, 1990, p. 246.

59 These titles all appear in the Palam Baoli inscription.

60 The title *Mahārājādhirāja* given to Sultan Mahmud Khalji figures in two inscriptions, dated 1437 and 1446, in Deogarh fort in UP; Prasad, *Sanskrit Inscriptions*, pp. 201–2.

61 Palam Baoli and Sarban inscriptions.

62 *Paramabhaṭṭarāka*, an epithet of the sovereign ruler, is used for Shamsuddin Iltutmish (1210–1236) in Mahoba fort copperplate inscriptions from Uttar Pradesh; the dates on the inscriptions are AD 1227 on one side and 1234–50 on the other. Prasad, *Sanskrit Inscriptions*, p. 80.

63 Note, in this context, the interesting passage in a fifteenth century sale deed of a girl and her son from Tirhut in north Bihar: 'in Tīrabhukti, which is protected by

*Mahārājādhirāja*, the prosperous Bhairavasiṃhadeva, a Nārāyaṇa against enemy kings like Nārāyaṇa against Kaṃsa, who is engaged in devotion to Śiva and is shining with all the insignia received through the favour and boon of the Sultan, the prosperous Alāvadina Śāha, the *Paramabhaṭṭāraka, Parameśvara:* supreme lord, *aśvapati:* the lord of horses, *Gajapati*, the lord of elephants, *narapati:* the lord of men and *rājatrayādhipati*: supreme lord of a triad of kings and the guardian of the east…': Mahes Raj Pant, 'Six 15th- and 16th-century Deeds from Tirhut Recording the Purchase of Slaves', in Bernhard Kölver (ed.), *Recht, Staat und Veraltung im Klassischen Indien* (The State, the Law, and Administration in Classical India), München, 1997, pp. 164–5.

64 Palam Baoli inscription, verses 6–11.

65 These terms occur in a stone inscription, dated 1491 in the collection of the Lucknow Museum. The inscription belongs to the time of Sikandar Shah Lodi: the expressions relate to a minor family of rulers, which is called in the inscription as *Bahalīma-vaṃśa*, Prasad, *Sanskrit Inscriptions*, pp. 210–11.

The choice of particular expressions was designed to project the ruler as upholder of royal norms. The king was expected to keep his subjects happy: his wealth, lawfully acquired, was only the share he was entitled to as the protector of his subjects. See R.S. Sharma, *Aspects of Political Ideas and Institutions in Ancient India*, Delhi, 3rd rev. edn., 1991, chap. 5.

66 For example, the transformation, in the Lalitpur stone inscription of 1424, discovered in Deogarh fort, of the term Ghori into *Gaurī-kula*, to which *Śrīmān-Mālava-Pālaka, Śaka-nṛpa, Sāhi* Ālaṃbhaka (Hoshang Shah Ghori of Malwa) belonged; P. Prasad, *Sanskrit Inscriptions*, pp. 183–99.

67 Several short inscriptions at Qutb Minar in Delhi have the Form *Śrī Sulatrāṇa*. (P. Prasad, pp. 18–21), but this may not be taken to suggest that the form *Suratrāṇa* was arrived at through some intermediary stages. From the very widespread occurrence of the term *Suratrāṇa* in different parts of India, it would appear that it gained ready currency as the Sanskritic equivalent of Sultan.

68 The text (1.39) has the following:

*Tathā tat pālayāmāsa sāhiḥ Śrīmad-Akabbaraḥ*
*Nītyā yath-aiva nāsmārsit Kauśaleyaṃ jano-khilaḥ.*

M.R. Pant suggests that the form *Kauśaleya* (son of Kauśalyā) may have been used for reasons of metre.

69 P. Prasad, *Sanskrit Inscriptions*, pp. 144–8.

70 *Hammīramahākāvya* in Chandra Prabha. *Historical Mahākāvyas*, chap. 9.

71 E. Hultzsch, 'Hampe Inscription of Krishnaraya, Dated Śaka 1430', *EI*, vol. I, pp. 361–71. Chandra Prabha cites (*Historical Mahākāvyas*, p. 330 and fn. 3) the evidence of an inscription from Kolar district in Karnataka to show that the title Hindurāya-suratrāṇa dates to the time of Bukka I. Evidence of the use of the term *Hiṃdu-suratrāṇa* by a ruler of north India is provided by the Sadadi (west Rajasthan) inscription of 1439 of Guhila Rāṇā Kumbhakarṇa; he is mentioned as having received the title after defeating the Sultans of Ḍhillī and Gūrjaratrā. The title *Suratrāṇa* in this record is used with reference to Allāvadīna who was a contemporary and defeated adversary of Kumbhakarṇa's predecessor Bhuvanasiṃha: D.R. Bhandarkar, 'A List of Inscriptions of Northern India in Brahmi and its Derivative

Scripts, from About 200 BC', *Appendix to Epigraphia Indica and Record of the Archaeological Survey of India*, vols 19–23, Delhi, rpt., 1983, pp. 109–10, no. 784. See, in this connection, the interesting discussion in Phillip B. Wagoner, '"Sultan among Hindu Kings": Dress, Titles, and the Islamicization of Hindu Culture at Vijayanagara', *Journal of Asian Studies*, vol. 55, no. 4, 1996, pp. 851–80.

72 See *Rāṣṭrauḍhavaṃśa-mahākāvyam*, passim.

73 Lucknow Museum Stone inscription, see n. 70.

74 Palam Baoli inscription.

75 The translation is slightly modified from what is available in F. Kielhorn, 'Two Chandella Inscriptions from Ajaygadh', *EI*, vol. I, p. 329.

76 Prasad, *Sanskrit Inscriptions*, pp. 92–3.

77 Ibid. Inscriptions also refer to installation of new images to replace broken images. One can cite in this context the evidence of a Kiradu (west Rajasthan) inscription of 1178–9 which records the installation of an image by the wife of a subordinate official Tejapāla working under Mahārājaputra Madanabrahma, ruler of Kirāṭa-kūpa (Kiradu). during the time of Caulukya Bhīmadeva, to replace an image broken by the Turuṣkas, D.R. Bhandarkar, 'A List of Inscriptions', p. 56, no. 381.

78 The citations made here are not extracts from the translation of the text; they are paraphrases, taken from publications cited below.

79 Prabha, *Sanskrit Inscriptions*, p. 339.

80 K.A. Nilakanta Sastri, *The Pāṇḍyan Kingdom, From the Earliest Times to the Sixteenth Century*, Madras, rpt., 1972, p. 213.

81 K.H.V. Sarma and T. Krishnamurty, 'Annavarappadu Plates of Kataya Vema Reddi', *EI*, vol. 36, pp. 167–90.

82 N. Venkataramanayya and M. Somasekhara Sharma, 'Vilasa Grant'.

83 D.C. Sircar, 'Rashtrakuta Charters from Chinchani'.

84 G. Bühler, 'The Kangra Jwalamukhi Prasasti', *EI*, vol. I, pp. 190–5.

85 This is how the kingdom of Durgabhānu, a local Chandrawat ruler of Mandasor, has been described in an inscription of the early seventeenth century. The Chandrawat rulers claimed to have obtained many countries from the *Dillīśvara*, 'Lord of Delhi' (*Dillīśvarāt-prāpta...deśān-anekān*); Sadhu Ram, 'Two inscriptions from Rampura. Saṃvat 1664', *EI*, vol. 36, pp. 121–30.

86 *Bhānucandra-carita*, 1.39.

# Contributors

**Kunal Chakrabarti** is Professor of ancient Indian history at Jawaharlal Nehru University, New Delhi. He specializes in the study of the social history of religion in pre-modern India. In addition to several research papers published in scholarly journals, he is the author of *Religious Process: The Purāṇas and the Making of a Regional Tradition* (2001).

**B. D. Chattopadhyaya** studied and researched at Calcutta University and Cambridge University and has taught at the University of Burdwan, Visva-Bharati, and Jawaharlal Nehru University. Apart from several edited volumes, he is the author of *Coins and Currency Systems in South India* (1977), *Survey of the Historical Geography of Ancient India* (1984), *Aspects of Rural Settlements and Rural Society in Early Medieval India* (1990), *The Making of Early Medieval India* (1994), *Representing the Other? Sanskrit Sources and the Muslims: Eighth to Fourteenth Century* (1998), and *Studying Early India: Archaeology, Texts and Historical Issues* (2003).

**Noboru Karashima** is Professor Emeritus at the University of Tokyo and at Taisho University, Japan. He has been President of the Epigraphical Society of India, the Historical Society of Japan, and the Japanese Association for South Asian Studies, and is currently President of the International Association of Tamil Research. His publications include *South Indian History and Society: Studies from Inscriptions, A.D. 850–1800* (1984), *Towards a New Formation: South Indian Society Under Vijayanagar Rule* (1992), *A Concordance of Nayakas: The Vijayanagar Inscriptions in South India* (2002), *In search of Chinese Ceramic Sherds in South India and Sri Lanka* (ed. 2004), and *South Indian Society in Transition: Ancient to Medieval* (2009).

**Hermann Kulke** did his PhD in Indology from the University of Freiburg. He has been Reader in Indian history, South Asia Institute,

Heidelberg, and Professor of Asian History, Kiel University, Germany. His specializations include pre-colonial state formation in South and Southeast Asia and Indian Ocean studies. His publications include *Kings and Cults: State Formation and Legitimation India and Southeast Asia* (1993), *The State in India 1000–1700* (ed.,1995), *Nagapattinam to Suvarnadwipa: Reflections on the Chola Naval Expeditions to Southeast Asia* (ed., 2009), *A History of India* (co-authored with D. Rothermund, 5th edn 2010), and *Rituals and the State in India* (ed., 2010).

**Sheldon Pollock** is Ransford Professor of Sanskrit and Indian Studies at Columbia University and former George V. Bobrinskoy Distinguished Service Professor at the University of Chicago, USA. He is founding editor of the Murty Classical Library of India (Harvard). His publications include *The Rāmāyaṇa of Vālmīki*, vol. II: *Ayodhyākāṇḍa* (1986) and vol. III: *Araṇyakāṇḍa* (1991), *Cosmopolitanism* (2002, ed. with Homi Bhabha *et. al.*), *Literary Cultures in History: Reconstructions from South Asia* (ed., 2003), *The Ends of Man at the End of Premodernity* (2005), and *The Language of the Gods in the World of Men* (2006). He was awarded the Padma Sri by the Government of India in 2010.

**Leslie C. Orr** is Associate Professor in the Department of Religion at Concordia University, Montreal. Her research expertise focuses on the religions of South India, with special reference to the social and institutional histories of medieval Hinduism, Jainism and Buddhism, and women in medieval South Indian society and religion. She is the author of *Donors, Devotees and Daughters of God: Temple Women in Medieval Tamilnadu* (2000) and has written a large number of research papers which have been published in various scholarly journals and edited volumes. Her current research project is titled 'Renovation, replication, recovery, and revival: Building temples and building histories in South India'.

**Devika Rangachari** is an independent researcher. She graduated from St Stephen's College, Delhi and did her doctorate in history from the University of Delhi. Her book, *Invisible Women, Visible Histories: Gender, Society and Polity in North India (Seventh to Twelfth Century AD)* (2009) underlines the pivotal importance of gender in the historical reconstruction of the early medieval period in north India. She has published several articles in distinguished academic journals and is also an award-winning children's writer.

**P. Shanmugam** is former Professor and Head, Department of Ancient History and Archaeology, and currently Director, Institute of Traditional Cultures of South and Southeast Asia, University of Madras. He is an active member of the Numismatic Society of South India. He has been involved in several research projects, including on the ports of the Tamil country, and has participated in excavations at sites such as Korkai, Kodumanal, Uraiyur, and Kanchipuram. His publications include *The Revenue System of the Cholas 850–1279* (1987), a monograph on the coins of the Sangam Period in Tamil Nadu (2004), and *Recent Advances in Vijayanagara Studies* (co-edited, 2005).

**R.S. Sharma** was Professor Emeritus, Patna University, and former Professor of History at the University of Delhi and at the University of Toronto. He was also Founder Chairman of the Indian Council of Historical Research; Member, University Grants Commission; Secretary and General President of the Indian History Congress; and Deputy Chairperson of UNESCO's International Association for the Study of Cultures of Central Asia. His numerous books include *Śūdras in Ancient India (1958), Aspects of Political Ideas and Institutions in Ancient India* (1959), *Indian Feudalism (1965), Perspectives in Social and Economic History of Early India* (1983) and *Rethinking India's Past* (2009).

**Upinder Singh** is Professor in the Department of History, University of Delhi. She is the author of *Kings, Brāhmaṇas, and Temples in Orissa: An Epigraphic Study (AD 300–1147)* (1994); *Ancient Delhi* (1999); *The Discovery of Ancient India: Early Archaeologists and the Beginnings of Archaeology* (2004); and *A History of Ancient and Early Medieval India: From the Stone Age to the Twelfth Century* (2008). She has edited *Delhi: Ancient History* (2006) and *Ancient India: New Research* (co-edited with Nayanjot Lahiri, 2009), and has written a book for children, *Mysteries of the past: Archaeological Sites in India* (2002).

**Burton Stein** was Professor of South Asian Studies at the University of Hawaii. He taught at the University of Minnesota; was Visiting Professor at the universities of Chicago, Pennsylvania, Washington, California and at Jawaharlal Nehru University, New Delhi; and was a professorial research associate at the School of Oriental and African Studies, London. His publications include *Peasant State and Society in Medieval South India* (1980), *Vijayanagara* (1989), *Thomas Munro: The Origins of the Colonial State and His Vision of Empire* (1989), and *A History of India* (1998).

**Y. Subbarayalu** is Head of the French Institute of Pondicherry and former Professor of Epigraphy and Archaeology, Tamil University of Thanjavur. He has been the Chief Investigator for the Historical Atlas of Tamil Nadu, Tamil University (2001–4) and is co-ordinator for the *Historical Atlas of South India*, French Institute of Pondicherry (2005–8). His publications include *Political Geography of the Chola Country* (1973), *A Concordance of the Names in the Chola Inscriptions* (co-authored, 1978), *Palm-leaf Documents of Tiruchirappalli District* (1989), *Studies in Chola History* (2001), and *A Glossary of Tamil Inscriptions* (2002–3).

**Cynthia Talbot** is Associate Professor of History at the University of Texas, Austin. Her earlier research focused on temple inscriptions from medieval Andhra, while more recently she has been exploring Rajput society and culture during the Mughal era. She is currently working on a book that examines historical traditions relating to the twelfth century king Prithiviraj Chauhan. She is author of *Precolonial India in Practice* (2001), *India before Europe* (co-authored with Catherine B. Asher, 2006), and editor of a forthcoming volume *Changing Conceptions of India's Past.*

**Kapila Vatsyayan** is Chairperson, IIC-Asia Project, India International Centre, and a nominated Member of the Rajya Sabha. Apart from being a scholar, she has also been involved in developing policy frameworks for art history, education, Sanskrit, Buddhist and Pali studies. She has been Secretary, Department of Arts, Ministry of Human Resource Development; Academic Director, Indira Gandhi National Centre for the Arts; Member, UNESCO Executive Board; and President, India International Centre. Her numerous publications include six monographs on the *Gita Govinda* and Indian miniature paintings; *Classical Indian Dance in Literature and the Arts* (1968); and *The Square and the Circle of the Indian Arts* (1983).

**Kesavan Veluthat** is Professor of History in the University of Delhi. He was educated in the University of Calicut and Jawaharlal Nehru University and has taught in the universities of Calicut and Mangalore. He was Visiting Professor at the École Pratique des Haute Etudes and at Maison des Science des L'Hommes, Paris. Apart from several research papers that have appeared in various scholarly journals, his publications include *Brahman Settlements in Kerala: Historical Studies* (1978), *Political Structure of Early Medieval South India* (1993), and *The Early Medieval in South India* (2009).